Bay Breezes

By **Glenn Neumann**

Published by
Elk Rapids Area Historical Society

Excerpts taken from the
ELK RAPIDS PROGRESS

A newspaper published in
Elk Rapids, Michigan

Volume II
Issues of: 1880, 1881 and 1882

Editor:
Benjamin F. Davis
1878 – 1894

Limited Edition

Number *343*

Glenn Neumann

Cover Design—By Linda (Neumann) Weinzapfel.

Cover Photograph—Elk Rapids Iron Company's Smelting Furnace. Built in 1872-73. On Monday morning June 23, 1873, the furnace went into blast and the following day the first pig iron was made.

Published By--The Elk Rapids Area Historical Society.

ISBN   0-9653504-1-x

DEDICATION

I dedicate this Volume II of *BAY BREEZES* to my grand children; Benjamin, Matthew, Jeffery, Eric, Renee´ and Aimee.

They are the next generation to enjoy living in the development of the Grand Traverse Country.

History Is Real

"Real stories, in distinction from
those we invent, have no author.
Although history owes its existence
to men, it is not 'made' by them.

**--Hannah Arendt,
American historian**

Introduction

Elk Rapids, Michigan is a unique and beguiling place.

Situated in the southwest corner of Antrim County, bounded by East Grand Traverse Bay on the west, Elk Lake to the east, Bass Lake to the north and bisected by Elk River, the town owes most of its development to man's love of the water and its power.

The area was originally home to Native Americans from the Ottawa and Chippewa tribes, who lived and played on its white sand beaches long before the first white settler appeared. That man, Abram Wadsworth, a surveyor from Durham, Conn., arrived in 1846 and built a sawmill across the river four years later.

First called Stevens, then later renamed Elk Rapids in honor of Wadsworth's discovery of a pair of elk horns in the river, the town soon became the lumber processing center of most of the region.

In those days lumber was king of the North Woods, and the kings of the lumber trade were the Dexter & Noble Co., who operated one of the largest mills in the north from the Port of Elk Rapids.

A company town in every sense, early Elk Rapids was populated by wealthy land barons, rowdy lumberjacks, ambitious businessmen, displaced Indians and rugged pioneer families. At one time, seven saloons and seven churches dotted its streets, an indication of the town's constant struggle to balance its bawdy boomtown reputation with more civilized society.

Taking advantage of Antrim County's large hardwood stands of maple, beech and ash, Dexter and Noble began another enterprise at Elk Rapids, an iron foundry that became one of the largest pig iron smelting facilities in the Midwest. As the town grew, so did its appeal to tourists.

Nowhere is the history of this colorful and exciting period better captured than on the pages of the local newspaper. The first issue of the *Traverse Bay Eagle* rolled off the press in 1865.

Over the next two decades it would change names several times before becoming the *Elk Rapids Progress*. Under each of its incarnations, the publication never failed to provide its readers with the essential news of the day as well as the often witty, sometime sarcastic opinions and observations of the various editors.

This book, and the others in the *Bay Breezes* series, offer a survey of the small town newspaper in general and of early Antrim County and Elk Rapids specifically. By cataloguing the old newspapers in this manner, the publisher is providing readers not only with a valuable tool for genealogical research, but also a highly entertaining tome that anyone with an interest in history and even the slightest connection to Elk Rapids and the Grand Traverse Country will want to have on his or her book shelf.

Amy Whitaker

—Editor of the *Town Meeting.*

Acknowledgments

Glenn Ruggles -- Author and advocate of Oral History. Thank you for the photograph for the front cover of this book and for your continuing support.

Amy Whitaker -- Thanks for writing the Introduction for this volume.

James Keller -- Thanks for the excellent job of proof reading.

Elk Rapids Area
Historical Society -- Thank you for continuing to support this series of *BAY BREEZES*.

Michael Neumann -- My computer 'Guru'. I appreciate your expertise.

Linda (Neumann) Weinzapfel -- Thanks for the graphics for the front and back cover designs.

Table of Contents

Note To Readers: The date leading into each paragraph of text of this book is the date of the newspaper issue in which it may be found.

Chapter 1
Antrim County

01 02 80 The Board of Supe's proceedings took up considerable space in our paper the past two weeks. If they would meet less frequently, have shorter meetings, put their proceedings into some kind of shape, not have such long-winded resolutions just to make the people believe they have been doing something, pay the publisher of *The Herald* (of course) legal rates for publishing them, it would be a good thing for the county and a good thing for the tax payers.

We are unable to get the proceedings of the Board of Supe's at the imaginary county seat, Bellaire, on the 18ᵗʰ ult., consequently we shall not be able to dish up another toothsome morsel this week.

01 09 80 The Board of Supe's have at last adjourned sine die[sic]. It is about time. They have saddled on to the people a big load in the shape of taxes and the county seat matter. They have spent for Supervisors services since their last June meeting over $800, while the Grand Traverse county Board only spent $158 for services.

01 09 80 We have searched the records and have found therein many grave errors and many big bills. We have read our exchanges and have found in them that the Clerk is sitting at the "imaginary county seat, Bellaire," that the Board of Sup's have held a meeting of no special importance except to audit to themselves a few more bills and to vote praises to themselves for doing so. We know that the Treasurer and Judge of Probate are here yet and are likely to remain at the county seat.

01 09 80 Wonder if they have a regular mail at the "imaginary county seat Bellaire", now. When the County Clerk left the county seat they hadn't for his mail had to be forwarded to Mancelona.

Mr. Nelson Todd of N.Y., has purchased the Antrim County Poor Farm.

01 16 80 Sheriff Cameron came down from Bellaire Saturday last, and told us that no mail route had been established. Lively town for a C.S. But county seats don't generally bring much business, but they make taxes high, particularly when a removal is tried.

01 23 80 The county seat matter is hot in Wexford county, so we see by *The Manton Tribune*. It is hardly time for it to get very hot here, but we expect some one will be whooping it up before long.

01 30 80 M.F. Gates recently sold farm near the "imaginary county seat" for $400.

01 30 80 We learn that the County Clerk is copying the parts of the Supervisors records which the writ of certiorari [sic] from the Supreme Court calls for. Hope he enjoys it as well as we did when we copied the entire October meeting so to be able to present it to our readers.

01 23 80
        Judge Hatch will hold Court
          In the County somewhere,
        But never said, I'll hold it
          In the Town of Bellaire.

        The Supreme Court says, Hold!
          To the Supes up there,
        'Till it settles the question
          In regard to Bellaire.

        Oh break the news tenderly
          To the Supes up there,
        That a S.C. Injunction
          Broods over Bellaire.

01 30 80 James Briggs and son are rebuilding the chimneys at the Court House. They had become so very unsafe that Sheriff Cameron was obliged to order the work done.

01 30 80 A new mail route has been established between Eastport and Mancelona, which will take in the offices of Keno (Bellaire), Arkona, Snowflake, Central Lake. They have at last a mail at Bellaire.

01 30 80
        We'll wager a cent 'gainst an old gray mare,
          That the Supers' of the County up at Bellaire,
        Everlastingly pulled their thin lank hair,
          When they read the injunction that was served on them
             there.

02 06 80 By Chove! We have forgotten to say anything about Super's or taxes for a long time. The solution of the problem $3 to $1 is this: If we had raised taxes at the same rate on our evaluation that Grand Traverse County did on hers, where we now pay $30 taxes on property in this county we would only have to pay $10 on the same.

02 06 80 From *The Leelanau Enterprise*: The temper of neighbor Ben Davis, of The *Progress,* is slightly roiled at the removal of the county site from Elk Rapids to Bellaire, and the consequent enormous taxes to which the people are subjected. We would suggest to Ben. the following hymn as appropriate to the occasion:

        Oh think of a home over there,
        Where we've voted the new county site,
        Where the orbs of wild animals glare,
        And the woods make perpetual night.
        Where the bear with her cubs has her lair,
        And the County Board lingers to fight;
        Oh think of the home over there,
        At the sweet sylvan site at Bellaire!
        Closing with the Benny diction.

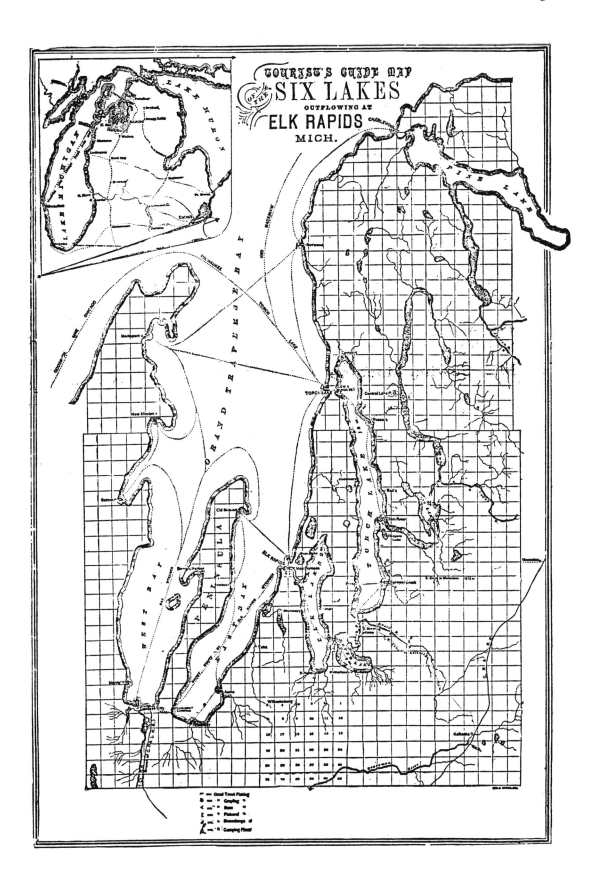

02 13 80 We learn that the County Clerk has lost the key to the vault doors in his office.

02 13 80 Last December the Board of Supervisors drew about $200 from the Treasury, putting it into Leavitt's hands and ordered him to use it in the commencement of suits against the County Treasurer to make him remove his office from Elk Rapids. He drew the money; but has commenced no proceedings. They have authorized the Chairman and Clerk to issue the bond of the County for $500, get the money on it, put that into Leavitt's hands to be disbursed according to his discretion. What right have the Board to take any such proceedings at Keno, Bellaire, or any other "imaginary" county seat after the Supreme Court has commanded a stay of all proceedings? What right have they at any time to make Leavitt, Getty, or any other man, who is not County Treasurer, the disburser of public funds of the County? We think the Supreme Court had better issue another stay to such illegal proceedings.

The building committee sold $140 worth of bricks which they claimed belonged to the County, and disbursed that money as they pleased, without paying that money into the County Treasury as the law requires. The same committee sold the County Poor Farm and a payment of $150 has been or is to be soon to be paid. Will the committee illegally spend that or pay it into the County Treasury where it properly belongs? Is it not about time the people should know where the money is going to and should demand it should be paid into the Treasury and paid out in a legal manner and after the bills are audited and allowed? Things are getting to be decidedly mixed.

02 13 80 The Board of Supervisors met last Tuesday and resolved that they could not obey the commands of the Supreme Court in answer to the writ by next Monday.

02 20 80 As near as can be found out County Clerk, Harriman, lost his keys to the vault doors in his office and sent to Detroit for some new ones. They not arriving, Harriman and Leavitt got into a considerable sweat about it. It seems that a stranger, who claimed to be a jeweler came there Wednesday of last week, and as near as we can gather from the reports, found a couple of keys tied together with a string. Suspecting, but not having positive knowledge whose keys they were, and wishing to have some fun at Harriman and Leavitt's expense, it is said that he offered to open the doors for $25, that he afterwards went in and examined the lock and again offered to open the doors at that price. Harriman and Leavitt having determined to burst the doors open the on Friday night if the keys did not come, and having little faith in the Jeweler's ability as an expert in such business, or not wishing to draw on their own pockets, refused to pay anything, so the Jeweler gave Harriman the keys he had found and the doors were opened.

Suspecting that they had struck a big mare's nest they got out some papers issued by Wm. W. Johnson, J.P., and early Saturday morning arrested the Jeweler on some charge, and spent all Saturday trying to develop something in said mare's nest. The fellow proved to sharp for the whole crowd of them. He denied having stolen the keys, said he had committed no crime, defied them, tantalized them, black-guarded them and made fun of them all day. By night they got enough of him, retired from the contest, beaten at that little game — at Keno.

It seems to us that the Supreme Court of this State has no rights which the majority of our Board of Supervisors are bound to respect. They just yell "Keno" and then proceed with their proceedings.

04 09 80 John Hartwell is Supervisor of Helena again.

Geo. H. Bender is supervisor for Mancelona township for the next term.

D. H. Stebbins of Banks will meet at "Bellaire, the imaginary County Seat" for once more as Supervisor.

Mrs. John Harriman of Keno was candidate for the office of town clerk of Forest Home against Austin, the old clerk, and was beaten by one vote.

At Torch Lake they had a pretty hot time. Daniel Blakely was elected over P. M. Russell. The County Seat matter gave Blakely the majority of three votes.

At Milton there were two tickets in the field. Wm. Cameron was elected over Alex. Campbell for Supervisor.

04 23 80 L.G. Evans of Eastport has taken the contract to carry the mail from here to Charlevoix, and entered upon his duties Wednesday.

04 23 80 Is it not pretty near time for the supers to meet again over there? Should think they would be pretty near out of funds now.

06 04 80 A stump speaker of the Greenback persuasion is laboring with the people in the vicinity of Bellaire.

06 11 80 ELK RAPIDS—During the storm last Saturday night the wind blew the nuts off from a cast iron stove which was riding at anchor on the walk between S. Yalomstein's store and the Lake View House. Only the bottom of the stove could be found next morning.

06 11 80 Last Saturday evening about 7 o'clock a tornado or a what do you call it struck this village, blowing off about 360 feet of the roof from the stock house at the furnace and blowing in some of the glass in the fronts of some of the stores. The damage at the furnace was between $1,500 and $2,000.

CENTRAL LAKE—Considerable damage was done by the storm at this place. Whole fields of wheat and potatoes were washed out of the ground and the fall of rain was immense.

Vances—At the head of the five mile lake was the scene of another overturning. Mr. Vance's mill was taken from its foundation and moved about 15 feet. His dam was washed away and considerable other damage was done.

EASTPORT—Wm. J. Henry's dam at this place was washed away.

KEARNEY—The bridges down in Kearney were all washed away. Some of the bridges at Intermediate Lake were washed away. Damage is impossible to estimate, but will reach several thousand dollars.

06 11 80 We learn from a telegram received by a gentleman at this place that the proceedings of the Board of Supervisors of this county were sustained by the Supreme Court in regard to the removal of the county seat from this place to Keno—Bellaire. Although the decision does not please us, we certainly hope it is for the best. While we opposed the removal and could see no good reason for removing, nor can we yet, we have opposed it because we thought it right, because we thought it would be a bad thing for the county, and for the reason that the movement was premature.

06 18 80 We have encountered one enthusiastic Garfield man since the nomination who offered to bet us $100 that Garfield would be elected President. We hadn't the money and we don't think our friend had either. All bets should be declared off in Antrim county this year as every tax payer in the county will need his spare change to pay taxes which will be high enough goodness knows for the next decade.

07 02 80 D.H. Stebbins of Banks, has been appointed by the Board of Supervisors Treasurer of the County in place of R.W. Bagot, resigned, who will enter upon the duties of the office the 15th inst., or as soon after as possible.

Last Monday Mr. R.W. Bagot, sent in his resignation to the Board of Supervisors as Treasurer, together with a statement showing the financial condition of the county. The Board met Monday and passed a resolution the effect of which was, they sent a special messenger Thursday from Bellaire requesting him to meet the Board with the books and vouchers and then his resignation would be acted upon.

07 16 80 The population of Antrim county is 5,200.

09 17 80 There were 61 marriages, 43 deaths and 129 births in Antrim County during the year 1879.

09 24 80 A Mr. Stover, of Kearney has just built a new grist mill, and it is in running order.

10 01 80 We learn that the Cameron school house on the Torch Lake road was burned Wednesday night. Some of the people in the district are glad of it. Cause of fire unknown.

10 22 80 NORWOOD—Mrs. Jane Lucia, of Norwood, died on Sunday morning from the effects of a cancer under her tongue. She had been treated some months ago by Dr. Evans who pronounced her incurable, but more recently by bogus Dr. Spayne who had flattered her friends that he could produce a cure. She bled to death from the cancer eating off an artery under her tongue.

10 29 80 Frazier, (Rep.), is the knight of the rostrum. When he warms up to his subject, people have to skootch a little to escape the torrents of eloquence and things. He ties loose the blood-hounds of war! Waves the tattered appendages of the crimsoned waumasetta [sec] and gesticulates and squeals like 200 lbs. of calico on her first pair of skates.

The most ridiculous mess of hash the Rep's offer to a hungered people is "Payment of Rebel Claims." It looks too pitiful to see a stalwart mossback weeping and gnashing his teeth over an improbability if not an impossibility. We feel for them just as we do for the poor simple domestic, who sat weeping as if her heart would break, until her mistress heard the moaning and sought the sorrowful maiden to ascertain the cause. "Biddy Jane, what causeth thy grief? Why those pearly tears? Come confide in me, reveal to me the secret of thy woes. "I-I-was just thinkin' (boo-hoo) if I had a baby and if that baby should die--how-how bad I'd feel--boo-hoo!

10 29 80 It is reported that Stebbins the appointee of the Board of Supervisors as successor to R.W. Begot as treasurer is not clear headed enough to do the business of the office. If that is the case voters had better cast their ballots for Cameron the Greenback nominee who, we will warrant can do the business satisfactorily.

10 29 80 The Supervisors were in session the fore part of this week. Among other bills past were two raising the salary of the District Attorney from $200 to $800... and that of County Treasurer from $400 to $600.

The county jail at Bellaire is fast nearing completion. It stands on a stone foundation and is built of 2x6 inch scantling laid flat, one on the other. The Sheriff's residence will be erected on the south end of the jail building.

11 05 80 The county ticket will stand as follows:

Sheriff	C.W. Doolittle.
County Clerk	John Harriman
Treasurer	James Cameron
Prosecuting Attorney	Roswell Leavitt.
Judge of Probate	William Getty

11 12 80 The old Court House and grounds at the Elk Rapids are now for sale by Roswell Leavitt, who is ready to receive offers for the same, and will sell as soon as a favorable offer is received.

11 26 80 TORCH LAKE – The large saw mill at this place has called for labor not to resume again until the sound of the whistle in the spring. Many of the employees have dispersed to various lumber camps, and the hum of the saw, the gentle voices of the tracksman holding conversation with their horses, and the general business like activity of the town become as things of the past, and settled to a calm repose.

11 26 80 The present storm has proved to be one of the most relentless and tempestuous in the history of this section; highways are impassible and all transportation temporarily blocked up, the snow from Atwood to Norwood is from 3 to 10 ft. deep and commands even the U.S. Mail to halt.

12 03 80 Their was a meeting of some interested persons at the head of Torch River last Monday to plan bridging the river at the point. The county donated $25 for that purpose and persons interested will build the bridge and furnish material. The bridge will only be a temporary structure.

12 17 80 The temporary bridge across Torch River has been completed and is now in good condition for crossing with teams.

01 06 81 SPENCER CREEK — A pleasant dance was had at Joseph VanCamp's Christmas eve. About 100 persons took part and enjoyed the dance and supper.

The people of this place had a Christmas tree at the Angel school house, and the building was so crowded that several persons could not obtain entrance. An enjoyable evening was had.

01 06 81 If the editor had said to look up the interests of the "Antrim County Poor Farm," or Alexander Campbell, of Milton, we could have believed that he had taken a holiday for the last six months.

01 21 81 There is some talk of organizing a Historical Society. Mr. W.W. Johnson, of Snowflake, has proposed it. Let the people get together and organize one and we think it would be highly interesting and profitable both to old and young. Central Lake would be a good point at which to meet, and the time of meeting can be made known through the columns of the county papers. Let us see what can be done.

01 28 81 We have received the 15th semi-annual price list of the Lake Side Farm, Snowflake, this County. W.W. Johnson is doing a large business with farmers of the West, selling them seedlings and cuttings. By the business in which he is engaged, he brings into the county quite a sum of money, which he invests here.

02 04 81 THE COURTS — Anna Charlott Lawson *vs.* John Peter Ogren was arrested and proposed to settle, and went to Charlevoix to procure money with which "to settle the bill", which was $100. On his return without the money the case was resumed. Friday last the sheriff left him for a moment while he was eating his dinner and Ogren made tracks for some fairer clime, and has not been since heard from.

Wm. H. Riley *vs* Chas. A. Newton — trespass on the case, before Justice McLaughlin Saturday. This action was brought for selling the carcass of a "gentleman porker" for food. The case was settled without trial.

02 11 81 SNOWFLAKE — The Snowflake P. O. has recently been supplied with a letter scale for weighing letters, &c.[sic], and the P. M. is happy.

03 11 81 A bill has been introduced in the legislature, detaching a small portion of Kalkaska county and adding the same to Antrim county. The bill proposes to make Torch river the boundary line, and the specific object is to place our county in a position so as to help erect and maintain a bridge across the river. This would be a great advantage to quite a large portion of Kalkaska county as well as to southern Antrim. Farmers living in the vicinity would have the privilege of marketing produce at Elk Rapids or Kalkaska. Considering the benefits that would arise from the passage of the bill we are strongly in favor of it. -*Herald*.

03 11 81 A man by the name of Fred K. Powers, of Kearney township, has left for parts unknown in company with a daughter of Roswell Jacobs. A wife and three children mourn his departure, and the parents of the erring girl are deeply afflicted on account of the strange conduct of their child.

The school under the efficient management of Miss Gates, of Elk Rapids, is progressing finely. The house is a new one, got up on the old fashioned red school house plan, all except the paint. The chimney barely projecting through the roof gives the whole thing a kind of bobtailed apearance.

05 20 81 Mr. Ed Stafford, of Norwood, has been moving some building for Lowell Sours and Perry Stocking this week.

      A new arrival at Eastport in the person of a fine little daughter, at the home of Mr. and Mrs. Jno. W. Pearl.

05 27 81 Republicans, subscribe for the *Antrim County Herald.* $1.50 per annum; fifty cents during the campaign. Address *Herald,* Mancelona, Mich.

06 17 81 TORCH LAKE – F.J. Lewis returned from Chicago about a week ago. He is now prepared for the Summer Campaign, everything within and about the hotel is in the best of order, particularly noticeable is the well trimmed and tastfully laid out grounds, which render the Lewis House so pleasant and attractive. Among other spring improvements Mr. Lewis has just erected a wind mill pump, for supplying the hotel with water.

06 24 81 TORCH LAKE – "Chubb" Bargy, had his left hand cut off a few days ago while working in a saw mill in Hillsdale county, this state. His brother Peter C. Bargy, of Central Lake, left here Monday to visit him.

      The *Queen of the Lakes,* made us the first visit of the season last Saturday, taking down a lot of freight on her return for Dexter & Noble.

      The schooner *Duval* loaded with lumber for J.H. Silkman and left for Milwaukee last Saturday evening.

07 22 81 One of the finest Summer Resorts is at the Lewis House, Torch Lake. The hotel has over one hundred rooms and the appointments are good. The grounds about the hotel which are very large, are simply beautiful. Mr. Lewis has put a good deal of work on them this year and success has crowned his efforts. In connection with the hotel is a fine bowling alley, and billiard room. For rest and quiet, for a good time generally, take in Torch Lake, and the Lewis House.

08 05 81 The boilers and machinery for a steam saw mill, are near the site of the saw mill, two miles South of Alba during the past two or three weeks.

08 05 81 The new steam saw mill is in operation at Spencer Creek and doing a good business condiering the size of the mill.

08 16 81 SNOWFLAKE – A new school house is being built at Snowflake. The size will be 20x30, and it is a very neat building. George Washburn has the contract for building it.

10 28 81 Fitchville is located in the town of Custer on section 30, about 8 1/2 miles east of Spencer Creek. It has a good water power, which is used by Fitch Brothers in driving a saw mill, pump factory and turning shop. It has a weekly mail, supplied from Westwood on the G.R. & I rail road. We understand there is a good opening for a store at that point, and that the proprietors of the place will donate lots to those who will erect buildings upon them.

11 04 81 The post-office of Snowflake, this county has been discontinued, the mail going to Bellaire.

11 18 81 SNOWFLAKE — The new school house is nearly completed and school will commence in a few days. Miss Ella Sliter, of Central Lake, has engaged the school for a four month term and from present indications the house will be well filled with scholars.

12 16 81 In Antrim county there are 571 acres of U.S. land; 12,369 acres of State land, and 196,207 acres of Railroad land for sale.

12 23 81 The post-office of Elgin, Antrim county, has been discontinued, and all persons getting mail at that office, can hereafter receive mail at the Elk Rapids office.

01 06 82 We are happy if the snow we now have has come to stay, and hope there will be more with it. Every inch of snow on the ground in this county means so many dollars. If we have six weeks sleighing there will be a difference probably of $150,000, in the business of the county, that much at all events will be paid for wood and labor.

The Congregationalists of Banks are preparing to build a $1,200 Church, and to have it done in the spring.

The recently discontinued post-office at Snowflake has been re-established.

01 13 82 About three o'clock Thursday morning, Jan. 5, the village of Wetzell was alarmed by the cry of "fire." The store of Wetzell Bros. was in flames. The fire making such rapid progress that those sleeping in the building did not have time to secure their personal effects. The stocks was insured for $4,000. Loss above insurance about $3,000.

If you wish to live in a healthful country, where all kinds of vegetables and fruits grow to perfection come North and settle in Antrim, Benzie, Charlevoix, Emmet, Grand Traverse or Kalkaska counties...

02 03 82 Wetzel, the first station north of Mancelona, appears to be progressing splendidly. Calling at the place one year since I saw only a dwelling house, a small house for the men and other appurtenances usually seen about a lumber camp; while passing the same place a day or two since I saw twenty houses all of them one story, but built with a view to neatness and order which speaks well for the residents.

Last week we published in our Eastport correspondence an item relative to the proposed removal of L.G. Evans from the mail route between Elk Rapids and Charlevoix, and that another carrier would take the route. We can only reiterate what our correspondent has said, that Mr. Evans has been the most prompt and efficient mail carrier we have had for several years and that no reason is known here for the change.

02 03 82 EASTPORT — The wood inspector was here inspecting wood for the Iron Co. on the 27th. Reports say that he has returned to Elk Rapids to have his "jaw" inspected and "docked."

The saw mill between Wetzell and Alba is doing a lively business, employing one double circular saw and twenty men.

02 10 82 Alba is about to rise from the obscurity of a flag station; books, receipts etc. having arrived there February first. T.R. & J.E. Vanwert denote the building and ground for a station.

02 24 82 The arrival of the U.S. Mail at Snowflake, Mich. Feb. 15, was celebrated by the shooting off of several fire crackers and other demonstrations. W.W. Johnson is the post master.

03 10 82 Why doesn't some great big politician go about it and have the northern boundary lines of Antrim and Charlevoix counties straightened? —*Petoskey Record.*

The question asked by all desiring to travel from home to the "Corners" or Brownstown — Shall we go with a sleigh and carry a wagon, or vice versa?

03 17 82 EASTPORT — J.W. Pearl has been buying a "Patching Trotter."

03 24 82 Silkman's mill at Torch Lake commenced running Feb. 27, for the purpose of sawing timber and lumber for a new dock which Mr. Silkman intends building on the bay at that place this spring.

03 31 82 TELEGRAPHIC — A Project that Should Receive the Support of Elk Rapids and of every Town Along the Line.

In connection with our local last week in regard to the telegraph line from this point to Central Lake *via* Williamsburg, Spencer Creek and Bellaire, we can now say that it is a dead, sure thing, and is bound to go through. This town has also communication by navigable lakes with all these points, except Williamsburg, which is only a few minutes drive from Elk Lake, and is so near to the lake that the lumber manufactured there this summer will go down the lake to reach the seaboard at this place. All the other towns have direct water communication, and will soon have telegraphic.

03 31 82 It has been hinted to us that there was a movement on foot to try and remove the county seat from Bellaire to some out-of-the-way point on the eastern part of the county, and that Elk Rapids was looked upon as a town that would help to do it. Unless we mistake the temper of the Elk Rapids people, they do not care particularly where the county seat is, so long as the business of the county is done up in some kind of shape, and so far as moving the seat to some other point we believe they would say, "Let it stay where it is, and thus avoid further and useless expense." Bellaire is now, perhaps, the best point in the county for the seat, aside from Elk Rapids, and we would not give more than fifty cents to have it back here again. To the agitators and removers, we would say, go into some honorable business and you could make more money than at county seat removing.

03 31 82 S.F. Hill has resigned his position as Chairman of the County Board of Examiners, on account of not having the time to attend to the business of the Board.

EASTPORT – Best & Co. have purchased land here for their saw mill site, and expect to be here next month with their mill. They also intend to put in machinery for staves and heading.

03 31 82 There is a vacancy in the office of justice owning to the misprinting of a name; Oscar L. Craw, instead of Oscar H. who was elected over George D. Wycoff.

SNOWFLAKE – W.W. Johnson, proprietor of the Lake Side Farm at Snowflake, received last week 400 pounds of tree seeds from Germany.

In speaking of the telegraph line from this place to Bellaire. The *Breeze* says: This sounds like business, and Bellaire will heartily co-operate.

Town Hall carried in Kearney by 26 majority.

Forest Home Town Hall was voted down by 17 majority.

EASTPORT – Chas. Hultz of Torch Lake, is closing out his goods, and intends to go out of mercantile business. He has purchased a fine little steam boat which he will run on Torch Lake, principally for passengers, we believe.

EASTPORT – The "Town" has met." For Supervisor, James Cameron; Treasurer, Archie Cameron; Clerk, C. Acker; School Inspectors, John Pearl; Highway Commissioner, P.C. Bargy; Constables, R. Eagleton, and H. Blakely.

04 14 82 To-day it is expected that the prominent men of Central Lake, Bellaire, Spencer Creek, and Williamsburg will meet at the store of Ruchmore & Holbrook, for the purpose of making arrangements in regard to the telegraph line, which is to be put up connecting these places with Elk Rapids. The line will to through.

04 14 82 The following is the new board as far as we have been able to obtain the same:

Banks	L.M. Kanagy,
Central Lake	R.R. Wilkinson,
Custer	A.J. Jackson,
Chestonia	John Harmon,
Echo	J. Hackett,
Elk Rapids	James J. McLaughlin,
Forest Home	Johnson,
Helena	Henry W. Stewart,
Jordan	
Kearney	George W. Montgomery,
Mancelona	Bender,
Milton	Campbell,
Star	A.J. Clark,
Torch Lake	James Cameron.

04 21 82 *Mancelona Herald* A man named Saddler, employed by the Pine Lake Iron Co., while leading one of the horses belonging to that firm, into stable at Ironton, was bitten by the animal, upon which, he pulled out the horse's tongue, and by some means either cut or tore it from the creature's head. He then fled to the house of an acquaintance, in Echo, but was followed and arrested. He is now in jail at Charlevoix. The horse was shot, and the man will probably have plenty of time to learn lessons in humanity before he is free to drive another team.

04 21 82 Specifications should read as follows for telegraph poles: Not less than 25 feet long, 42 inches at the top, good sound cedar timber, and not less than 27 to the mile.

04 21 82 Subscriptions for the Elk Rapids and Central Lake telegraph line will be received at the *Progress* office at $1 each. Now walk right up and pay your cash.

04 21 82 Seventy-five real-estate owners are requested to pay in to Rushmore & Holbrook $1 each to aid in constructing the telegraph line from Elk Rapids to Central Lake.

04 28 82 A pleasant trip to take, we think, and one that will become a popular one before long, would be from Elk Rapids through the Nineteen lakes. We understand that in the near future boats will so run that this can be done.

The Clam River bridge, which cost the county $800 is a disgrace to the county, and proper steps should be taken to level the whole concern.

04 28 82 Be sure and pay your $1 at Rushmore & Holbrook's store to assist in building the telegraph line from Elk Rapids to Central Lake. We know one firm in Elk Rapids which paid $800 in cash to bring the line here. The above firm have showed all the public spirit they should in the matter of telegraph lines and now it is time for some one else to make a move. Come right up and pay your $1 and really show up if you have any public spirit.

05 05 82 The telegraph line which we have heretofore spoken of still boometh, and the work will commence in a week, probably. The line will be a great benefit to the towns through which it will pass, and that is what Elk Rapids and the *Progress* want.

The *Progress* congratulates the towns of Williamsburg, Spencer Creek, Bellaire and Central Lake, upon the bright prospects of their soon having a telegraph line.

05 05 82 Work is now progressing finely on the building to be occupied by the Shugart House, and Mr. Shugart hopes to be able to open it for the accommodation of the public by June 1. *-Breeze.*

05 05 82 The Antrim county jail at Bellaire, is a perfect terror, and persons who are inclined to take the wrong path, are respectfully invited to take a trip to the above town and take a peep at the aforesaid jail. It seems to us that it is one of the "jailiest jails" we ever heard of or saw before. We have never been incarcerated; (newspaper men are such models) but that jail strikes terror into our inmost gizzard. The floor is of 2x4's spiked together and the cells are of bar iron riveted. The outside of the building is not unpleasant to look at, it being about 40x80 and is painted white; but that jail!

14

05 05 82 The Chairman of the Board of Supervisors, L.M. Kanagy, of Banks, has the happy faculty of expediting the business of the Board of Supervisors, and consequently is the right man for that place.

05 05 82 Resolved, That we, the Board of Supervisors of Antrim County, don't care about the public knowing anything about our proceedings; therefore don't print. — Carried.

05 05 82 County Clerk Harriman has the most complete and convenient arrangement in the fire-proof vault that we have ever seen for keeping the many large books of the county, one feature being that it saves all wear on the covers of the books. –*Breeze.*

THE FIRE-PROOF VAULT? BUILT AT BELLAIRE, (KENO) THE "IMAGINARY COUNTY SEAT."

01 30 80 We learn that the County Clerk is copying the parts of the Supervisors records which the writ of certiorari [sic] from the Supreme Court calls for. Hope he enjoys it as well as we did when we copied the entire October meeting so to be able to present it to our readers.

05 12 82 We have an advertisement in this issue, of a notice to contractors to build three miles of road including the Torch River bridge. We have seen plans of this bridge and if made according to plans and specifications it will be quite handsome.

05 12 82 TORCH LAKE — James R. Nichols met with quite a serious accident on Friday, while throwing his arm upwards in the act of striking an ox with a whip he dislocated his shoulder joint which luxation [sic] proved a very painful and difficult one to reduce.

05 19 82 The insulators for the telegraph line from Elk Rapids to South Arm to the number of 1,200 came on the *Faxton* Tuesday. Nine miles of poles had been set at Wednesday's writing.

05 19 82 We have so far been able to learn the names of the lakes and rivers outflowing at Elk Rapids: The names are Elk River, Elk Lake, The Narrows, Round Lake, Torch River, Torch Lake, Clam River, Clam Lake, Grass River, Grass Lake, Intermediate River and what is known as Intermediate Lake is a chain of lakes and rivers, the names of the rivers being the same as the lakes. They are named Central, Clow, Hanley, Sissons, Wilson, Bowers, Sinclair, Mathers, Wells and Scott. We have heretofore mentioned that there were nineteen, but we believe that we have given them all. Bowers Lake is sometimes given as Gotham and Bowers, but that is really one Lake. Fifteen lakes are enough anyway.

05 26 82 The *Breeze*: Deputy Sheriff Maxfield says to tell "Ben" that the Antrim county jail is a jail, that it was made to hold folks, and that no prisoner has ever escaped from it.

06 02 82 The Lewis House grounds, at Torch Lake, are lovely this spring. Frank certainly has the most beautiful location for a hotel that we have ever seen. For the past two or three years the proprietor has expended a large amount in beautifying his elegant grounds, and now it seems that almost perfection has been reached.

06 02 82 The Mancelona correspondent of the the *Breeze* is right on the war path in trying to make sinners "flee from the wrath to come." He gets right up and howls. Wake up snakes and crawl!

06 02 82 Blakely & Blakely have opened a general store at Eastport. Both members of the firm called on us Tuesday before going to Traverse City where they purchased their goods.

06 02 82 Three divorces granted at the last term of the circuit court for this county. Evidently this is a poor climate for married people.

06 09 82 We learn that the new bridge to be built over Torch River, will only leave a channel 38 feet wide. This, if it is so, is decidedly wrong, as it will allow the passage of only the smaller boats. The specifications in regard to dredging the river several years ago, was to the effect that the channel should be widened 50 feet. We hope that this matter will be looked into by those most interested, and that the river at that point will be left at the width heretofore mentioned.

06 16 82 EASTPORT — Dr. Coolman's pretty ponies trot through our town very frequently. The Dr. has quite a practice in Antrim county.

We have ten dwelling houses, two stores and two blacksmith shops, and would have a saw mill if it could get here from Traverse City.

06 23 82 We have in mind an inland route from this point to Charlevoix which will eventually receive considerable attention. Now if Charlevoix parties will take hold of the matter we shall be most happy. By looking closely at the map you will find that only about three and a half miles of land interrupts inland navigation from this point to Charlevoix...

06 23 82 SPENCER CREEK — Mr. Barber, of Summit, Traverse Co., passed through town on the 16th inst. He had in his possession a piece of pure copper weighing 13 lb. We were informed by Mr. Barber that this was only about (?) of the piece and that several such pieces were disinterred near the head of Torch Lake, by parties digging a ditch.

06 23 82 The steamer *Bellaire* has delivered at Drayton's landing three cargoes of the stone for the court house, and to-day they are being hauled from thence to the grounds with teams.

06 30 82 EASTPORT — Does the moon look down on a more beautiful sheet of water than our Torch Lake?

Work on Messrs. Hull & Best's saw-mill is going steadily on. The building will be 40x80 — a hoop and shingle factory attached.

06 30 82 The road between this place and Torch Lake is in very good shape. Considerable work having been done on it lately.

07 07 82 SPENCER CREEK — The steamer *Ida* carried from Spencer Creek and Clam River, 79 people on the 4th, to Bellaire.

As the *Progress* is fond of fish stories we will try and submit a few which are hard to beat. J. Cawley and C. Brown caught 100 bass and perch in Clam Lake on the 18th ult.; R. Holibert caught 27 speckled trout in J.H. Berry's mill pond on the 20th ult.; R. Holibert and J.D. Angell caught 50 trout in Rapid river on the 24th ult.; A.B. Probasco caught 28 trout in Coy's mill pond on Monday; B.L. and C.E. Smith caught 26 trout in Coy's mill pond Tuesday.

07 07 82 About 50 miles of wire came on the *Faxton* last week for the telegraph line to South Arm. The poles for the line have been set as far as Central Lake and the stringing of the wire will commence next Monday.

07 07 82 On Saturday, July 1, John H. Silkman, of Torch Lake, received a telegram from Milwaukee, informing him of the death of his only son, Samuel H. Silkman. Mr. Silkman left Sunday, for Milwaukee.

07 28 82 Our correspondent from Central Lake hinted to us some weeks since something which occurred in room number three in the Wilson House, Torch Lake. The following from the *Petoskey Record* will probably explain the "blind joke": Early this spring Mr. E.F. Wheeler, who has resided in Petoskey some four years, and who kept the Park House here for the last two years, went to Charlevoix and leased the Fountain City House for the season. Among his boarders was a gentleman doing business there for a Chicago lumber firm, named Andrew W. Hutchins. An intimacy sprang up between Mrs. Wheeler and Hutchins, and Mr. Wheeler began to suspect that his wife and the lumber dealer were altogether too friendly. So Monday night last, July 10th, his suspicions were fully verified, as on the occasion Mr. Wheeler, in company with an officer from Charlevoix, and the proprietor of the Wilson House, at Torch Lake, found his wife and Hutchins quietly sleeping the happy hours away in a room in that hotel.

07 28 82 The new mill, at Eastport, has commenced operations. It is owned by Hull & Best.

07 28 82

The wonderful Hubbell,
  Is causing much trouble,
In quarters official they say,
  With his voluntary tax,
Backed up by the ax,
  To decapitate heads that don't pay.

The Boys will remember,
  The sixth of November,
Your wicked unscrupulous plan;
  To bolster up self,
With ill-gotten pelf,
  Besides stabbing a much better man.

08 04 82 The *Charlevoix Sentinel* thinks that country papers should not publish the news, like the little episode which occurred at Torch Lake, recently.

08 04 82 The Wetzell saw mill with boarding house, black smith shop, etc., was burned recently. The loss was $10,000, which is partially covered by insurance.

08 04 82 EASTPORT — The tug *Elk Lake*, belonging to the Iron Co., is taking the cord wood from our shores very rapidly.

08 11 82 CUSTER — The brick yard recently started by John Call, of Custer, is in running order, and first class brick are being made.

08 18 82 Thomas Crow, the person incarcerated in the county jail for larceny, escaped Sunday night but was captured Monday night the other side of Mancelona. It will be remembered that he stole some tools from A. Pollock's tool chest.

08 18 82 It is about time that Antrim county patriots began itching for office. We hope that both the Republicans and Greenbackers will put forth their best men — we have not heard that the Democrats will do anything- so that the offices can be filled with those competent to discharge the duties.

08 18 82 We learn that Phil. Russell has the contract for building the Torch river bridge for $2,750.

09 01 82 We hope that it will never be said again "that the only way to convict a man of murder in Antrim county would be to cut up the corpse and feed it in chunks to the jury."

09 08 82 Chas T. Hickox has been retained by Antrim county in the murder trial, People *vs.* Martin Martinson.

09 08 82 The frequency that murder has been committed in Antrim county, and the easy escape of the murderers is a great cause for alarm among all classes of people. It seems as though a murder was looked upon as a big joke, and the murderer one who was awfully fond of joking. People may talk of the frequency of murder in the South or West, but we do not believe there is a county of only 5,000 inhabitants anywhere in this country, where more than 4 murders have been committed in 10 years. We believe a sentiment should be worked up, a right kind of a sentiment, whereby justice, not prosecution or malice, should be meted out to every criminal great or small. We take great pride in our County in some regards, but the frequency of murder is one cause of great regret among all classes of people, and it is about time a rebuke in some shape should be administered.

09 08 82 EASTPORT — The firm of Blakely & Blakely have dissolved partnership. F. Blakely having sold his share in the business to J. McPherson.

09 08 82 A team belonging to L.G. Evans, stage driver between this place and

Eastport, ran away last Monday. No damage done except breaking the forward axle of the wagon.

09 15 82 TORCH LAKE — Last Friday while Mr. Thompson's son and a couple of other boys were sitting on a log near the village, a bear made a rush for them and knocked young Thompson off the log, scattering his basket of vegetables. The boys fell promptly back to a more secure position, and bruin acting on the Jacksonian principle appropriated the spoils.

09 22 82 SPENCER CREEK — The telegraph poles are all set between this place and Bellaire.

John McAllister is getting out the timbers for the Torch River bridge.

Another Angell in our midst — 9½ pounds without the wings — to J.D. Angell and wife.

09 22 82 We hope the farmers of Antrim county will take right hold and make the Fair, to be held at Bellaire in October, a success. No reason why this county should not have a good fair.

09 22 82 O.J. Holbrook, with men started out Monday stringing the line from this place to Central Lake.

10 05 82 The telegraph wire is being stretched from this place to Bellaire.

10 05 82 P.M. Russell has commenced operations on the State road and bridge across Torch River. We understand he will commence driving piles this week.

10 13 82 To A Republican — We should suggest that he go and look at the criminal records of the county for the past correspondent of the *Breeze* who signs himself "A Republican" that two years, and see if he cannot there fine some "food for reflection."

In the first case of People *vs.* Welch, he will find a large expense incurred and no convictions — acquittal on some technical grounds.

The second case he will find never reached the jury- prisoner discharged because of defective papers made by the Prosecuting Attorney.

The case against Peterson charged with highway robbery never reached a jury — was thrown out of court because the Prosecuting Attorney had not brought it properly.

Look at the expense incurred and see if you find any convictions, during the past two years.

Here we witness the humiliating spectacle of the Prosecuting Attorney of the County of Antrim bringing a prosecution for the violation of a liquor law, after the law had been repealed.

For such ignorance of the laws to our mind there can be no excuse.

In each of these cases the Prosecuting Attorney has shown himself incompetent and wholly unfit for the office.

Elect him again if you want him, but excuse us from helping. We have the interests of our county too much at heart.

10 13 82 EASTPORT—Best & Hull's mill is sawing lumber for the town buildings at Bellaire. Timber for the lumber is still being landed. It is 30 feet long.

10 20 82 The Elk Rapids and Central Lake telegraph line will soon be completed to East Jordan. The people along the line can thank Mr. O.J. Holbrook, of this place, for it because he has worked night and day to accomplish this object.

10 27 82 SPENCER CREEK—R.W.Coy is shipping lumber to Torch Lake by tug *Silkman*.

11 03 82 The iron work for the new Torch River bridge will be done at the Iron Co.'s machine shop and foundry.

11 03 82 Alba has 293 inhabitants.

11 03 82 P.M. Russell informed us yesterday that he would have the Torch River bridge completed inside of a month, and is now ready for the iron work, all of which will be manufactured at Elk Rapids.

11 03 82 P.M. Russell has the bridge across Torch River well under way, and has commenced cleaning the bed of the road on the west side of the river, Phil. expects to have it so teams can cross by the first of December.

11 10 82 *Kalkaskian*--The Antrim county jail now contains six prisoners— three charged with murder, two with burglary, and one with grand larceny. Wicked county!

11 17 82 The *Breeze*: Chestonia and Star are building some excellent roads and their highway commissioners seem to understand that it helps a road to remove the roots from the wagon track.

12 01 82 The *Breeze*: New comers from Indiana and Canada are coming and settling in the northern part of Central Lake and Banks townships quite rapidly. Hardly a day passes without a new resident being added.

12 08 82 SPENCER CREEK—Winter has come and the merry chime of the bells is again heard.
Twelve new seats have been put into the school house, which some what relieves the crowded condition of the school.

12 15 82 TORCH LAKE—The Torch Lake property is advertised for sale, which includes store, saw mill, several hundred acres of land, tug, and other property. The price asked is $50,000, and we consider Torch Lake about the best point in Northern Michigan, for a capitalist. We have no advertisement but the property is for sale, nevertheless.

Chapter 2
Agriculture

03 11 81 Potatoes and apples are coming from Old Mission these days. The sleighing is fine on the bay.

06 17 81 Jacob Kaiser who purchased the farm South of town which formerly belonged to Mr. Geo. E. Steele arrived here from Germany Wednesday to take possession of the place.

06 24 81 The Grand Traverse county Agricultural Society will hold its fair October 4, 5, 6 and 7.

06 24 81 Mr. E. Newcomb, of East Bay, has invented a hay fork for hoisting hay from the load into the loft which was made at the furnace.

09 02 81 $1.12 is being paid for No. 1 wheat.

11 11 81 Mr. Edwin Elliot's threshing machine is stuck in the mud about 9 miles from Eastport in the "ox-bow" and the threshing contracts that he has on hand will have to lay over until the machine can be gotten out.

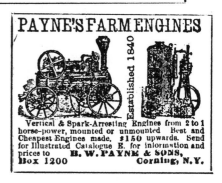
12 02 81 R. Swift exhibits, from his farm in this township, (Forest Home) a pie-melon, which measures two feet and twelve inches around, and three feet long, its weight being fifty one pounds. He also thrashed 120 bushels of rye from just five acres sown. Nine potatoes of the Shaker Russett variety were shown which filled a half-bushel measure. One of the nine weighing four and one-fourth pounds. The united weight of the nine being twenty-seven pounds.

12 23 81 Isaac Daw raised a new log house yesterday on his farm, in Whitewater.

01 13 82 A year or so ago a farmer living near Round Lake came to the drug store which then belonged to Mr. R.W. Bagot and wished to know if he would buy some opium, as he had some to sell, which he had taken from poppies on his farm. Mr. Bagot replied that he could not buy it, but he would send it to Powers & Weightman, of Philadelphia, and whatever they would pay he would give to him, the farmer. The firm to whom it was sent, said that it was the best kind of opium and wished Mr. Bagot to be sure and secure all of it he could, and paid for it about $7.00 or $8.00 per pound. We further learn that the farmer had sown wheat, which winter killed, and poppies came up instead, and that he gathered the gum. The amount gathered was eleven pounds and was rich with morphia. If this is so and we have no reason to doubt it, as Mr. Bagot told the facts to Mr. Watson, who is with Messrs. Rushmore & Holbrook, a profitable business can be made of growing the above plants for opium in this country, as there are few places where they can be grown successfully.

01 27 82 About fifty persons attended the Grange oyster supper at Mr. Sours' last Wednesday evening, and report a very enjoyable time. One hundred and seven persons partook of the supper, and the receipts for the evening can be found in another column. (Receipts -$29.38, Disbursements $12.47, Profit, $16.41.) A large number were from Williamsburg and adjoining towns and Mr. Sours' large farm house was thoroughly packed with people.

02 03 82 An enterprising farmer, a vender of the lacteal fluid, fluent in speech and as wise as old probabilities himself, made a serious mistake a few days ago. Suggestions having been made to him that it would be well to change his stock of cows for some that would give a better grade of milk, became indignant, and forthwith submitted a sample quart for analysis. The report was given when to his chagrin, he discovered that he had given for analysis, milk out of the wrong can.

02 17 82 Below we give the articles of the Antrim County Agricultural Society. As we have before stated the next meeting will be held at Central Lake...

03 17 82 That the Antrim County agricultural Society is securing a sure foot-hold, and that it will develop into a substantial, wide-spread and harmonious institution, is we believe, assured. Difficulties were met at the start. Officers had to be elected for members of the society, and those joining at the start were all from one small portion of the county. This, of course, located all of the officers in one neighborhood, and other portions of the county took the inference that it was a Bellaire concern, etc. This could not be helped at the time, but the officers were, however, elected with the understanding that they were to resign as soon as members were secured from other portions, and the society would thus be able to fill the offices as to fairly represent the whole county. The recent meeting at Central Lake did much to further the growth of the society, and perhaps more real headway was gained at this gathering than at all the others combined. This society will prove a grand thing for Antrim county, and should receive members, support and encouragement from all.

03 17 82 The firm of Dexter & Noble have purchased 90 tons of hay this winter which is being baled. The hay was all brought into town by our farmers, which speaks well for Antrim and Grand Traverse counties.

04 14 82 Isaac Love and George Lackey sold a young team of horses to Dan Phillips, Thursday. Consideration $200.

05 26 82 We used to be disgusted with a cloudy sky but since the clouds have saved us from impending frosts and thereby secured a good prospect for an abundance of fruit in this region, we are grateful to the fleecy visitors, and they can come and go at their pleasure.

06 23 82 While returning from a fishing trip last Saturday the publisher was very nicely entertained by W.H. Fife, of Yuba. Mr. Fife took pleasure in showing us his fine stock and over his beautiful farm. In the barn we saw two head of the celebrated Holstein cattle, a yearling bull and a two year old heifer, the two costing $575.

07 21 82 The first reaper and binder will commence work on the peninsula next week.

07 28 82 John Carns and Neil Munroe are making some valuable additions and improvements to their barns.

08 25 82 On C.D. Hollenbeck's farm in Milton, the proprietor, Chester Holenbeck and John Winters bound in 30 minutes, 720 sheaves of fall wheat, about 8 sheaves apiece a minute. The sheaves were already raked. Who can beat this?

09 01 82 John Carns has a new wind mill erected near his elegant farm house.

10 13 82 To-morrow an informal exhibit of fruits, vegetables, etc. will be held at this place, at the Lake View House. Mr. Dyer has offered the use of the verandah of the house which will allow a display of about 300 plates. Very likely, a room or so will be opened if necessary.

10 13 82 Great boom in the hop market and prices high. Over $2,000 worth shipped from Old Mission last week.

Grand Traverse apples have been sent to England to be used as models for painting.

10 20 82 Neil Munroe, of Whitewater township, has constructed a silo in which he has put about four tons of green hay. This he proposes not to open until spring. Should the result of his experiment prove satisfactory he will enlarge his operations in this direction another season.

10 27 82 M.F. Gates brought to us Monday several fine samples of apples, among them the Pound Sweet, Man, Greening and other varieties.

12 08 82 We have been longing for an old fashioned Grand Traverse winter. Not one of your slushy, sleety, half warm, half cold ones, when every body feels as if business or pleasure were a nuisance, and the less to do of either was a blessing. We are glad to remark that there is every prospect that our wish will be abundantly gratified. Premonitory symptoms began about the 25th of November, and culminated at this writing, Thursday, in one of the liveliest wind and snow storms that we have seen at this time of year in a long time. The farmers, God bless them, who are the mainstay and support of all business look happy and contented, well knowing that a cold snug winter, with months of good sleighing, affords them nearly as rich a harvest of the wherewith as their broad acres do under the genial rays of the Summer's Sun. When farmers are prosperous, as they generally are in the Grand Traverse country, all other classes, in a greater or less degree, feel the effects of their prosperity.

Chapter 3
Bangor Chemical Company

04 01 81 Mr. Frank Lombard, of Chicago, is in town and will superintend the erection of the Chemical Works. From him we learn that the main building will be 96 feet long, 48 feet wide, and 45 feet high. The alcohol house will be 84x48, 28 feet high. The size of the other buildings has not been decided; but we will give a more extended notice of the Works hereafter.

04 29 81 The Elk Rapids Chemical Co., have commenced clearing the ground for the erection of their works.

05 20 81   THE WORKS
The Clearing House will be 100x48, 3 stories high.
The alcohol house will be 48x84, with 24 foot posts.
Timbers are being framed at the ship yard for the Chemical Works.
There are two copper-smiths fitting pipes in the Cooper building for the Chemical Works.
Ten carpenters from Bangor this state are employed in the erection of the Chemical Works.
$10,000 of copper piping came in on the barge *Leland* and is now stored in the Cooper building.
The Cooper building has been thrown open and carpenters in the employ of the Michigan Co., are making 75 tanks for the Chemical Works. Several of them holding thousands of gallons.
The ground where the Chemical Works will be erected, will immediately be broken and preparations made for the building. The works will be erected just above the furnace on the banks of Elk River.
The engine and pump and fan house will be 50x75. There will be a Buckeye engine 14x24 and a Blake pump which is 24x20x12.
There will also be a battery of six return flue boilers.

05 27 81 There are twenty-three carpenters working under Mr. Frank Lumbard, framing timbers and making tanks for the Chemical Co. Besides these employed in the construction of works there are as many more at the furnace and about town.
Five more carpenters from Grand Rapids, came here Tuesday, on the *Faxton*.

06 03 81 It will take 8,040 feet of copper piping for the condensers alone, at the Chemical Works.

06 03 81 There will be over three miles of copper piping used for the Chemical Works.

06 03 81 Jerome Wilcox, a coppersmith, in the employ of the Chemical Co., had his hand badly burned with hot rosin [sic] Wednesday morning while filling the pipes before bending them.

06 03 81 The work of grading the lot where the Chemical Works are to be erected commenced Tuesday and the stones for the foundation are being drawn.

06 03 81 We learn that one small store house for the Chemical Works will be 20x40, and it is expected that three more of the same size will be built. The drying house will be 60x80.

06 10 81 The raising of the alcohol house will be commenced next Monday.

The foundation has been laid for the alcohol house, and work commencenced on the foundation of the clearing house. There are ten masons at work.

06 24 81 The alcohol house has been shingled and is now enclosed.

07 22 81 The copper piping for the alcohol house which have been put together in the Cooper building is being taken to the Works.

All the outside carpenter work on the alcohol house has been done. There have been 11 tanks set up and the work is being pushed.

07 29 81 Over fifty mechanics are now employed at the chemical works.

07 29 81 Mr. E.J. Burwell, of Bangor, will be the foreman of the alcohol house instead of C.J.Garrett, as erroneously reported last week.

08 05 81 The Chemical Plant — Nearly three miles of hoop iron has been used for bands for the tanks.

No one can have any idea of the immensity of these works, until they visit them.

It will take about one ton of paint for the outside of the buildings of the works.

The trestle work for the gas main has been put up from the kilns to the fan house.

The engine house is nearly completed, and the engine is in the house all ready to be set up.

All the outside work on the clearing house has been done and the painting of it has been nearly completed.

The evaporating house will be commenced next week. It will be 48 feet wide, 20 feet high, and 84 feet long.

The stone for the foundation of the boilers was being drawn yesterday. The boiler house will be 24 feet west of the alcohol house, and will have six return flue boilers.

The alcohol house which is 48 feet wide and 84 feet long has 21 tanks, some of them holding thousands of gallons connected together by copper piping. This building has been painted and the work about it is nearly done.

The clearing house is nearly painted and the floor on the upper story is being made water tight, 200 pounds of white lead has been used on this floor. The floor below will also be water tight, and 100 pounds of white lead will be used.

08 12 81 These works will be the longest in the world.

 08 12 81 From forty to fifty barrels of lime of the purest quality will be used each day.

There are 28 tanks in the clearing house some of them holding 3,000 gallons. Others will hold 5,000 gallons apiece.

The foundation to the engine will be 4 feet solid masonry and is being built this week. The engine will be bolted to the foundation.

Last Friday while laying floor in the clearing house Fred Debbingham severed the large artery in his left leg with an adz which he was using.

The diameter of the gas main from the kilns to the fan house is 4 feet outside and 44 inches inside measurement. It is 650 feet long. The smoke is drawn from the kilns through this main and forced into condensers.

08 16 81 The clearing house is the highest building in the county being 61 feet from the wall to the peak.
200 feet of the gas main has been placed on the kilns. 600 feet more will be put up. The main is 44 inches in diameter.

The evaporating house has been completed, and the evaporating tanks are being made. There are two evaporators 45 feet long and two 30 feet long. Through this building passes what is called the long box to the alcohol house.

08 25 81 The boilers have been placed into position and the mason work is going on for the foundation to the others.

09 02 81 The alcohol house will be heated with steam.
About 2,000 kerosene barrels will be used a year for barreling the alcohol.

09 02 81 About three sections of the gas main is being rolled out a day. Each section is 16 feet long and 44 inches in diameter.

There will be four chimneys which will be 70 feet in height. Three of these will be at the drying house and one at the boiler house.

09 09 81 The foundation for the condensers is being laid. There will be 24 stone walls, each being 45 feet long. The condensers will be placed in pairs upon this foundation. Several walls have been built.
The gas main is being placed upon the trestle work to the kilns, and the fans connecting therewith are being put into position in the fan house. The work on the main has been done by thorough mechanics, and every bit of the work about the works shows a master hand.

10 07 81 Six boilers have been placed on their foundations.
There have been six condensers to put up and three more are to be placed on foundations.

The building of the fan house has been commenced, and it will be situated between the engine and boiler houses. The green liquor pump will be in the same building.

There are 58 men in the employ of the Chemical Co. 15 more carpenters could find employment.

Last Thursday night during the storm one of the stacks was blown down, making the second time that it has occurred.

The roof to the drying house is nearly finished, and the furnaces for drying the acetate of lime have been completed.

10 28 81 On Monday all the pumps and the engine were tried at the Chemical Works, and all worked to perfection. Hose were attached to the hydrants and the pumps forced the water clear over the clearing house. The large pump that feeds the condensers, which condenses the smoke into the green liquor, sends an eight inch stream.

10 28 81 The Chemical Works start to-day, taking the smoke from one kiln.

11 04 81 Mr. Frank Lombard returned to his home at Bangor to-day. He came to Elk Rapids early in March and superintended the re-construction of the Furnace Co.'s pier. About May 1 he began the work for which he came to Elk Rapids namely the construction of the Chemical Co.'s buildings. During the past six months he has had from 75 to 100 men under his supervision. Mr. Lombard has won the entire approbation of the B.C. Co. and the respect of those under his direction and of the citizens of Elk Rapids.

11 04 81 The refuse from the Chemical Works, which is very little, will not affect the fishing interests here.

07 01 81 Mr. S.S Spaulding has a bakery in connection with his boarding house and keeps fresh bread constantly on hand at Spaulding & Philip's meat market.

11 04 81 All day Sunday persons from the village could be seen wending their way to the Chemical Works, to see the process of making 10 gallons of liquor every minute out of smoke from charcoal kilns.

11 04 81 The Chemical Works made a successful start on Saturday morning last. Exactly at half-past ten steam was allowed to enter the cylinder of the handsome Buckeye engine. Almost simultaneously the big fly wheel began to move, the fans caught the motion from the shaft above and but 42 seconds elapsed between the first stroke of the engine and the puff of the uncondensed smoke breathing from the head of No. 4 condenser. Five minutes later a steady flow of liquor began and from that time until 4 A.M. Wednesday the quantity never fell below 6 gallons per minute and rising at times to 12 and 13, and this from 1 kiln at a time. The main being laid over five kilns when those that happened to be burning "came down," of course the Works were compelled to stop and await the further building of the main. This once accomplished no more breaks will occur and a steady run of at least 14 gallons per minute will be procured.   The acetate and alcohol departments will be in running order early next week. In next issue we shall give a general description of the process, and also publish some matter which is new and of general interest.

The works have been running only on two charcoal kilns and from the smoke taken from them has been manufactured 36,000 gallons of liquor, or 18,000 gallons for each kiln. It is claimed that the green liquor manufactured is the best ever turned out. It will take 90 bushels of lime to neutralize this.

11 18 81 A full column description of the new Chemical Works. The largest production output of acetate of lime and wood alcohol in the world. — Ed

11 25 81 The gas main is being laid over several more kilns.

12 16 81 It is hard work for the furnace and Chemical works whistles to keep together.

12 23 81 Wednesday afternoon John Coggin was seriously burned on his left hand and arm in one of the graining pans at the Chemical works. He had let the steam onto the pans and was walking across a plank on top of them when he stumbled and fell and had the misfortune to fall with his hand into the boiling liquor. The steam was so dense in this department that it was impossible for him to see and for that reason he made the misstep.

12 23 81 100,000 pounds of acetate of lime has been stored in the store houses besides several thousand pounds at the works.

12 30 81 The product of the Chemical Works is taken by contract for five years. It is really too bad that they are not compelled to advertise at all but such is the naked fact.

01 13 82 At the Chemical Works, the vapor from the alcohol has something of the effects of ether. If a person gets too much it renders him delirious, and causes blindness. Mr. D. Church and four others took in more than they could hold one day this week causing the effect above mentioned.

01 20 82 Dr. Pierce made a flying trip to Traverse City Thursday to superintend the shipment of the Chemical Co.'s first car load of alcohol...

01 27 82 The Chemical Co. intended shipping 25,000 lbs. of their acetate product weekly, but have been compelled to abandon the idea on account of the thaw, inopportunly spoiling the sleighing. Is it right we should thus be dependent upon the state of the roads in sending our products to outside points? As we have so often and earnestly said, a rail-road would remove every difficulty, and prove a most profitable investment for the corporation and a solid benefit to our manufacturing concerns.

01 27 82 The great benefit arising from a railroad from this point to Traverse City has been demonstrated the past two weeks. Last week 3,000 gallons of wood alcohol was shipped from Traverse City, which had to be carted to that place from this point, and the fact that outside parties wish a car-load of acetate of lime a week for the next three months is another reason.

02 03 82 The Chemical Company shipped three carloads of acetate to Philadelphia Wednesday. This entire shipment, 72,000 lbs., was transported to Traverse City by teams. Seven sleigh-loads, carrying each 4,200 lbs., leaving Friday morning alone. Others followed until the car-lots were complete. Oh for that rail-road!

02 03 82 The Chemical company started four loads of acetate of lime to Traverse City last Saturday morning about one o'clock. Each load means 4,300 pounds of the product.

02 17 82 Monday the smoke was being pulled from three kilns, and 20 gallons of liquor a minute was the result.

03 17 82 The Bangor Chemical Co. have shipped the past seven days by the tug *Ryan* 328,000 pounds of acetate of lime.

03 24 82 *Bangor Reflector.* The Elk Rapids Chemical works show the following enormous out-put for February: Acetate, 13,000 lbs. per day, or a total of over 350,000 lbs. Alcohol 200 gallons per day or a total of 5,600 gallons.

03 24 82 The Chemical Works of this place have about completed some important improvements. Mr. H.M. Pierce, of Elk Rapids, has been here and superintended changes which will greatly enhance the value and capacity of the works. New condensers and tanks have been built upon an enlarged scale, so that there will be a daily increase here-after of about 1000 lbs. of acetate and 15 gal. of alcohol. The works have been thoroughly cleaned and every thing is put in good preparation for the future. On account of these essential improvements the works have lately been shut down, but will again resume operations in a few days.- Bangor *Advance*.

03 24 82 Last week in connection with our notice of the new method of carbonizing wood, we had no room to speak of the contrivance Dr. Pierce has patented, for cooling off charcoal kilns. The cooler is placed on the outside of the kiln, which bears a resemblance to the condensers at the Chemical Works. It is connected to the kilns by 8-inch pipes. The hot air comes from the kilns at a temperature of 500 degrees, passes through the cooler and returns to the kiln at a temperature of 60 degrees, reducing the time for cooling from nine days to three.

03 31 82 The grounds about the Chemical Works are being raked and graded, and everything outside being put in better order.

A new No. 2 smoke fan has been purchased and put up in the fan house.

03 31 82 In a late number of the *Bangor Advance* we found an item which stated that Dr. Pierce, of this place, had patents covering the manufacture of turpentine, and that in a few weeks he would go South to superintend the erection of works, etc. A recent rumor has it that the Chemical Co. has purchased $124,000 worth of pine land in Louisiana at $1.25 an acre. Col. F.H. Head of Chicago, president of the Bangor Chemical Co., and Mr. H.H. Noble, of this place, one of its members, were in the South recently, looking up lands, as considerable has been said lately in regard to the wonderful pine land of the south. We suppose the next rumor in regard to the Chemical Co. will be, that it has purchased the rocky mountains, and by some peculiar process will extract elephant's milk out of them.

03 31 82 Tuesday night at 11 o'clock the Chemical Works was hitched on to Kiln No. 26.

04 07 82 The Chemical Works hitched on to kiln No. 18 Tuesday.

04 14 82 The Chemical Works commenced drawing smoke from kiln No. 12 Tuesday. The condensers are all being cleaned which will make the flow of liquor larger.

04 21 82 The chemical works was drawing smoke from kilns No. 1, 6, 19 and 20 yesterday. The new process of burning was in operation on No. 20.

05 05 82 The Chemical works for the past two weeks have averaged an out-put of 5,000 lbs. of acetate and 60 gallons of alcohol, daily. The chambers in the kilns are somewhat out of repair, and brick have been ordered to put them in proper shape. When this is done it is expected that the rate of production can be still further increased.

05 19 82 Dr. H.M. Pierce has built a small charcoal kiln near the chemical works, on an improved plan.

05 19 82 Dr. H.M. Pierce was experimenting with wood tar Wednesday when our reporter was at the chemical works. Several barrels of this tar is made each day and it is thought that better use can be made of it than using it for fuel. It is thought that for roofing it can be used, and also for cement for pavements. Several samples have been sent to Chicago for trial.

05 19 82 We should not be surprised if our local in regard to turpentine manufacturing by the Chemical Co. in the South had more truth in it than was at first imagined.

05 26 82 The Chemical Co. resumed actual operation yesterday, after an extended "shut down", caused by a similar state of affairs at the furnace. Many improvements have been made during this interval; and now an increased output, and that of even a better quality than previously manufactured is confidently expected.
    Not only in the running of the works do we notice an onward stride towards perfection, but the Co.'s late experiments have proved peculiarly successful. We refer particularly to the reduction of wood to charcoal by the new process of carbonization. All the knowing ones unite in pronouncing the coal superior to any produced by usual burning. A like increase in strength of distillate, raises the Chemical Works percentages also.

06 02 82 The Chemical Works has drawn on kilns 17, 19, 20, 21, 23, 24, and 25. This week smoke has been drawn from 7, 19, 20. and 21.

06 09 82 The chemical works drew smoke from six kilns Sunday and the flow of green liquor was 26 gallons a minute.

06 09 82 The Chemical Co. are talking of building a store house for storing the winter's product of the works. Nothing definite as yet in regard to size.

06 09 82 Charles Mackey is the new fireman at the chemical works, and hails from Ohio.

06 09 82 The Superintendent of the alcohol house, chemical works, Jerome Wilcox, informs us that 400 gallons of alcohol was the Sunday's product in that department.

06 23 82 N.K. Fairbanks inspected the Chemical Works, Tuesday. Mr. Fairbanks is a stockholder of both the Chemical and Iron Co.'s.

06 30 82 Tanks have been received by the Chemical Co. for the purpose of boiling the tar, and preparing it for shipment. About 30 barrels of wood tar a day have been manufactured and the tar has heretofore been used for fuel. Now it will be put through different processes, barreled and shipped to cities where it is used on wood pavements.

07 07 82 The Chemical Company are building a new stock house. The work commenced on it yesterday.

07 14 82 For the past eight months, in fact ever since the chemical works began operations, the entire tar product, amounting to between 20 and 30 barrels per day, has been used merely for fuel. While realizing fully that the tar is valuable for many purposes if properly worked, the managers of the company, being busy in the extreme, with the vast amount of detail works, incident to the starting of such a large enterprise, were satisfied for the present,in using the product as an aid in steam generating. Lately, however, Dr. Pierce has made a determined effort to raise the tar above the level, of a fuel. The result justifies expectations, and a ready market is found among asphalt contractors, "japan" men and many other industries, where only a supply is needed to create a demand. The tar is first concentrated, by boiling, to such a consistency that on cooling it becomes a solid jet-like mass, easily transported, in barrels, kegs, or even paper flour bags, and also worked with facility. Thus a new industry has sprung up in our midst, that bids fair to play an important part among the products of the Elk Rapids Chemical Works.

07 21 82 The Chemical Company are building an immense store house, the size of which is 64x110. It is estimated that the building will hold 10,000 sacks of acetate, although 5,000 or 6,000 sacks is all that will be stored in it at once, so as to leave plenty of room for drying and handling the product.

07 21 82 A very large chime whistle for the Chemical works is being made at the Iron Co.'s foundry.

07 28 82 The Chemical works are in splendid running order. More and better alcohol and acetate are being produced than ever before. We notice many improvements also, among the most prominent we mention the repainting of the entire main. A big work, but adding much to the uniform neatness of the Company's plans.

08 04 82 Twenty barrels of wood tar were shipped on the *Reindeer* by the Chemical Co.

08 04 82 Last fall the Chemical Company built only a temporary boiler house at the works. They are now building a new one 56x67- 14 foot posts. The new one will be a frame building with an iron roof.

08 04 82 The Chemical Co. have erected a tar still near their works, which will hold about 50 barrels of the product, and the work of boiling and barreling has commenced.

08 18 82 The new boiler house of the Chemical Co. is of corrugated iron, both the roof and the sides of the building.

08 18 82 440,000 pounds of acetate of lime and 2,940 gallons of wood alcohol was shipped on the schooner *City of Chicago*, to Chicago.

09 22 82 A new tar still has been built at the chemical works, which holds about 30 barrels of tar.

09 22 82 The Chemical Co. have about 400,000 pounds of acetate in their store house. One hundred barrels of alcohol were shipped on the *Leland*.

10 20 82 The Chemical Company shipped by schooner *Ellen Spry*, Sunday, 300 tons of acetate of lime and 77 barrels of alcohol to Chicago.

11 24 82 The fire protection at the Chemical works is very nearly complete. Three hydrants with proper pipe connections have been put in the past week.

12 15 82 Norman M. Pierce has had his laboratory removed to Chicago.

12 15 82 The Chemical Co. are building another store house back of the alcohol house.

12 29 82 We understand that Mr. Stewart Church will assume the duties of Superintendent of the Chemical Works after January first 1883.

Chapter 4
Village of Bellaire

01 02 80 If you wish to become a huge millionaire, buy lots in the swamp around Bellaire.

01 09 80
<blockquote>
If you wish to escape
   Much trouble and care,
Don't buy city lots
   In the town of Bellaire.
</blockquote>

01 30 80 From Sheriff Cameron and Pros. Att'y, Leavitt, we learn that the lumbering business at Bellaire, the "imaginary county seat," is booming. We are glad to see business in that condition everywhere. Messrs, Lyon & Son is the firm that is engaged in the lumber business there. We also learn from the same source that the hotel at that place is "chuck full" of transients all the time.

02 06 80 Post-office Keno, Town of Bellaire, Township of Kearney, County of Antrim, State of Michigan. There is nothin' like havin' things explicit, you know, when you want to send your letters to Bellaire (Keno) you know.

POST-OFFICE. KENO, TOWN OF BELLAIRE, TOWNSHIP OF KEARNEY, COUNTY OF ANTRIM, STATE OF MICHIGAN.
As seen by our Special Artist.

02 06 80 How the people at Bellaire got the name for their post-office we don't know nor do we care. But going into our post-office the other day we saw a huge flaming poster of Beadle's Half Dime Library, which read, "Deadwood Dick's Double," and a picture of two men lying full length with revolvers in their hands and underneath was this inscription: One! git ready. Two! say your Kittenchism. THREE!! balance for the final send off. And lastly KENO!!!!

04 02 80 This week we produce two beautiful engravings of the natural scenery in the vicinity of Bellaire. They were drawn by our Special Artist, and are true to natur'. We will save the cuts and any of the citizens of Bellaire who wish copies can have them at a low price. We shall issue several more during the coming month, thus giving our neighbors a chance to adorn their homes with local subjects.

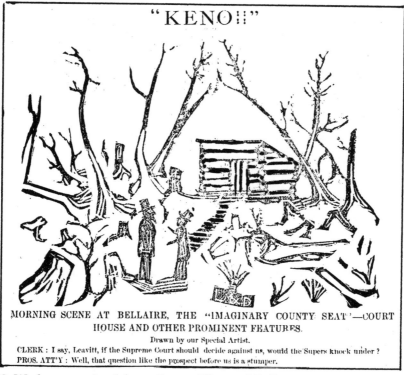

"KENO!!"

MORNING SCENE AT BELLAIRE, THE "IMAGINARY COUNTY SEAT"—COURT HOUSE AND OTHER PROMINENT FEATURES.

Drawn by our Special Artist.

CLERK : I say, Leavitt, if the Supreme Court should decide against us, would the Supers knock under ?
PROS. ATT'Y : Well, that question like the prospect before us is a stumper.

06 26 80 We have received from Crazy Allcott of Bellaire, two postals which are really as good productions as the Bairs! Bairs! Bairs!" article was which he sent to this paper some years ago and which some of our oldest readers will remember. At that time Mr. William Getty wished the author of "A blast from Forest Home—Bairs! Bairs! Bairs!" placed in a lunatic asylum at the expense of the county. We support that motion now as the stuff on the postals are as senseless as the article was, and we question if H. Alcott could not be held responsible for sending such matter through the mails. If there had been any point to them like there was on the postals that Wm. W. Johnson of Hen Bay sent out, we should not have cared. We have them pasted up in our office so that any one who wishes to see something more from the author of the article "Bairs! Bairs! Bairs!" can do so.

08 06 80 We paid a brief visit to the village of Bellaire on Saturday last and was quite surprised to see what a place had grown from almost nothing in so short a time. A place about 80 by 100 rods has been cleared of trees and on one end of this is erected a row of fine looking wooden buildings which are mostly occupied as stores. Around the edges of the clearing are several dwelling houses. We also notice several places being prepared for building. The place is situated on the east bank of Intermediate River, just below the point where Cedar River empties into it. The river furnished abundant water power and is navigable for boats of light draft as far as the village. If it continues to improve at the present rate it will soon be a place of considerable importance.

10 01 80 The Bellairites expect to erect a new school house this fall.

T.W. Nelson and Charles Farrand have taken the contract to erect the new jail at Bellaire.

10 29 80 A Greenback speaker spouted at Bellaire last Tuesday evening. Roswell Leavitt answered in behalf of the Republicans.

L.C. McKinstrey, formerly of your place, will soon open a saloon at Bellaire, and now the Super's won't have to go dry while doing the public business.

01 06 81 Nixon Bros. have opened a general store and are having a good trade.

W.W. Johnson, of Snowflake has just issued his tree and seed catalogue for the season of 1881. He is doing a large business in the tree line with the prairie farmers of the West.

Bellaire is improving but there is still room for a big improvement yet. One thing that is badly needed is a hotel. Deacon Cook has a small boarding house, but it is run too much on the private family scale to be a success. If a good man should open a house here he would be well patronized.

02 11 81 Some parties from Sidney, Ohio, talk of putting in a dam and grist mill here in the spring.

The lumbering firm of Cook & Hayes have contracted with Wadsworth & Thurston, of Central Lake to put in a million feet or less of hard wood logs, and have commenced operations.

03 11 81 Business is very dull. The saw mill is standing idle. The men who proposed putting in a flouring mill here have concluded to go somewhere else, owing to the lack of A.E. Palmer, who owns the water power.

03 18 81 The iron work for the inside of the jail is being hauled from the R.R. to-day.

We understand that the saw mill at Bellaire is to be started soon by Mr. Thomas, of Central Lake, and we hope the gentleman will be able to furnish the lumber needed at that place. We wish him success in the business.

T.W. Nelson, the pioneer merchant of Bellaire, who has been operating in ship timber this winter has not been visible at any of his usual haunts for the last week or ten days and his creditors seem to think he has "skipped out." As town clerk of the township of Kearney he has very carefully concealed the files of chattel mortgages belonging to the office and where they are nobody interested can find out. His assets are few and small while his liabilities make a very respectable showing.

03 25 81 Town politics are raging in a mild form, and the afflicted candidates are allowed to run at large.

Mr. Jacobs daughter, the one who eloped with Fred Powers, has returned home and says that Powers has gone to Colorado.

04 08 81 Our people are very much elated over the arrival of the Wooden Ware Manufacturing firm of Richardi & Bechtold who have recently located here and who will put in a large amount of machinery and utilize the immense water power which the Intermediate river affords at this point. They will give employment to about 75 hands at the works. Besides using a large quantity of hard wood logs from up the lakes which will be likely to cause a rapid settlement of the excellent timbered lands along the shores above here.

08 16 81 Mr. Bechtold, of Bechtold & Richardi, is building a fine house.

The saw mill is running in connection with the wooden ware factory. It runs nights.

There are thirty tons of freight at Mancelona, for this place, all for one firm.

The company of Bechtold & Richardi are going into the manufactureof shingles. They will also manufacture broom handles.

08 25 81 The wooden ware works are doing a thriving business. They are making at present bowls and scoops.

One member of the wooden ware works Co. is putting up a large square house north of the village and across the river.

Court house square has recently been cleared and grubbed. Now let it be plowed and seeded.

Two brief years have passed. A village literally hewn from the wilderness, "has risen upon this wild bit of nature" a busy thriving village, with nearly three hundred inhabitants. A wooden ware manufactory, two saw mills, a planing mill, shingle mill, blacksmith shop, gunsmith, hotel, three general stores, one hardware store, a grocery, drug store and printing office are now full-filling their missions where less than two years since primeval quiet reigned.

10 14 81 Jas. Wadsworth, of Central Lake, has started a lumbering camp on section six, Chestonia township.

Antrim county's jail is finished and ready for the sheriff and family to occupy. Now for a court house.

Richardi & Bechtold have commenced the erection of houses on the north side of the river for the accommodation of their workmen. S.C. Cook has the building of the same.

A peddler by the name of Acker, living in Forest Home is out of pocket to the amount of fifteen dollars. While traveling through the country he was overtaken by evening, and was obliged to seek lodging at some distance from his place. At night he had about twenty-five dollars, and in the morning he found only ten in his pocketbook. He has taken measures to recover his money as he thinks he knows where it is.

10 21 81 The jail is being plastered. It was quite an engineering feat to place the scaffolding in position, but Lyman Drayton and James Sacket were equal to the occasion.

11 04 81 Bellaire prays for a daily mail and a telegraph line.

Twenty thousand small hemlock trees, and ten thousand white cedar ones, from W.W. Johnson's seed farm at Snowflake, passed through Bellaire this week on their way to one of his customers in the east.

11 11 81 The post office building has received many improvements recently, the latest being a shingle roof.

Four of Bellaire's prominent business men have formed a stock company for the purpose of erecting a large hotel. This is a good move, and with the natural advantages which Bellaire possesses, it should develop into a summer resort second to none in the state.

11 18 81 The school house has been completed this fall and school is now in operation. About thirty pupils are in attendance.

Mr. Wadsworths line of steamers is running from Central Lake to Elk Rapids and Torch via Snowflake and Bellaire and proves a great advantage to our merchants and others besides a profitable investment to the owner.

01 06 82 Bellaire is destined to receive a share of the tourists and pleasure seekers the coming season. The steam yacht *Ida*, owned by J.M. Wadsworth, will make trips between Elk Rapids and Bellaire, passing through the beautiful chain of lakes and rivers, and at this point will connect with the little steamer*Wah-wa-tay-see*, which will ply through Central and Intermediate lakes. The steamer*Mah-sha-mah-goos*, owned by C.W. Farrand, will, we understand, be rebuilt the present winter, and at the opening of navigation make regular trips to and from Elk Rapids, also connecting with the boat north from this place. This makes a delightful inland trip, and, as good hotel accommodations, excellent trout and grayling fishing,(to say nothing of bass, pickerel, etc.) can be found on the route, it should become popular, and we predict it will.

02 10 82 The *Breeze*: Antrim county's first fair will be held in Bellaire, beginning Oct. 3, and ending the 5th.

02 17 82 Scoops and trays from Richardi & Bechtold's factory, are being hauled to the railroad for shipment in large quantities.

Bellaire contains at present a wooden ware manufactory, two saw mills, (one in operation), planing mill, shingle mill, blacksmith shop, gunsmith, hotel, six stores, printing office, is between two and three years old, is surrounded by a fine farming region and will double in population in the next two years.

03 03 82 Mr. Richardi, of Bellaire, came near loosing his house by fire last Wednesday, a week. A large hole was burned in the roof before it was extinguished.

04 07 82 We learn that Bellaire will have a $1,200 town hall.

Not a licensed saloon in Bellaire, and yet men reel along our streets nearly every day.

Bellaire has the county seat by a hard fight, and now Bellaire is going to keep it.

04 28 82 Men are at work in the brick yard on John A. Harriman's farm, and this vicinity will soon be supplied with first-class brick at a reasonable price.- *Breeze*.

04 28 82 The Bellaire House, the only hotel at Bellaire, is soon to receive great alterations and improvements. A large addition will be built to the house, and when finished the proprietor thinks he can more successfully accommodate tourists who go up the inland route.

Bellaire voted $1,200 for a town hall and at the last session of the Board of Supervisors a resolution was made to rent the upper story of the town hall for a court room, and to finish the lower story of the building for county offices, so that Bellaire's town hall will cost about $2,500 or $3,000.

Bellaire, the county seat of Antrim county is geographically situated in the center of the county, on Intermediate river, and bids fair to become one of the busiest towns in Northern Michigan; The excellent water power there afforded for manufacturing purposes, and the fact that it is not only geographically situated, but it is in the midst of as choice farming lands as any town in this northern country. The town has one hotel which is open to the public and will soon have another; a large wooden ware factory, several grocery and general stores, printing office, and numerous dwelling houses.

A remarkable fact about the town is that when the county seat was voted there a little over two years ago, there was not a dwelling house nor a building but it was an unbroken wilderness. Bellaire has the same general wildness of appearance, which characterizes all new towns in Northern Michigan, but as our reporter is an "old settler" in this part, this wildness did not have the same weight which it sometimes has on newcomers, when coming into some parts of this region. One side of the river is the town, and on the other side the banks rise quite sharply for a few feet, and then with a gentle rise for some distance. This side of the river is covered with a grand old forest, which will before long be cleared, and sold for village lots. Several houses have been recently built, and more are to be erected. A fine brick block is soon to be constructed, the machine being already purchased to manufacture the brick. Aside from a little wildness our county seat is beautifully situated, will in time become one of the prettiest places in the county, and although the moving of the site was premature, still it has had the effect of settling up that part of the county more rapidly.

Not a village in Northern Michigan has a prettier location than Bellaire. Let the stumps be removed as rapidly as possible.--Breeze

04 28 82 J.A. Harriman, of Bellaire has purchased the brick machine of Dexter & Noble of this place. It was taken to Bellaire Tuesday by the steamer Bellaire.

Richardi & Bectold are running their wooden scoop and bowl factory slow on account of scarcity of logs. The firm have a nice business and do much towards making Bellaire a busy town.

05 19 82 Bellaire is not a "Leadville," "Manitoba," or anything in that line; but is having a steady, substantial growth that augurs well for its future. Its location is excellent, its industries permanent, and it is keeping pace with the development of the country, and escaping that feverish, mush-room growth that has proved so fatal to other towns.

05 26 82 It is rumored that the wooden ware factory at Bellaire will shut down in a few weeks, because the workmen demand higher wages than the proprietors can profitably pay.

05 12 82 Arrangements are nearly completed which will give Bellaire a mail from the south four days each week. *–Breeze.*

MAIL *EN ROUTE* FOR KENO, (BELLAIRE),
By our Special Artist.

06 02 82 Richardi & Bechtold have had surveying done this week, preparatory, we believe, to putting in another race, more buildings and additional machinery to be used in connection with their business.

06 16 82 Richardi & Bechtold have recently platted on the north side an addition to the village of Bellaire. The addition consists of about fifty lots, 50x150 feet, and 80x150 feet, and embraces some very desirable locations. *–Breeze.*

06 16 82 John A. Harriman returned from the south last Saturday. He secured a brick-maker at Kalamazoo, and in order to supply the immediate demand the company will put up a pony kiln and burn at once; later they will burn a large kiln for future sale.

07 14 82 The Shugart House at Bellaire opened Monday.
About 1,000 people attended the celebration at Bellaire the 4th.

09 01 82 Geo. M. Jackson, an Elk Rapids photographer, is in town and has pitched his tent near L.M. Lester's store.

09 15 82 Chas. T. Hickox, Esq., was summoned to Bellaire, Monday, as counsel for defendant on case of People vs. Michael McCusker charged with assault and battery upon Frederick Barber. Jury trial before A.S. Abbott, J.P. Jury rendered a verdict of guilty but recommended that mercy be entended the prisoner. Prisoner fined 30 cents and costs.

09 21 82 The brick Company at Bellaire will soon burn a kiln of brick.
Richardi & Bechtold of Bellaire are building an addition to their factory.

11 10 82 *Breeze*: The Bellaire Post-office has been removed to Mr. Stebbin's building formerly occupied by L.M. Lester & Co. The building has been repainted and renovated generally and presents a very much improved appearance.

11 17 82 A man by the name of Quick, who had contracted to build the Bellaire town hall, has skipped out it is supposed, with the greater part of the funds, in all, amounting to about $750. As near as we can find out about it, he was to receive so much money to commence building, and when the hall was partially completed he was to have more. He had the frame up, and a small amount of material around and drew the cash, and at last accounts he could not be found. The Bellaire folks can do nothing as yet, because the time for the building to be finished has not expired, and if he should be arrested he might say he had gone after material, as that is the reason he gave for wishing to draw money. After getting the money he got away Quick.

04 23 80 Some of our readers have spoken to us in regard to the name Keno properly belonging to Bellaire. It is a fact that the name on the post-office is Keno, town of Bellaire, in the township of Kearney, County of Antrim, State of Michigan, Universe Earth. So, if you want to send a letter to Bellaire, send it to Keno. We have some engravings of Bellaire, beautifully executed, that we will send to inhabitants around Bellaire for a one cent stamp, all others will be charged two cents. To further the interests of Keno-Bellaireites we will send the above engravings upon application.

Chapter 5
Businesses of Elk Rapids

01 09 80 Geo. Goodhew has rented a part of Jas. Cullyford's harness shop and is now prepared to repair all boots and shoes that are brought him.

01 23 80 When we have no barber we wonder why it is we can't have a good one as well as other places. Now should this barber leave let us never talk about why we can't keep a good one, but say to ourselves, we didn't know him when here, but got our friends to do our barbering and expected him to live on wind. We don't know as he has any intentions of leaving, but should he, we could not think hard of him for so doing. While in town he can always be found at the Lake View House.

01 23 80 Benj. Yalomstein left this place Saturday for Traverse City to take a position in his father's store at that place while his father will attend to the business interest here. Benj. has lots of friends in town.

01 30 80 Birney Horvitz has a nice assortment of goods on River Street. Patronize him.

02 06 80 Chas. Wendell has rented for a couple of weeks a window in the *Progress* building, where those wishing to get their clocks, watches and jewelry repaired can bring them. He is a first-class workman, and will be prompt in repairing all articles brought him.

02 27 80 On Monday last Messrs. Goldman & Alpern purchased the stock of school books, jewelry, etc., belonging to G.H.Bakley. They took possession of the stock that day and will continue business at the old stand, having rented the building for a term of years. The business will be continued under the name of Mr. Alpern and as he is gentlemanly and obliging, it will probably be profitable to them.

03 05 80 We learn from Mr. Jas. W. Beadle, of Beadle & Son, of Detroit, that he will visit this place some time next week for spring orders. He will have a full and complete line of goods for the spring and summer season, and will be pleased to wait on his friends and patrons for their orders. Prices to suit the times.

03 05 80 The "Great Wardrobe" man will be here March 15, with a selection of over two hundred samples of foreign and domestic cloths cashmeres for spring and summer wear. Be sure and let S.K. Pierce have your order.

03 05 80 A. Newton bought last Monday O.J. Powers' livery stable so that now he controls that business in town. Mr. Powers will remain here.

03 19 80 S.K. Pierce has been in town the past week soliciting orders for the "Great Ward-robe," and of course received a good many.

04 02 80 Trying to do business without advertising is like winking at a pretty girl in the dark. You may know what you are doing but nobody else does.

04 09 80 Mrs. E. Little, who has opened a millinery establishment in the building formerly occupied by the County Clerk, left for Chicago last evening on the *Leland* to purchase a stock of new goods. Her advertisement will appear upon her return.

04 23 80 We notice that Mrs. Jas. Davidson has a fine new lot of millinery goods that she purchased in Chicago last week for cash.

04 30 80 We see that C.A. Newton has taken down the sign "Cheap Livery," and has put up one in its place "Livery and Feed."

05 07 80 We call attention to the advertisement of the New York Clothing House on this page. Mr. Yalomstein has two stores, one in Traverse City and one at this place. His two sons, Benj. and Max manage the store here while Mr. Yalomstein runs the one at Traverse City. Their store here is located in the large three story building on River street next door to the Lake View House. If you want anything in the clothing line you will do well to call on them.

05 14 80 Another jolly little fracas occurred in Newton's saloon last Saturday afternoon. We learn that no one was very badly hurt, but one man had his clothing nearly torn off, and the scene on the street was not especially interesting. We wish we had officers in this town who had "sand" enough to stop a row when one was commenced, and, if we are obliged to have saloons, we wish the keepers of them would try and preserve order.

05 14 80 Mr. Towne has decided to remove to this place and for that purpose has rented one side of the building where the post office is now located. He will put in a stock of jewelry, and as he is a fine workman and a pleasant gentleman we think his venture will prove advantageous to himself and to our people. Mr. Towne knows every branch of his trade, and that is something that the majority of the jewelers coming to this place did not. He has been long and favorably known to the publisher of this paper, who was instrumental in getting him here. He will be prepared to fill all orders by the 1st of June.

05 14 80 Mr. Joseph Cox is alive to the wants of his customers. He will commence to build shortly an addition to his meat market which will be 67x24 feet and 3 stories high, making an ice house for the purpose packing meats in the summer, so that farmers can sell to him as well in hot weather as any other time.

Mr. Joseph Cox has put in his meat market a nice little assortment of canned goods.

The post office has been removed from the Lake View House to the building where G.H. Bailey formerly had a jewelry store.

Mr. R.W. Bagot has his soda fountain charged and now you can get a good glass of soda for 5 cents.

05 21 80 Will Briggs who took the contract from the Elk Rapids Iron Co., to make several hundred thousand bricks commences work this week.

05 21 80 C.A. Newton, returned from Chicago the first of the week, bringing with him some fine horses for his livery stable.

05 28 80 Wanted—Two good masons to work in Elk Rapids, with two months work guaranteed, at current wages. For particulars inquire of James Briggs.

05 28 80 Andrew Dougherty has put a neat little stock of school books, tobacco, cigars, confectionery, etc., in the building east of the P.O. We hope he will sell lots of goods.

06 11 80 C.A. Newton has removed his livery stable to the barn in the rear of the Lake View House.

06 18 80 Peter Williamson has moved his photograph gallery from the rooms over S. Yalomstein's store to the building west of the *Progress* office. It will be a week or more before he will be ready for business.

We saw a new bus on our streets Wednesday which will go to all boats that stop at this place. It is owned by C.A. Newton.

06 26 80 George Goodhew has removed his boot and shoe shop from the building east of the *Progress* office to the building one door east of J. Cox,s meat market.

06 26 80 The Cooper building on River Street which has so long stood without being used for the purpose for which it was built it having been used for a store house for several years, will in a short time be used for the business it was originally built for. John Hughes a practical workman, has rented a part of it and will carry on the business of carriage and wagon making and repairing and blacksmithing. He has recently purchased a new lot of tools and has engaged men to help him along in the work. Mr. Hughes has been in business here and people are acquainted with his work.

07 02 80 Peter Williamson is having the building next door west of this office fixed up for a Photograph Gallery. Workmen are painting and papering and when all the work is completed the interior will present a neat appearance.

07 23 80 We noticed some cholera-morbus [sic] in one or two show windows the other day in the shape of some little green apples. The less you have to do with this festive fruit the more you have to be thankful for.

08 06 80 C.A. Newton is building a barn on his vacant lot on Traverse avenue.
    The Elk Rapids Retail Liquor Store—C.A. Newton Prop.
    John Hughes has commenced work in the Cooper building. As he is one of the best of workmen he will probably have a good share of blacksmithing to do. He intends soon to add a carriage factory to his business.

08 20 80 C.A. Newton brought in 10 horses and a span of mules on the last trip of the City of Traverse. He has now 23 horses at his livery and sale stables.

08 20 80 Joseph Cox has the foundation laid for the addition to his meat market and the building will commence as soon as bricks can be had.

08 27 80 Mr. J.P.C. Church, who has been connected with Messrs. Dexter & Noble so long, has accepted a position with R.W. Bagot, our popular druggist and grocer. As Mr. Bagots business has rapidly increased during the past few years, we think under the new arrangement it will be better, as Mr. Church is one of the best salesman in the country, and a pleasant gentleman. Mr. Church, was found at his new place of business Wednesday morning.

09 03 80 O.J. Holbrook fills the position in the dry goods department of Messrs. Dexter & Noble's store made vacant by the resignation of Mr. J.P.C. Church. Milton Lang takes Mr. Holbrook's former position, in the grocery department, and Henry Ballard fills Mr. Langs "vacant chair".

09 03 80 S. Yalomstien has gone to New York to purchase his fall stock of goods for his stores at Traverse City and Elk Rapids.

09 10 80 The suit of Newton *vs.* Donley has been an absorbing topic of conversation for the past two or three days. We don't know any thing about the merits of the case. We went to see the horse after it came off the vessel and it looked as though 1,000 bricks had struck it sideways, but then Newton will doctor him up and sell him for $75 in a few days, probably.

09 10 80 John Hughes now has a horseshoer at his blacksmith shop in the Cooper building. He is now doing a fine business.

09 10 80 The case of Newton *vs.* McLane — trespass on the case, which was to be tried on 11th inst., has been settled by the payment of $15. The defendent hired a horse and buggy to go a certain distance. He overdrove the horse and brought back buggy in a damaged condition. Plaintiff brought suit before Justice McLaughlin which resulted as above.

Newton *vs.* Donley — trespass on the case. This trial came off before Justice McLaughlin Wednesday of this week. Capt. Donley contracted with C.A. Newton for the use of a horse to draw timbers into the schooner *Prussia* for which he was to pay $15. The horse came home under the weather, and Newton brought suit, claiming $75 damages. A judgment was given Plaintiff of $40.

09 17 80 A.B. Dougherty is doing a nice business in the building east of the Post-office. He deals in confectionery, choice cigars, and has school books for sale. Give Andy a call.

10 01 80 Work has been stopped for the season at the brick yard. Two kilns have been burned and there is another on the yard that has not been set up. 300,000 bricks have been manufactured this year.

10 01 80 Joseph Cox has put up in front of his barn, one of Forsyth's platform scales. They differ from Fairbank's in construction, but are said to be as good made. There is one remarkable feature about them, and that is, if a person buys those kind of scales he will be obliged to build a house for them.

10 15 80 The addition to Joseph Cox's meat market is being rapidly built. When completed his market will be a handsome two story building 152 feet long, 35 feet wide. The addition will be an ice-house and store-room, so that pork packing can be carried on successfully at all seasons of the year.

10 15 80 Mr. R.W. Bagot is receiving new goods every day, and we won't forget to mention that he is selling them, too.

10 15 80 Mr. Joseph Cox has just built a new granary which holds nearly 2,000 bushels of grain.

11 12 80 Mr. Joseph Cox our enterprising meat market man, bought over $160 worth of hog meat last Tuesday.

Mr. John Hughes is turning out a few nice cutters from his blacksmith shop. It is his purpose to manufacture goods as soon as he gets a good wood-worker.

11 12 80 The brick work has all been done on the addition to Mr. Joseph Cox's meat market.

11 19 80 Mr. O.J. Powers came home last Friday from, Canada with a number of horses.

11 19 80   A Puff APIECE

Dr. Evans is busy with numerous calls.

Dr. C.R. Keach is having calls night and day.

C.A. Newton has some good drivers in his livery.

Chas. Grammel brews "the boss" lager beer.

L.O. Simmons makes good fits for all who go to him.

Wm. Riley, the barber should be liberally patronized.

C.A. Newton receives a good many orders from abroad for cigars and liquors.

Peter Williamson will take your phiz [sic] if you go to his gallery.

Dr. Bailey is back and his friends are mighty glad of it.

John Hughes, "the village blacksmith," is doing a lively business.

The ladies should call on Mrs. James Davidson and see her complete stock of millinery.

George Goodhew makes new soles and repairs old ones, and he knows just how to do it.

The New York Clothing House is "chuck full" of goods and will have more for the Holidays.

Geo. D. Wyckoff has a nice stock of confectionery and canned goods which he offers the public.

Andrew B. Dougherty "beats the town" on cigars. Try them. He also has a stock of school books. Buy them.

If you want turkeys, chickens, or any kind of meats for Thanksgiving, Joseph Cox can supply you.

R.W. Bagot, Druggist and Grocer has a full and complete stock of goods. If you don't believe it just walk into his store.

The Lake View House is open, and if you are in town call in and the genial proprietor will show you where the dining room is.

S. Goldman's store always looks as neat as "a new pin." He has a large stock of dry goods, boots and shoes, clothing.

Mr. Geo. A. Dyer has filled in the shelves in the post office with beautiful Christmas goods. People should call and examine.

Kramer & Manwarring appear to be busy repairing and manufacturing sleighs about now. They do their share of the work we should judge.

The lawyers will probably have pretty good picking this winter.   Hon. F. R. Williams and Roswell Leavitt, Esq. appear to be on the move continually.

Attention is called to the two adv.'s of C.D. Towne. Persons wishing Christmas Goods that he does not carry in stock need not send away for them. Give him a call.

The "Old Reliable," Messrs. Dexter & Noble have an immense stock of goods in every department of their store. Dry goods, boots and shoes, clothing, hardware, crockery, groceries, and agricultural implements.

We call attention to the advertisement of M. John Silkman, of Torch Lake, who has a fine store at that place which is "cram full" of seasonable goods. In adopting the cash system he is doing a good thing for himself and also for those that trade with him.

The *Progress* is a good advertising medium. Give us a call.

Last but not least the preachers. Rev. A.C. Lewis in visiting friends in Buffalo, and Rev. S.G. Blanchard is busy.

11 19 80 If our business men don't like the locals we give them this week, they can pay us for them. We set 'em up in this way.

11 19 80 This winter will be a good one in a business way in our county. With getting out cord wood and logs our farmer friends can do nicely, and in the spring some of them will be a good many dollars richer. The prices paid for wood at different points are good ones, and we are sure logs will bring fair prices.

11 26 80 E.S. Noble has a new Insurance Agency...

12 03 80 The steamer *City of Grand Rapids* brought new goods for C.D. Towne's jewelry store last Saturday night, and he is now showing a fine lot of clocks, jewelry and silverware etc.

01 06 81 John Acker purchased recently the store building near the Lake View House of O.H. Ellis, Traverse City, for $1,000. He takes possession May 1.

Geo. D. Wyckoff recently sold the brick store he now occupies too C.A. Newton for $1,200, possession to be given May 1.

01 28 81 We have been shown the plans of the store and dwelling which Geo. D. Wyckoff has contracted to be built. The main building will be 16x40; with a wing 12x28, two stories high. He intends to occupy it about the 1st of May, and will keep a fuller stock of canned goods, confectionery, cigars and tobacco than he does at present. One feature, which will be added, and which will meet with approval, will be the ice-cream parlors which he intends to have for ladies and gentlemen.

02 11 81 Chas. Schuler intends keeping a butcher shop in the building on River St. formerly owned by Goldman & Yalomstein. We see he is making a start by building an ice house, and he is also building a slaughter house on the bay shore above Chas. Grammel's brewery.

02 18 81 Ice houses are being rapidly filled. The ice cut from Elk Lake is from 18 to 20 inches thick.

02 26 81 Blacksmithing and Woodworking, at the old Cooper Shop by John Hughes.

03 04 81 C.A. Newton, will ship by cars in a short time a number of horses for his sale stables at this place. We would like to know what he does with all the horses he ships in- must be a ready sale for what he buys.

03 11 81 Roswell Leavitt, Esq., moves from the old office into the new to-day, Phillips brothers go into the old office.

03 11 81 Chas. Schuler brought 15 head of cattle from Chicago Monday. The train was delayed and he could not get any further than Kalkaska with his stock so he was obliged to "hoof it" from Kalkaska.

03 11 81 We learn that Mr. James Ryan intends to start a harness shop in the building one door east of The *Progress* office.

03 18 81 We should not starve- three meat markets in town. Casper Schuler opens his meat market Monday where people can get the choicest cuts.

03 18 81 A stone foundation is being built under Casper Schuler's building on river st. Casper says he will have a good cellar if it costs him a thousand dollars.

      C.A. Newton returned from Chicago Wednesday evening, with sixteen horses for his Livery, Sale and Exchange Stable- not "city plugs," but good, sound horses, "and don't you forget it."

04 08 81 Mr. W. Youman has started a harness shop in the Cooper building.

04 08 81 Geo. D. Wycoff has moved his fruit and confectionery store from the brick building which he has been occupying to his new building. Mr. Wyckoff will now give two sticks of gum for a cent. The new store is not unlike other stores, having the customary shelves and counters, but we are of the opinion that Mr. Wyckoff's business will increase rapidly in his new quarters. It is of wood and is neatly arranged for the business in which he is engaged, lunch room, fruit and confectionery.

04 08 81 AD—Schuler & Veit, dealers in Fresh, Salt, Smoked Meats, Bolognas, and all kinds of sausage...

04 08 81 We call attention to the advertisement of Manwarring & Kramer on second page. They will keep on hand a full stock of agricultural implements. For the reception of these goods they intend putting up a temporary building near the old shop. Later in the spring they will commence building the shop heretofore described in the *Progress*. We wish them success in the new branch of their business.

04 29 81 C.A. Newton has moved his saloon from the building next to S. Yalomstein's store into the brick building formerly occupied by G.D. Wyckoff.

04 29 81 John Hughes now has a wood worker in his blacksmith shop and is doing considerable work in that line.

05 06 81 Passing by the Wagon and blacksmith shop of Manwarring & Kramer one day this week we could not help but be impressed with the rapid growth of their business, showing what fair dealing and strict attention to business will do. They need and we believe they soon intend to have more commodious quarters for their constantly increasing trade.

05 06 81 Schuler & Veit's smoke house burned Monday.

05 06 81 John Acker has removed his saloon into the building formerly occupied by Chas. A. Newton.

05 13 81 C.A. Newton intends building an addition to his billiard hall 22x40 which will make the building 22x70. He will very soon place in the hall two Monarch billiard tables.

RETAIL
Liquor
Store,

WM. DEARING, PROPRIETOR,

CHOICE WINES AND LIQUORS

AND

C. Crammel's

AND

Milwaukee Beers

ON DRAUGHT·

BILLIARD HALL IN CONNECTION.

The Elk Rapids

Retail Liquor Store

have constantly on hand a choice selection of

Wines and Liquors

CHOICE BRANDS OF

CIGARS.

Orders by mail will receive prompt attention.

C. A. NEWTON,
Prop.

I **HAVE ON HAND**

And will sell the following

Brands of Liquors

For a beverage, or any amount
Less Than Five Gallons.
Whisky :
OLD RYE,
BOURBON,
XXX,
STAR,
CONCORD,
MONARCH,
NORDHAUSER,
PLEASANT, VALLEY,
Brandy :
PEACH,
CHERRY, AND
IMPORTED COGNAC.
Gin :
OLD TOM, WHITE ROSE,
INPORTED GENEVA.
Wines :
PORT, SWEET CATAWBY,
CHERRY AND
IMPORTED SHERRY.

NEW ENGLAND RUM,
APPLE JACK AND
JERSEY LIGHTNING.
John Acker.

---

82. Spring & Summer. 82.

We are now showing

The Latest

PATTERNS IN

DRY GOODS,

—AND—

CLOTHING,

For Spring and Summer Wear.

Our Stock of Hosiery, Gloves, Ties. Edgings Etc. is Complete.

WE HAVE THE LATEST STYLES
OF BOOTS AND SHOES,
HATS AND CAPS, CAR-
PETS AND OIL-CLOTHS.

Come and see us and Examine Goods and Prices. Remember, PLAIN FIGURES on all our Goods, one price to all, and that th Lowest.

S. Goldman.

05 20 81 C.A. Newton received several thousand lath last week from Traverse City for the addition to his billiard hall.

05 20 81 Manwarring & Kramer received a consignment of farming implements, wind mills, etc., Monday by boat.

05 20 81 Spaulding & Phillips have moved into the Cox building and will hereafter have their market there.

05 20 81 Chas. Schuler recently purchased the lot east of his market of James Spencer. Consideration $300.

05 20 81 Schuler & Veit have dissolved partnership, and Mr. John Veit will continue business at the old stand. Look at change in advertisement.

05 27 81 Peter Williamson, our photographer, is in very poor health this spring. We hope he may recover soon.

06 03 81 C.A. Newton has put in to his billiard hall two monarch billiard tables, the best made by the Brunswick Co. He expects to put up a nine pin alley east of his hall before long.

06 24 81 New boxes have been received for the post office.

06 24 81 After the 1st. of July, the Elk Rapids post office will be an International Money Order Office:

NOTICE TO THE PUBLIC.

Money orders can be obtained at this post office, payable at Money Orders post offices in the following countries to wit:

Italy, Norway, Sweden, The German Empire, France and Algeria, The Netherlands (Holland), The Dominion of Canada, Luxenburg (The Grand Duchy of), United Kingdom of Great Britain and Ireland.

07 01 81 R.W. Bagot, has sold his Drug, Grocery and Provision store in Elk Rapids to Messrs. Fred Holbrook and Wilson Rushmore. The purchasers will take possession within thirty days. —*Eagle* Traverse City.

All the above is true with the exception of the facts in regard to Mr. Bagot's selling out, and the time to surrender property. Mr. Bagot informs us that he has not sold.

Mr. S.S Spaulding has a bakery in connection with his boarding house and keeps fresh bread constantly on hand at Spaulding & Philip's meat market.

07 08 81 The Elk Rapids post office is about as neatly arranged as any in this country. Post master Geo. A. Dyer has all patent boxes and tries and does please the public.

07 22 81 John F. Veit has a new sign for his meat market.

54

07 29 81 Mr. R.W. Bagot sold his drug and grocery store to Messrs. Rushmore & Holbrook last night. The new firm are well known to the people of this and surrounding country. They have engaged the services of Mr. C. Watson, of Cheboygan, as their drug clerk, who is a competent druggist and a pleasing gentleman. Mr. Holbrook has gone to his new quarters and Mr. Rushmore will leave the employ of Messrs. Dexter & Noble in the course of a year or more. We wish the new firm every success imaginable, and the people will do the rest as they are competent business men.

08 05 81 The new firm of Rushmore & Holbrook, successors to R.W. Bagot, of the drug and grocery business, start out with the most encouraging prospects before them. Long may they wave. A rumor has been in circulation that the firm of Dexter & Noble was in some way connected with the firm, which has no foundation in fact. No doubt it would be greatly to the advantage if the new firm to be associated with an institution of such proportions as the firm of Dexter & Noble has attained; but as this is not the case we bespeak for the firm of Rushmore & Holbrook, a fair share of such patronage, as fair dealing and prompt attention to business will secure.

08 05 81 C.A. Newton's new livery barn has been inclosed and is now nearly completed. It is 48x96 and is one of the best barns in the county. Mr. Newton has purchased several new buggies, and means to keep a first class livery stable.

08 05 81 The Western Union Telegraph office has been removed from Messrs. Dexter & Noble's store to Rushmore & Holbrook's store. The U.S. signal office has been removed to the same place.

08 12 81 C.A. Newton brought home ten horses from Chicago Tuesday by way of steamer *City of Traverse*.

08 12 81 The Lake View House barber shop will next week be presided over by a new tonsorial artist.

08 16 81 Mr. J.P.C. Church is fitting up the Hughes building on River Street, and intends stocking it with a line of general groceries.

08 19 81 C.A. Newton sold his saloon yesterday to William Deering for $4,000, possession to be given in a few months.

08 23 81 S. Goldman has completed the addition to his store and now has one of the best appointed dry goods stores in town.

Mr. Norman Pierce has rented the whole upper story of Messrs. Rushmore & Holbrook's store and intends having his laboratory there.

08 23 81 Messrs. Rushmore & Holbrook have their delivery wagon running and deliver immense quantities of goods.

08 25 81 S.S. Spaulding is doing a nice bakery business. Breads can be obtained at Spaulding & Phillips' meat market.

08 25 81 G.M. Jackson will commence putting up a building this week on the lot of Lawrence Sweeny, at the east end of River Street, for a Photograph gallery. The building will be 14x26.

08 25 81 Mr. S. Goldman intends building 40 feet to the building in which he has his clothing and dry goods store, making the building 90 feet long. The work will commence this week.

09 02 81 Mr. Geo. Manwarring is making a machine which is neither a bicycle, a tricycle or a velocipede, but appears to be a cross between bicycle and a tricycle. There are three wheels to the machine, a large one in front and two smaller ones behind. The crossicle (machine) will be propelled by a crank with each hand which are over the forward wheel, and it is to be guided with the feet. Right between the cranks are two pulleys upon which runs endless chains to pulleys on the hub of the large wheel. We are anxiously awaiting developments.

09 02 81 Rushmore & Holbrook's soda water fountain is always charged, and Mr. Watson, their druggist understands how to make good soda. In the winter they propose to dish it up hot.

09 02 81 C.A. Newton's livery stable is nearly completed. The office and waiting room have been plastered and will be nicely fitted up. It is one of the best barns in the country and "broke" $2,000.

09 09 81 Messrs. Rushmore & Holbrook will commence this week to deliver every thing bought at their store. The enterprise of the new firm is commendable.

10 07 81 Manwarring & Kramer have commenced building their wagon and blacksmith shop on Traverse Avenue and expect to be in it this fall. The foundation has been laid and the framing of the timbers is being done this week. The building will be 30x60, two stories. The firm have sold a good many agricultural implements this year and expect a large increase to their business for the year to come.

10 07 81 The post-office did $530 money order business Wednesday.

G.M. Jackson, our Photographer, is in Traverse City this week with his tent.

10 21 81   OYSTERS ! OYSTERS ! OYSTERS !

At Rushmore & Holbrook's store. September, October, November, December — Oysters. These are the first of the season and are fresh. Take a couple of cans for your Sunday dinner. Just in to-day by express.

"After Tea" "Checkered E.B." and "Manhatta" Cigars on sale at the Lake View House Billiard Rooms.

11 11 81 The bread manufactured at Spaulding bakery of the finest patent flour, and the Boston baked, Rye, and brown breads cannot be beaten. We have sampled them and know whereof we speak. All kind kept on sale at Spaulding & Phillips meat market.

11 11 81 We shall be thoroughly glad when navigation closes and we shall not have freight brought by boat, as it costs nearly as much for freight from Traverse City to this place as it does from Chicago to Traverse City by rail.

11 11 81 Attention is called to the notice in regard to business at the post-office. The public should observe it. Our post office is the neatest in appearance of any in Northern Michigan. Mr. Dyer proposes to have better mail facilities next season than now.

11 25 81 As far as manufacturing interests are concerned Elk Rapids now turns out more manufactured product than any town in Northern Michigan. When all our places of business are in running order our manufactured product will be greatly in excess of what it is now. The furnace makes 14,600 tons of iron a year. The chemical works will turn out 52 million pounds o acetate of lime, and 100,000 gallons of wood alcohol a year, and the saw mill, will make a cut of at least 30,000 feet of hardwood lumber a day. The grist mill does a mighty good business, and one year shipped away 18,000 bushels of wheat; but this year the surplus wheat is all used by home consumers. Who says Elk Rapids does not need or will not get a railroad?

11 25 81 The firm of Spaulding & Phillips has been dissolved. Look at notice in another column.

11 25 81 We learn that Mr. Oliver Powers has the contract with the Chemical Co., to convey the product from their Works to Traverse City for shipment. Whether the statement is true or not, a good "moral" from the local can be learned, and that is, the two towns should be connected by rail, and they will be if that road at Manistee ever points towards Traverse City. A road from the above named town would be just as advantageous to that village as it would to this. Elk Rapids will eventually get a railroad.

12 02 81 Hughes & Sharp have dissolved partnership.

12 09 81 Oliver Powers returned from the Southern part of the State last Friday with ten horses, which he went out to purchase.
12 16 81 Manwaring & Kramer have removed into their fine new building, and are doing lots of work. They have our best wishes.

12 23 81 W.W. Youmans & Co., have removed from their old quarters in the Cooper building into the room at the west end of the building. They are settled and display a nice stock of goods in the harness line.

12 30 81 We print on first page this week a card of the new law firm which has been recently formed, Pratt, Hatch & Davis, who will commence doing business Jan. 2, 1882.

01 13 82 The beautiful snow is falling this morning giving us enough to make sleighing good, causing gladness in the hearts of the trader and the lumberman. Bring on your poetry.
01 13 82 Messrs. Lang and Walker recently purchased of Mr. Geo. D. Wyckoff,

his store building on River St. Consideration, $1,800, possession given Jan. 1, 1882.

01 27 82 Post-master Geo. A. Dyer has obtained a lease of Dr. Geo. H. Bailey's building until April 1, so that the post-office will not be removed until that time. We presume by April 1 that arrangements will be made for a commodious office.

02 03 82 Chas. Grammel is filling his ice house at the brewery with ice from Bass Lake.

02 24 82 Mr. John French has purchased Messrs. Dexter & Noble's twelve row boats, and is painting them for the summer campaign.
03 03 82 Some weeks ago we mentioned that the post-office would before long have a commodious building expressly for it. We now make a note of the fact that Mr. George A. Dyer has leased the large Cooper building on River street and will fit it up for a post-office and rooms for hotel purposes, in connection with the Lake View House. Mr. Wm. M. King has the supervision of the work. We shall mention this matter more fully in a later issue.

03 17 82 The work of preparing the Cooper building for the post-office has been in progress some few days. A room 35x35 has been partitioned off, and will be completed at once for the P.O., stationery and news depot, and for C.D. Towne, Jeweler. The other work on the building, as proposed will give about 20 new rooms for the Lake View House; a large dancing hall and dining room. Now if the building could only be raised one story, and the post-office removed to the old Lake View House we could have a hotel that would accommodate 80 or 100 guests.

03 24 82 John Acker is grading his lot on River Street one door east of the *Progress* office.
    W. Riley intends building a barber shop, 15x20, west of R. Leavitt's law office. The lumber is on the ground for the building.

03 31 82 C.A. Newton brought in 18 head of horses Wednesday night from Chicago.
    The carpenter work on the Cooper building has been rushed, with "no monkeying." Any one having any building to do should get Wm. M. King's figures, as it does not take him all summer to do a job.
    Spaulding & Son have rented Lang & Walker's store building on River street and will keep a bakery and a confectionery store at that place. Their business will be a successful one.

04 07 82 The post-office was removed Wednesday from Dr. Baileys building to the Cooper building.

04 14 82 The room where the post-office has been taken is the handsomest in town. It is 35x35 with new white walls and ceiling, and the floor is laid in 3 inch strips of maple and cherry, one strip of cherry and two of maple, alternate.

04 14 82 Emery Reese is back on the stage route between this place and Traverse

City. We are glad to mention this as he is prompt, reliable, and has the respect of every one in town.

04 21 82 George E. Sharp has removed his blacksmith shop into the old Ed. Gillard shop on church street.

Manwaring & Kramer are making a new bus for C.A. Newton.

C.A. Newton will extend his livery barn 47 feet. It will then be 52 feet wide by 124 feet long. Increase of business.

Messrs. S. Goldman, W. Riley and Geo. A. Dyer were to have new advertisements in this issue, but they will appear next week.

L.O. Simmons has moved his shoe shop into the building where Geo. Manwaring formerly had his wagon shop.

Wm. Riley has moved his barber shop into his new building on River street. He expects to put veneer on to the walls as soon as it is dry.

05 05 82 Wm. Deering has purchased of C.A. Newton his saloon building on River street with all the stock, fixtures. Possession was given May 1st .

05 12 82 Chas. Grammel has opened a saloon on River street, with Frank Howe as manager.

05 26 82 Charles Hickox, Esq., arrived last Saturday from Medina, O., and will commence the practice of law in our village. As we have before mentioned, Mr. Hickox has fine abilities, and will no doubt meet with success here.

The publisher, B.F. Davis left Wednesday afternoon for Chicago, to attend the May Festival. If any thing goes wrong, the readers of very often.The *Progress* will excuse it on the grounds that Ben does not take a vacation

06 02 82 Charles Grammel is painting his saloon building on River street.

06 09 82 Owing to increase of business Wm. H. Riley has placed another chair in his barber shop.

06 09 82 Geo. M. Jackson has received a new camera for his photograph gallery.

06 09 82 The piers for the addition to Newton's livery barn have been completed. C.A. has also a new shed for his buggies.

06 09 82 The Lake View barber shop has been moved from the office into the basement. A cool and comfortable place to go.

06 16 82 Newton was out with his fine new 'bus' yesterday. Made by Manwarring & Kramer, and upholstered by W.W. Yuman & Co.

06 16 82 R.W. Bagot informs us that it is his intention this summer to loan money in sums of from $100 to $1,000, and that this is all the business he intends doing at present.

06 30 82 Chas. T. Hickox, Esq., is having an office built in the Cooper building.

Rushmore & Holbrook have their soda fountain charged and you can get a glass for only 5 cents.

Williamsburg parties are shipping lumber to Chicago *via* Elk Rapids.

07 07 82 M. Alpern, of Detroit, has purchased the harness business of W.W. Youman & Co. and took possession Monday. He is a young man, practical workman, and should be well patronized. Mr. Alpern has recently ordered a new stock.

07 14 82 Chas. T. Hickox, Esq., has moved into his handsome new office in the Cooper building. The office is painted in the latest style- olive green and Indian red.

08 04 82 F.R. Williams is building the main part to his law office, which will be 14x24. The carpenter work commenced yesterday.

08 18 82 Wanted—A boy to learn the harness trade. Inquire of M. Alpern.
About 500,000 brick have been molded at the brick yard, and a kiln of 250,000 has been burned.

08 18 82 G.M. Jackson, photographer, was home Saturday, from Eastport, where he had his tent pitched.

09 08 82 C.A. Newton has commenced excavation for his new store building on River street, and in consequence R. Leavitt, Esq., and Wm. Riley have been compelled to move their buildings on other lots.

09 15 82 The Jewish residents have their stores closed and are celebrating their New Year.

09 22 82 Monday night Wm. Riley's barber shop was blown from its foundations. The building fell against the Landon house, near which it was standing, putting a good sized hole in the side. No damage internally except a few broken mugs.

09 22 82 Geo. F. Manwarring has rented his wagon shop to Wm.M. King, possession of which will be given October 1.

09 29 82 C.A. Newton's Charlevoix saloon business was not a success, so he has shut up shop.

10 13 82 Geo. M. Jackson has sold his photograph gallery, on River street, to Truman Carns, and will close it in about two weeks.

10 27 82 Chas. Grammel is having a new fence built around his brewery.
O. Powers is building a new barn on the lot he recently purchased on Traverse avenue.

11 17 82 Mrs. J. Cox is fitting up the rear of her brick building on River street for a store. The space for a glass front is being cut through the brick wall.

11 24 82 J.W. Davis—Real Estate, money to loan, and collections.

12 22 82 George Sharp has his blacksmith shop just around the corner and is doing a good business.

The Hoxsie bros. are establishing a stage line between Traverse City and Elk Rapids. The stage is covered and is heated by a coal stove, and they invite every body to "go warm." They make their trips here from Traverse City, Mondays, Wednesdays and Fridays, and their return trips, Tuesdays, Thursdays and Saturdays.

The "go warm" stage makes daily trips between Traverse City and Elk Rapids. It is a comfortable convenience for travelers in cold weather.

Chapter 6
Maple Grove Cemetery

01 09 80 By a vote of the Board, persons wishing to purchase cemetery lots or to procure a permit to inter, will apply directly to the Town Clerk.

Michael Butler was appointed sexton of the cemetery.

01 16 80 The Board of Health are studying how they can enlarge and beautify the Cemetery, and so modify the old plan and improve its appearance in the future. They are also attempting to get a complete record of the interments which have been made and keep it up hereafter, so that all necessary information can be obtained as to each interment, somewhat after the Woodmere Cemetery Record, of Detroit. This is a work of much importance to friends, and it will be of greater importance as time rolls on. Now we find that very few have any marks to show their resting place; soon they may be ruthlessly disturbed. If friends do not choose to mark the resting place of the dead- to neglect to do it- by all means have the Record show it. We are entirely unable in many cases to know who to call upon for the needed information and it would be esteemed a favor if those having friends there would call upon the undersigned, or make it convenient to so mark the graves to show name, age, residence, disease, birthplace and place of death- certainly the name and age. We find also many interments have been made in alleys and other places which may subject the remains to removal. We desire to make some alterations with a view to disturbing as few as possible.

Board of Health,
Geo. E. Steele, President.

04 02 80 Job to Let—We want to plant a lot of native shade trees on the Cemetery and do some grading there. Bidders inquire immediately of
Board of Health, of Elk Rapids.

per Geo. E. Steele, Pres't. Elk Rapids, April 1st, 1880.

04 14 82 Mr. John Rogers of Yuba has erected during the past week a neat monument at the grave of his wife and son, in the Elk Rapids cemetery. The monument is of blue polished marble, and though not large, (about six feet high,) the design is in good taste, and the work well executed. It was prepared in the factory of V.N. Pearsall of Grand Ledge, Mich. and was obtained through the agency of Rev. S.G. Blanchard, who will forward all orders for such work, and guarantee satisfaction at very low rates.

09 29 82 We have been spoken to several times about one or two persons who have been known to desecrate the graves at the cemetery. We did not know that this town held such contemptible creatures, and hope we shall never hear the like again. We have not yet been informed the names of the parties, or we should publish them.

06 01 82   FROM MISS TO MISTRESS.

She who fails Mrs. to change from Miss,
Has Mr. chance of wedding bliss.
          - *Cincinnati Gazette.*

But she who changes from Miss to Mrs.
Has solved the Mr.y of kisses.
          - *Nycum Advertiser.*

When a Miss Mrs. to kiss a Mr.y,
A Miss is Maid in modern history.
          - *Gorham (N.H.) Mountaineer.*

Tho' a Miss, 'tis said, is as good as a mile,
When a Miss misses Mrs., Misters do smile.
          --*States.*

Chapter 7
Village of Central Lake

01 02 80 Mr. John Hanley is erecting a building 18x24 in Central Lake, which will be used by him when completed for a grocery store. The frame work was raised Monday last.

10 01 80 Nearly all the people of Central Lake have been attending Circuit Court this week, the trial of the case of the People *vs*. Thomas H. Groh, having a hearing.

The trial of the case of the People *vs*. Thomas Groh- assault with intent to murder, at the last term of the circuit court for this county, resulted in a sentence of three years in state prison.

10 15 80 The People *vs*. Michael Wealch- incest and adultery- had a hearing before a justice of the peace at Central Lake last Thursday, Friday and Saturday. The complainants- Wealch's two married daughters make a bad, bad man of him. It seems from their testimony that he has had sexual intercourse with them, both before and after marriage. The evidence given by them goes to prove that their mother assisted the father in the fulfillment of his depraved wishes. The case is a horribly disgusting one. Wealch was brought here Sunday and placed in the county jail, and denies, of course, the crime, and proposes to fight the charge.

10 22 80 W.W. Smith is building an addition to the Central Lake Hotel. It is two stories high, and presents a fine appearance.
Central Lake is now blessed with six stores. They are running under the following names and branches of trade: Henry Sissons, Grocer; Caleb Green, General store; Wadsworth & Thurston, general merchandise; John Parr, druggist, Mrs. C. Green, millinery store.

10 29 80 No murders, no marriages, no fires, no elopements, no nothing except politics ruffles the peaceful bosom of our burgh. From the numerous political meetings and the decease of so many fine dogs that have barked themselves to death at candidates for office, the people are beginning to think there is to be an election this fall and are getting interested in the issues of the day.

11 12 80 There was a runaway up in Banks last Tuesday. We understand that Mr. Parson drove up to Flannagans store and got out of his buggy, leaving his wife and baby in it, and stepped in the store for a moment. There was quite a crowd around the horses and they gave a hurrah for Garfield the team started down the road on the run. Mr. Yettan managed to catch one of the reins but was dragged under the buggy before he could do any good. Mrs. Parsons seized the other and after the team had run about 30 rods she pulled the horses around a stump so short that it upset the buggy. Mrs. Parsons was hurt severely and it is feared that she will not recover. Her baby escaped uninjured. The horses after rounding the stump. Started on the back track and ran about two miles. Completely demolishing the buggy.

02 26 81 Competition runs high among our merchants here and occasionally leads to unpleasant results. A collision between two rival dealers one time last week seemed imminent but the assailant after having made a flourishing display of his clenched fists in the immediate vicinity of his opponent's nose finally hesitated to strike the threatening blow...cooled off a little, and out of sympathy for the oppressed tax payers of Antrim County resumed an attitude of peace.

03 25 81 Wadsworth & Thurston have sold out their winter's stock of feed and are now hauling from Mancelona.
Ansel Green has sold out his stock of merchandise to Henry Sissons. The business will be conducted at the old stand, Mr. Sissons having rented the building.

05 20 81 Michael Wealch, of Central Lake, who was acquitted at the last term of the Circuit Court for incest, has been taken again for the same offense, committed some time ago.

08 16 81 Green Bro's. new hotel is nearly completed.
James M. Wadsworth is fitting up a building for the post office, and for a business office, and is making preparations for his lumbering business this winter.

08 16 81 A writ of *Certiorari* has been issued out of the Circuit Court against the school inspectors of Central Lake and Forest home to review their proceedings in establishing school district No. 5, of those townships.

10 21 81 The work on the new post-office building, is so near completed that the post-office has been moved. Wm. M. Covert will take charge.

02 10 82 The *Intermediate Valley* is the name of a small paper published by Geo. L. Thurston, Central Lake.
I took a trip to-day a few miles north-east of this place to see the country and I was astonished. Not more than three miles from here I saw the cars quite plain in the vicinity of Mancelona- a distance of 15 miles. The scenery was beautiful to behold from the top of Somerville hill.

02 24 82 The 20th inst. was pay day for logs. Plenty of gold in circulation.

03 10 82 New goods are constantly arriving at Sisson's store. New attractions in "old styles."

03 31 82 We want grist and saw mills. A good location for both at this place.
We expect a blacksmith from Torch Lake. We hope he will not disappoint us.
John Crawford, of Banks, has been in town. It is a pity he cannot get a wife.
C. Green has traded a mill for a livery horse, and has loaned him out until the 1st day of April—if he lives. Later—dead. Wm. H. Easton was the purchaser of the once noble animal. Cause of death, was fast driving.

04 07 82 R.B. Hays, while out boat riding on Grass Lake got caught in a snow storm, and was lost, a few days ago. He is suffering from mental depression.

04 21 82 Our town blacksmith has arrived.

C. Green and J.M. Ogletree went to the Colby bridge to put in a pine log, to be cut in to lumber for small boats, for the use of tourists this summer.

05 26 82 At this writing a raft of square timber, got out by James M. Wadsworth, for a foreign market is just passing by.

Central Lake was rather boisterous the day of the eclipse. One woodchuck was killed, a red squirrel was shot off the liberty pole, one dog fight and several men were seen reeling on the streets under the influence of snake poison.

06 16 82 Dr. Blakesley has a fine new sign up on his drug store.
F.H. Thurston has carpenters at work building a new store house.

C. & A. Green have their new hotel completed and are now ready for business. The Smith Hotel has been enlarged, and is now open to the public.

06 23 82 Jas. M. Wadsworth, of Central Lake, informs us that as his square timber is off his hands all that he has now to do is to get his log drive down then prepare for winter. The logs will be down the last of this week.

07 07 82 Jesse A. Cary will run a stage between Russell's landing and Central Lake, to connect with all boats stopping at either place.

10 20 82 The post-office has been moved to F.H.Thurston's store.

12 01 82 Our saw mill blew its first whistle Wednesday night.

12 08 82 J.A. Cary and Joe Minnie are stringing the telegraph wire between here and South Arm.

68

11 04 81   THE PEANUT.

A large and healthy peanut
  Lay cozily abed.
And it chuckled, O so gleefully!
  And to its self it said:
"There's a great big world before me,
  And my mission yet to do;
And up I'd be doing it
  Ere the sun has dried the dew.

"There are greedy boys to conquer,
  And hungry girls as well.
What a world of power I've hidden
  Within this little shell.
Though they slay me in the battle,
  Though they crush me like a worm,
Though they bake and crunch my body,
  If I can I'll make 'em squirm."

And the small boy grabbed that peanut,
  And he cracked it 'tween his teeth;
But, when he would have swallowed it.
  It choked him e'en to death;
And the peanuts work was ended-
  It had fallen in the strife —
It had done its mission nobly,
  Though the doing cost its life.

Chapter 8
Churches of Elk Rapids

01 02 80 The heating apparatus of the Presbyterian Church is being repaired. Workman are putting in another register, as the building has not been sufficiently heated.

01 09 80 There will be a mite (sic) social at the residence of Rev. A.C. Lewis next Tuesday evening. All are cordially invited.

01 16 80 The mite (sic) social at the residence of Rev. A.C. Lewis last Tuesday evening, was like all that are given very enjoyable. The time coming for departing the young ladies made the most of Leap Year, and we hear said that they played some pretty good jokes on each other.

01 23 80 Last Tuesday night, services being held in the M.E.Chapel, two rowdy's of boys tried to play a trick that any fool could do. They put a stick across the frame of the door and tied the door to it. It was a mean contemptible trick that they should be prosecuted for, and we shall publish their names if they don't keep quiet in the future.

02 06 80 The social at the residence of Hon. F.R. Williams last Tuesday evening, was the last but one that will be given by the Ladies of St. Paul's Church this winter. Despite the driving storm there was quite a number present. One of the pleasant features of the social was the excellent rendition of "Mrs. Malony's Opinion on the Chinese Question," by Mrs. Geo.Dyer.

02 20 80 The citizens of Elk Rapids and vicinity are cordially invited to attend a donation party for the benefit of Rev. J.R. Bready at the Parsonage Wednesday evening, Feb. 25. No pains will be spared to make the occasion a pleasant one to all.

02 27 80 Mr. Editor—Permit us through your columns to tender our thanks to the good people of Elk Rapids who assembled at the M.E. Parsonage on Wednesday evening, Feb. 26, and after a season spent pleasantly in social converse and partaking of a nicely prepared supper, furnished by the ladies, left us in possession of $62.43, which we trust is a token of good will. -J.A. and L.N. Bready.

03 26 80 A very pleasant donation party was given at the residence of Mr. John Carns, a few miles south of this village, last Friday evening, for the benefit of Rev. J.R. Bready. The amount of $40 was subscribed.

04 23 80 On account of ill health the Rev. A.C. Lewis has been absent from this place for over seven months. He arrived home last Sunday and will remain about ten days, and then return to Chicago where he has spent part of the time. We learn that he is gaining slowly, which will be gratifying to his many friends.

04 30 80 The Bishop will visit St. Paul's church, Elk Rapids, Sunday next, May 2d. There will be morning service, sermon, communion and collection for expenses. The Bishop will meet the Sunday School immediately after service.

05 07 80 It's a noticeable fact that although the ministers of the gospel find it necessary to take a vacation, the devil keeps right on working on full time through the Summer months- and he don't draw a double-breasted salary either.

05 14 80 Rev. R.W. Fletcher last Sunday tendered his resignation as pastor of the Presbyterian church at this place to take effect two weeks from that time.

05 21 80 The ladies of the Presbyterian Aid Society, will give a farewell social for the Rev. Mr. Fletcher, at the Church next Wednesday eve. the 26th.— By order of the President.

05 21 80 As is customary in the M. Church, the ladies of that body in this place have formed a "Ladies Society," which meets every two weeks with Mrs. Reynolds Landon as President and Mrs. Andrew Morton, Secretary.

05 28 80 A very pleasant ice-cream social was given at the Presbyterian Church last Wednesday evening—a farewell social to Rev. R.W. Fletcher, $31.00 realized.

06 04 80 We publish the following by request: Sir—The following preamble and resolutions were unanimously adopted by a rising vote at a fully attended association of the Methodist Episcopal Church of the Grand Traverse District, at Traverse City, May 18 to 20.
    The Committee authorized to publish and forward them to your respectful attention append the testimonials to this circular.
    Whereas, there is a general state of Sabbath desecration in that part of Northern Michigan embraced within the bounds of Grand Traverse district; and
    Whereas, such desecration is opposed to good morals both public and private, and is also socially degrading and injurious to the health of the community, being productive of great mental and physical deterioration; and...

06 11 80 There will be services at the Court House on Sunday, the 13th at 10:30 o'clock. Also a collection for deficiency in Pledge to Missions in the Diocese.

06 18 80 There will be services in the Presbyterian Church next Sunday at 10'clock a.m. Rev. S.W. McGregor of Dearborn, Wayne Co., Mich., will conduct the service. There will also be service in the Yuba church at 2:30 o'clock.

07 16 80 Sabbath School Association— According to previous announcement a public meeting was held at Central Lake, on Wednesday June 20, for the purpose of organizing a Sabbath School Association for Antrim County, auxiliary to the State Association...

10 01 80 The Methodists of this place will have for their pastor the coming year, Rev. J. Blanchard. He was stationed at Norwood last year.

09 24 80 At the last M.E. Conference at Muskegon, the following appointments were made for the ensuing year for the Grand Traverse District:

A.J. Eldred, P.E. :

Almire and Inland	J.W. Arney.
Bliss	Supplied.
Boyne	B.H. Whitman.
Bear's Lake	W.W.F. Smith.
Cadillac	E.H. Dou.
Cadillac Circuit	S. Stephens.
Charlevoix and Indian Mission	J. Blanchard.
Fife Lake	W. Heath.
Frankfort	J.H. Staley.
Kalkaska	O.J. Golden.
Leroy	L.D. McKee.
Little Traverse	E.F. Newell.
Manton	S. Steele.
Mancelona	S.H. Hewett.
Monroe Center	E.P. Howell.
Norwood	C.M. Smith.
Northport	A.M. Eldred.
Indian Mission	Supplied.
Petoskey Circuit	Supplied.
Petoskey and Indian Mission	W.S. Sly.
South Arm	Smith.
Spencer Creek	Supplied.
Sherman	H.P. Blake.
Traverse City	J.W.P. Carlisle.
Williamsburg	L. Dodds.

10 22 80 The Methodist Quarterly Meeting will be held in the Sour's school house on Saturday and Sunday the 23rd and 24th.

11 26 80 There will be a Sunday School picnic at the Court House this evening for the benefit of the scholars of St. Paul's Sunday School.

12 24 80 Divine Service, Sermon, Annual Collection Fund for Aged and Infirm Clergy, and Holy Communion next Sunday, being Sunday after Christmas, at half past ten o'clock, at the Court House.

04 01 81 IN MEMORIAM—Of Pastor, Rev. A.C. Lewis by the members of St. Paul's parish, Elk Rapids, Mich., held March 23, 1881...

04 08 81 It is very probable that the Methodists of this district will buy the Court House at this place.

04 15 81 The Methodists of this District have purchased the Court House at this place for a house of worship and for a parsonage, the sum of $1,500 being paid over to the County yesterday. The building which the Methodists have bought is at the least calculation worth $2,000, it having cost $7,000 and it stands in the center of ten lots, which go with the building, and each lot is worth at least $100. To say that they have made a good bargain is drawing it mild.

04 22 81 At the annual meeting the following persons were elected vestrymen of St. Paul's Church:

Richard W. Bagot.

Senior Warden	J.M. Pennock.
Junior Warden	James Ellis.
Secretary	Orin J. Holbrook.
Treasurer	Edwin S. Noble.

04 22 81 Rev. Mr. Belden left Monday, for Iowa, for his family, he having accepted a call as Pastor of the Presbyterian Church at this place.

05 06 81 The Methodists took possession of the old Court House last Friday. Prosecuting Attorney Leavitt giving a bond for a deed until such time as a deed could be given.

The M.E. Church Society have come in possession of the Court House property and will at once proceed to make some alterations in the audience room that will make it more convenient for religious worship.

05 20 81 There will be service of the Episcopal Church in the M.E. Chapel Sunday morning at 10:30 o'clock and at 3 P.M.

05 20 81 The Methodists will at once commence work repairing and arranging the Court House for a house of worship. The trustees will hereafter give notice, the limit of time they will allow publicentertainments in their building. The Methodists have acted wisely in this matter, as the hall has always been used for entertainment's, which they will not put a stop to until it has been dedicated.

05 20 81 We expect to remain in our present place of abode for some time, as we have sold the M.E. Chapel to the Episcopal Church, and they will hold services there shortly.

05 20 81 The Court House is to be kalsomined and thoroughly renovated, before being occupied by the Methodists as their church. The work begins to-day.

05 27 81 There have been two Guilds formed for St. Paul's Church. One is the St. Agnes' Guild for ladies, and the other, the St. Alban's Guild for gentleman. The object of these Guilds is to promote the interests of the church in the parish.

05 27 81 Rev. G.H. Drewe has secured rooms over R.W. Bagot's Store where he can be found hereafter.

06 10 81 Rev. S. Dodds, of Williamsburg, has bought the house and lot in this village formerly owned by Rev. Mr. Stinchcomb. Mr. Dodds was in town on Saturday last on business connected with said property.

06 10 81 Hear ye! hear ye! The Methodists have vacated the Chapel and the Episcopals have taken possession.

06 17 81 The Court House has been kalsomined and was to be used last Sunday evening by the Methodist people and would have been had the pastor not met with the accident we speak of elsewhere.

06 17 81 While coming from church at Milton last Sunday Rev. S.G. Blanchard was thrown from the wagon in which he was riding and had his shoulder blade broken by the fall. It was caused by the tongue of the wagon falling while the wagon was going down a gentle slope. Dr. Bailey was called who set the bone, and Mr. Blanchard is as comfortable as could be expected, and expects to sufficiently recover so as to be able to preach in the Court House next Sunday evening.

06 17 81 The Methodists at this place have purchased a new chapel organ of the Mason & Hamlin Organ Co., and will probably use it at service Sunday evening.

07 01 81 The Antrim County Sunday School Association held a Local Convention in the Knight's school house, in the town of Banks, Tuesday evening and Wednesday of last week, June 21 and 22...

07 22 81 Dexter & Noble have kindly presented ministers of this village with passes on their steamers for the season.

08 12 81 Presiding Elder Eldred, will dedicate the M.E. Church Sunday. There will be service at both morning and evening.

08 19 81 Very interesting service was held in the M.E. Church last Sunday morning. Presiding Elder Eldred preached the dedicatory sermon and the Church was formally dedicated.

08 25 81 Rev. J.R. Savage, pastor of the Union church at Kalkaska has resigned. Cause; too little salary for even a preacher to live on.

10 21 81 Rev. Abel Anderson, pastor of the Norwegian Lutheran Church, Muskegon, was in town Monday, and held services at the furnace Monday evening.

10 28 81 The Episcopal Church has a new chimney.

12 02 81 The Methodist and Presbyterian Sunday schools have decided to hold a Union Christmas service.

12 16 81 The New England Supper given by the ladies of St. Pauls' Church at Lake View House was a success so far as pork and beans, pumpkin pie, and receipts at the door were concerned. All voted a good time.

12 24 81 We see the *Traverse City Eagle* mentions that the Episcopalians of this place intend building their church. We hope that measures can be taken so that it can be built this season. The plans if carried out will give them one of the handsomest little churches any where.

12 30 81 A Christmas tree and oyster supper was held in the New Methodist Church in North Milton Christmas eve. A large number were present, and the tree well loaded with presents. Everything passed off pleasantly and $32 was raised to pay for work done on the Church. Good for North Milton.

02 10 82 We hope that Mormonism will be thoroughly crushed in the next year or so, and the only reasonable way to do it is to send a force of 25,000 men into Utah and stop it by force. We wish, of course every one to enjoy their religious liberty in the United States, but sensual gratification is not religion, and that seems to be the basis on which Mormonism rests. If we are not right in regard to the basis, we are right in characterizing the whole pack of them a dirty lot.

02 17 82 Some of our enterprising ladies are getting up an entertainment for the benefit of the three religious societies of this place. It is proposed to give it next Monday and Tuesday evenings at Lake View Hall, and the proceeds will be divided equally among the Episcopal, Presbyterian and Methodist Episcopal churches. The entertainment will consist of an operetta, mimic opera, and one novel feature will be the broom drill, which will be executed in true military style. Crowded houses expected, and for particulars look at small bills.

02 24 82 There will be a donation party, Tuesday evening, March 7, at Mr. S.S. Spaulding's boarding house for the benefit of Rev. S.G. Blanchard. All are invited.

02 24 82 The amount of money raised for the three religious societies by the opera given at Lake View Hall last Monday and Tuesday evenings was $20 for each society or $60 in all.

03 24 82 The third annual session of the Inter-Denominational Ministerial Association of Northern Michigan, will be held in the Presbyterian Church in Petoskey, beginning Tuesday evening May 30, 1882, and continuing the two following days.

04 14 82 The Easter offering at St. Paul's church amounted to $52.00.

04 14 82 The new seats for the Presbyterian church have come, and now that church has good seating.

04 14 82 Rev. S.G. Blanchard will preach to the Indians at Indian Town on Sunday.

05 19 82 Last Sunday Rev. L.M. Belden's residence caught on fire from a defective flue. Neighbors discovered and extinguished the flames. On the evening of the same day burglars tried to effect an entrance but were frightened away.

05 19 82 Rev. S.G. Blanchard is getting lumber on the ground for a new house.

05 26 82 Indian Quarterly Meeting in Indian town, June 3rd and 4th. Presiding Elder Eldred will be in attendance.

06 16 82 Rev. W.F. Binder, of Petoskey, held service at the Brand school house last Sunday morning. While in town he stopped at the Hughes House.

06 30 82 St. Paul's chapel has been newly kalsomined, and put in pleasant shape.

06 30 82 Efforts are being made by the Episcopalians to build their church this summer. It will be of brick, and if built according to the original plans, which we had the pleasure of seeing some few years ago, it will be an ornament to the town and a credit to the society.

06 30 82 The Episcopalians have received deeds from H.H. Noble and R.W. Bagot of the two lots where the chapel and the foundation to the new church stand.

08 18 82 The vestry of St. Pauls church have decided to commence building their new church immediately. The original plans will be carried out as near as possible, with the means they can command. It is intended too build the body of the church at once, leaving the outside ornamentation until a later day. On Wednesday morning over $800 in subscriptions.

08 18 82 Rt. Rev. George D. Gilllespie, D.D., Bishop of the Diocese of Western Michigan, will visit St. Pauls Parish, on Thursday, the 24th inst. at 8 P.M., to administer the apostolic Rite of Confirmation. In the afternoon at three O'clock, the corner stone of the new Church building will be laid, with religious ceremonies by the Bishop, assisted by other clergy.

08 25 82 Laying the Corner Stone of St. Paul's Church.-
The corner stone of St. Paul's Church was laid yesterday at 3:30 P.M. by Rt. Rev. George D. Gillespie, Bishop of Western Michigan, assisted by Rev. J.N. Rippey, of Lancaster, O., and Rev. J.S. Large, of Traverse City. The stone was laid at the south eastern corner of the proposed building, and beneath it was placed a hermetically sealed box containing the list of papers and articles named below...Copy of the Journal of the 8th.
Annual Convocation of the Diocese of Western Michigan.
Copy of the *Church Helper*, Aug. 7th, 1882.
Copy of the *Living Church*, same date.
Copy of the *Young Churchman*.
Copy of the *Elk Rapids Progress*.
Copy of a resolution of the vestry to build the Church.
List of Officers and members of St. Paul's Church Elk Rapids, Mich.
Copy of the charter and organization of the Church.
One 10 cent scrip, issued by Dexter & Noble, Elk Rapids.
One 25 cent United States coin, 1882.
   " 10 "   "   "   "   "
   " 5 "   "   "   "   "
   " 3 "   "   "   "   "
   " 2 "   "   "   "   "
   " 1 "   "   "   "   "

08 04 82 Rev. P.R. McLellend, of Northport, will occupy the pulpit in the Presbyterian church Sunday morning. Rev. L.M. Belden will conduct the service at Northport.

09 01 82 A social will be held at the residence of J.W. Davis, on Friday evening, for the purpose of assisting in making the last payment on the organ in the Methodist Church. All are cordially invited to attend.

09 08 82 At the M.E. Social given at the residence of J.W. Davis, last Friday evening, Mr. Frank Stevens, of Evanston, Ill., a very fine baritone singer, rendered three selections. There were ten pieces on the program (and refreshments) and receipts were about $17.00.

10 27 82 Messrs. Peale & Sterling have taken the contract to build the Episcopal church and will commence work on it as soon as the lumber for it can be sawed.

11 17 82 Consent has been attained from the school board to have the school bell rung for religious service. The services at the Presbyterian Church will begin promptly at 11 o'clock, the first bell will ring at 10:30 and the second at 10:50. Services at the M.E. Church Sunday evening at 7:30, first bell at 7:00, second bell at 7:20.

11 24 82 Rev. F. Miller, of Bay City, Presiding Elder of the Evangelical Association, will preach in the German language at the Brand school house, next Sunday morning, at 10:30 o'clock. All German families are invited to attend.

12 01 82 The Thanksgiving services at the M.E. Church yesterday were of unusual interest. The audience though much larger than usually attends thanksgiving services here, was much to small to speak well for a community of over eleven hundred persons. We cannot account for the meager attendance at these services in this town, only in two ways, either the want of time or an utter indifference in regard to the proclamation of the Chief Executive of the Nation and State, appointing the day for the purpose therein named.
    The sermon by the Rev. Mr. Belden, pastor of the Presbyterian Church, from the text, "Say not thou what is the cause that the former days were better than these, for thou dost not inquire wisely concerning them," from which he drew a comparison between the present and the past, very much to the advantage of the present, showing conclusively that there has been a steady advance from the earliest times down to the present; in science, literature, the arts, religion, morals, politics, and agriculture- and in every-thing that tends to make men better and happier. He gave those chronic grumblers, who are forever sighing for the "good old days of yore" a scoring that they will not soon forget, if any of that class were present.

12 08 82 The M.E. Church trustees have placed seven lots of the ten, which forms "Court House Square," on to the market. J. Ward Davis has the sale of them.

12 15 82 The Episcopalians, Presbyterians and Methodists will have a Christmas tree together this year.

Chapter 9
Charlevoix County

01 30 80 From the *Sentinel* we learn that President Cherrie and Superintendent Sprong of the Pine Lake Iron Co., have been in Charlevoix making arrangements for wood and material for the furnace.

11 19 80 Archie Buttars who has just been elected State Senator from this District, came to this region a poor boy in 1856. He was steady and industrious, and by strict attention to business he became one of the leading business men of Charlevoix.

11 26 80 The *Charlevoix Sentinel* came to us this week. The *Sentinel* is one of the oldest and best papers in this north country enlarged to a six column quarto and otherwise improved, and it is the wish of the *Progress* that it may continue to thrive. While we do not believe in "stalwartism" not thinking it honest, Smith can run his paper to suit himself. It is a good paper, has a genial gentleman for an editor — when he isn't on the rampage and we wish it and it's editor success.

01 14 81 The Chicago-Charlevoix Summer Resort Association have organized a joint stock, and will as early as possible in the Spring send a landscape gardener there to lay out, grade and beautify the grounds.

    The Board of Supervisors of Charlevoix Co. by a vote of ten to five, submitted to the people of the County at the annual Spring election, the question of the removal of County Seat to the village of Boyne Falls, twenty-one miles East of Charlevoix, and six miles East of Boyne City.

02 11 81 The Pine Lake furnace, Charlevoix county, went into blast last Saturday, and on that day the first cast was made which amounted to five tons of iron.

02 18 81 The *Boyne City Standard* has collapsed.

    The proprietors of the *Boyne City Enterprise* want a second-hand Washington hand press, as they have got tired of their wooden one. They make a pretty good looking paper with the wooden one.

04 15 81 Charlevoix is to have a sash and door factory.

    At the last election the people of Charlevoix county voted against the removal of the county seat from Charlevoix to Boyne City.

05 13 81 *The Charlevoix Sentinel* is now a little over thirteen years old, it having reached its thirteenth year last week. It is one of our most valued exchanges, and we hope time will deal well with it. It is a neatly printed well, edited paper, and deserves the very best support that the people of Charlevoix County can give it.

08 16 81 The *Boyne City Enterprise* begins another year of its existence.

10 21 81 East JORDAN — The Monroe mill dam, on the Jordan, has given away once more with a heavy loss to the proprietor of the mill.

A woman by the name of Tooly, living at South Arm, was found drowned [sic] on Sunday evening last. It is supposed that she committed suicide in temporary insanity.

11 04 81 Amos Fox has the piles down for the extension of his dock in Round Lake, which will be completed this fall. G.W. Crouter has also had piles driven for a dock in the rear of his drug store.
The bridge is now completed. Teams crossed on Saturday for the first time since one week ago Thursday. There is talk of lengthening the bridge instead of raising the approach which were the intentions when work was commenced.

11 25 81 The Monroe mill dam on the Jordan river is now entirely gone, and the mill has been taken down. Mr. Monroe is negotiating for a site at the head of the Arm upon which to place it, and make a steam mill of it. This solves the problem of fish ladders for the Jordan, as the stream is now entirely unobstructed.

12 30 81 J.B. Babcock broke through the ice and was drowned near Empey's dock, at East Jordan, Saturday. His body was recovered. He resided near Elm Rock, and leaves three orphan children.

01 20 82 Norwood is booming this winter, the new mill Co. are paying $3 a cord for shipping wood and $3 a thousand for hemlock logs and $5 for hardwood logs delivered at their mill.

03 24 82   THE HISTORY.
To the Editor of the *Charlevoix Sentinel.*
        Thanks for your kind notice in last week's paper of my efforts to collect historical notes relating to this part of Michigan. You were correct in stating that my ambition is to collect material enough for a history of this region in book form. No special reference is had to the settlement of the Beaver Islands by the Mormons, though that will come in, and will receive the attention justified by its importance. My plan embraces the collection of historical facts in relation to the whole Grand Traverse Region, from the time of its first occupation by white men up to the present time. The early settlers are gradually passing away. With them will perish a fund of valuable and interesting knowledge of early times, unless their experiences and observations be put on record for preservation. Any information bearing on the history of the country will be thankful received. I may never have the pleasure of putting it into book form, but I promise that whatever is furnished shall at least be put into a suitable form for preservation, so that it may be available to some future historian.
        Newspapers in Grand Traverse region please copy.
                                        M.L. Leach.
                                        Charlevoix, March 13, 1882.

03 24 82 W.A. Smith, editor of the *Sentinel* of Charlevoix was elected President of that village, Monday, a week.

03 24 82 *Charlevoix Sentinel:* The merchants of Harbor Springs have formed a Board of Trade, to establish a uniformity of prices. In other words they have put "up a job" on the trading public.

04 07 82 Charlevoix will retain her county seat by about 100 majority.

05 12 82 C.A. Newton has started a saloon at Charlevoix.

10 27 82 NORWOOD—George Jacques, of Norwood, has burned a kiln of 6,000 brick from clay found on the farm of Maxim Genett. They burn nearly the color of Milwaukee brick, and are of a superior quality.

11 10 82 One night last week a crowd of furnacemen at Ironton, destroyed the house of a notorious prostitute, the "Spanish Doctress" and tarred and feathered and rode on a rail both her and her companion, Frank J. Davlin.

12 01 82 *Charlevoix Sentinel:* Another ripple of excitement is created in the Advance region by a renewal of the "coal discovery" on the farm of Geo. M. Wood. Material at least closely resembling coal has been unearthed on the place several times in the past few years, but interest in the matter has died out suddenly each time. It is now asserted positively that a large vein of good coal has been uncovered about forty feet below the surface of the ground which is said to be of good quality. Steps are being taken to investigate the matter further.

Chapter 10
Dexter & Noble Enterprises

01 09 80 In passing through Messrs. Dexter & Noble's store the other day we saw "heaps" of new goods.

02 13 80 Messrs. Dexter & Noble are building a large ice house on the road leading across the river, which will be 18x32x12 feet high.

02 20 80 On Friday the Quinn brothers will leave for Elk Rapids to raise 800 tons of iron which was in the schooner Two Fannies when she went ashore last fall. The work is done under contract with the Elk Rapids Iron Company. —*Det. Free Press.*

03 05 80 Owing to the very unfavorable weather the Quinn brothers have been unable to remove much iron from the wreck. They have, however, removed all the deck load or about 100 tons. They have not examined the vessel to see how badly she is damaged. At first they only kept one pump going, but we learn from them that they have two suits of armor, and that they will keep two pumps running the next time they visit the wreck.

03 05 80 Those that put up ice this year did so at the right time. Messrs. Dexter & Noble have completed an ice house all but painting which is stored with clear and beautiful ice. All who have houses have them filled with this luxury.

03 05 80 We learn that Messrs. Dexter & Noble have contracted with parties for timbers to build a boarding scow to replace the one that burned last fall.

03 12 80 It being very changeable weather, the Quinn Brothers resolved to take a survey of the wreck Two Fannies last Sunday. They went to the wreck and after getting there the wind began to blow pretty fresh from the north so that they could not do anything but take some of the iron from her. About 12 M. the breeze freshened up so that when they returned to shore it was pretty hard work to land with 17 in the boat.

03 19 80 We learn from Mr. Quinn that the wreck Two Fannies, is in a bad condition. In making an examination Monday, he found that her keel was all "chawed off," butts all open and most of the seams on her bilge are open. On visiting the wreck yesterday, we could see that her deck is all gone and the cabin is all washed away. The divers have removed 300 tons of iron and calculate to remove about 50 tons a day.

05 07 80 Messrs. Dexter & Noble have had a force of men at work the past week clearing the land back of our village. Drains have been laid and in a few weeks the lots will be salvable and we think that where they are having the land cleared, will in a short time be the most desirable building spot in town.

The company are also clearing and laying out a village a little north and east of the furnace, this side of Mr. Jas.P. Brand's farm. The lots will be sold on the installment plan. There will be an acre in each lot. They will be sold cheap, and men working at the furnace or those in the employ of Dexter & Noble, or any one else wishing a nice little piece of land to cultivate after work is done, should speak to the company at once. Part of the land is on a bluff and the rest on the flat below, so those that live there can be called bluffers and flats. But really it would be a good thing. There are perhaps one hundred houses at the furnace and are all huddled together, not giving any one a door yard. By this plan the company propose to give those working for them a nice large lot on reasonable terms, where they can build a house and make a pleasant home.

05 21 80 Mr. E.S. Noble has sodded the bare places along the river bank on his lawn which improves its appearance very much.

06 04 80 We have received from Mr. Pat Fogarty a copy of *The Iron Port* published at Escanaba for which he will please accept our thanks. Mr. Fogarty is a wholesale dealer of flour and feed at that place and does a rushing business. He has handled for some time Messrs. Dexter & Noble's flour.

06 04 80 A span of horses belonging to Dexter & Noble began the week's business by running away early Monday morning. They ran up the Elk Lake road several miles and were making first rate time when we saw them.

06 26 80 Messrs. Dexter & Noble are paying 30 and 35 cents for wool.

08 27 80 The grist mill is running night and day.

10 08 80 Mr. E.S. Noble left for Chicago Wednesday where he has gone to purchase goods.

10 15 80 Messrs. Dexter & Noble are barreling potatoes for shipment to Chicago.

11 05 80 Wanted—Men to cut wood. Steady employment given until spring. Better wages than going to the woods. Inquire of Dexter & Noble or of Quincey Thacker.
Yuba, Mich., Nov. 1, 1880.

11 12 80 A new floor is being laid in Messrs. Dexter & Noble's store.

11 12 80 Messrs. Dexter & Noble received a "big lot" of goods on the steamer *City of Grand Rapids* Wednesday.

11 19 80 Messrs. Dexter & Noble will this winter rebuild their saw-mill for the manufacture of hardware lumber, and men are at work getting out the timbers for the proposed work. The Company will issue a circular in about two weeks giving their prices for logs.

12 31 80 Messrs. Dexter & Noble's store will be closed to-morrow afternoon.

01 06 81 After the saw-mill of Dexter & Noble is rebuilt it is expected there will

be 10,000,000 feet of lumber cut a year. The furnace makes an average of 40 tons of iron a day and the Chemical works will turn out about 15,000 pounds of acetate of lime, 180 to 200 gallons of wood alcohol, and 30 barrels of wood tar. The daily average of freight won't be small.

04 08 81 Messrs. Dexter & Noble are rebuilding the dock.

04 29 81 Mr. John Shaw is putting up 20 rods of wire fence on Messrs. Dexter & Noble's farm.

05 06 81 The barge Leland from Chicago is expected to make this port some time this week with grain and merchandise for Dexter & Noble.

05 13 81 The device invented by Mr. T.S. Noble for the more rapid and economical transfer of cord wood from the banking ground to wood scows is reported to be a complete success.

05 20 81 The old saw mill of Dexter & Noble is trying to run, and makes pretty good time; but it will as soon as convenient for its owners be pulled down and a new circular mill put in its place. The Company have bought quantities of logs this year and it is expected that some work will be done on them this season.

06 10 81 The spearing of fish is prohibited from any of the lands belonging to Messrs. Dexter & Noble and some one will be arrested for trespass some of these days.

06 10 81 W.L. Morman, of Grand Rapids, has accepted a position in Messrs. Dexter & Noble's store and arrived here Saturday, and can be found in the dry goods department.

07 22 81 New turbine water wheels for the saw mill were brought here Sunday by the *Jennie Sutton.*

07 29 81 We have heretofore spoken of the proposed rebuilding of Messrs. Dexter & Nobles' saw-mill. We are informed that operations will begin two weeks from next Monday, under the supervision of Mr. S. Canfield, a mill wright, from Grand Rapids. As soon as the mill is rebuilt new and improved machinery will be put in and then the firm will have a first class circular mill.

07 29 81 Owing to the increase of trade in Messrs. Dexter & Noble's store, Mr. Joseph Butler has been employed in the office of the firm.

08 05 81 Mr. William Macey had his right foot cut in a fearful manner at the clearing house last Thursday afternoon, by a board falling forty feet. The cut was sewed up by Mr H.H. Noble and he is doing nicely.

08 05 81 Messrs. Dexter & Noble are having the logs and slabs removed from Elk River below the chute.

08 12 81 Messrs. Dexter & Noble had five acres of Lancaster wheat that went 36 bushels to the acre. The whole crop was very fine, both Lancaster and Jenning's white.

08 12 81 The fare on the *Queen of the Lakes* will be reduced to a single fare for the round trip for teachers who wish to attend the Institute.

08 25 81 Mr. S. Canfield of Grand Rapids, the millwright who has the contract for rebuilding Messrs. Dexter & Noble's saw mill, arrived here last Thursday and commenced work Monday.

09 02 81 The new saw mill which Dexter & Noble are to build will be 44x130, with large circulars and two edgers, and it is expected that the cut will be 30,000 of maple a day. The work of tearing away has been commenced. The old siding mill will be allowed too stand. There have been rumors to the effect that a veneering mill would also be built, but nothing of the kind will be done immediately.

10 28 81 The work on the saw mill begins to show some, a bridge is being built over the race and preparations being made to put in the foundations. An engine is running night and day to keep the water out of the flume that is to be. When completed, it is said that the company will have one of the finest curricular mills in the country.

11 11 81 The frames of Messrs. Dexter & Noble's saw mill have been partially raised, and it begins to assume some proportions. The two turbine wheels have been put in and the engine which has been pumping water from the pit has been stopped. Work will now seem to count more than before, because it was anything but an easy job do clear away the old mill and get things in readiness to begin on the new.

11 25 81 Messrs. Dexter & Noble have recently put a package room in their store, where all goods to be delivered by the dray are put in and labeled.

12 09 81 A span of horses belonging to Messrs. Dexter & Noble ran away Monday. They became frightened at the steam escaping from the pile driver and ran out on the dock. When near the ware-house they collided with Wm. Morrison's team nearly killing one of his horses.

12 16 81 The Searles Bro's were engaged Tuesday fitting and putting in pipes to supply Mr. Norman Pierce's laboratory with water. The pipes were connected with the large tank in the grist mill which is supplied with water from the furnace pump. This will enable Mr. Pierce to do much more work than he has been able to do and in consequence he is as happy as it is possible for him to be.

12 16 81 The acetate of lime stored in Messrs. Dexter & Noble's river warehouse caught fire Monday, but the fire was discovered and promptly subdued.

02 03 82 It is now understood that the large tract of pine belonging to Dexter &

Noble, in Boardman and Orange comprising about fourteen million, will be made into board timber and that Messrs. Dexter & Noble will commence cutting it next summer. —*Kalkaskian,* Kalkaska.

02 17 82 We learn that Messrs. Dexter & Noble intend running their brick yard this season, and that men are engaged getting out the clay at the present time.

03 10 82 We learn that Messrs. Dexter & Noble are to purchase a brick machine to be used on their brick-yard the coming season. This company have one of the finest yards in this country for the manufacture of brick.

03 17 82 It is expected that the new saw mill of the Iron Co. will commence operation next Monday. We shall present a description of the mill in a later issue.

03 24 82 Dexter & Noble have sent by the barge Leland 6,000 bushels of wheat to Chicago. The barge left yesterday.

03 24 82 The Elk Rapids Iron Co. will pile all their hard wood lumber on the bay shore in front of Mr. H.H. Noble's residence. Men and teams have been at work the past week, drawing sand and grading the space for a lumber yard.

03 24 82 As we promised in last issue we will give our readers some idea of the fine new mill recently built at this place by the Elk Rapids Iron Co. The length of the mill is 134 feet, width 44 feet, and is built for a double circular mill.

The logs first enter the mill through the log slide, on an endless chain, with alternate hooks, a new patent of M.N. Garland, of Bay City. This method of drawing the logs into the mill allows them to be put into the slide at any time. After arriving at the log deck they are ready to be rolled on the carriage, which is done by Rogers' improved log turner. The double circular mill consists of Stearns, Clark & Co.'s improved make. After the log is cut on the carriage, it is passed along on live rolls to the gang edger, where part of the log goes to the gang edger, part to the gang slabber and part to the trimmer. The edger was made expressly for this mill is double, and made to accommodate two circulars.

The motive power comes from two large 74 inch Leffell turbine wheels, which will furnish about 150 horse power, and when the mill is run up to its fullest capacity, it will cut about 80,000 feet of hardwood lumber a day. For keeping the saws in order the Co. have purchased a new improved swedge, also a new saw gummer. The mill is painted a dark brown color, with the window casings white. All the timbers for the machinery and the railing around the stairs are painted, The Co. have not spared any expense to make this mill one of the best of its kind, it being strong and handsome.

Mr. S. Canfield, of Grand Rapids, had charge of the building of the mill.

03 24 82 Dexter & Noble will build on to the end of their dock about 100 feet; but will do nothing more than that this season, although some talk of their running a dock across to the furnace, thus forming a "T" may not be without some foundation. If this is done next season Elk Rapids will have a good harbor.

03 24 82 Dexter & Noble's grist mill will receive extensive alterations and repairs this spring. Some of the improvements needed are, two middlings run burrs, improved flour packer, rollers, more bolting capacity, more hopper bins, etc.

03 31 82 The Iron Co.'s mill is now sawing "stuff" for the Chemical Works and for a tram-way to lead from the mill to the yard.

03 31 82 While sawing at the Iron Co.'s mill yesterday one of the dogs slipped and fell on the saw. A few sparks flying around made some of the bystanders make lively steps for the outside.

04 07 82 Timbers are being taken from the river to the lumber yard for spiles for the extension of Dexter & Noble's dock. It will be extended 100 feet this summer.

05 05 82 W.J. Light returned from Chicago Tuesday where he has been purchasing the spring stock for Dexter & Noble.

05 05 82 The cut at the Iron Co.'s saw mill yesterday was 52,474 feet of hemlock. That is not so bad for one circular, and hemlock at that.

05 12 82 The Iron Co. are building a 60 feet tramway back of their saw mill with slides for lumber. This is only a temporary way of taking away lumber. It is being piled at the ship yard.

05 12 82 For nearly a quarter of a century a firm has done business in Elk Rapids, and has not during that time taken money out of the country, but has on the contrary brought thousands of dollars into this region, investing it in different industries and enterprises. It has conducted its affairs on strictly business principles, and consequently it has thrived and prospered until to-day the firm of Dexter & Noble, stand prominently as one of the richest and most enterprising firms in the country.

Besides their interest in various industries they have one of the most complete retail and wholesale stores in the North-west. Calling there one day this week we found that they were indeed dealers in everything. The new spring stock recently bought for cash, has been unpacked and shelved and one sees in every department shining new goods. This firm retails and wholesales crockery, glassware, boots, shoes, dry goods, clothing, hats and caps, groceries and provisions, and make a specialty of hardware. As they buy directly of the manufacturer for cash they can afford to sell for cash to the consumer and buyer at very close figures.

05 19 82 The Company have discovered that some of their pressed hay is becoming seriously damaged from being baled when too damp.

05 26 82 Frank Wollin now drives Dexter & Noble's delivery wagon.

06 02 82 E.R.I. Co.'s mill is running on maple and Mr. Wm. Chandler informs us that they are turning out lumber of a fine quality and that they have maple enough for sixty days sawing.

06 09 82 John Coggan was the recipient of a severe blow from a piece of slab from the gang slabber Wednesday. John Dunham is not working on account of a lame back, caused by another chunk which hit him in the back.

06 09 82 Dexter & Noble are having the railing and framework of the upper bridge painted.

06 23 82 Several changes have been made in Dexter & Noble's office this week. Horatio Lewis takes the position of cashier, and his brother William, who had the position now takes Henry Cooper's place as the Iron Co.'s book-keeper; Henry in turn takes Dexter & Noble's books and C.N. Hurlbut, who formerly had them, has a new position made for him as general office manager.

06 30 82 Dexter & Noble now have their steam brick machine in operation, and are turning out 27,000 brick a day.

07 07 82 Dexter & Noble are getting ready to burn their first kiln of brick.
Dexter & Noble are building an addition to the barracks on the farm to receive the new hay of this season.

07 28 82 Dexter & Noble's spile driver was being moved to the end of the dock, Wednesday, to drive spiles for the extension of their dock.

08 04 82 The work of repairing Dexter & Noble's grist mill will commence immediately, and the plans now made if carried out will give them the most complete mills this side of Grand Rapids, with a capacity of 125 barrels a day. J.A. Scott, a mill-wright, of Detroit will superintend the work. The improvements intended will give them a new packer and sacker, bolting capacity for 125 barrels a day, cockle machine, a Smith purifier, three sets of rolls and a forty horse power machinery wheel. The mill will only shut down during the time the new wheel is being put in, as nearly all the other work can be done while the mill is running. With the improvements mentioned, the Company can congratulate themselves upon having a complete though small mill, and one that will turn out a quality of work second to none.

08 04 82 W.J. Light, traveling agent for Dexter & Noble...

08 25 82 The new machinery wheel for Dexter & Noble's mill is now being put in.

09 01 82 800 bushels of winter wheat was threshed out on the company's farm last week, in good condition.

09 08 82 The Iron Co.'s saw mill now saws 50,000 feet of hemlock lumber a day.

09 15 82 The new castings for Dexter & Noble's grist mill show some very fine workmanship, and speaks well for R.D. Round and Joseph Parks, of the Iron Co.'s foundry and machine shop. The castings referred to are the wheels for the upright and main shafts, and are perfect in construction.

09 15 82 The improvements at Dexter & Noble's mill are more extended than when we first noticed. A new double floor is being laid in the basement, and a new bulkhead and wheelpit have already been built.

09 22 82 The Bell telephone is in use here. The furnace and chemical works are connected with the business office of both in Dexter & Noble's store.

09 22 82 The Iron Company are putting in another wheel for their saw mill. The Iron Co.'s saw mill has commenced to run nights.

09 22 82 Dexter & Noble are building a new flume for their grist mill, commencing the work on the same, Tuesday.

09 29 82 The Iron Co. have about 1,000,000 feet of logs sunk in the river above the furnace, and will raise them by means of a derrick, which has been built recently by A.K. Dougherty. The logs will be hoisted on to scows and brought down the river. The power to be used will be the spile driver engine.

09 29 82 W.J. Light left Monday for Chicago to purchase Dexter & Noble's fall stock if goods.

10 05 82 A gang of burglars forced an entrance into the store of Dexter & Noble last Wednesday night, some time between 12 o'clock and morning, they made themselves exceedingly free with dry goods, groceries, candy and cigars, but their especial attention seemed to be directed to the safe which contained the article they were in quest of, *viz.* money. Appearances did not indicate that they were professionals, but new beginners, as they picked up most of the tools used in cracking the safe in the store. Still this may have been a blind. The outer door of the large safe was blown open and all valuables taken. The books were some damaged by the explosion. Apparently the inner or burglar proof safe resisted their attacks as it remains securely locked and probably will have to be forced open before it will be known whether its contents were abstracted. The loss is not known at present but if the contents of the burglar proof safe are all right it will be comparatively small. It is supposed that the near approach of morning compelled them to skip before the work was completed as Mr. E.S. Noble remained in the store until midnight. They stole a horse, wagon and new harness from Chas. Grumble with which they made good their escape. No clue has, as yet, been obtained as to the direction the rascals took on leaving town.

10 13 82 W.J. Light returned from Chicago, Tuesday evening, where he has been purchasing the fall stock of goods for Dexter & Noble.

10 13 82 How many Greenbackers are going to vote for Dexter & Noble's candidate for Prosecuting Attorney?—*Breeze*.

The above "war cry" has had its day and become too old and stale to require notice. The editor of the *Breeze* is of course a man of too much sense to believe it, and only allows it to appear no doubt, through courtesy to the man who howls such clap-trap out of force of habit.

10 13 82 Chas. Grammel's horse, which was taken by the burglars last Wednesday night, was found Saturday last near Monroe Center and the buggy was found three miles East of Traverse City.

10 13 82 The amount taken from Dexter & Noble's safe, last Wednesday night, a week. though not known yet positively is supposed to be about $200. There were $14,000 or $15,000 in the burglar proof at the time.

10 20 82 Go and see Dexter & Noble's grist mill. Quite a sight since it has been overhauled.

11 03 82 The brick making season has closed, and Dexter & Noble's machine is being rebuilt at the Iron Co.'s foundry.

11 03 82 Dexter & Noble have a new time lock on their burglar proof safe. With this arrangement even the proprietors cannot open the door until the time set for opening has expired.

11 17 82 The extension of Dexter & Noble's dock was completed last Sunday, giving plenty of room for handling freight.

11 24 82 Dexter & Noble have been purchasing large quantities of wheat for the past few days.

11 24 82 Capt. Boner, from Beaver Island, is in port with about 700 bushels of grist work for Dexter & Noble's grist mill.

12 08 82 The Iron Co.'s saw mill has shut down for the season.

Chapter 11
Doctors

02 20 80 Mr. Editor: I have noticed an article in the *Progress* stating that the diphtheria cases were all getting along well in Elk Rapids. I am positive that there have been no cases of diphtheria in Elk Rapids this winter. There have been quite a number of cases called diphtheria which were nothing more than canker sore throats.

Yours Resp.
G.H. Bailey. M.D.

Ed. *Progress*:

The above article appeared in the *Antrim County Herald* of Feb. 12. As I know personally of at least four cases of Diphtheria namely, Andrew LaForge, Mrs, Judge Hatch, Mrs. Wilson Rushmore and myself, not one of whom G.H.Bailey ever examined, I wish to contradict his statement that he is positive that no such cases have existed in Elk Rapids this winter. As he appears to posses the remarkable faculty of forming positive opinions without evidence, I would ask if he is positive that the title of M.D. which he affixes to his name may not belong to another instead of himself...if he assumes the title of M.D. wrongfully it is base deception...G.H. Bailey can allay this doubt if he is a graduate of Victoria University by publishing such a letter as I have mentioned, for that institution delights in protecting the interests of its graduates and will freely give him one if he is entitled to it. — Edwin S. Noble.

03 12 80 Dr. Evans showed considerable skill as a marksman with a revolver Monday by putting a hole through a large black dog that had invaded his house. Wish that some one would knock over the rest of the curs in town.

04 16 80   Arthur, Ont., 29th March, '80
Neil Munroe, Elk Rapids.
Dear Sir: I received your letter, but not thinking it of vital importance I delayed answering. I may state to you how ever that Geo. Bailey lived with me about eight years, and left me to go to college to study medicine, he went to Victoria College and I supplied him with money and books two winter sessions he assisted me in my practice and made many warm friends about here not only socially but as a successful practitioner. I consider him better qualified to practice medicine than nine tenths of the medical men in Michigan.

Victoria College or as it used to be called Rolphs School of Medicine is now out of existence, old Dr.Rolph has been dead some years, but there are still enough of the Professors remaining to supply Dr. Bailey with papers sufficient to prove assertions, and if required when in Toronto I will call on some of the Professors with whom I am personally acquainted, & get the necessary certificates, still he must if he has not lost them have all the necessary papers now.

Yours truly,
Walter Henderson,
M.R.C.S. Ed.

We publish the above letter by request of Mr. Neil Munroe, who informs us that he wrote to Dr. Henderson asking him about Dr. Bailey's standing as a physician and surgeon and gave the letter to Dr. Bailey to send to Dr. Henderson. Upon comparing the Henderson letter with Dr. Bailey's writing and having also submitted it to several persons who are somewhat expert in comparing handwriting we have reasonable grounds for believing that the Henderson letter was written by Dr. Bailey himself and therefore publish it for what it is worth.

Our columns are always open to both sides in any controversy and if we are mistaken in this we be very glad to do Dr. Bailey or any body else full justice. — Ed.

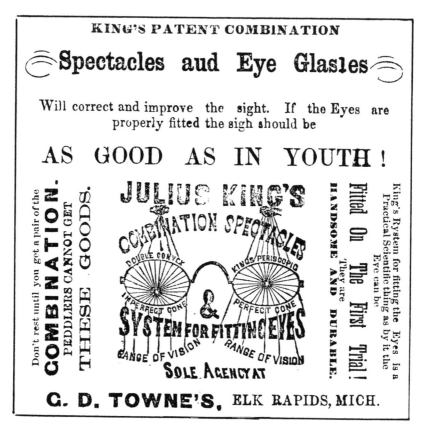

04 23 80 More about the Bailey Affair.

Mr. Editor: I notice in your last issue, a letter from Walter Henderson, M.R.C.S. Ed.

This is a high sounding title, and might impress people as coming from a source not to be questioned: but it does not answer my question. I asked G.H. Bailey "if when he swore that he was a graduate of Victoria College" he was sure that it was true?

He may have gone to "Dr. Rolph's school two winter sessions" may be better qualified to practice medicine than nine-tenths of the physicians in Michigan, (although I suspect the members of that profession might object to the statement) but did he graduate at Victoria? He swore in the Circuit Court that he did.

Dr. Henderson M.R.C.S. ED. says that Victoria is out of existence. I have a letter from the President of Victoria which says, "The name of G.H.Bailey does not appear among the list of graduates." This letter has the seal of the College upon it and I consider it good evidence that G.H.Bailey never graduated there and also that Walter Henderson, M.R.C.S. Ed. has made a misstatement when he says it is out of existence. It never was in a more flourishing condition than to-day, and is a college of such renown that nearly every quack and impostor from Canada claims it as the school from which he graduated.

In conclusion I wish to say this: If G.H.Bailey can prove that he graduated at Victoria College I will beg his pardon for having ever called his sworn statement in question, and do all I can to publish the fact to the public that I was mistaken, but I must have better evidence than a letter from this man with a high sounding title! The diploma, or duplicate (if the original be lost: Not a lecture ticket or diploma from a veterinary college but a diploma from Victoria, where he swore he graduated.

It is the man's character for truth and veracity, not his ability as a physician that is called in question. — Edwin S. Noble.

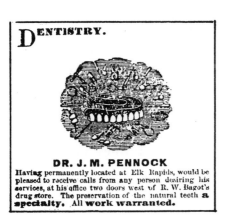

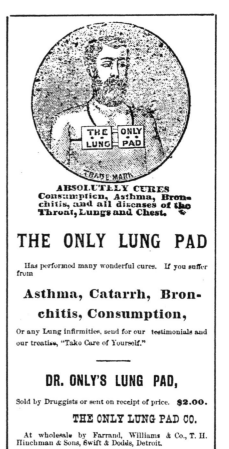
07 16 80 Dr. G.S.Kimball, of Ypsilanti, is at the Lake View House this week. He has had considerable dentistry work to do, and we hope that he can be induced to remain here. If you wish good work done call on him at the Lake View House.

08 27 80 Dr. O. Pennock, formerly of Otsego, has located at this place.

Dr. C.R. Keach formerly of Troy, Vt., has located at this place and can be found at the Hughes House, where he has his office at present. He is of the homeopathic school, and will have his full share of the practice around here we have no doubt, as there are many believers in Homeopathy.

10 29 80 A span of horses belonging to Dr. George Bailey ran away Sunday morning. The horses started when in front of his residence and went through the alley by S. Goldman's Store and ran wildly up the Elk Lake road passed Mr. L. R. Smith's farm where they were stopped. The horses were not injured but the carriage was quite badly smashed. Phy Bailey who was holding them was dragged a considerable distance, and was at last forced to let go the lines.

04 29 81 Dr. Kirby Kittoe, formerly of Hazel Green, Wis., has located at this place.

05 06 81 Dr. Kittoe, late of Hazel Green, Wis., has come to Elk Rapids with a view to permanently locate and practice his profession here. The Dr. seems to have already acquired quite an extensive practice.

06 03 81 A new Doctor in town — Dr. Kirby Kittoe, for nine years a student of St. George's Hospital, London England; and acting assistant apothecary to the same hospital, for six months; Member of the Royal College of Surgeons, and Licentiate of the Apothecary's company of the above City, since 1843, has permanently located in Elk Rapids; and offers his professional services, as Physician, Surgeon, and Accoucheour [sec], to the residents of town and country. Calls in either, will be attended to promptly, Night or Day. Office for the present over Mrs. Cox's store. Side Entrance.

06 03 81 AD — For Spectacles and Eye Glasses at J.D. Towne's. in E.R.

06 10 81 The household goods belonging to Dr. H.M. Pierce caught fire while coming from Traverse City on the *Jennie Sutton* yesterday. The fire was discovered and subdued when about four miles out. Very little damage.

08 23 81 Dr. J.M. Pennock, of this village has just returned from a trip to Eastport and Central Lake, and has had remarkably good success, making eight sets of teeth, besides filling and drawing many more. The Dr. is working up a large practice in the county.

12 23 81 Phy Bailey vaccinated 54 Indians at Deroucher's, and it worked on 53. All that could be done, has been, to alleviate the sufferings of the Indians there, and to prevent the spread of the disease.

02 10 82 Dr. Bailey was at Charlevoix twice last week, being summoned by telegraph to see Mr. David Spaulsbury, who has been dangerously ill of typhoid pneumonia.

03 24 82 Dr. Pennock has been at Old Mission for several days — pulling molars for the Peninsulars.

03 31 82 Dr. Bailey will open a drug store here some time in April. He has engaged I.C. Terry, druggist, of Muskegon, who will be here next Tuesday before going out to purchase stock. The store building owned by the Doctor will be fitted up and painted as soon as the post-office is removed to the Cooper building.

05 05 82 Dr. A.B. Conklin, formerly of Manchester, has located in town and has a card and a notice in this issue of the *Progress*.

05 12 82 Dr. J.M. Pennock is back from a trip around the county. We learn that he has done a good deal of carpenter work on the jaws of the Mancelona and Bellairettes.

05 26 82 Dr. A.B. Conklin will build an office east of Rushmore & Holbrook's store, 16x24. The work was commenced yesterday morning.

06 30 82 Sam Crampton received one day last week, circulars for Sister Agnes' Cure, together with a postal containing on order for 2 dozen bottles of the tonic. Sam, being considerable of a joker, wrote to the firm on the postal, "never mind the medicine, but send Sister Agnes along as soon as possible."

07 14 82 One of the men at the Company's new camp, on Elk Lake, while felling a tree, Tuesday forenoon, was struck upon the head by a falling limb, cutting a three cornered gash through the scalp, exposing the skull. His back was also considerably hurt, but his injuries are not serious. Dr. Conklin was called and dressed the wound.

07 14 82 Dr. A.B. Conklin moved into his pleasant new office last week, and can be found there when he is not attending to his numerous calls. The fact that the doctor has built, is evidence that he intends to remain here permanently.

Chapter 12
Emmet County

05 20 81 The Post-office of Little Traverse has been changed to Harbor Springs.

06 10 81 The contract for building the Petoskey and Gaylord State road has been awarded to C.P. Sweet of the *Kalkaskian*. He has also secured the contract for building the Boyne Falls and South Arm State road. He will commence work on both roads during the present month.

08 16 81 Petoskey is troubled with burglars and close watch has been put upon them. Thursday night the sheriff and another man came up to three of the gang in the woods and stepped forward to arrest them, when the Sheriff received a shot in the mouth the ball coming out through the cheek. The other fellow was lowered with a sling shot and the crooks retained their freedom.

12 23 81 The water works are a complete success in every particular, as has been demonstrated by the use of the hose, and exceed the most sanguine expectations. The mammoth new hotel that is now being erected in Petoskey is to be know as The Arlington, which is a good one. Work has commenced in earnest and will be pushed with all possible diligence, looking to its completion at as early a day next season as possible and consistent with the substantial character of the building to be erected as a strictly first class hotel.

01 06 82 A new post-office has been established at Carpenter, Emmet Co.

01 27 82 The newly platted addition to the village of Petoskey, owned by Wachtel, Quinlan & McCarthy and surveyed by Geo. E. Steele of this place, embraces the ancient and historic Indian camping grounds of Little Traverse bay. Where erst,[sic] (an not so very erst either), the red men gathered about their council fires and in the weird light planned savage raids upon the thinly peopled frontier settlements of Michigan, Petoskey's busy streets are now laid out. — *Herald* T.C.

03 24 82 Petoskey *Record*: J.G. Braun, saloon-keeper, is in jail at Harbor Springs for selling liquor to a habitual drinker. The wife of the man entered the complaint. Fine and costs amounted to $28.

03 31 82 *Petoskey Record*: Saturday after noon an intoxicated Indian standing in front of the bank, on Mitchell street, fired a revolver for fun. The ball struck the walk opposite, in front of Saulsbury's market. A lady had just passed the spot. Rather lawless and dangerous fun we should say.

03 31 82 *Petoskey Record*: Peter, son of Simon Petoskey, died of consumption Thursday night of last week. The last request he made was for a piece of pie plant pie.

06 23 82 The *Emmet County Independent,* which was started four years ago at Harbor Springs, then Little Traverse, now comes out in a new dress and with a new name. It is now the *Northern Independent* and is printed with a new type on a new press...

07 14 82 *Petoskey Record:* The Elfin Star Comedy Co. filled an engagement of the successive nights at Bump's Hall, closing last evening with the fine emotional drama of "Camile." This is one of the finest troupes that has ever visited Petoskey. Miss Effie Johns is without doubt one of the finest actresses traveling, and she is well supported by a first class company.

07 21 82 On Sunday the corner stone of a new Episcopal church was laid at Harbor Springs by Bishop Gillespie. R.O. Crandall, of Laporte, Ind., furnishes the lot, and Charles Scott, of New Haven, Conn., pays for the church.

08 04 82 Senator Thomas W. Ferry has secured an appropriation of $15,000 for laying a cable from Mackinac City *via* St. Ignace to Mackinac island, by an amendment to the sundry civil bill.

Chapter 13
Village of Elk Rapids

01 09 80 The Drain which was lately put through the village is a success, as quite a volume of water passes through it now although it is not yet completed.

01 23 80 William Morrison recently purchased two lots on Traverse Avenue of Lawrence Sweeny for $200.

01 23 80 A lively horse race occurred Saturday last on River Street, between the horses belonging to James Cameron and O.B.Sackett. The horse belonging to the latter gentleman came out ahead.

01 23 80 The recent fall of snow has started the business at this place. During the month of January trade had quite a set back by the warm weather, but now booms again. We learn from tradesmen that business has not been so good for years as at present.

01 30 80 We notice that a snow plow has been shoved along the street after each fall of snow.

01 30 80 Yesterday Joseph Cox bought of Alexander Kuntz the farm formerly owned by James Briggs, on Elk River near the furnace. The farm is now intended as a pasture in connection with the business of butchering. Cox and Kuntz have been trying to come together in this matter for some time and about two years ago Kuntz made a proposition to trade which was kept open for some time, and Cox entered into negations but the matter was not closed at the time, and whether Cox backed out or Kuntz withdrew we are unable to report. Now the bargain is closed and the title passed.

02 13 80 Although the Elk Rapids Band never disbanded, it has not had a meeting since last Summer until last Wednesday evening, when "the boys" met and we hope they will meet often. Something should be done to help them along. Although never hearing a word from them, it is and has been a considerable expense to each individual member. Our people should agitate the matter, because while in practice they were a great help, as a band is to every town. We propose that they receive a benefit of some kind.

03 05 80 We hope that as soon as it is convenient the horse that was drowned in Elk River will be removed. Horse flesh although it is highly spoken of as article for food, still we think that if the juices were extracted in some other way it would be preferred by the good people of this place who are in the habit of drinking the water from the river.

03 05 80 Look out for that Gossamer Rubber Ulster that perambulates our streets. It is 58 in. long, 34 in. shoulder, 38 in. bust measure. "We said we would," make a local of it, "and so we will, upon our sacred honor."

03 19 80 We publish this week the "Tourists Guide Map." Around Elk Rapids can be found the best fishing. We would say something of the hotels but we have only one open and that is "chuck full" all the time and consequently needs no advertising.

03 26 80 We understand that Sweden is about to invade the Grand Traverse Region. John Brown, the man who ran the Iron Co.'s boarding scow last summer, and who went to Sweden last fall, is about to return at the head of fifty natives.

04 09 80 Several pickerel have been shot in the swamp near the furnace.

04 16 80 Sweden invaded our town to-day.

04 23 80 The Swedish nation which invaded this region recently are a strong healthy looking lot of men.

04 30 80 If we have no railroad at this place the tide of immigration is setting in. Seventy-five Swedes, some of them with families, have settled at or near this village. A good many of them have obtained employment with Dexter & Noble and some with the Iron Co. Messrs. Dexter & Noble have a number clearing a fifty acre lot near the village. With her natural advantages Elk Rapids will soon become a very prominent place in Northern Michigan.

05 07 80 We notice in the street before a few places of business in our town a pile of boards or something else which gives our town away. Probably this year we will see a larger crowd of tourists than ever before, and we ought to in favor of our village take a little pains in making things look a little better.

05 07 80 The post-office is soon to be removed into the elegant new building recently occupied by G.H. Bailey. Mr. Dyer, the P.M. is having the room prepared, the carpenter work having been done.

05 07 80 Burglars entered the office of the *Elk Rapids Progress*, last week, and didn't get a dollar! It must be that Bro. Davis had just paid his wash bill. — *Tribune*, Manton.

We had not paid our wash bill, but we had drawn an order on a delinquent subscriber for the amount, and they took that.

05 14 80 Mr. Rushmore is having his house painted, and has had the pile of sand removed from his front gate. Now if one or two shops in town would remove the pile of boards from in front of their shops it would be a good thing.

05 14 80 We see that the pound has been completed and if you miss any of your swine you had better look them up.

People having swine should be careful how they let them run or they may find them in the pound some fine morning.

05 21 80 The bad holes in the sidewalk between the post-office, and Dexter & Noble's store have been fixed.

05 21 80 Workmen are grading the cross street west of the Lake View House. After the grading is done, a covering of slag from the furnace will be put on.

05 28 80 A great deal of work has been done on the streets in our town this spring. Besides the "filling in" that has been done, Adam Schuler, Esq., has raked all the rubbish off of them.

07 09 80 A neat new fence has been put in front of the vacant lot opposite the Lake View House in place of a high board fence.

07 16 80 The population of Elk Rapids is 741.

07 23 80 If there were two or three sail boats here that could be rented it would be a very good thing.

09 10 80 Our Jewish residents observed their New Year, which was last Monday. Their stores were closed that day. We wish them a happy New Year !

09 17 80 The new house which Messrs. West & Wait of Traverse City, are building for Mr. L.R. Smith, is beginning to loom up. It will cost when completed about $1,900.

10 15 80 We see from a distance that some one is building a frame house at Muckle-town.

10 15 80 Owing to the fact that the telegraph lines are down no election news has been received to-day.

11 19 80 Pond-ice Wednesday morning was plump 3 inches thick. It froze 1¾ inches in two days.

11 19 80 We learn that a good many changes and improvements are contemplated here another year, and Elk Rapids, although never back ward, will be apt to go along with such a jog as to make all our heads spin. With the large saw mill running another season, together with our other industries, everything looks bright indeed, for our village.

12 10 80 Elk Rapids is now blessed with a street sprinkler-not to lay the dust exactly, but to sprinkle the street. During the winter the gentle zephers play among the trees some times, and blows the beautiful snow from off the highway so that the slippin' is pretty poor, and the sprinkler acts as a irrigator as it were, making the slippin' good. Wish they would run the thing once or twice in the summer to irrigate the sand.

12 24 80 A Meteor of unusual size passed over Elk Rapids on Tuesday evening at ten o'clock. The moon at its full would scarcely have equaled its brilliancy. Its course was South East to North West.

01 06 81 S. Goldman recently purchased the house and lot on River Street formerly owned by Wm. B. Chandler for $1,000.

102

01 06 81 The activity in the real estate business is due to the extensive manufacturing interests which will begin operation in the Spring. Everybody looks more hopeful, and well they may. A railroad will probably be the next move and then—!

01 06 81 The fine sleighing we are having makes the cord-wood business remarkably brisk. Thirteen teams with big loads of wood went along the street Wednesday following each other. Quite a procession.

01 21 81 The Bay froze over Sunday night last, the mercury at seven o'clock Monday morning indicated 12° below zero.
     Several persons were skating on the Bay Tuesday. Elk Rapids now has a big skating rink.

02 26 81 The ice on Elk Lake and the Bay appears to be perfectly safe for teams. Parties are drawing hay from Old Mission to this place, and teams cross Elk Lake with heavy loads of wood.

02 26 81 Elk Rapids must look out or it will be the wicked "city" of Grand Traverse Region. We surely have more nasty suits than any other town or newspapers of our exchange do not publish them.

03 04 81 THE OLD SETTLERS—The following invitation will be sent to every "old settler" in the Region this week, and it is expected that an immediate reply will be given so that the committee will know how many will be present:
     Yourself and family are respectfully invited to attend a General gathering

of the old settlers that have been in the Grand Traverse Region twenty years or more, to be held at Elk Rapids, on the 15th day of March, at 1 o'clock P.M. Oyster Supper and a good time is expected.

03 04 81 "The worst storm we ever had" is what old settlers say in regard to the storm of Sunday, Monday and Tuesday. Sunday it commenced to snow and Monday we had a fearful blow. The snow in front of the Lake View House, and from the Post Office to Chas. Newton's Saloon was from 10 to 15 feet high Tuesday morning, and men were at work most of that forenoon shoveling out snow so that the roads were passable. The stage from Traverse City did not come Monday, on account of the storm but arrived here Tuesday at 4:30 P.M. The North stage always on time- arrived here on Monday. In every direction roads were impassable, by the great drifts.

04 22 81 We hope that all of our citizens and those citizens of surrounding towns will celebrate the new holiday — Arbor Day.

04 22 81 $15.00 has been subscribed for a band stand in front of the Lake View House.

05 06 81 Mr. A. Dunning who recently purchased the house on River St. formerly owned by S.B. Spencer is grading and improving the looks of the lot.

04 22 81 Spring has come.
       Roads are bad.
       Side walks are clear.
       The band wants a new tenor horn.
       Be sure and plant your tree Arbor Day.
       It will soon be time to go trout fishing.

05 06 81 The ice has disappeared in the Bay and inland lakes and navigation was fairly open in this section last Monday morning. There will be a change in the way of doing business, that's all. Business is always lively in Elk Rapids, Winter or Summer.

05 06 81 Houses in our town are a scarce article. For the past two weeks we have had person after person inquiring for houses to rent. Some one should build fifteen or twenty to supply the market.

05 13 81 Elk Rapids has now three saloons, and the ladies complain they cannot walk out in the evening without being insulted. —*Sentinel.*
   The above is a nice item to be found in the State papers, in regard to our village. We have not heard of any ladies being insulted, but we certainly have enough saloons, and we hope that if we are to have such places licensed, the authorities will see that the laws are enforced.

05 20 81 Several parties have been burying the carcasses of horses in the vacant lots west of R.W. Bagot's residence. They should have been taken farther out from town and buried deeper.

05 20 81 The road beyond the Court House which has always been so sandy is having a layer of cinders from the furnace placed upon it.

05 20 81 Village lots are going off like hot cakes. A boom, as it were, has struck town.

05 27 81 Dr. H.M. Pierce has purchased the lot below R.W. Bagot's residence, and has commenced building a dwelling with main part 22x32 two stories.

05 27 81 We forgot to mention last week the concert given by the band on Monday evening. Some pieces they played nicely.

06 03 81 Considerable rowdyism is displayed on our streets evenings by a few young men which should be stopped. We hope that it will be as we should dislike to hear that they had been placed in the "cooler."

06 03 81 Adam Schuler, Esq., is engaged this spring raking the streets.

06 03 81 Tourists began coming to Elk Rapids before our hotels were quite ready to receive them. Pretty good for E. R.

06 03 81 James Beer is building a house on Water St. The house will be 18x24 two stories, the foundation of which is already laid. Mr. Beer is from York State, and has only been in town a few weeks.

06 03 81 F.O. Aslett recently purchased a lot on Water St. and intends building a house on it with the main part 16x26. Work was begun on it Monday.

06 10 81 The boxes at the Post-office have all been taken and Mr. Geo. A. Dyer, the P.M. will shortly add two hundred and fifty more boxes. This is an indication that E.R. is growing.

06 10 81 Dr. H.M. Pierce of the Chemical Co. returned from Grand Rapids Thursday with his family. They will occupy the cottage which the Dr. has recently built on the bay shore at the West end of River St.

06 10 81 We clip the following from a long communication to Forest and Stream:
        Take the spring wagon which meets the boats, and you will be whirled along the long dock, piled with iron ore high on either side, down onto a short stretch of level road, around a mill over a stream nearly above a fish chute, and in about five minutes brought up whirling at the Lake View House, a clean homelike little inn, where you will be treated well by a very gentlemanly land lord.
    I have made this sketch a flying one. You can well lengthen it to good advantage by making a longer stay at Traverse City, Elk Rapids or Lewis House.

There is more sport and more to interest one at Elk Rapids, however, than at the other mentioned points.

Excellent fishing may be had at any place you may choose to stop. At Traverse City, deep water fishing, and near the town trout, bass, etc. At Elk Rapids shoulder your rod at the hotel, and you can be back again with quite a respectable string, and undoubtedly the same at the head of Torch Lake. At Elk Rapids I know you can, for I have tried it.

Go, take this trip, see and be convinced.

06 17 81 Some party stole "Jo Minnie's" skiff last Saturday night.

06 17 81 Elk Rapids has been designated a signal station.

06 24 81 Elk Rapids is in great favor with Kentucky people as a summer resort.

06 24 81 We mentioned last week this place was a storm signal station. We learn that Post-master Geo. A. Dyer, has appointed Mr. Orin J. Holbrook as observer.

07 01 81 Traverse Avenue is being graded.

Cedar Street is being graded and cinders from the furnace put on. Our village will have fine roads.

Kenneth Campbell has purchased the house and lot on Traverse Avenue formerly owned by Willis J. Mills for $310.

07 01 81 The Elk Rapids Band go to Spencer Creek the Glorious Fourth.

07 08 81 The east end of River Street is being graded.

The old open sewer running parallel with the Elk Lake road is reeking with filth and the germs of disease, and it should be cleaned out or filled up altogether, as it is no good for drainage purposes. Official duties are not always pleasant or profitable; but gentlemen of the Board of Health, you are the only source of relief in these emergencies and to you we appeal.

07 15 81 The thermometer marked 100° in the shade last Friday. In the sun it marked 115°.

08 12 81 A Fisherman's Paradise- Petoskey may be just the place for a camp meeting, and Newport and Atlantic City all right for surf bathing, but Elk Rapids is the paradise of fishermen... (full column)

–Correspondence of the *Richmond,*(Ind.) *Telegram.*

08 19 81 McAllen, the Chimney sweep, discoursed some sweet music to the inhabitants of this village this week.

10 21 81 With the great manufacturing interests centered here, the future prospects of this village are bright. With the lumber, iron and Chemical business the amount of money that will be paid out for wood, logs and labor will reach many thousands of dollars. There is no chance for one to be idle here, for there is always plenty of work for those who choose to labor.

10 21 81 We take the following from a letter written to the *Alliance*, published in Chicago:

For three summers past the writer has ended his vacation, and the annual cruise of the canoe *Nepenthe*, by a brief stay at the Lake View House at Elk Rapids... having fought mosquitoes, no-see-ems," and fleas throughout the tedious hours of more than one sultry night (tents and bars to the contrary notwithstanding), having wielded the paddle manfully for consecutive hours against wind and tide, and found the well-earned rest only on the "soft side of a plank"...

-H.W.J. Chicago, Sept. 20, 1881.

10 28 81 As there is always danger of fire in a village, there should always be proper means at hand to subdue it, and we make the following suggestion in regard to it. If the people on river street will lay a pipe connecting with the Chemical Co.'s main pipe that runs through the river and will tax themselves enough to pay for hose we have a sure protection from fire. The company will not agree to furnish water for the town, but for fire if one should break out. Let us hear from you.

11 04 81 We again call the attention of the village to the means almost given them for protection against fire. The Chemical Co. are willing to furnish power if the people of the town will lay the pipes and furnish hose. Will you take hold of the matter now or will the whole town have to be burned before you wake up.

11 04 81 Shoot your dogs! Some of the boys moved all the signs about town Tuesday night.

11 04 81 The large drain which runs through the village to the River should be fixed so that it would carry off more water from the swamp east of the village. It only takes off about half the water that it should.

11 18 81 Ben. Davis of the *Elk Rapids Progress,* pays $1.50 per cord for wood. We burn wood that costs $5.00 and get trusted when we can.
- *Ypsilantian*, Ypsilanti.

12 09 81 During the severe storm Tuesday night the break-water in front of R.W. Bagot's house was torn away and the waves washed about 30 feet of the shore away destroying a part of the little grove in front of Mr. Bagot's residence.

12 09 81 The *Elk Rapids Progress* seems to have the right name. It has buoyant hopes of the future prosperity of its town, and speaks of it in glowing terms. — *Advance*, Bangor.

You are right we have hopes of the future prosperity of our town. There is nothing to hinder it from being the strongest and largest in this section of the country. Its slow growth is in a measure due to its citizens, but there will a time come when nothing can keep it from becoming what it should be today, the metropolis of Grand Traverse Region. The *Progress* in a small way tries to advertise Elk Rapids and Antrim county. And as it grows older and stronger it will do the town and county more service, and the only recompense we ask is a just appreciation of it. We like the town, people and county; expect to grow with them, and if the *Progress* is rightly named we are very glad of it.

12 16 81 The U.S. Signal station will be discontinued at this point for the season, after the 15th inst.

12 23 81 If we have no snow this winter, we are of the opinion that times will be harder than was looked for. A few weeks of good sleighing would put a different look on all kinds of business. Give us snow, Oh ! give us the beautiful snow.

12 23 81 A sewer is being built from the Hughes House to the pond.
　　　　The back streets of our village are being quite rapidly built up. C.A. Newton put up his large livery barn and was followed by Manwarring & Kramer who built their fine new wagon shop. Several residences have been built, and we predict that this street, Traverse Avenue will, before long become the principle street in our village.

01 06 82 Rents are high and houses are scarce.

01 20 82 The street sprinkler is on the move again. Elk Rapids is more highly favored in winter than in the summer, as our roads are sprinkled in winter to make sleighing better.

02 10 82 One reason why we think that Elk Rapids is on the gain is the fact that lots for business purposes are held at from $600 to $1,000 and are on the gain.

02 10 82 Mr. Benj. Dunning is having stone drawn for a new foundation to be built under his house on River St. It is also his intention to raise the house one story and make other improvements.

02 17 82 The dancing bear arrived in our village Tuesday evening, with his two keepers and quite a little excitement was observed on our streets.

02 24 82 In reply to the many rumors of the waste products from the Chemical Works, affecting the river's purity, we would say that we have interviewed the Company's chemist with the following result: He states recent analysis made by him, of the water, fail to show anything possibly attributable to the Works. Tests fail to reveal even one part in a million of delteerious[sic] substances.

02 24 82 Some of the young men in the village talk of getting up an entertainment, the proceeds to go towards building side-walks about town. It is proposed to give an entire change of program each night and give an entertainment one night out of a week. The charge for tickets will only be one penny, with the privilege of paying more if persons wish. As soon as arrangements are made, bills will be circulated.

02 24 82 We have heard frequent complaints in regard to the refuse from the Chemical Works affecting the water of Elk River so much as to render it unfit for household purposes.

02 24 82 The ups and downs of life are never so faithfully portrayed as when our solid citizens attempt to reach their homes *via* the side-walks of Elk Rapids.

03 03 82 NOTES BY THE WAY — by the Rambler.

During my rambles I stumble not only on our sidewalks, but upon a few things that will doubtless interest us all — I noticed that a boat house was being built which will be a great convenience to our towns people and the tourists. I would suggest the addition of a pair of shells, and the formation of a boat club. We have young men who have fine physiques and a friendly rivalry in this direction will meet with encouragement. The boxing club have already succeeded in demolishing one set of gloves, and several sets of noses, also a few eyes are in deep mourning as a consequence to numerous friendly encounters.

I notice a few people regard the alley ways as public property, and set their buildings in the midst thereof. I notice boys of tender years playing pool; wonder if their parents know it. I notice that Doctor Pierce wears a happy, smiling face, and well he may, having achieved a success in manufacturing charcoal that time cannot efface. May he live long to wear the honors that have been so thickly strewn about his pathway during the past year.

I notice that we are to have a donation party next week, and hope the entire proceeds won't be eaten up -in cake- leave a generous contribution and a big basket full for the Domina, for they can't live on souls, though some appear to think so.

03 03 82 I notice the whistles of the Chemical Works and furnace vary as to their daily blows, which is doubtless owing to the difference in time between Bangor and Elk Rapids.

03 10 82 The drain which was stopped up, thereby flooding the back part of the town, has been opened, and no danger from a flood can now be feared.

03 17 82 W.H. Smith has purchased of L.R. Smith his house and lot on Traverse Avenue.

03 24 82 TELEGRAPHIC.

A Project that Should Receive the Support of
Elk Rapids and of every Town Along the Line.

Some time ago O.J. Holbrook, manager of W.U. telegraph at this place, conceived the idea of uniting this place with Williamsburg, Spencer Creek, Bellaire and Central Lake, by telegraph. He at once commenced negotiations with prominent men all along the proposed route, and from every one has received their earnest co-operation, the line will connect at Elk Rapids, with the Western Union Telegraph line, and will give the above named places direct communication with the outside world. At present it is safe to say that it will be pushed to completion at the earliest date. We shall speak of this further in a later issue.

04 07 82 When Elk Rapids needs a railroad real bad there is enough capital here to build it to Kalkaska. Traverse City probably spends three times the above amount, and had better save it up for that furnace, long talked of.

04 07 82 Elk Rapids has patronized saloons to the extent of $20,000 during the past twelve months. She might better have saved it up towards a railroad. — *Herald,* Traverse City.

04 07 82 The *Traverse Herald* should commence its temperance work, at home, as that town has twice as many saloons, and twice as much drunkenness as has Elk Rapids, to say nothing of the other evils

04 07 82 Monday afternoon a cow belonging to J. Ward Davis meandered into Mrs. Mary Morrison's wood shed, and broke through the floor into the cistern beneath. By a little effort the cow was taken out with very little injury. The cistern is never used and the only damage done was the braking of the floor which has been repaired.

04 07 82 Elk Rapids is quite a town. A fire, an election and a cow in a well, all in one day. We should have the Ovid railroad.

04 14 82 Elk Rapids has the finest water power in the State; ships more manufactured product than any town North of Grand Rapids; is in the center of the best sporting country of this region; has three good churches, a $12,500 school house; will soon have a $3,000 town hall; has the largest works in the world for manufacturing calcium acetate and wood alcohol; has a charcoal furnace which has the finest record of any in the world; has one of the finest saw mills in Northern Michigan. The town is backed by as good a farming country as can be found in Michigan, and has water communication with some of largest towns in the county. The water power gets its head from ninety miles of lakes and rivers, and fifty miles of rivers and lakes are navigable. To those who wish to settle in a growing town, come on; and to those who wish to farm, buy a farm on any of the "Nineteen lakes."

05 05 82 Chauncy Hollenbeck, of Creswell, brought us a clover root one day this week which was four feet and a half long. Now if there are any of our exchanges, particularly the *Detroit News,* who do not believe this root story we will pass the root around, if they will pay express charges. We do not propose to pay out any money to prove that we cannot tell a lie.

05 05 82 For one or two years one of our business men has hired a man to rake River Street. We do not know whether he will do it this summer or not, but if he does not, persons should have the street raked in front of their yards or stores and all rubbish removed.

05 05 82 We have wonderful and it is indeed glorious news which we will impart to our readers. A new sidewalk will be built the whole length of River Street, and the good part of the old walk will be put down on Traverse Avenue. The work commenced this morning.

05 05 82 There is plenty of room in this village for any one who wishes to commence business, and we believe there will be plenty of trade too.

05 05 82 The side-walks in our village long have had our earnest support in their behalf. We have sighed over them; walked over them; fell over them; written and talked about them, but to no purpose. Why is this thusly? They have done their duty well and faithfully, and now that they are getting old and feeble, why are they not replaced with younger and stronger ones. Lay the poor old boards quietly away that they may rest.

05 12 82 A festive drummer comes to our town frequently.

05 12 82 The side-walks are now being built at a great rate and we are glad that the work on them was begun so soon.

05 12 82 Elk Rapids is enjoying a permanent, steady growth, and is one of the best towns in the North to locate in. Almost any business could be successfully carried on.

We are glad to notice so much building in different a parts of the town, and believe more would be done if the lots in the southern part of the village were in a marketable shape.

05 12 82 A number of buildings are in the alley back of River street. These should all be removed so that teams could go through.

05 12 82 About a year ago the firm of Dexter & Noble cleared a small tract of land belonging to them, on the east side of Elk River, platted the same, and offered the lots for sale. Quite a number of lots were taken, and houses erected. The *Progress* man took a walk to East Elk Rapids yesterday and found it a really pleasant spot. The land is high and dry, and this part of our village is being rapidly built. About seventeen nice new houses have been erected, lots fenced in, and trees set out and other improvements such as grading lots etc. If one thinks the town has not improved walk to East Elk Rapids.

05 19 82 Elk Rapids has increased its population by 500 inhabitants the last two years. That is a pretty good per cent.

05 19 82 A good many shade trees have been set out about town.

05 19 82 The *Breeze* says that Bellaire has escaped that feverish mushroom growth. We can bear witness that Elk Rapids has too. This town is 35 years old and all it has grown has been by force of circumstances, as no one has ever tried to push it. It is growing out of itself now though.

05 19 82 A side-walk has been built from River street to the chute.

05 19 82 W. Sterling has contracts for building houses for Mrs. Spaulsbury, Chas. Rex and A. Morrison.

05 26 82 The President of the Board of Health, will be inspecting your alleys and back yards these days. Don't wait for an order to clean them up, and remove everything that will endanger the health of your family and neighbors.

06 09 82 The heavy sea of Saturday and Sunday, washed away the breakwater in front of R.W. Bagot and Dr. Pierce's residences. The damage done to the shore was considerable, as several handsome trees were washed away.

06 16 82 New cross walk on River street near Bridge.

06 16 82 Dexter & Noble are putting slag from the furnace on the road leading from the upper bridge to River street.

06 23 82 It seems as though every one in town used the public streets for their buildings. A few days ago C.A. Newton commenced building his barn and had all the timbers right in the middle of the street. The Commissioner of Highways should speak to Mr. Newton and compel him to remove all the rubbish from the front of his buildings. The streets are not made for hay scales or buildings and every one living on River street have some sort of a shed in the alley or on the street. Newton has timbers; Mrs. Cox has scales; The Lake View House has a laundry and Benj. Dunning has his house and barn right in the alley.

06 30 82 Traverse Avenue is having considerable work done on it this spring. Every lot on this street has been sold this spring by Dexter & Noble to different parties in town.

06 30 82 Dexter & Noble have put lamps on both bridges, at the chute and at the saw mill. This example should be followed, along River street.

07 07 82 After paying all expenses for the Fourth there were $10.00 left. The committee propose buying a flag to be used on public occasions.

07 07 82 Several new one story houses have been built at the furnace.

07 28 82 A call is made in another column for the people of Elk Rapids to make some movement to provide water to supply the town for household purposes and in case of fire. The water in Elk River is not so pure as it might be. The call cannot be found, as there is no place to hold a meeting, but that is no reason why people should keep right on drinking wood alcohol. Talk up the subject of water works for fire and household purposes.

08 04 82 However efficient may be our laws of health, or however well we may understand the necessity of conforming therewith to secure to ourselves the largest portion of health, yet through negligence and indifference there are no laws of which the masses live in such open violation as the laws for the regulation of our sanitary conditions... It is true that the many unhealthy surroundings that are insidiously generating sickness and death among us, are allowed to exist and remain unabated until they have sown the deadly seeds that must bring a certain harvest for the reaper, Death... It is a duty that belongs alike to the health officer and every law abiding citizen... There are two cases of typhoid fever in our midst at present that have been living for weeks with in the pernicious presence of decomposing animal and vegetable matter, and subjected nature to a stench that would stifle a buzzard... Suffice to say it should be your

care to see that no animal or vegetable matter be allowed to remain upon your premises to decompose and make impure the air you breath, or settling into the earth drain into your wells and contaminate your drinking water...the two most fruitful sources of zymotic diseases with which we have to contend...
    -Dr. A.B. Conklin.

08 04 82 Many pretty building spots can be found west of the Methodist Church. Some of them on rising ground command a fine view of the bay. We suppose it will not be long before this property will command fancy prices.

08 11 82 Since our notice some weeks ago, a movement has been started to raise money to put in water works for supplying the town with water. Something like $1,500 stock has already been taken and it will be an easy matter to raise the amount to $4,000 or $4,500, the amount estimated to lay a main through the principle street and put in the works. Some have spoken of taking the water from the bay, and others from Elk Lake. When a meeting is called, of course each one will have the privilege of offering suggestions. Mr. Parks has a plan and informs us that the amount above mentioned will cover the cost. From what we can learn the power to be used will be a turbine wheel, placed below the chute, to drive two large pumps which will be placed there, one for feed and the other for forcing the water through the mains. The matter is yet in a crude form, but Elk Rapids is going to have water works, and as soon as the matter takes a tangible form we will at once place it before our readers.

08 18 82 A side-walk is being built from F.R. Williams' towards the chute.
    C.A. Newton bought of S. Goldman, the lot on River street, known as the Chandler lot for $1,500, and will commence the building of a 63x100, two story building on it week after next. Not decided yet whether he will build a brick or frame.

08 18 82 At last a movement has been made towards supplying the town with water, the notice in another column calling for citizens to a meeting should bring out every property owner. The movement started has received the support of our strongest men, financially, who have not yet taken stock, but who will probably subscribe last, making up the deficiency.

08 18 82 Chas. T. Hickox, Esq., has bought the two Parkinson lots on River street fronting the bay, and has plans of a very handsome cottage. The lots owned by him are located near the south end of River street, near the corner of Elm.

08 18 82   WATER ! WATER ! WATER !
A meeting of the citizens of Elk Rapids will be held in Lake View Hall on Monday evening next, 21st instant, for the purpose of organizing a company to supply the town with water. — A. K. Dougherty.

08 25 82 What good is there in having a health officer unless the business of the office is attended to. We have heard complaints from almost every quarter in regard to the sanitary condition of the village. The Board of Health has been spoken to but know good comes from it. There is a penalty attached if the health officer does not attend to his duties, and we would advise our friends to complain to the Prosecuting Attorney, instead of coming to us.

08 25 82 A couple of tramps are hanging about town, near the old grave yard.

09 01 82 We did not mention last week the result of the notice the week before for the citizens to meet at Lake View Hall for the purpose of talking up the water works question. Various plans were talked of and a committee was appointed to investigate the cost of wood and iron mains and other matters relating to the subject.

09 01 82 The slaughter house south of town causes considerable annoyance to residents on the southern part of the village, particularly when we have a south-west wind. The health officer will look after this.

09 01 82 Several of the village cows broke into the crops of Fred Burberry's farm last week, and the Supervisor was called upon to appraise the damages.

09 01 82 The health officer of the township said to us on Saturday last, that when ever a complaint had been made to him, he had notified parties to remove or lessen the offense against the general health of the township, and that hereafter he should serve a written notice on persons and if the terms of the notice were not complied with in twenty-four hours, he should take measures to prosecute, we are very glad if we have been misinformed in regard to the sanitary condition of the village, but at the time of publishing last week's paper, we knew of several places in town where perfumery of a very questionable smell arose.

09 15 82 Work on the town hall and the Episcopal church commenced Monday morning.

10 20 82 Dry block wood brings $2.00 a cord in Elk Rapids.

10 20 82 The Elk Rapids W.U. Telegraph office has been in connection with the Williamsburg office this week. About election time we can probably hear from the whole county the same night. Whoop la! If for nothing else this line is a benefit in November.

10 20 82 The following persons have built residences in this village this season, either for rental or to live in: O.J. Powers, P.S. Brinkerhoff, Mark King, A. Pollock, H. Andrews, D. Wood, Joseph Drake, Mrs. Spaulsbury 2, Wilson Rushmore, A. Morrrison, Fred Nackerman, Chas. Durkee, N.R. Morman, Wm. Brush, J.R. Speidel, J.J. McLaughlin, Sam Price, Wm. Morrison, Chas. Marriot, Chas. Rex, Mrs. Winnie and 2 Swede houses.

10 20 82 What do the people say about incorporating Elk Rapids?

10 20 82 The swamp back of the village is causing considerable sickness this year. Several hundred dollars worth of draining would help matters. Who is going to do it?

11 03 82 Since Dexter & Noble's safe was burglarized, a month ago, detectives have been at work to bring the guilty parties to justice and on Wednesday A. McManus, of Traverse City and Wm. Wiley were arrested at the above place, on suspicion and brought here. The same day they were taken to Bellaire and lodged in the County jail.

11 03 82 A Pinkerton detective has been in town the past two or three weeks and has unearthed considerable deviltry.

11 24 82 *Commercial Advertiser*: Elk Rapids has a "Poker Club" according to the *Progress*, sinfulness there, but that is not so. The members only gather about the stove in the grocery and tell wonderful yarns while they rustle the embers with the poker.
     'Bout time for a "Jack-pot."

12 01 82 Joseph Drake is veneering his new house with brick. This is a new method of using brick in this section. Houses built in this way are as warm and comfortable as solid brick walls without the danger of dampness.

12 01 82 *Evening News*: Elk Rapids has no lock-up, and when a wild whooper-up from the forest vastnesses comes into town to soak up his hide with bug juice, he does it and "runs the village" to suit himself.
This is perhaps laying it on pretty thick, but we should have a lock up and an officer who had nerve enough to jug the wild whooper from the forest glade.

12 01 82 The stage from Traverse City came in on runners Monday. The prospect is good for an old fashioned Grand Traverse winter- good sleighing; no slush.

12 08 82 We wish the town board would contract with some one to have snow put on to the bare spots on the side-walks, so to even them up, as it were. Shoveling snow from the sidewalk is a rare occurrence in Elk Rapids.

12 15 82 Thursday afternoon, 2 o'clock. The Nor'wester that opened its batteries upon us yesterday, continues with unabated fury. Wind dead ahead, and blowing a gale, with snow until you can't rest. Locals non comeatibus [sic]. Our local Editor, muffed to the chin, sallied out with blood in his eye, in search of one local item to grace this space. Item: Blamed cold, locals snowed under.

12 15 82 Another Nor'wester Wednesday, a two forty wind with lots of the beautiful. Let it come, it is enough sight better than mud or bare ground.

12 29 82 J. Ward Davis has 134 village lots for sale in Elk Rapids. Some will be sold for $20.00 each and some for from $300 to $1,000.

Chapter 14
Elk Rapids Township

04 09 80 At the township election last Monday the following persons were elected for township offices:

Supervisor	Henry H. Noble.
Clerk	A. K. Dougherty.
Treasurer	Wm. B. Chandler.
Highway Comm	John Denahy.
School Inspector	J.C.P Church.
Township Superintendent of Schools	C. M. Ranger.
Justice of the Peace	J. Ward Davis.
Constables	John Acker, O. Powers, John Spencer, J.P. Davidson.

09 09 81 The bridges between the village and Indian Town need repairing badly. Two of them which cross Elk River are regular old traps

11 04 81 The cranberry marsh at Tobago Lake ought to be made to pay. Some good man should invest. Cranberries can be found there now in quantities.

03 03 82 Elk Rapids has no town hall, and is it not about time we had one?

03 24 82 A notice has been posted about town signed by twelve or more freeholders of this township, notifying voters that at the next town meeting day the question of whether Elk Rapids would have a $3,000 town hall or not. Of course this is only according to law and we are fully confident that not a dissenting vote will be cast.

04 07 82 The following ticket was elected:

Supervisor	James McLaughlin.
Clerk	Archibald K. Dougherty.
Treasurer	Andrew LaForge.
Highway Commissioner	John Denahy.
Township Sup't. of Schools	George A. Dyer.
School Inspector	Fitch R. Williams.
Drain Commissioner	Henry H. Noble.
Justice of the Peace	Oscar L. Craw.
Constables	Oliver Powers, Charles A. Newton, John E. French, John Acker.

04 07 82 Elk Rapids will have her $3,000 town hall. At the township election Monday, 118 votes were cast for the motion, and 4 votes against.

05 12 82 A committee has been appointed to locate and commence building the town hall. We will not publish names until acceptance has been filed.

05 19 82 The town has purchased the lot on the corner of River and Pine streets, of Casper Schuler, for a site for the town hall, for $400. It is a fine location for the hall.

05 19 82 The committee appointed by the town board to build the town hall is, E.S. Noble, S. Goldman and Wilson Rushmore. These gentlemen will undoubtedly see that the money is well spent and that Elk Rapids will have a first class building.

05 19 82 The town is bonded for the sum of $2,500 to raise money to build the town hall. Casper Schuler takes $2,000 and J.J. Winkler $500 at 7 per cent.

05 19 82 Supervisor McLaughlin, who has just taken the census of Elk Rapids township informs us that there are 1,120 inhabitants in the township, and a little over 900 in the town, which is an increase of 300 inhabitants the past year. During the year 1881 there has been only 8 deaths; and 26 births in the township.

06 02 82 We hope the committee appointed to build the town hall will rush the work as fast as possible, so that it could be used, at least once or twice in the fall.

07 21 82 The plan of the town hall building has been approved by the town board, we understand, and the building committee will commence operations immediately. The building, the elevation of which was submitted to the inspection of the board will be a fine one and will show to advantage when erected on the corner of River and Pine streets.

The specifications are as follows; 40 feet wide and 100 feet long. The entrance hall will be 15 feet wide and 20 feet long, and on each side will be two rooms (for cloak room and ticket office) which will be 11x20, except the room on the left, which will lose a part of its length to allow the passage of a six-foot stairway to the gallery. The gallery will be 20x40 allowing a few feet for the stairway. The main room will be 40x60 leaving a stage 20x40. In front of the stage will be a six foot platform to be used for lectures, public meetings etc., and on such occasions the stage can be used for seating.

The basement will extend the whole length of the building, and will be 7½ feet high, allowing plenty of room for furnaces, wood room, also two rooms directly below the stage 19x20, which could be used by troupes, and shows of various kinds if there should not be room enough in the dressing rooms on the side of the stage. The seating capacity is estimated at from 600 to 700 people. The building will be 20 feet high without the mansard roof, which will add 15 feet to its height. The front door and windows will be high enough with handsome transoms to light the gallery.

The building will be brick, and will give Elk Rapids one of the finest audience rooms in Northern Michigan, and an ornament to the town of which we may all be proud. The work on it will commence at once. The plans were drawn by Charles H. Peal.

07 28 82 Excavation for the town hall commenced Tuesday.

08 04 82 Stone for the foundation to the town hall has been drawn this week.

08 18 82 The health officer of this township should pay some attention to his duties or else resign.

09 22 82 The foundation of the town hall is nearly completed. The brick work will probably commence next week.

09 29 82 Joseph Corkey has taken the brick contract on the town hall, which includes rubbing and penciling, and the plastering of the interior. There will be two coats of plaster, dry sand finish.

William Briggs laid 15 perch and 5 feet of stone on the town hall foundation one day last week.

10 13 82 Mr. Charles H. Peale showed us the plans of the new town hall yesterday, and as we have already given the size we will now give something of an idea of how the building will look, when completed. The foundation, which is left in rough cast work is to be cemented, and blocked off as imitation of cut stone work. The exterior of the brick work is broke up by pilasters, with ornamental galvanized iron caps. The front entrance is gained by a door way 5x8 with a heavy half circle transom. On each side of the entrance are two large windows, circle top, ornamented by brick cap projections. Over the entrance door is a triangular window to light gallery. The sides are also broken up by brick pilasters, with six large windows on each side, same as the front windows with cap projections.

Entrance on the stage can be gained by a large door 5x8 in the rear. The roof is supported by five large trusses, being mansard, and is covered with shingles ornamented by diamond shaped blocks. The building is 38x102 feet, and the rear 22 feet is taken off for the stage, and on the front 16 feet is taken off for office rooms and main entrance hall which is 13x16 leaving an auitorium 38x62. Under the stage are two large dressing rooms, the entrance to which is gained by stairs leading from rear of stage. Over the offices is a gallery 17x38. The entire interior is to be wainscoted three feet high, with molded cap and base, of hardwood. The stage front opening is 22x132 high, finished by splayed panel jams, and is also lighted by sunken foot lights. The building is ventilated by four large flues running from floor line to a point 3 feet above the entire roof. The hall will be heated by furnaces. Estimated seating capacity about six hundred people.

10 20 82 The brick work on the town hall will be completed next week.

10 27 82 It has been said that the bidding on the work to be done on the town hall has been so low that no contractor will more than make good fair wages.

12 01 82 We understand that no lock-up will be constructed in the basement of the town hall building. If there are serious objections to having one there, then the town should build one independent of the town hall. Officers complain bitterly of having to sit up with arrested persons night after night with-out any comfortable place to do even that. We hope the town board will act in this matter before it is too late and if there are no serious objections have one built in the basement of the hall. It would cost less and answer the purpose just as well as a building independent of the hall would.

12 15 82 The town hall is being lathed. One furnace has been finished and it warms the building nicely.

Chapter 15
Native Americans

03 12 80 Tuesday is the day for the Indian trade, and the day that some persons make their living by selling them whisky. Some one will be "snatched up" some of these days.

03 19 80 As some of our readers in Southern Michigan wish to know something of the Indian language, we publish the following, by request, which is:

HOLD THE FORT.

NUGUMOWIN 2. 8s & 5s

Ew ke wa oan wan bun dum oak
 Neej ke wa e took!
Tuh gwe shin oag wau che wung ook,
 Shah ge che wa tah!

Che--"Soan ga ta aig, nim pe tuh gwe
 shin."
 E ke to Je sus.
Nuh qua tow ik ew ish pe ming
 "Wee che' yahng ka gait".

Wau bum ik pah nah goo zi chig.
 Muh che mun e toag.
Shin ge shin oag o ke che tahg,
 Shah go che int wau.-

'Nah! ke wa oan wa wa bah sing,
 Noan dum oak bi bi gwun.
Ow Ke ni gah ne zee me nahn
 Waic ji shah go ji 'waing.--

A ne goak on ji me ga dim,
 Ba sho dush Je sus;
Pe tug we shin wa to gi mah 'm yung
 How, sah sah qui tah.--
Translated by Jacob Greensky.

(for English translation see
"*Bay Breezes*" Vol. 1, page 219.)

03 26 80 The hymn "Hold the Fort," which we published in our last issue was in the Ojibway language. A remnant of that tribe are now living in the vicinity of Elk Rapids. We shall publish other hymns in their language occasionally.

05 21 80 Some years ago a gentleman by the name of Kelsey, from Southern Michigan, was visiting this part of the country and had occasion to cross the bay to Old Mission, having an Indian who went by the name of "Big Dave" to take him across in a canoe. When nearly across a squall come up and the canoe was overturned throwing both into the water. They both came up and caught hold of the canoe, and before Dave had the water out of his lungs he yelled out: Mr. Kelsey! Mr. Kelsey! If we be drowned, put it in de papah! Put it in de papah! As Mr. Kelsey told us this afterwards, and as we saw Big Dave yesterday and having never seen a notice in de papah, we conclude that they arrived at Old Mission safe.

05 21 80 "Big Dave," the Indian preacher, speared nearly 100 fish one night this week.

06 11 80 A couple of Indians whose names are Tom Fisher and Jacob Allen broke into E.H. Hale's store at Indian Town last night and proceeded to smash things. They were captured and Hale and a man by the name of Campbell who brought them to this place and lodged them in the jail.

08 27 80 A good many Indians have left this place this week to attend camp meeting at New Mission which is being held this week. We learn that an excursion is to be given to New Mission Sunday.

10 01 80 Col. Geo. W. Lee, Indian Agent, has been in town this week.

12 03 80 One night last week an Indian soaked in the river for an hour, and yelled lustily for help before the help came nigh.

01 28 81 That troublesome Indian, Sitting Bull, has again made his escape into Canada with about 1000 followers. It is thought on request of proper authority the Dominion Government will surrender him and his followers to this Government.

05 20 81 Indians are spearing large quantities of suckers these days.

08 12 81 An Indian by the name of Brown had his satchel cut open Tuesday and fifty-five dollars in a pocket book stolen.

John Cameron was arrested yesterday for cutting open Indian Brown's satchel and stealing $55.

08 25 81 Two Indians who had been drinking yesterday, got into a quarrel and Peter Wanageshick struck Jacob Allen in the head with a piece of cinder cracking his skull. Dr. G.H. Bailey dressed the wound.

10 14 81 Mr. Mon-ow-o-quot, of Harbor Springs, died at Elk Rapids a few days ago. He thought he was 115 years old, and was one of the original landed proprietors of this state. —*News*.

11 04 81 The Indian who was reported to have had the small pox died on Friday. It has been pronounced not to be small pox but the result of sleeping among poison ivy.

11 25 81 A case of small pox has been reported at Indian Town. Every precaution has been taken to prevent its spread.

12 02 81 Ten Indians have died of small-pox at Indian Town, and those that have been exposed to the disease are kept away from the others.

01 06 82 We think, in the way of retrenchment the Government should abolish that sine [sic] cure known as the "Mackanaw Indian Agency." Geo. W. Lee is fond of calling the Indians "his children," but when they have the small pox he is confined to his house with typhoid fever. It has been often demonstrated that the Michigan Indians can get along with out the aid of an agent, and we know now that they can get along with out Geo.W. Lee, and the sooner his self-constituted paternity is annulled the better.   --*Sentinal*, Charlevoix.

05 19 82 Several squaws came into town Wednesday evening and reported that James Miller had killed Jim Fisher. The only truth about the matter was that Miller and Fisher got tight that afternoon and in the fight that ensued, Fisher received a bloody nose.

06 02 82 George Tob-a-sha-ge-go, son of the old Chief Squa-ga-na-ba, died at his home at Indian Town, last Saturday and was buried Monday. Although he was the hereditary chieftain of the Indians here, they paid no particular attention to him, or even the old chief for some time before the former died and much less attention to the latter.

06 30 82 *Charlevoix Sentinel:* Moses Wa-baw-gon-a, of Harbor Springs, while full of fire-water, amused himself by overturning and injuring the grave stones of the pale faces, for which crime he is in the stern clutches of the law.

07 28 82 Tuesday night an Indian who goes by the name of Brown, went to Pete Wa-na-gi-zic's hut and commenced pounding on the door, when Wa-na-gi-zic opened the door and struck Brown with an ax several times, cutting a gash about an inch long in his upper lip, and another peeling off his left eyebrow, and also slight wounds above and below his right eye.

07 28 82 Some one is selling liquor to Indians. It will be a severe thing if some one gets caught at it.

07 28 82 Capt. E.P. Allen, of Ypsilanti, has been nominated by the president for the office of Indian agent for the state of Michigan, vice [sic] Geo. W. Lee, deceased. Mr. Allen is an able man. — *Evening News*

08 18 82 Indian camp meeting commenced at Northport Tuesday.

Chapter 16
Fish & Game

05 14 80 We hear that there will be more boats to let this year than there was last year, so that fishing parties will not be obliged to fish "straddle of a log."

05 21 80 John Denahy caught a trout below the chute Sunday which weighed two pounds. Fishing parties stopping at Elk Rapids are not obliged to go several miles in the country, but can go two or three rods from the hotel and find good bass, pickerel, trout and muskellunge fishing.

05 28 80 Over 100 beautiful speckled trout were caught below the chute Sunday. For the benefit of friend Sprague of the *Eagle,* we will remark that there are two kinds of fish, the religious fish and the secular fish, and "better the day, better the deed," so that the fish caught Sunday, the religious fish are larger than the secular, and they bite a mighty sight better. However, if there are as the *Eagle* says, people who do not fish Sunday, and we believe it for we never do, nor do we approve of it, we will tell him and the people who do not fish Sundays that the secular fish bite. Ben Yalomstein caught 30 trout below the chute Monday in about fifteen minutes.

05 28 80 Messrs. Dexter & Noble had a fish ladder placed in the chute Monday.

06 04 80 Ben Yalomstein has caught nearly 200 speckled trout this season.

06 18 80 Messrs. Rockfellow, Skinner and Philips shot about 35 pigeons apiece back of the furnace Wednesday morning.

07 02 80 We have spoken very often of the excellent trout, bass and pickerel fishing around Elk Rapids, but never particularly of the bass fishing. Near Messrs. Dexter & Noble's grist mill the water in Elk River passes through a chute. Below the chute in the bed of the river there is a hole about thirty feet deep and about the same width. As soon as the water is shut off the fun commences. It is nothing unusual to see twenty-five or thirty persons there just hauling out the bass. Just away from the dock and in the current from the saw mill race is another good point, also at the mouth of Elk lake, Elk river and Bass lake. A Mr. Beesley of Cincinnati, who has fished 19 years at the "Thousand Islands and other noted fishing grounds, says that in all his experience he has never experienced such good success in bass fishing as he has at this point. The other morning he caught sixty fine bass in a short time.

07 09 80 E.A. Kemp, engineer on the steamer *Jennie Sutton,* received a card from J.B. Stickney, of Mazomaine, Wis., the gentleman who caught so many trout in Rapid River recently, which had on it the following: "I shall probably visit Elk Rapids and Old Mission every season as long as I can, as I think there are no places like them in the U.S. for health, rest and trout fishing.

07 23 80   FISH NOTES.

Messer. J.W. Beesley and J.J. Knight, two gentlemen stopping at the Lake View House, caught 75 trout at Yuba creek yesterday.

Robbie Williams, a six-year old son of Hon. F.R. William's, has commenced early in life and bids fair to become a successful sportsman. He caught 24 bass and one 3 pound pickerel at Bass Lake last Saturday.

Mr. J.W. Beesley, of Cincinnati, Prof. Rust of Kenyon College, and a gentleman by the name of Roberts, all stopping at the Lake View, caught 85 trout at Yuba Wednesday. Mr. Beesley caught 52 of them.

Fish, fish, fish, fish, fish, fish, fish, fish,
fish, fish, fish, fish, fish, fish, fish, fish, fish,
FISH, FISH, FISH, FISH, FISH, FISH, FISH, FISH, FISH, FISH,
FISH, FISH, FISH, FISH, FISH, FISH, FISH, FISH, FISH,
FISH, FISH, FISH, FISH, FISH, FISH, FISH, FISH, FISH,
fish — stories told at the Lake View House.

ELK RAPIDS,
The best Black Bass
Fishing Point,
IN THE WORLD !

---

07 23 80 Miss Katie Beeslley received a refreshing bath yesterday below the chute. She had gone down to fish for bass and while walking across a piece of timber she made a mis-step and stepped into the water, and very gracefully, too. Before getting out, which she did unassisted, she carefully adjusted her eye-glasses and her back hair comb, while Mrs. C.D. Town, who was with her, screamed for help "or she would be drowned." The water was only three or four feet deep at this point.

07 30 80   FISH NOTES.

Messrs. Hanna and Miner, of Bloomington, Ill., caught 362 trout in a creek near Williamsburg, Monday last.

Messrs. Hanna, Miner, Platt, Beesley and Jonas gave a trout breakfast and supper to the Lake View House guests on Tuesday.

Contradiction — Prof. Jonas did not fall into the River last week. He had a small fish on his line and it pulled him in. Selah!

Mr. and Mrs. N. Sid Plate returned Friday last from their fishing expedition to Rapid River and furnished all the guests at the Lake View House with a trout breakfast Sunday morning.

Prof. Rust went fishing at Central Lake the first of the week and brought back a bass Thursday that weighed 6 pounds and 132 ounces, and measured 23 inches in length, and 173 inches around the body. Mr. Kerr, of Louisville. Ky., who was with him did not have such good luck, while his son Jimmie grew just one inch taller as he pulled in a 3 pound bass.

As there has been some question whether fish could run the ladder placed in the chute this season by Messrs. Dexter & Noble, we have had the matter settled to our entire satisfaction by making inquiry of Mr. W.W. Griffith, President of the Fish Commission of the State of Kentucky, who has been a guest at the Lake View House. This gentleman informed us that he considered it excellent means of ascent, which the representatives of the finny tribe would not be slow to improve.

08 13 80   FISH NOTES.

A party of three caught 94 in Rapid river Tuesday.

Mr. B.F. Frink of Burlington, Ill., caught some very large bass in Elk River last Monday.

J.E. Lippincott, Isaac Kinsey, and Irene Kinsey fished last Friday at Battle Creek near Williamsburg and caught 75 trout in that stream. We are informed that the fish averaged the largest of any that have been brought here.

Messrs. Thruston and Fosdick, of Louisville fished all day in Elk Lake yesterday and did not catch a fish. We cannot tell a lie. We learn the reason the gentlmen didn't catch any. He said damme, he said damme, and according to "Jo. Minnie" fish won't bite if you swear at them.

08 20 80   FISH NOTES.

C.D. Town and John Archbold went fishing at Battle Creek the 15th inst. and caught 119 speckled trout.

We learn that 3,200 trout have been taken from battle Creek this season, and there is good fishing there yet.

08 27 80   FISH NOTES.

Messrs. Beesley and Neff, Cincinnatians, caught 158 speckled trout at Battle Creek Tuesday. One weighed 1 pound and 2 ounces dressed, and the rest were a large average.

The editor of the *Traverse City Daily Eagle* evidently does not know much about the geography of his own county. We think when he learns that Battle Creek is in that county, and that there is good fishing there, the fact of there being one good fishing point in that county will make him sick. We have been so used to big catches in this place that nothing can affect us.

Will the *Progress* be kind enough to tell us where this particular Battle Creek is? — *Eagle*.

We Will. It seems to by the above that the *Eagle* is inclined to doubt our fish stories. Battle Creek is in Whitewater township, Grand Traverse county, and flows into the head of Elk Lake. There are three creeks flowing into the head of this lake, which are, Follett's, Battle Creek, and one other, the name of which we are unable to give. We will right here mention that we can back up any fish story that we have told. Do you rise for any more information, Mr. *Eagle*?

09 03 80   Fish Notes.

J.W. Beesley caught 50 trout in Rapid River Monday which were of a large size.

Ben Yalomstein, Andrew Dougherty and James Morrison caught 75 trout at Rapid River Sunday.

The September bass fishing season opens good. Every day nearly, some one goes along the street with a big string of black bass.

The boatman familiarly known as "Jo. Minnie," caught 30 pounds of bass in Elk Lake Sunday. He caught one which weighed six pounds.

The trout fishing season is now over. A great many have been caught by parties stopping here, at Yuba, Follett's, Battle Creek, and at Rapid River.

10 15 80   There is good fishing at this place now. A great many perch are being caught off the end of the dock, and herring can be captured in numbers back of the grist mill. Some of our Ky. friends should be up here.

10 22 80   Partridges are so thick in this part of the country that they fly right into people's wood sheds. Mr. Michael Butler caught one under these circumstances Wednesday.

02 11 81   A good many are enjoying the duck shooting around the mouth of Elk River. Eugene Cross shot four "Beauties" yesterday and others have been equally successful. The large flock that has hung around the races and the mouth of the river is being thinned.

04 22 81   Pickerel have commenced to run, and several have been shot in the creek near the furnace.

04 29 81   We learn that some swans were in the bay in front of our village Sunday.

"Big Dave" caught 100 pounds of black bass last Friday, and one of them weighed 6 pounds and 2 ounces. It is about time for our tourists to come.

05 27 81   Our "tourist friends" will be glad to learn that "Joe Minnie" is awaiting their arrival.

05 27 81   Fishy Items.

William Dumphrey speared a 2-pound speckled trout last Friday.

Prof. Ranger, John Archbold and Horatio Lewis caught 75 speckled trout in Rapid River last Saturday.

Harry Alpern caught several fine black bass below the chute yesterday morning, a number of them were 3-pounders.

Charley McLaughlin speared 26 white fish in Elk Lake Friday night, weighing in all 109 pounds, besides several bass, pickerel and other fish.

116 trout caught in Rapid River Wednesday. Ben Yalomstein caught 45; C.D. Towne, 36; and John Archbold 35.

06 03 81   Fishy Items.

Albert Reed caught 36 trout below the mill Tuesday.

Mr. J.W. Beesley caught 16 trout off the dock Thursday.

Frank Warren speared a 5 pound bass last Sunday eve.

Lyman Price caught 36 speckled trout at the chute Friday.

Richard Pratt caught 46 speckled trout at Rapid River last Sunday.

Two Louisville, Ky., gentlemen caught 15 fine bass below the chute Wednesday morning.

Over two hundred speckled trout were caught in Elk River below the chute last Sunday.

Frank Warren caught a muskellunge last Tuesday night at the chute which weighed 17 pounds.

Harry Alpern and Joseph Butler caught 50 pounds of black bass below the chute Monday Morning.

Messrs. Rosengarten and Carley of Louisville, Ky. caught 560 trout at Rapid River Thursday.

William Briggs caught 75 trout at Rapid River Sunday. Harry Briggs caught 62; and Lyman Price caught 42 at the same place.

Elzor Fortin, more familiarly known as "Jo Minnie" caught 75 beautiful speckled trout at Rapid River last Friday. He brought themto this place alive.

Prof. L. Denny, of Kalkaska, who is stopping at the Hughes House caught 60 trout off the dock yesterday, and it was not much of a day for trout either.

The bass fishing at this place has commenced, and promised to be the best we have had. Two Louisville gentlemen captured 15 before breakfast the other morning besides the quantities they caught during the day.

The next time we go fishing with a party which has all the luck and catch all the fish we won't eat a single fish. Nary a trout did we catch at South Boardman Tuesday, but there was a good mess on our table the next morning. Our first trouting in over two years, and no luck. It was annoying to see how easy the thing could be done, and not be able to get them. *Leader,* Kalkaska.

It is fearfully annying as the boss of this shop knows. He fished all afternoon at Yuba Creek, and only caught two trout both of which measured three inches. The trouble of it was, we think, he fished most of the time for a big sucker, which he thought was a big trout and did not catch the "blarsted" sucker. Editors "never have no luck."

06 10 81 Dr. Turner Anderson, of Louisville, Ky., caught a 6 1/2 pound bass below the chute Tuesday. Dr. Anderson does not hesitate to plunge right into the water after his fish, which probably accounts for his catching the most. He "wears the feather" for catching more fish than any other Louisville gentleman here.

06 17 81 391 bass, 233 speckled trout, and 116 lake trout were reported caught last week. The small ones weren't counted.

There are too many fish caught here for us to "catch on" to every item. If you make a good catch, let us hear of it.

06 24 81   FISHY ITEMS

The *Elk Rapids Progress* is of late filled with fish stories-stories that would make Annanias, or even the editor of the *Detroit Post*, blush with shame. – *Evening News.*

We clip the above from our esteemed contemporary the *Detroit Evening News*. George Washington could not tell a lie. Mark Twain claims to be a better man than Washington, because he can tell a lie, but won't. Our ancient friend Annanias stands next to these two worthies, as there is only one recorded against him, so the comparison so far as our ancient friend is concerned, is not so very odious [sic] after all. But we confess to a little nervousness when the editor of the *Post & Tribune* is mentioned, and had the editor of the *Evening News* been included in the comparison also, we should have quaked with fear lest these same fishermen should sue us for libel forthwith.

The cool weather has interfered with the fishing. The "June fishing" will probably take place in July this season.

The number of fish caught below the chute last week was over 600.

J.B. Stickney and party of Mazomanie, Wis., caught 396 fine trout in Rapid River.

E.L. Sprague, of the *Eagle*, declined fishing at this place, because he never fished on Sunday. We will admit that fish do seem to bite better.

The *Elk Rapids Progress* now each week publishes from a half to a column of fish stories. Ben tells some good ones, too. —*Tribune*, Traverse City.

06 24 81 Some of our fishermen here say that if they had the State news paragrapher of the Evening news here they would chuck him in the hole below the chute.

The *Progress* is well filled with fish stories these days. Some of the accounts of the exploits of the disciples of Isaac Walton are so marvelous, but are no doubt all true. Elk River is no doubt one of the best streams in the state for bass fishing. —*Eagle* Traverse City

07 01 81 Over 400 black bass were caught below the chute last week. Not counting the catches of three or four. More than 100 speckled trout were also caught.

"Jo Minnie" caught a black bass at the chute Tuesday which weighed 4 pounds.

Lemuel Smith, son of L.R. Smith caught with his hands six fine bass below the chute last Saturday.

Elzor Fortin, or "Jo. Minnie" caught a speckled trout below the chute Tuesday morning which weighed 2 pounds and 4 ounces and was 172 inches long.

We notice by the *Progress* that large quantities of black bass are being taken at the chute at Elk Rapids, mostly by pleasure seekers from a distance. The *Progress* is getting "fishy." —*Leader*, Kalkaska.

Atoine Lindenlief, head sawyer in Messrs. Dexter & Noble's saw mill caught eight large black bass under the saw mill last Saturday afternoon. He used no hook or spear but took them out with his hands. As soon as the mill shuts down at night the men go below and stand on the turbine water wheels and pick out the black bass.

07 08 81 FISH NOTES.

462 black bass were reported caught below the chute this week.

At Bass Lake last Friday after noon Howard Tebbets, of Harrodsburg, Ky. caught 112 bass.

Dexter & Noble have forbidden the spearing of fish around the chute.

Mr. John W. Beesley and "Jo Minnie" caught 161 speckled trout at Rapid River Tuesday afternoon and Wednesday morning.

On Sunday C.D. Towne and Ben Yalomstein caught 125 speckled trout at Battle Creek.

07 22 81 FISH NOTES.

The fishing will hereafter be transferred to the foot of Elk Lake. Bay fishing will be good, and Bass Lake will afford some sport. The fishing at the chute is not as good as last week.

The number of fish caught as reported in the Progress last week was 1344; also three dozen frogs.

Any one reading the *Progress* and *Kalkaska Leader* would naturally infer that bears at Kalkaska, and black bass at Elk Rapids (just below the chute, you know) were thicker than mosquitoes at Bellaire. If you are going to dish it up so often, boys, give it to us in smaller doses. —*Herald*, Mancelona.

07 29 81 The score of black bass caught by tourists at Elk Rapids as reported by the *Progress* already has gone up into the thousands. The sporting reporter of *the Progress* is engaged upon the basis that he believes there is no hell. —*Evening News.*

We have accepted the new revision and shall continue to publish the number of fish caught here. It would be better for hell and for the News if that paper would leave hell alone.

Bait your hooks with grasshoppers these days.

Judge Beattie and Mr. John B. McFerran, of Louisville, caught 20 trout and 1 grayling at Cedar River on Tuesday. The fish were caught from a boat at the mouth of the river. The grayling weighed 1 pound. Judge Beattie, who caught the grayling has preserved a fin.

425 black bass, 50 speckled trout, 3 muskellunge and 1 pickerel were reported caught last week.

07 29 81 ADMIRALTY BUREAU OF THE MUNICIPALITY OF ELK RAPIDS.
GENERAL ORDER 10,001.
ELK RAPIDS, July 25, 1881.

Recognizing the piscatorial ability and success of our devoted subject and present commodore, John W. Beesley, and the hardships which he encountered with the mosquitoes on Rapid River in his successful campaign against the trout then gathered to defy him, and his exertions and skill in numerous contests with the Pesces along our shore hereby demonstrating to the world the great advantages possessed by our municipality as a place of resort for those who delight in fishing, and as thereby great gain has come to our citizens. And further recognizing the fact that in our service, and from his physical exertions on Rapid River, his hair turned yellow, a before unknown phenomenon, it is our pleasure to create for him and to promote him hereby to the rank of Admiral of our fleet, and be will be honored accordingly.

By order of the Municipality of Elk Rapids. Esox Lucius. Sec.

08 05 81   FISH NOTES.

Last week only 153 bass were reported caught in the river and Bass Lake.

529 speckled trout were reported caught in Yuba, Folletts, Battle Creeks and Rapid River.

Mr. John W. Beesley has caught 951 speckled trout this season All caught at Rapid River with the exception of 100 which were caught at Battle Creek.

Last Sunday as a German was fishing at the short dock, a mink run on the dock and stole two of his fish. Mr. N. Sid Platte, of Louisville, baited his hook with a bass and had the satisfaction of hooking Mr. Mink. He wiggled from the hook, however, and the sport of fishing for minks came to an end.

08 12 81   FISH NOTES.

Three persons from this office went fishing last Saturday afternoon and brought back 150 speckled trout.

People who want to beat this journal on fish stories must get down to business pretty soon. A Charlotte man named Haskins got drunk a few days ago and vomited up a live sunfish 5½ inches long. If you don't believe it call on hosts of Charlotte people who have seen the fish and Haskins' mouth. —*Evening News*

08 12 81 The fish ladder in the chute should be repaired so that fish could get up into Elk River and Lake, or our fishing at this point will be soon "played out." Post-master, Geo. A. Dyer, has the plans, and specifications of the ladder adopted by the state, and the one at the chute should be repaired or a new one put in. If this is done we may enjoy the fine fishing here indefinitely but otherwise, we fear our fishing will be spoiled.

Only 38 reported bass caught last week and 280 trout.

08 25 81 An Indian anchored off the channel bank in the bay Tuesday and caught 15 Mackinaw trout still fishing. Several of the trout would weigh 25 pounds each.

09 09 81 Will Briggs shot 5 partridges Sunday.

Saturday Mr. Charles Bremaker, of Louisville, brought home 2 mallard ducks, 1 teal, 1 grouse, 1 Virginia Rail, 1 Pigeon.

Messrs. Beckham and Bremaker caught 38 bass, perch and pickerel. at the mouth of Elk River Tuesday after noon.

Narrow Escape-Mr. H. Bowers, of Rochester, N.Y. had a serious mishap yesterday at Elk Lake. It was neither a bass, a pickerel or a perch that took his hook; but while standing in the boat, he went over into the briny deep. His cries were heard at the village intermingled with Joe Minnie's "wah wah wahs." When he arrived at the Lake View House he had a part of the appearance of a mermaid and a drowned rat.

10 07 81 Mr. Geo. A. Dyer has recently received several bushels of wild rice which he intends sowing about Torch River, and other places in this county where wild ducks congregate, and it is expected that duck shooting will be one of the attractions to the many sportsmen that visit this famous fishing resort.

10 21 81   FISHERMAN FISHERMAN'S PARADISE.

From May 27, to Sept. 2, the number of black bass caught as reported in the *Progress* was 4,200, and trout 3,810. This does not include any of the other catches made.

Boats, Bait, and Guides.

As the *Progress* is devoted mostly to the plans for next season, it would be well to mention in this connection the conveniences which can be had at moderate prices for those who wish to fish. Mr. John E. French will purchase this winter several sail and row boats, and will build a boat house and also a minnow house, and those who wish to fish can find at his house pails for minnows, rods, hooks and lines, and if they wish experienced guides. At the mouth of Elk Lake he will anchor a lighter, which will have on it a cabin, and those who like still water fishing can go there. The lighter will be made so that it can be towed up to Rapid River, and having a cabin on it tents will be useless. The cabin will be furnished with a stove and other conveniences for camp life. Mr. French has other plans which will be made public as soon as he perfects his arrangements.

10 21 81 Mr. G.M. Jackman shot 17 snipe near the village the first of the week.

10 28 81 John E. French caught 75 large perch off the end of the dock yesterday.

10 28 81 Snipe, woodcock, wild geese, wild ducks and all kinds of game are very plentiful in this part of the country this fall.

12 23 81 Louie Wilcox caught 25 herring off the end of the long dock yesterday morning.

We learn that Mr. Williamson caught nearly 100 herring at the dock yesterday.

12 23 81 If the good perch and herring fishing does not stop we suppose the state editor of the *Evening News* will be shieing his quill at us. During the summer he tried to say some hard things about our sporting editor, but that person is alive now.

02 10 82 Fish-ladder, side-walks, bridge. Fish-ladder, side-walks, bridge.

02 17 82 Mr. John French has a minnow house built near the chute and has conveniences for keeping 10,000 of this kind of bait. As soon as the frost leaves the ground he expects to build his boat house, which will be on Elk River, just above the chute.

02 24 82 We must impress it upon the minds of fishermen that no brook trout can be taken from the water that is less than six inches in length. If caught it must be thrown back. This new law goes into effect this spring.

03 10 82 As the fishing season is near at hand we will dispose of our surplus railroad stock cheap. Only those who mean business need apply.

03 17 82 John French has six of his row boats painted and fitted for the summer.

03 17 82 Wild rice has been sown in Round Lake and it is being prepared for Petobago pond. Ducks to quite a number fly north, and are found around the places above mentioned.

03 24 82 Eastport—Last week Mr. A. Richardson killed a badger weighing 40 pounds, on his farm.

04 14 82 The *Elk Rapids Progress* gives fair warning that it will resume its weekly fish stories this summer. They are designed to attract fishermen, can all be verified under oath, and are alike good evidence of the good fishing in the Traverse Bay region and of the elasticity of the truth thereabouts. —*Evening News.*

The *News* has such a delightful, gentle way of telling any one they like. It leads up to it by degrees, which is much better than the common and we might say vulgar way. "Elasticity of the truth," indeed, how charming.

04 14 82 John E. French caught three pickerel last Saturday in the creek which runs from Bass Lake into Elk River.

04 14 82 The Supervisor of East Bay should see that there is a fish ladder placed in Yuba Creek. This is one of the best trout streams in Northern Michigan and if a ladder is put in there this spring it will so continue to be. We hope this matter will strike the owner of the mill just right, so that the Supervisor need not go to the trouble of looking up the matter.

04 21 82 We do not think that the sawdust from the mill will drive the fish away, as the fishing was fine when D. & Noble's mill was running full blast. If sawdust going into the river does seem to affect the fishing we have no doubt but that the Iron Co. will stop it.

04 21 82 The pickerel are biting in Bass Lake...
Last Saturday night there were nine fishing lights out on Round Lake, and about 1,000 pounds of fish were taken out.
Last Friday W.H. Smith caught 15 speckled trout with his hands. He was filling in a ditch on Traverse Avenue, and had to take the trout out.
Well, Ben, here is our start on fish items. A party composed of A.C. VAnTassel, A.J. Clark, L.M Lester, R.S. Abbott, and ye editor, captured from Grass Lake, in two hours and thirty minutes, sixty-one fish (black bass and pickerel), weighing from six pounds down.— *Breeze*.

04 21 82 Some parties are putting nets in the mouth of the river and that way of fishing should be stopped.

04 28 82 It has been told us that the owner of the Yuba dam and one of Yuba's prominent men have decided that after the fish chute is placed in the dam that tourists can fish there by paying for it but the editor of the *Progress* cannot fish there at all. We again call the attention Supervisor Pulcipher to that dam.

05 05 82 John E. French caught five speckled trout at the chute Wednesday morning, and two on the following morning.

05 05 82 Several fish were at the chute the other morning inquiring about the fish ladder.

05 05 82 The wild rice has arrived and will next week be sown in Intermediate and Grass Lakes. —*Breeze*.

05 05 82 A supervisor is made an inspector of fish chutes and while in that service he is allowed $2.00 per day. If he notifies a firm or corporation to put in a chute, and they refuse or neglect to comply they are liable to a fine of $200 or imprisonment or both at the discretion of the court. Every thirty days after the notice has been given, the person, firm or corporation are liable for each offense. This is according to the law on the subject. We mention this as a reader at Central Lake sent to us for information. We will also say that we sent him a copy of the "Michigan Sportsman's Journal."

05 05 82 It is said that an angle worm cannot dig more than one inch per hour, but he is always an inch beyond the shovel when you want fish bait.

05 12 82 We learn that 10,000 salmon were deposited in Torch Lake, Tuesday. Our fishing is already fine, but this gives us another item about our "fisherman's paradise."

Two very good trout streams enter Round Lake. One is Barker's Creek and the other which is near, goes by the name of Big Creek.

05 19 82 The Indians are netting a great many black bass at Petobago pond.

05 19 82 This is for the *Breeze*: Call the names of the fish caught there. Suckers, rock bass and sun fish are not fish for items. Catch all the black bass, pickerel, muskellunge and speckled trout you are a mind to, but don't gag us with suckers and sun fish.

05 19 82 The Indians are spearing suckers and herring by the boat load in the river.

05 19 82 Charles McLaughlin and Willie Daw are taking some fine whitefish and trout in Elk Lake these calm nights. They speared 13 Tuesday night and 15 Wednesday night.

05 26 82 The fishing days have come, the scaliest of the year.

05 26 82 Dr. Conklin and J.C. Green caught 35 speckled trout one day this week.

Harry Briggs, of this office, and Hulburt Russell caught 23 trout one day the first of the week.

Lon Langworthy and George Arnold caught 48 trout in a creek near Williamsburg one day this week.

06 02 82 Elzor Fortin (Joe Minnie) has returned to Elk Rapids, and will be employed during the season by tourists and sportsmen. He has contract with John E. French & Co.

"Mossy" Moore caught a 2 pound perch at the dock Tuesday.

C.D. Towne captured 20 trout May 26 which he brought home with him.

Ben Yalomstein and C.A. Newton caught 44 trout in one of our streams May 25.

J.C. Morse of Milford, caught 5 speckled trout at the chute. One weighed 13 pounds.

BELLAIRE — Not less than 500 trout have been taken from the river at this point during the past four days. A few of the catches that have come under our observation are as follows: Sam C. Cook, an even fifty; Warren Wood, one hundred and three; A. Van Tassel has been four times, the result being eighty-six, forty-three, seventeen and sixteen; one caught by him weighed two pounds and five ounces another two pounds and three ounces, and he had twelve that weighed from one pound to one pound and eight ounces each. Byron Fulller caught eleven in a short time. R.E. Maxfield and Henry Pinney also made large catches, as have also Chas. Richardi and George Wallace. And last and least ye editor with Mr. Van Tassel's kind assistance, captured twenty in about two hour's time. — *Breeze*.

06 02 82 The fish commissioner may make it a point to raise a rumpus with some of these folks who spear fish.

06 02 82 A party of Rockford, (Ill.) boys will be here about the middle of July, and will camp out near town. John Boyd, who formerly lived here is their pilot, and they will probably have a fat time.

06 02 82 One of our Yuba friends says that if we had kept our mouth shut we could have fished up there this summer, but that we cannot now. That is all right, sonny, but it is mighty mean that others can fish there and we are shut off from it.

06 02 82 Max Yalomstein is mad, and we do not blame him a darn bit. Monday his brother Ben and Dr. Conklin went over to the chute for a fish, and just as they were leaving Max said to Chas. Hickox, "I'll bet you the cigars, Hickox, that they don't catch two fish. "Take it up!" said Mr. Hickox. The Dr. and Ben fished around or an hour and never had a bite. Hickox in the mean time was not idle, but hooked two speckled beauties from the Lake View House aquarium, and took them in a pail to the fishermen, who soon returned (with the stolen fish) bragging of their luck. Max paid the bet and when he learned the joke he pulled four bushels of hair from his head and in the evening was heard to sing,
>I wish I had sum'un to luv me;
>Sum'un to be faithful and true,
>Sum'un to raise h--- with those fellers,
>Who with Hickox, went fishing for two.

06 02 82 Dexter & Noble prohibit persons spearing fish on their premises.

06 09 82 Thousands of minnows at J.E. French & Co.'s minnow house.

06 09 82 The very best place to fish in Yuba creek is on some railroad land near the upper bridge. We fished there last summer and expect to this, if the weather continues.

06 09 82 This spearing fish ought to be stopped, and sportsmen about town should see to it that the law in regard to spearing fish is enforced.

06 09 82 An Indian caught a 16 inch speckled trout at the chute Monday.

06 16 82 The *Daily Nashville* (Tenn.) *American* has the following to say about the Nashville fishermen stopping at this place: It is said that the highest evidence of a perfectly truthful nature is to be able to go fishing and report the exact facts as to the size and number of fish caught. No fish biting at the hooks of any of these gentlemen need have any fear that his weight will be reported double or his number multiplied by three.

06 16 82 The black bass have not been biting very well this week because they are so mad about the fishway not being built for the chute before this time. We owe this apology to, and for them, because we mentioned some time ago that the

136

fishway would be built before May 1st. We do not blame the poor, dear things very much because it is natural for them to feel hurt and disappointed. Is was our first lie, and we hope to be pardoned for that one offense, as we have tried to do our duty by them and we think they really and truly ought to bite.

06 16 82 The Nashville party to the number of ten are fishing at Petobago pond to-day.

A.B. Dougherty and Ben Yalomstein caught 40 trout at Yuba one day the first of the week. Ben also caught 8 trout at the chute the same day.

Last Saturday evening, Joe Minnie and Ira Sharp returned from Rapid River with 200 trout, which weighed 20 pounds. Joe caught 165 and Ira 35. Joe brought back alive a 13 and a 10 inch trout for the Lake View House aquarium.

William Porter, of Nashville, Tenn. caught a 20 pound lake trout, Monday, off the bay dock, with an 8 ounce rod, and common sea-grass line. It took about 15 minutes to land the big fish, it having to be towed to shore, and four persons gave their help. A telegram was sent to Nashville telling of the fine fishing at this place.

06 23 82 Catches reported for the week; Black bass 446; Speckled trout 366; Lake trout 7, weighing up to 10 lbs.
C.E. Hillman, of Nashville, Tenn., who has fished for forty-five years, in every part of the country, remarked to us, one day this week, that he had never seen such a fishy place as Elk Rapids. Finest fishing he ever had.

06 23 82 The fishing has been unusually fine the past week, for the commencement of the season. We claim, and rightfully, that we have the best bass fishing in America.

06 30 82 Reported catches for the week: 425 bass, 61 speckled trout, 1 pickerel, 3 mackinaw trout.

06 30 82 The fishway for the chute is almost completed and is approved by the State Fish Commissioner.

07 07 82   FISH NOTES.
Reported catch for the week: 311 black bass and 44 speckled trout.

07 07 82 Don't see how the *Progress* manages to keep up with the count of the fish catch. If we should attempt it here it would require the best efforts of our reportorial staff. How is it, Davis, do you ever "bunch 'em?"   – *Breeze.*

The first thing necessary, of course, is to have the fish. Then it is very easy to count them. John E. French & Co. employ six or seven men and when they come in from a days fishing they report at the office, and bring in the fish. We publish probably, accounts of one-third of the fish caught here. Aside from John E. French & Co.'s record, Winfield Scott, clerk of the Lake View House, keeps a record for us, so that there is no possibility of a mistake arising.

07 21 82 We received the *Manton Tribune* too late last week to notice that friend Cooper had been in town and are sorry that he did not make himself known. On the 4th he fished at the chute and says: Leaving Old Mission about 10 A.M. we arrived at Elk Rapids at 11 and at once repaired to Ben. Davis' "below the chute" and there landed seven nice black bass, weighing from one to three pounds apiece, when we were summoned to again board the boat. (We had hoped to call on the *Progress* to allow Ben. to count our string, but it was not so ordained, and therefore we must submit to have this portion of our article questioned). Aboard the boat again with only one man missing- he could not leave "Fisherman's Paradise"- we at once "went below" and refreshed the inner man with good wholesome food.

07 21 82   FISH NOTES.

Reported catches for the week - black bass from the chute and river, 208; speckled trout mostly from Rapid River, 335.

07 21 82 When David said in his wrath that "all men are liars," his prophetic soul must have had AuSable fisherman in view. —*Evening News.*

The fishermen that come up this way, can see that the above is not intended for them, and David did not really and truly know anything about our chute.

07 28 82 Last week we had not time to mention more than the number of the trout catch made by Messrs. Lee Smith and W.F. Abrams, of Cincinnati, at Rapid river. There were 133 in all, the largest weighing 1: pounds. Captain Johnson, of the *Queen*, says that they had the finest string of fish taken from the above river in eight years, and Joe Minnie says their big fish was the largest taken from the river in two years. All admit here that it was the finest string of fish ever brought to the Lake View House, and that is saying a good deal. We do not mean in number but in the size of the fish caught.

07 28 82 On the 23rd inst. Joe Minnie caught 133 trout at Rapid river.

J.C. Green and John LaLone caught 69 trout at Yuba Wednesday.

08 04 82 Deep water bass fishing has commenced in good earnest. The mouth of Elk lake and in the bay at the mouth of Elk river, and yet at the mouth of the mill race good bass fishing can be found. Bass lake, Petobago and several other points can be mentioned.

08 11 82 A 7 pound sheephead was speared in the river Sunday.

08 18 82 On the 7th Joe Minnie returned from Rapid river with 250 trout.

08 25 82 On Tuesday, several sportsmen were shooting clay explosive balls in front of the Lake View House and made the following record: J.M. Barbour, of Louisville, Ky., 16 straight; Wm.T. Barbour,of Louisville, 10 out 13; J.C.Green 3 out of 13.

08 25 82 The reported weekly catch:
Bass, 77; Speckled trout,299, all from Spencer creek, Acme creek, Yuba creek, and Rapid river.

08 25 82 On the 19th Big Dave caught 20 lake trout (Mackinaw) in the bay, deep water fishing.

On the 18th Joe Minnie returned from Rapid river with 275 trout.

09 01 82 On the 25th Joe Minnie caught at Rapid river 300 trout.
On the 31st J.C. Green and A.W. McElcheran caught 100 trout at Rapid river.

On the 26th an Indian caught 5 Mackinaw trout deep water fishing the largest weighing 50 pounds.

No more trout stories this season.

09 08 82 Partridge and duck shooting after the 16th.

09 08 82 "Joe Minnie" returned from Rapid river with 350 trout on the 1st. He has caught this season 1,793 speckled trout, which is a good record.

09 29 82 It is now about time for perch and herring fishing. Perch are biting first-rate.

10 05 82 Over ten thousand speckled trout were caught by Traverse City guests and residents during the past season. –*T.C. Herald.*

We call for a "bill of particulars."

10 15 82 Sports may fine the following of interest: Squirrels may be killed from September 1st to January 1st; partridge, from October 15th to January 1st ; woodcock, from July 1st to January 1st; railbirds from September 1st to December 1st; wild turkeys, from October 15th to January 1st; wild fowl, from September 1st, to May 15th; deer, from October 1st to December 1st.

11 17 82 *Kalkaska Leader.* A son of J.W. Chaney, of Clearwater township, met with a singular and painful accident recently, while out deer hunting. A powerful, double spring bear trap had been set in the woods without the customary pen around it, and the first the young man knew of its presence he had one foot in it with a sharp spike driven through the flesh of his leg, above the ankle. He proved equal to the emergency, however, and with true grit picked up the lever used for setting the trap, and pressing down one of the springs, tied it with his handkerchief and then pressing down the other, managed to extricate himself.

11 17 82 Wednesday, in Charlevoix, a Mackinac trout weighing ninety pounds was taken from the nets of the Cross boys.

Chapter 17
Entertainment and Festivities

01 02 80 Those who attended the ball at Traverse City New Years eve from this place report that a fine time was had.

03 05 80 A handsome young widow applied to a physician to relieve her of three distressing complaints, with which she was affected. "In the first place," said she, "I have little or no appetite. What shall I take for that?" "For that, madam, you should take air and exercise." "And, doctor, I am quite fidgety at night, and afraid to lie alone. What shall I take for that?" "For that, madam, I can only recommend that you take—a husband!"—Fie ! doctor; but I have the blues terribly; what shall I take for that? "For that, madam you have—besides taking air and exercise and a husband—to take the newspaper."

03 12 80 One of the pleasantest parties for some time was given at the Lake View House last Friday evening. The friends of Mr. and Mrs. Geo. A. Dyer assembled at the above place about half past eight, and they "tripped the light fantastic" until about half past twelve. The dining hall of the house makes a fine place for dancing, and it had been very nicely arranged. The parlors had been thrown open for those who wished to have a quiet game. Every one there had an "immense" time.

04 02 80 We should think that by the complaints in town by some people about the thin milk that it would be a good plan for other people to shingle their cows before a rain.

04 30 80 A dance came off in the new carpenter shop at the furnace Monday night.

05 07 80 He goes home with her; wants to go in; no; yes; she shuts door in his face; dog called; young man runs; wood-pile in the way; falls; brimstone; blue fire; slow music; curtain.

05 21 80 A dance came off at the residence of Mr. Spaulsbury, on the Elk Lake road, Tuesday night.

06 04 80 An excursion was given on the steamer *Queen of the Lakes* Thursday evening. The cornet band furnished music.

07 02 80 Our people will celebrate the Fourth of July by a basket pic-nic on Me-ske-go-nog Point, between Elk and Round Lakes, on Monday the 5th. The steamer *Queen of the Lakes* will leave here at 9 and at 11:30 A.M., and at 2 o'clock P.M. for the point calling at Sherman's and Curtis' landing each way. Returning the steamer will leave Me-ske-go-nog at 10:15 A.M. and at 12:45 and 6 P.M. The steamer *Jennie Sutton* will arrive here on time for the 10:30 A.M. trip of the *Queen of the Lakes*. The *Sutton* will not leave in evening until the *Queen* arrives. The fare on the Queen of the Lakes will be 20 cents each way and the fare on the *Sutton* will only be one half of the usual amount. We learn that there will be boat, foot and tub races and that a small prize will be given to each. There will be no celebration, no stump speech making, but every one will go in for a quiet, pleasant time.

07 09 80 The fourth of July was celebrated as advertised by a basket pic-nic at Ske-ge-mog Point the 5th. Quite a number of people took the *Queen of the Lakes* on her 9 o'clock trip and others followed on her later trips. Ske-ge-mog Point is a beautiful place between Round and Elk Lakes. Just the right place for a summer hotel. The *Queen* was enabled to land her passengers without the help of small boats as there is deep water there. After the two o'clock boat the racing began with the following result:

BOAT RACES.
Double scull-
1st prize, $5, Edwin Cooper and Frank Noble.
2nd prize, $5, H.N. Cooper and Joseph Butler.
Single scull-
1st prize $3, Edwin Cooper.
2nd prize $2, Frank Noble.
SWIMMING RACE – 2 MILE
1st prize $3, Frank Noble.
2nd prize $1.50, Joseph Butler.
THREE LEGGED RACE.
1st prize $2, Frank Noble, Joseph Butler.
TUB RACE.
1st prize $3, Edwin Cooper.
2nd prize $1.50, Phy Bailey.

07 16 80 Prof. Von Vreeland and wife have their parlor entertainment and concert at the court house last Friday evening to a fair audience. Prof. Von Vreeland has a very fine voice and sings very low. In his magic he introduced several interesting and novel tricks. As a ventriloquist he has but few equals. His planning mill illusion was a decided success and called forth loud applause. His character sketches were very natural. Mrs. Von Vreeland has a wonderfully full clear voice, especially in the upper register, and at once becomes a favorite with the audience. Should they stop here again we predict for them an overflowing house.

07 23 80 "The Famous Continuous Moving Mirror Panorama," from New York, illustrating Bunyan's *Pilgrims Progress* was shown in the Court House last Monday night. We don't know any thing about the Panorama except from hearsay, but those that attended pronounced it first-class in every respect, and we pronounce the fellow that shows it a first-class fraud. He engaged some of the boys to distribute his bills and help him at the Court House. They worked a part of two days and two whole evenings and he paid them off with dumb watches and celluloid scarf pins worth about a cent and a half a bushel. Sheriff Acker hearing the complaining about their treatment went up and "sat down" on his goods until he had paid them. He advertised to show in the Methodist Church, and just here let us remark that Methodist Churches better leave him alone, but the Chapel was too small. By representing to Mr. Acker that it was for the benefit of that Church he got the County House free. After the entertainment was over he refused to give any thing; but we believe he was prevailed upon to hand over about $7. Methodist churches in neighboring towns should have as little to do with him as possible.

07 23 80 Empire Stites of Williamsburg furnished music for the Lake View House party last night.

08 13 80 Bills have been circulated announcing an entertainment at the Court House Monday evening Aug. 16, by J. Randall Brown, the great mind reader. His entertainment is highly spoken of by leading papers, and by some of the most noted men of our country. Our citizens should not fail to be present as the entertainment is well worth attending.

08 13 80 The dancing party given at the Lake View House Tuesday evening by the E.J.D.C., was one of the pleasantest affairs of the season. A number of the towns people, guests of the hotel and quite a large party of Old Mission people attended. The music was furnished by the Elk Rapids Quadrille Band of which Mr. Empire Stites is leader. There were five pieces and the music was excellent. The hall looked very pretty, owing to the fine taste of Mr. Jas. Lewis. A few beautiful plants were arranged in the room which gave a pleasing effect. All voted that they enjoyed themselves and were anxious for another.

11 19 80 We learn that there is fine skating on Bass Lake which fact is hailed with delight by the girls and boys, and by some of the older people as well.

12 24 80 There will be a social dance in Lake View Hall on the evening of Dec. 24, 1880. Music by Morrison's Band.

12 31 80 The skating on Elk Lake has been fine, and Christmas Day quite a party went up and enjoyed it. When one can skate 10 miles long, and 3 miles wide in some places, and was covered with ice from three to five inches thick, and was just as glarey as a skater could wish. Come up North if you want to skate.

12 31 80 After the skating party had adjourned Christmas night a favored few were invited to the rooms of Mr. and Mrs. C.D. Towne, at the Lake View House, and enjoyed a chocolate. These chocolates are delightful as those who have gone to them will know.

01 28 81   THE MASK PARTY.
There is a certain fascination to the average American in a carnival, just as attacks of measles, whooping cough and scarletina are duly expected during the years of infantile progression, so in the maturer years of incipient mustaches and adolescent puffs and crimps, do there occur periodical breaking out of mask-fever, which, in case of males takes the forms of outward eruption, of gorgeous raiment supposed to represent the times of the merry monarch, or in other instances of these nondescript garments which are supposed to convey to the eye accurate description of the daily attire of the native and foreign elements of our

population; while the ladies—"God bless 'em!" burst out in all the colors, of a rainbow, in every conceivable costume, that taste and ingenuity can invent. The mask fever was at its height, caught I think from our neighboring City, when it was announced a Mask Party would be given at Lake View Hall Monday Evening Jan.17, 1881. At 8:30 on that evening Prof. E.Stites Orchestra- which, by the way is first class, struck up one of its excellent selections, where upon the sixty masked who were gathered in the parlors of Lake View Hall marched in, in fantastic array. A more motley crowd could not be imagined, nobody knew anybody, for the disguises were complete. Young appeared old, old appeared young, and no one was like him or herself. The costumes were not, perhaps, as elegant and expensive as our City friends', but were sensibly and ingeniously gotten up, showing that our ladies and gents' energies and ingenuity can be used in more ways than one. We venture to say that, comparatively little money was spent on fashioning their picturesque and becoming costumes, which also shows the young men that our ladies are equal to emergencies, and can make themselves lovely and attractive with very little outlay; let them remember this.

At 11 o'clock all masks were removed and exclamations of surprise were heard; "why was that you?" "I thought 'twas Blanche,"and,"well I declare I thought you had on sister's bonnet." "Was that you in that jesters costume?" "I took the wire masked man for you!" Those not in costumes looked on with sparkling eyes, and all were happy as good music, good dancing and a good company could make them. At 2 o'clock the party dissolved, while congratulations on all sides were heard for the "splendid time" they had had. And as we looked on, we said. Where can be the objection to a Mask Party and what could be more orderly, more decorous and enjoyable than this, and for our part we say, may the next year bring a return of the same and we thank certain gentlemen for giving us the pleasure?—A Lookeron.

02 26 81 The party given by the E.R.D.C. last Friday evening was by far the pleasantest of the series given this winter. At 9 o'clock the gay maskers were in the Lake View House parlors when the line of march was taken for the hall. Arriving there, they all felt as though they could stay until morning, and it is seldom that you can find a more joyous company than was there that evening. Considerable ingenuity was displayed by those that made their own suits, and those that rented costumes from Chicago, were of course' handsomely dressed. It would not be advisable or interesting to give a detailed account of the costumes, but all looked well, all appeared well and the gentlemen of the club giving the party are to be complimented for the pleasant arrangements. Prof.Stites' band played their best music and all unite in thanking the gentlemen who afforded them the evening's pleasure. The committee giving the party was Messrs. Hurlbut, Holbrook and Cooper. At 2 o'clock the party dissolved, with every one feeling that they had had a "glorious time," and that with the return of the year they may have another as pleasant an evening.

04 08 81 The Elk Rapids Cornet Band have never disbanded, but for some months they have not met as they had no leader. We are now very glad to announce that they will continue their practice under the leadership of Mr. J. Gevish, formerly of Traverse City.

04 15 81 We have a new instrument added to our tortures. It is a dulcimer.

04 15 81 The Elk Rapids Cornet Band is making excellent progress. We suggest that it receive a substantial benefit.

04 22 81 Some of the young lads in town have organized a ball club.

05 06 81 The Peck & Wildman Theater Company will be in Elk Rapids all next week beginning with Monday evening.

05 13 81 On Tuesday night the Wildman & Peck Opera Company played "Fanchon, the Cricket," to a full house. Wednesday night "East Lynn" was the play. Last night the company played "Rip Van Winkle." The company consists of eleven ladies and gentlemen, and their rendition of the above plays was very good. The company will probably visit our village again next fall, and if they do they will be greeted with full houses.

06 17 81 Look at notice in another column of the Great Exposition Circus, which will visit Elk Rapids June 24.

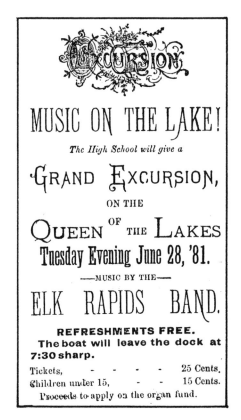

05 20 81 The Wildman & Peck Company played to full houses five nights last week. It is certainly a fine troupe and we hope they may visit us again. On Saturday night they played the laughable farce, "Our Boarding House," with F.J. Wildman as Col. M.T. Elevator, and Al. E. Peck as Prof. Gillipsie, and all the parts were nicely taken. From here they went to Charlevoix and Petoskey, and will return here later in the season.

07 22 81 About forty of our people attended a dancing party at Old Mission Tuesday night. At five o'clock that afternoon a number went over on the *Jennie Sutton.* The ride over was delightful, made more so perhaps by the Elk Rapids Band. Arriving at Old Mission, carriages were in waiting to take the party to one of the most delightful spots in Michigan, Rushmore's. This summer hotel stands about a half a mile from the dock, in a clump of beautiful beech and maple trees, charming spot. After the Cornet Band had played some of their best pieces, the musical sound of the tea-bell was wafted to our ears by the gentle breezes, and the whole party adjourned to the dining hall and enjoyed one of Rushmore's famous Teas. At nine o'clock carriages took them to the ware-house on the dock where the dance was given and a jolly good time was had until 12 o'clock when the party dissolved. The ride coming home was but a repetition of the one going over. A number of guests at the Lake View House were prevented from going at 9 o'clock by the threatening weather. A number of pleasant people from Grand Rapids and Cincinnati are at Old Mission and enjoyed the party. Elk Rapids people will long remember the very pleasant party at Old Mission and Rushmores charming summer house.

07 29 81 A German [sic] was given at the Lake View House Wednesday morning at 10:30. So many young people in town makes it lively, as there are dancing parties every evening, and mornings are now being devoted to dancing. Elk Rapids is lively these days.

07 29 81 A "sheet and pillow case" dancing party was given in the Lake View Hall Wednesday evening.

08 12 81 A harvest dance will be given in Newton's new livery stable this evening.

09 02 81 The Lumbards gave an entertainment at the Hughes House Tuesday night. They show all they advertise to, and have had good houses through the country. They went from here to Torch Lake.

12 23 81 A merry party of young people went skating at Bass Lake Tuesday evening. Two fires were built, one on the point and another on the bank towards the furnace. The ice was as smooth as glass and the jolly party did not come to an end until 11 o'clock.

01 06 82 Chas. Grammel gave a big dance at the brewery Monday night. The dance was held in the new ice house, and the music was furnished by Morrison's band.

01 27 82 "The Cardiensis Club" is an organization in our midst which meets every Friday evening for a quiet game of whist. Last Friday evening was the 10th meeting of the club. It has a President and Secretary, who are: President, Mr. Wm. C. Lewis; Secretary, Mr. Norman M. Pierce. The club have a constitution and bye laws to govern them, and the members thereof seem to enjoy themselves to a perfectly unlimited extent. Whist!

02 10 82 One of the most brilliant social events of the season was given by Mr. Edwin S. Noble at his fine residence last evening. Invitations were issued early in the week, and about 9 o'clock the guests assembled. The pleasant parlors were thrown open for dancing to the music of the cornet band, which continued until 11 when refreshments were served. The guests began to depart at half past one with pleasant thoughts of him who had contributed so much to their enjoyment.

02 24 82 The entertainment given at Lake View Hall on Monday and Tuesday evenings for the benefit of our three religious societies proved not only a financial success, but has developed the fact that our little village possesses both musical and histronic talent of no mean order... We must mention, however, that in "College Ned," Mr. Grey sustained his part in a creditable manner. His make up being perfect. Mrs. Grey acted the wife and mother with true dignity... The Broom Drill was well done, and is to be hoped that through life the young ladies may never have occasion to use the wrong end of the broom...

02 24 82 The E.R. Opera Company return thanks to Mr. and Mrs. Lang for the use of their organ at the late entertainment.

03 03 82 The *Traverse City Eagle* had the following to say in regard to our quadrille band in last issue:
The writer was not a member of the dancing party but dropped in for a few minutes to look on and listen to the music, which was furnished by the Elk Rapids Quadrille Band, and was certainly the finest we have heard for a long time. We think that any unprejudiced person who heard the music at Front Street House Tuesday evening will admit that Elk Rapids has the best Quadrille Band in Grand Traverse Region. Mr. Empire Stites, the leader, may well feel proud of the degree of perfection attained by his band.

04 28 82 A dramatic society has been formed in the village with A.K. Dougherty as manager. The first play that the society will tackle is "MichaelErle," the characters having been assigned to members of the organization.

05 12 82 The Great Interior Circus will make their magnificent march through the streets at 10 o'clock A.M. May 15.

05 12 82 The Great Interior Circus and Roman Hippodrome will be at Elk Rapids, Monday, May 15, and will present to their patrons the finest display of Arenic and Equestrian talent ever witnessed in any show on Earth. Grand street parade at 10 o'clock A.D. Usual prices of admission, Children under nine years half price.

05 12 82 The Great Interior circus and Roman Hippodrome is coming and will give two shows in Elk Rapids Monday May, 15.

06 02 82 The Dramatic club has rented the old Lake View Hall from S. Yalomstein, and used it for rehearsal last night.

06 02 82 There will be a dance in Lake View Hall this evening- the last of the season. Floor manager, Adam Laubscher. Good music in attendance.

06 02 82 The Elk Rapids drama club will appear for the first time in about three weeks.

06 16 82 The Dramatic Club have a new stage in Lake View Hall.

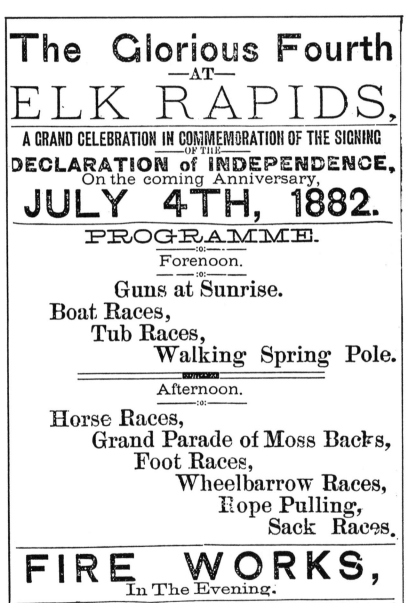

06 30 82 C.A. Newton has a couple of 2:40 trotters.

Boat riding on the bay and river now almost every evening.

06 30 82 On Wednesday and Thursday evening our people witnessed the play and afterpiece of "Michael Erle" and "Old Gooseberry" by the Amateur Dramatic club. While not mentioning any of the characters particularly, the entertainment as a whole was quite enjoyable. To our minds the afterpiece was much more cleverly acted than the regular play, although some characters in the play, were well sustained. The club have only been rehearsing for a few weeks and considering this fact, it was much better than was expected it would be. The stage was nicely arranged, and our scenic artists are deserving of the highest praise, The receipts for the first evening, about $50.

07 07 82 Last evening quite a number enjoyed the fireworks which were fired on E.S. Noble's grounds.

07 07 82 The Fourth happened to be a beautiful day. The usual salute at sunrise awoke the inhabitants of our town, making some of them growl about the 4th coming so often. About nine o'clock teams came pouring in, until we had, what seemed to be a general uprising of the people... In the afternoon about 2 o'clock the grand parade of Moss-backs occurred, and really it seemed as though they were the mossiest kind of moss-backs. The only one thing lacking was the absence of leek hooks [sic] to make the parade a success. Owing to the freshening breeze no tub, boat or spring pole races could be indulged in, but the time was agreeably filled up with horse racing. In the evening the fire works took about an hour of time. And all adjourned to their homes except the young folks, who danced till the following morn at Lake View Hall. We think all enjoyed themselves, and none were desturbed by drunkenness or bad order.

In conclusion we desire to say that if all the committees appointed, had furnished the amusement that A.K. Dougherty did, as committee on moss-backs, our enjoyment would have been complete.

07 14 82 The concert by the children at the M.E. Church, last evening was well attended, and all went away satisfied with the work which has been done here by Prof. Greenlee. The choruses, "Don't Forget the Old Folks," "Merrily over the Snow," "The Headlight," "Be sure you are right then go Ahead," were decidedly good. The solo, "The Blue Bird," by Miss Ola Welch, was very nicely sung; Miss Alice Bago, "The Lark," sang very sweetly. Miss Nora Burrell sang a sweet little ballad, "Riding on a Load of Hay," and she has such a charming little voice that she was recalled. Miss Nellie Lewis sang the solo, "Goodnight Little Nell," very effectively her upper notes being especially fine. Harvey Pierce as the "Fisher Boy" did some very good work and Harry Noble did bravely as the "Newsboy." Both have sweet voices. The duet "Reuben and Rachel" between Miss Alice Hughes and Harvey Pierce was well rendered. While we cannot mention more owing to the lateness of the concert all did well considering the time they have been at work.

07 14 82 The Elfin Star Comedy Company will play in Lake View Hall to-night.

07 28 82 A.K. Dougherty received a letter recently from a Detroiter, asking the privilege of opening our new town hall with some entertainment. We do not know how people generally feel about it, but we think, and so does Mr. Dougherty, that we have home talent enough.

07 28 82 John E. French takes a party out in his sail boat nearly every night. The boat has been newly painted and fitted with new sails and will accommodate about forty persons. Mr. French knows how to sail a boat and his charges for taking a party for a sail on the bay are very reasonable.

10 05 82 Masters' Troubadours gave a show at Lake View Hall last Friday evening to a "sold" audience. The time has gone by when an Elk Rapids audience will take in a snide, and not growl. We have always gone to everything that came along, because we were so isolated from the rest of the world that even a snide would break the monotony. The time has gone by, we want good entertainment or none.

Chapter 18
Grand Traverse County

01 30 80 L.M. Beers has plated a village at Old Mission. Old Mission is rapidly becoming a popular summer resort and it is to meet the demand for lots that he has platted the village. Several cottages there are owned by Grand Rapids business men.

06 11 80 A.T. Allen & Son of Yuba, have machinery and material on the ground for the purpose of building a saw mill at that place. The ground has been cleared and the work on the dam would have been commenced this week but for the late severe storm which made the creek raise so rapidly that work was impossible. We learn, however, that work will begin as soon as the water in the creek lowers.

06 11 80 John McDonald, of Yuba, has built a cheese factory on his place and has commenced manufacturing that article, which we learn is of a fine quality.

07 02 80 75 dozen pigeons were shipped on the steamer *City of Traverse* to Chicago Wednesday night, by the pigeon hunters at Yuba. A large flock of them are there feeding on beech buds. The hunters have several dozens of them on hand. One of them told us that he caught three dozen of them at one time last Sunday night.

08 20 80 Henry Shores of Old Mission, has commenced shipping fruit to this place. If you wish to get the best apples, pears, or in fact any fruit grown in this country you should speak to Mr. Shores.

10 15 80 Old Mission—Mr. John Drew is making a half acre flower garden, and has sent to Scotland for certain plants, flowers, etc.
There are two or three fruit buyers at this place, and have shipped here 15,000 barrels, which they expect to fill with apples. The apple crop is estimated at 30,000 bushels. They pay 70 cents and furnish barrel.

01 06 81 All persons in the Grand Traverse region who are interested in the organization of a Pioneers' and Old Settlers' Association are invited to meet in the Grange Hall at Traverse City on Tuesday, Jan. 18, at 2 p.m. for the purpose of effecting such an organization. A general attendance is requested.
John McDonald, Michael Gay, L. Miller, John Black, S.V.Northam, H.D. Campbell, H.S. Campbell and E.L. Sprague.

02 18 81 Fred Hall, the owner of the island in the bay heretofore known as "Hog Island" and "Harbor Island" has succeeded in getting a bill passed by the Legislature changing the name to "Marion Island."

03 11 81 We learn that the hotel accommodations at Old Mission will be better than last year. Mr. Rushmore, the proprietor of the Old Mission hotel, informed us that he would enlarge the dining room of his house and otherwise improve it by the addition of several rooms. Old Mission is a quiet, beautiful place to while away the summer, and has many attractions as a resort.

04 22 81 Lowell Sours is building a new house on his farm in Whitewater, on the Elk Lake road. It will be 16x24.

08 05 81 We learn that John McHarry, keeper of the Mission Point Light House committed suicide Sunday night by jumping from the steamer *City of Traverse,* in the West Bay. We learn that the cause of the rash act was domestic difficulties.

08 12 81 The work of clearing, grading and putting in order the new trotting track in the fair grounds has been commenced. The track will be put in condition for use at the coming fair.

The work of excavating for the stone foundation for a large new shingle mill to be erected by Hannah, Lay & Co., just east of their saw mill on the north side of the river, was commenced Thursday morning.

08 12 81 The dedication of the new Methodist Church at Williamsburg will take place on Sunday, the 28th inst. Rev. A.J. Eldred will preach at half past ten A.M., Rev. J.W. Miller at half past two P.M. and A.P. Moores in the evening. A cordial invitation is extended to the public generally.

08 25 81 The frame of the saw mill at Yuba has been raised and the mill will commence running as soon as the roof is laid and the machinery is in; and then will saw the lumber to side it up.

03 17 82 S.H. Sayler, of Yuba, intends building a new house. The size of it will be 30x36, and the stone work will commence about April 15.

04 21 82 The woolen mills owned and operated by Buller Bros., at Acme, for something over a year, will this spring be greatly enlarged. The firm will also put in new machinery and run a steam engine in addition to their excellent water power; the steam being used mainly for heating and dyeing. This business has so far proved an excellent investment, far surpassing the expectation of the young men, who felt it, at first, to be something of a venture. Beside their carding and yarn manufacture, they have finished and sold some fifteen hundred yards of cloth, during the year they have been in operation. The wool used by them has all been produced in this section and their clothe finds ready market here in Traverse City.

04 28 82 Mr. T.J. Johnson, of Wayne Co., this State, has bought and moved on to a farm in Whitewater township. Grand Traverse Co. He bought of J. Curtis, compensation $2,000.

06 09 82 The Hoxsie mill dam at Acme, broke away last Saturday night, but did not do very much damage.

06 23 82 Acme now has chemical works which produces Acme Bitters, Magic Oil and Acme Pain Killer. The three articles will cure any complaint that a man can think of.

07 21 82 The third cargo of lumber from Scofield & Son, arrived here Monday and is being shipped on the *Reindeer*, to Racine.

07 28 82 Captain Lane, keeper of the Mission point light house, killed a very large lynx one day this week. He had set his trap for foxes but the lynx strayed in. After a hard fight the lynx was killed.

08 04 82 After a six month residence in Colorado, Mr. O.E. Scofield and family, of Williamsburg, have returned to their latter place fully convinced that Michigan has attractions and advantages that he had previously overlooked. –*Fife Lake Eye.*

09 08 82 The *Fife Lake Eye* has just commenced another year. We hope that the "all seeing *Eye*" will protect it, and keep it free from delinq's and other wicked people. It was enlarged twice the first year, and keeps its eye on all local happenings in Fife Lake.

09 15 82 Henry Shores, of Old Mission has a horse that can trot a mile in three minutes. Never been on the track, but she's a daisy.

09 15 82 Ben "takes In" Old Mission.
        Monday by previous arrangement we took a trip over to Old Mission and visited the famous fruit farms on the peninsula. Henry Shores, with whom we had arranged to meet us was at the dock with his horses and buggy, and we were quickly taken to his farm a short distance from the dock...

10 05 82 The *Fife Lake Eye* has woodbined,[sic] on account of insufficient patronage. We are sorry because it was a first-rate local exchange.

10 20 82 Traverse City will have a new court house.

12 29 82 Ninety-four teams were on the road Tuesday hauling lumber for Hannah, Lay & Co. from their Long Lake mills. The average for the week has been 80 teams, and the average amount of lumber hauled by each has been 40,000 feet per day. The price paid is 90 cents per thousand feet. There is still nearly 8,000,000 feet to be hauled. The teams make two trips a day. —*Eagle.*

12 08 82   Miss Lollipop's Housekeeping.

Little Miss Lollipop thought she must help
To wash up the dishes, and wipe up the shelf,
To brush up the table and sweep up the floor,
And clean off the stains from the paint in the door.
She put on her apron and pulled up her sleeves-
She didn't want work that was only make believe:
"For muzzers who've dot yittle chillens," said she,
Must have yittle housekeepers: dat's what I'll be"
Little Miss Lollipop went through the room,
Whisked the dust high with the edge of the broom,
Broke the poor cup which she dropped on the floor,
Left the paint twenty times worse than before,
Spattered and splashed- but oh! how could I chide
The little heart swelling with sweet, helpful pride?
"For how would my muzzer be able," said she,
"To get free work if she didn't have me?"
Dearer the love in the sunny blue eyes,
Than the dust she is raising, which fades as it flies;
Better to miss the best cup on the shelf,
Than chill the dear heart which is enjoying itself
Dear little Lollipop, we are like you
Spoiling the work we are trying to do-
But surely the Father who loves us will heed
And take in his kindnes the will for the deed.

Chapter 19
Elk Rapids Iron Company

01 02 80 The work on the Furnace is being pushed. Men are working day and night, and she will soon be in blast and puffing as hard as ever, while her "broom sweeps the world."

01 02 80 Report of Blast No. 7 ending Dec. 13th, 1879, of the Elk Rapids Furnace:
No. of days in blast, 557. Total Iron made during blast, 21,821 tons and 690 pounds, being an average per day of 39 tons and 298 pounds. The largest week's run, 335 tons and 2080 pounds. The largest day's run, 51 tons and 1585 pounds.

01 02 80 The Elk Rapids Furnace has been in blast 557 days, and has been in blast longer, made more iron on one hearth than any other furnace on record.

01 09 80 The machinery at the Furnace is all apart; but when she starts again it will be in first-class order.

01 09 80 The Elk Rapids Iron Co. is taking advantage of the pleasant weather to drive spiles for the enlargement of the Furnace dock.

01 16 80 The furnace was in blast 557 days and consumed 35,885 tons and 1510 pounds of ore.

01 16 80 We understand measures will be taken immediately to protect the schooner *Two Fannies* from further damage as it is hoped that she is not injured at present beyond repair.

01 16 80 Some of the young men at the Furnace opened the new carpenter shop at that place with a dance last Saturday night, which was very enjoyable to the large number that attended. We believe that there will be another one to-morrow evening.
 The Elk Rapids Iron Co., has purchased from the Insurance Agents the cargo of pig iron in the schooner *Two Fannies* which went ashore in front of this village some time ago.
 The Elk Rapids Iron Co. has contracted for 21,000 tons of ore for next summer's business.

01 23 80 It is probable that the Furnace will start Monday. While out of blast the stack has been relined and a new hearth built. The engine has been taken apart and new pieces put in, also some improvements have been made in it. The Furnace carries a broom on the top of the stack, planted by MichaelTobin, who, every time he looks at that "dom broom" is filled with so much joy that he can hardly stand up.

01 23 80 The Elk Rapids Iron Co. is bound to have good roads leading to their works. They have recently dug out the sand and are filling in with slag, putting abutments against the hill to keep the sand from blowing down.

01 30 80 A trial of the Furnace engines last Monday showed that they had been very successfully repaired. The stack was filled Tuesday and she goes in blast tomorrow.

02 06 80 The ball in the new building at the Furnace last Friday evening was well attended. The music was excellent and all had a fine time. The dance was held in the upper story of the new carpenter shop, which makes a good dancing hall.

02 27 80 The Quinn Brothers, of Detroit, arrived here Wednesday and commenced taking iron out of the *Two Fannies* yesterday.

03 12 80 Over eighty men are employed at the furnace.

03 26 80 Some months ago we mentioned the fact that parties in Buffalo were building a new tug for the Elk Rapids Iron Co. The tug is now nearly completed. We find the following in the *Detroit Free Press* "G.H. Notter is building, at Buffalo, for Messrs. Dexter & Noble, of Elk Rapids, Mich., a first-class shallow-draft tug 62 feet over all, 152 feet beam, and 5 feet depth of hold. This is to be a twin-screw boat, and will be driven by two engines with cylinders of 10x11 inches, each working independent of each other. She will have a steel boiler.

04 09 80 Messrs. James and William Briggs have contracted with the Elk Rapids Iron Co., to furnish them several hundred thousand bricks.

04 16 80 New track has been laid between the furnace and the dock.

04 23 80 The Quinn brothers completed their work unloading the *Two Fannies* last Sunday, and left this place Tuesday of this week for Detroit. Mr. John Quinn is employed by the government for the summer.

05 07 80 Calkers and Ship Carpenters wanted by the Elk Rapids Iron Co.

05 14 80 The E.R. Iron Co., have received an auxiliary blower to help the blast.

05 28 80 We saw a card in front of Dexter & Noble's store yesterday, which informed us that the Elk Rapids Iron Co. would pay $1.40 a day for labor after June 1st and until further notice.

06 04 80 Capt. Johnson of the *Queen of the Lakes* is measuring wood on Torch Lake.

06 11 80 Last Saturday evening about 7 o'clock a tornado or a what do you call it struck this village, blowing off about 360 feet of the roof from the stock house at the furnace and blowing in some of the glass in the fronts of some of the stores. The damage at the furnace was between $1,500 & $2,000.

06 18 80 All the wood banked on Elk Lake last winter has been brought to the furnace.

06 26 80 The new air pump is being put into position at the furnace.

06 26 80 The damage done to the Elk Rapids Iron Co.'s stock-house by the tornado, which occurred a couple of weeks ago is being repaired. DanielStafford of Norwood, and S.S. Spaulding of this place have taken the contract to re-roof it.

06 26 80 The Iron Co. have put up a new machine shop at the furnace.

07 02 80 The Elk Rapids Iron Company have commenced the erection of six new charcoal kilns at the furnace. Unlike the old kilns they will be round, and will hold but 50 cords of wood. It is claimed that kilns of this kind will make more coal with the same amount of wood than any other kind.

07 16 80 The new machine shop at the furnace has been completed and everything is now in running order.

07 23 80 A new smoke stack has been put on the hoisting engine at the dock.

08 06 80 A short time ago there was some mortar stolen from the new kilns at the furnace. The next night six men with lighted lanterns watched for the thief. Probably they would have found him if they had taken a half dozen more lanterns.

08 13 80 Mr. Spaulding completed the Iron Co.'s. stock house roof last Saturday. There were 108,000 shingles laid.

08 27 80 The Elk Rapids Iron Co. recently purchased of JohnsonGoodenow & Co., of Northport, three wood scows which were brought here last Saturday night by the tug *Payne*. The scows are being hauled over into Elk River this week.

09 17 80 Eight horses were brought here Tuesday on the steamer *City of Grand Rapids* for the Elk Rapids Iron Co.

09 24 80 Going to the ship yard Monday we found Mr. A.K. Dougherty with a force of men finishing up a boarding-house scow for the Elk Rapids Iron Co., which they have been working on for some time. The scow is 80 feet long, 24 feet wide and has 4 feet depth of hold. The house to be built upon it will be 50 feet long, 24 feet wide. This will be the largest scow that the company have built and will be the best finished.

09 24 80 Six more horses came for the Elk Rapids Iron Co., on the *City of Grand Rapids* Monday.

10 08 80   FURNACE PUFFS.
       The Iron Co. are having a 54 foot scow built.
       Slag is being drawn and put on to the road west of the furnace.
       A new bridge is being built across from the elevator to the stack.
       The large hot air oven is being rebuilt, and will be fitted with new hot air pipes. It will really be a new oven.

A new Cameron steam pump has been put up in the engine room to force water into the large tank. It will also be used to supply Messrs. Dexter & Noble's store and grist mill with water.

The work in the machine shop is moving on. It is toosmall, and we learn that it is the intention of the company to build a large brick shop as soon as the amount of bricks can be made. No work will be done this fall, however.

A new Cameron air pump has been placed in the engine room to assist in the blast. It was working nicely yesterday when we visited the furnace. Mr. Thos. Mariott, the capable and accommodating engineer, "showed" us around, and helped us to a few items which we are extremely thankful for.

The company now have 35 charcoal kilns. Twenty-five of them hold 100 cords, and 10 of them hold 54 cords, each. The round kilns, 10 in number, which have just been built, are 16 feet high and are 29 feet in diameter inside the kilns, and hold 54 cords of wood each. They are composed wholly of brick and iron, there being no outside wood-work about them like there is about the other twenty-five. Mr. Samuel Conkling, who has charge of the kilns, informs us that it only takes five days to burn a new kiln.

10 08 80 Col. Head, of Evanston, Ill., one of the Elk Rapids Iron Co., has been in town several days.

10 15 80   FURNACE PUFFS.

A pulley caressed a finger on Joseph Parks' right hand last Sunday at the furnace.

In speaking of the new wood scow being built for the Iron Co., in last issue, we made it read 54 feet long. It should have read 60.

The furnace is not making as much iron at present as it has made heretofore, on account of the rebuilding of the hot air ovens. Those which are now in use need repairing badly and will be rebuilt as soon as the others are finished. In a few weeks the daily average will be up to 45 and 50 tons.

10 22 80 Shipments of iron ore, pig metal, etc., from the Lake Superior region, aggregate this season to Oct. 7: From Escanaba 652,671 tons; from Marquette, 548,949 tons and from L'Anse, 45,276 tons- a total of 1,546,896 tons, and an increase of 513,181 tons over last year.

11 12 80 The Elk Rapids Iron Co. has purchased the scow *James T. Petrie,* which will be taken over in Elk Lake and used in the wood business.

11 19 80 The wood circular of the Elk Rapids Iron Co. was out the first of the week. The prices of wood on Torch and Clam Lakes will be $1.40 and on Elk and Round Lakes $1.50, and $2 in the furnace yard.

11 26 80 Two stoves were cast at the furnace for the furnace at the School house this week.

02 26 81 The furnace has been shut down for two weeks. It had been in blast just one year when it stopped for want of wood. The blast has not ended, but work will commence as soon as sufficient wood is on the wood yard.

03 04 81 A NEW DEVICE — Mr. A.K. Dougherty is building for the Elk Rapids Iron Company two 'Somethings', the designs of which are gotten up by Thomas Noble, the 'Something', which is not as yet, patented. We give a description of one below. In loading scows with wood it is sometimes difficult to bring the scows to land, and it requires considerable time to arrange things before the scow is ready to load. The wood is loaded in barrows and wheeled over 16 inch planks resting on horses, and by the use of which, a great deal of wood is over-turned and falls into the lake, by which a large amount is lost each year, and it requires skilled men to handle the barrows. The device is as follows: A cedar raft 40x18: the superstructure of cedar also. There is to be a platform on the inner side, of upright, which will be 16x52. On the top of the superstructure will be fourDoyle pulleys which allows the lowering and raising of the platform to suit any bank so that in loading a scow, it will do away with the running plank and will give instead a runway 16 feet wide. Those who have looked at the device speak highly of the inventive genius of Mr. Noble, and any one who has had any experience running scows can at once see the great benefit to be derived from the use of it.

03 11 81 Castings of all kinds are made at the furnace. We believe that all cast iron articles used by the Iron Co., and Messrs. Dexter & Noble are manufactured there. The propeller wheels, which we have spoken of elsewhere are a remarkable invention for shallow draft steamers or tugs. Plow points, stoves, cog wheels, and crusher plates have been successfully made out of the very best charcoal iron.

04 22 81 The wood yard at the furnace although nearly empty in the day time, is full of young men in the evening playing ball who seem to enjoy themselves hugely.

05 20 81 Last Saturday the furnace made its biggest cast, 53 tons and a half.

05 20 81 Joseph Parks, engineer at the furnace, had the misfortune to break a toe on his left foot last week.

05 27 81 The Elk Rapids Iron Co. is shipping iron to Connecticut.

05 27 81 There is a good demand for team labor at this place. The Elk Rapids Iron Co. can give employment to four or five teams, and an "all summer's job."

06 03 081 At the foundry adjoining the casting room, at the furnace they are now casting 1200 valves for the Chemical Works.

06 03 81 Last Sunday the furnace made 54 tons of iron — largest days work done.
     The Elk Rapids charcoal blast furnace made for the week ending May 28, 1881, 345 tons and 630 pounds of iron, an average of 49 tons and 730 pounds a day.

06 10 81 The carpenters in the employ of the E.R.I. Co., are making several coal boxes for charcoal which is to be drawn to this place from Q.Thacker's at Yuba, which was burned last winter.

06 10 81 The Elk Rapids Furnace made for the week ending June 4, 1881, 368 tons and 500 pounds—a daily average of 52 tons and 1351 pounds.

06 17 81 The machine shop at the furnace has been extended several feet.

07 15 81 The tenement house at the furnace was discovered to be on fire Wednesday evening about 10:30, by Sam Crampton who promptly subdued the flames.

07 22 81 Two very large boilers for the furnace were brought here Sunday.
    Last Saturday night the Elk Rapids Iron Co. lost 30 cords of wood and a wood barge by fire.

08 05 81 About 10,000 cords of wood is piled on the wood yard.
    A new wood barge is being built at the ship yard for the Iron Co.
    The furnace boiler house has been torn down preparatory to the building of a new one.

08 12 81   At The Furnace.
    A new pipe cutter has been set up west of the engine house.
The tug *Minnie Warren* is having her boiler and engine repaired.
    A new side-walk has been built from the black smith shop to the engine house.
    The boiler house is about half up. The dimensions of the house is 28x32. There will be four new boilers 44x28. The boilers will probably be set in this week.
    A lean-to has been built on the east side of the stock house for a passage way for charcoal buggies from the charcoal kilns to the elevator. It is 8 feet wide by 200 feet long.
    The charcoal kilns have had chimneys put upon them and are supplied with dampers. A kiln can now be burned in three days instead of eight or ten days as was formerly the case.
    We mentioned two weeks ago that the Iron Co., lost thirty cords of wood and a wood barge by fire. The fire was discovered by Edward Elliott who uncoupled the barge from the tug and then scuttled it. The barge has been raised and the hull is in good condition and is being repaired at the ship yard.
    The daily average output for the furnace last week was 48 tons and 2237 pounds.

08 25 81 In the foundry castings have just been made for binders for walls of the boiler house.

10 28 81 A new lime kiln has been built west of the furnace to burn lime for the Chemical Co. The lime will be burned with gas from the furnace.

10 28 81 The casting house is turning out from 3 to 4 tons of castings a day.
    Kiln No.18 at the furnace fell in one day this week and No. 16 has been torn down.

12 23 81 The Iron Co.'s boarding scow has been brought down and lays in the river for the winter.

01 06 82 The Iron Co. commenced building a new charcoal kiln Wednesday morning which will be number 36.

03 03 82 Elk Rapids has a railroad- from the furnace to the dock. The locomotive has been purchased, and "off brakes" will next be heard. Take cars from dock to furnace, 10 minutes ride. The E.R.I. Co., have purchased a dummy engine to convey their ore from the dock to the furnace.

03 10 82 The Elk Rapids Iron Co. are putting in a cupola for the molding shop at the furnace. This will give the company facilities for doing all kinds of casting.

03 17 82 The dummy engine lately purchased by the Elk Rapids Iron Co., has quite a history. A few years ago it was used in New York City on the 9th Avenue elevated railway, and later by H.O. Rose, of Petoskey, on his road between that town and Crooked Lake.

03 17 82 The Riverside, the engine for use on the Traverse Bay & Elk Rapids short line was taken to the machine shop at the furnace to be overhauled. When the track for cars and engine is completed from the dock to the furnace, Chemical Works, saw mill, grist mill, store, etc., the facilities for transporting freight from all these points will be perfect, employing a less number of hands, and doing the work in a much shorter time.

03 17 82 The recent experiments in the new method of carbonizing wood, have proved a perfect success, results exceeding even the inventor's most sanguine expectations. As we promised in a late issue, we intend giving some idea of the process.
  Instead of firing the kiln, as now, at the top and allowing the heat to circulate and extend 'til wood is reduced to charcoal- intensely heated gas is introduced and in this atmosphere the wood is carbonized.
  The time of charring is materially shortened- the weight of charcoal per bushel increased immensely — this pleases the Furnace Co. The strength and amount of liquor accruing from the waste gases, improve vastly the usual showing — this pleases the Chemical Co. So both companies are rejoiced, and at no far distant time we expect to find all carbonization carried on in this manner.

03 17 82 The Elk Rapids furnace went out of blast Monday night after a successful run of two years and two months.

03 24 82 The talk about the Iron Co., building a machine shop at the furnace is nothing more than talk at present, as they have not yet decided whether they will build or not. When they do decide we will at once place it before our readers.

03 24 82 The Elk Rapids Iron Company's furnace at this place has just blown out for repairs having run 702 days making 32,867 net tons of pig iron, being an average of 46 1639-2000 [sic] tons per day for full time. There was consumed during the blast 55,156 tons of ore and 3,232,310 bushels of charcoal.

The largest days work was 65 170-2000 [sic] tons.

The largest weeks' work was 435 335-2000 [sic] tons.

Largest months' (30 days) work 1758 899-2000 [sic] tons.

From May 8th to Dec. 3d. inclusive, (30 weeks) this furnace produced 11,584, 240-2000 [sic] net tons; being an average per day of 555 325-2000 [sic] tons.

03 24 82 The stack of the Iron C.o.'s furnace will not be lined up this year, as the brick work is almost as good as when put in two years ago.

03 31 82 Some very fine castings have been made at the Iron Co.'s foundry lately. Of one casting in particular we make special mention. It is a section of the circle pipe for the tuyers that goes outside the stack. This section was 10 feet long and 24 inches in diameter, inside measurement. While at the foundry, Wednesday we learned that 3,700 pounds of iron had been used for castings that day. The mounding shop is quite small and we learn that it is the intention of the company to enlarge this department, by throwing the blacksmith shop into a molding room.

03 31 82 Frank M. Lombard, of Bangor, returned to this place Tuesday, and will take the position vacated by L.W. Skinner, as one of the superintendents at the furnace. Mr. Lombard was accompanied by his two boys.

04 07 82 The hearth for the stack at the furnace has been built up four feet. The general plan is different than formerly, and will probably increase the amount of iron per day considerably.

04 07 82 The Iron Co. have talked of running a dock directly from the furnace to the bay, so that ore could be transported to the furnace with less expense. This no doubt will be done eventually.

04 07 82 All the Iron Co.'s ore cars are being repaired.

04 07 82 R.P. Rounds made some very fine brass castings at the Iron Co.'s foundry Wednesday.

04 07 82 R.P. Rounds, superintendent of the Iron Co.'s foundry informed us that the sand used in the foundry would bring in Detroit 40 cents a barrel without freight and dockage added. The company shipped in sand for this room, before Mr. Rounds came here, and one day he shouldered his shovel and succeeded in finding a valuable bed for this purpose near Indian Town.

04 14 82 New flooring is being laid in the Iron Co.'s stock house.

04 21 82 The last section of the circle pipe for the stack will be cast Saturday — the mounds for the same are all ready.

The hoisting engine has had a new foundation placed under it; has been taken apart and the proper work has been put upon it and now it is in position.

04 28 82 The Iron Co.'s saw mill is running every day now, and Wednesday's cut with one circular was 39,514 feet of hardwood lumber.

04 28 82 Fred Gribi and Fritz Kaizer met with accidents at the Iron Co.'s mill Wednesday. The former had his thumb smashed and the latter two fingers by heavy timbers.

04 28 82 A horse belonging to the Iron Co. fell off the dock into the bay last Saturday, and swam ashore.

05 05 82   AT THE FURNACE.

    Kiln No.9 has been torn down and will soon be replaced by a new one.

    There has been a fire in the stack for several days. As soon as the pipe fitting is completed around the stack the furnace will start up.

    Michael Nackerman was summoned to Leland yesterday, by telegraph to do some work for the Leland Iron Co., and left for that place last night. Mr. Nackerman is considered one of the best furnace builders in the country.

    The work in the engine room has been quickly, and as usual, nicely done, and all the work that remains, is the fitting of a few pieces of machinery. We learn that the company would have enlarged this room had they brick enough on hand.

    The furnace yard is being cleared of all rubbish, and the Co. will soon have fine looking grounds. The company are filling in the small swamp east of the furnace, and chemical works. Other work we notice, spiles have been driven along the river front, and to the spiles have been bolted heavy planks and back of this planking slag has been dumped. This makes a good breakwater and dock, and extends from the chemical works to Dexter & Noble's river warehouse, a distance of a quarter of a mile.

05 19 82 Tuesday evening kiln No.24 at the furnace "blowed." It was a little too full of gas and sent the cast iron doors on top a flying.

05 19 82 The stack at the furnace was filled Wednesday and fired. Both the hoisting and the large engine were successfully run.

06 02 82 The forest fires on Torch Lake, this week, destroyed some cord wood belonging to the Elk Rapids Iron Co.

06 02 82 The furnace is making 42 tons of iron a day. We will publish weekly reports as soon as they can be furnished us.

06 09 82 The Iron Co., are widening their stock house by putting on an addition towards the river.

06 09 82 The Iron Co.'s stock house is 336 feet long and 60 feet wide. They are at work making it wider by 14 feet, and are also laying a new floor in one half of it.

06 09 82 The tenement building at the furnace is having a new fence built around it, also a porch on the North side.

06 09 82 There are 5,000 cords of wood on the Iron Co.'s yard.

06 09 82 We learn that the Iron Co. at this place, have always paid more for cord-wood than companies way down in the Southern part of the State.

06 09 82 Monday between 50 and 51 tons of iron was the day's run at the furnace.

06 16 82 The Iron Co.'s tugs are now bringing wood from Clam Lake.

06 16 82 In the 23 days, commencing May 19th and ending June 10th, the furnace made 1,008 tons and 930 lbs., an average of 43 tons and 1891 lbs. per day.

06 23 82 W.H. Smith has a contract with the Iron Co., to whitewash all the kilns.

06 23 82 The Iron Co. have new lumber and dump carts at their saw mill.

06 30 82 The new lime kiln at the furnace was burned Saturday, with gas.

07 07 82 The Iron Co. are having a new boarding scow built 40x16.

07 21 82 On Sunday the furnace made over 56 tons of iron, and Tuesday the same amount was made.

07 28 82 As soon as brick from the yard can be obtained, engine and casting rooms at the furnace, will be built.

07 28 82 The lumber Co. are having lumber piled on the dock.

08 04 82 14,000 cords of wood have been brought to the furnace yard from up the lakes so far this summer.

08 04 82 The largest brass casting ever turned out at the furnace was cast one day this week, the weight of which was 150 pounds. It is a green liquor pump for the Chemical works. R.D. Rounds, the superintendent of the foundry, thoroughly understands his business.

08 04 82 The largest days work the furnace has done this blast was over 57 tons.

08 04 82 The Iron Co. received yesterday 18 head of mules from Kentucky. They will be used at their wood camp on Elk Lake.

08 11 82 A new charcoal furnace is being built in the rear of kiln No. 22 at the furnace.

08 11 82 Quincey Thacker, of Yuba, is sending considerable charcoal, burned on his place, to the furnace.

08 18 82 The *Leland* is now getting ore at St. Ignace.

09 01 82 The furnace is making from 50 to 56 tons of iron a day.

09 01 82 The Iron Company are extending the track from the stock house to the new lime kiln.

09 29 82 A new lime house 20x21 is being built near the new lime kiln at the furnace.

09 29 82 The Iron Co. are building a new brick engine house 30x40 with arch roof. The preparations were being made yesterday, and the work on the foundation will probably be commenced to-morrow.

10 05 82 The Iron Co. recently received patterns from a Chicago firm for castings to be made at their molding shop.

10 20 82 The engine room at the furnace is being enlarged.

10 20 82 Plates for crushers are being manufactured at the Iron Co.'s foundry for a Chicago house.

10 20 82 *Traverse City Eagle*: The Elk Rapids Iron Co. have one of the largest and best equipped hardwood mills in the region, if not in the State.

11 24 82 56 and 57 tons of iron a day is the amount the furnace is now making. Not less than 53 tons a day in several weeks.

11 24 82 The engine room, at the furnace when completed will be roomy and a much healthier place for the Iron Co.'s employees.

11 24 82 The last cargo of ore for the furnace is in.

11 24 82 The Iron Co. are making a turn table for the Torch River bridge, this week.

12 15 82 The Iron Company are drawing their iron to the dock on sleds.

12 29 82 One of the tugs of the Elk Rapids Iron Company keeps in the wood service between the furnace and the Co.'s camp, on Elk Lake. About one hundred men are engaged at the camp, cutting wood and logs.

Chapter 20
Local Industries

04 29 81 Broad tire wagons are coming into universal use in this section of the country. Manwarring & Kramer have manufactured several.

06 03 81 There have been 130,000 bricks made at the brick yard so far this spring.

07 01 81 150,000 bricks is the size of the first kiln being burned at the brick yard this season.

06 16 82 The brick machine came in on the steamer *T.S. Faxton*, Tuesday.

10 20 82 Dr. Dennis Church has erected east of the furnace works for manufacturing potash, with a capacity of about three tons a month. At present he has only five leaches with evaporating pans and kettles, but if ashes can be obtained the leaches will be increased in number. People in town should now save their ashes as they can dispose of them for five cents a bushel or from 12 to 15 cents a barrel. To the farmers round-abouts, where you burn a log heap save your ashes and bring them to the Elk Rapids Potash Works.

Chapter 21
Hotels, Resorts and Restaurants

01 09 80 The Lake View House will be closed after the 15ᵗʰ inst. for the winter. The House will be opened again the spring.

04 02 80 If oleomargarine is so nearly like butter that the difference can only be told by the brand on the package, why not let it pass as butter and have done with it? We dare say it is better than lots of butter made from the cream of cows milk. If it isn't it must be poor stuff indeed.

05 14 80 Quite a number of changes have been made on the interior of the Lake View House. The gentleman's sitting room has been enlarged by taking out the partition between that and the room formerly used for a post office. The parlor above has been enlarged. Other improvements have been made.

05 14 80 Carpenters are at work removing partitions and otherwise enlarging some of the rooms in the Lake View House, which will be opened for guests about the 1st of June. Mr. Geo. A. Dyer, who managed the house so successfully last year, will have charge of it this year.

05 21 80 The owners of the Lake View House have rented the up-stairs part of the building next to it, belonging to S. Yalomstein, and will use the rooms for sleeping apartments in connection with the house. A passage has been made connecting the two buildings. How many tourists will be here this year it will be hard to estimate, but we think they will find when they come good accommodations, plenty of boats, and the best fishing grounds in the world.

05 28 80 A neat picket fence has been built on the west side of the Lake View House.

05 28 80 The Lake View House is receiving a new coat of paint. Mr. Yalomstein's store building will be finished outside exactly in the same manner as the house. A number of fine rooms have been added to the hotel, also a hall for dancing.

06 11 80 Wm.G. Rice, of Ellsworth, Me., is installed as clerk at the Lake View House.

06 11 80 A party of five from Louisville, Ky., are stopping at the Lake View House. Also a party of nine from Cincinnati.

06 18 80 The rooms lately added to the Lake View House have been fitted up in exceedingly good taste and the hall for dancing is going to be a pleasant place to "trip the light fantastic."

06 18 80 Mr. H.H. Noble recently purchased 12 new row boats in Cleveland for the use of guests stopping at the Lake View House.

07 02 80 The old scaffold back of the Cooper building has been torn down which is a good thing for the looks of the building.

07 02 80 The Leland brought 12 row boats for the Lake View House on her last trip here.

07 02 80 A new Steinway upright piano came here on the steamer *City of Grand Rapids* Wednesday for the Lake View House.

07 09 80 The Lewis House at Torch Lake is one of the pleasantest summer resorts north and is on the most beautiful spot of any. Visiting the town one day this week we noticed that the proprietor had spent a good deal of time and money in beautifying his grounds, and we think that his labors will be rewarded. The hotel is near excellent fishing grounds and tourists regard it as the one place to spend the summer. There is a large number of guests at the hotel now and every boat is bringing more. It is a lovely place and it refreshes one greatly to visit it occasionally.

08 27 80 The Hughes House under the management of Mrs. John Hughes has this season done a fine business. The rates are low being only $1 a day, and a good many people traveling take that into consideration. Since purchasing the house she has added several rooms and many improvements, and it is a good house as the many names on the register will show.

10 08 80 The Lake View House will remain open this winter, instead of being closed as it was last winter. The house under the management of Mr. George A. Dyer, has gained a fine reputation with summer guests this season.

11 12 80 The Lake View House boasts of the prettiest storm house in town.

04 29 81 The water pipes leading from the river to the Lake View House, which were frozen this winter are now free from ice and drawing water by "mewel" [sic] power is now dispensed with.

04 29 81 The Hughes House is undergoing extensive repairs this spring, new floors being laid in several rooms and a stone foundation being put under the building. Mrs. Hughes, the proprietress, intends farther improvements another year. The house is well kept and is well patronized by the traveling public.

04 29 81 White fish, lake trout, and very fine black bass have appeared on the Lake View House "bill of fare" for the past few weeks.

05 20 81 The Lake View House is undergoing repairs, and some additions being made to the house. The dining room will be enlarged so as to seat twenty-three more guests and a new kitchen is now being built. Other improvements are contemplated and we will mention them hereafter.

05 20 81 The office of the Lake View House will be enlarged by the addition of a neat reading room.

05 20 81 The Wildman & Peck Company played for five nights at this place last week beginning Tuesday, and ending their engagement Saturday night. Each night they were greeted with full houses, and Friday night the house was so crowded that it was difficult to find standing room. They play well and we are happy to announce that they will appear here again.

05 27 81 WANTED—At the Lewis House, Torch Lake, a good woman cook. Will pay $6.00 or $7.00 per week, also a good pastry cook. Will pay $5.00 or $6.00 per week, and five dining room and chamber girls. Will pay $3.00 or $4.00 per week, and two laundry girls. Will pay $4.00 per week. I hire for the season of June, July, August and September. Apply soon.
    –Frank J. Lewis

05 27 81 The Lake View House dining room has been enlarged, painted, and papered, and is one of the coziest in the country. The house is not near large enough, although the management is perfect. We hope next season to announce that an elegant new hotel has been built, as the reputation of this village as a charming place to spend the summer is now fully established.

06 10 81 A laundry is being built in the rear of the Lake View House.

06 10 81 VISITORS.—J.S. Kline, one of Louisville Ky., best lawyers is in town, J. Banks McIlvain, of Louisville, of the oldest whiskey house in Ky., is here. J.B. Stickney, of Magomaine, Wis., registered at the Lake View House Monday. W.B. Haldiman, of the *Louisville Courier-Journal*, is stopping at the Lake View House.
    Dr. Turner Anderson, a prominent Physician of Kentucky is at the Lake View House. Thomas L. Barrett, of Louisville, Ky., Pres. of the Kentucky State Bank is in town. Dr. J.H. Sutherland of Pertrolia Pa. has been in town for a few days, guest of Geo. D. Wyckoff. "Jack" Cromie, of Louisville, the "Ice King" of the South is stopping at the Lake View House.
Major McDowell, of Louisville, a noted breeder of fine horses in Ky., is spending a few days in town. Dr. E.J. Foree, of Louisville, a very distinguished physician of Kentucky, and the South, is at the Lake View House. C.M. Thruston, of Louisville, Ky., a capitalist and probably the next Mayor of Louisville, is in town. Mr. Thruston was here for some time last season.

06 17 81 Nineteen gentlemen from Louisville, Ky., and Cincinnati, O., came on the *Sutton* Wed. evening, and stopped at the Lake View.

07 08 81 A speckled trout breakfast was served up to all the Lake View House guests Thursday morning, contributed by Mr. J.W. Beesley, the result of his trip to Rapid River. He captured the finest lot of trout we have seen for the season.

07 08 81 The Lake View House was very properly draped last Sunday and Monday on account of the great sorrow felt at the attempted assassination of President Garfield.

07 22 81 The Lake View house has been filled with guests since the opening of the season, and letters are being received each day by the manager of the house from people who wish rooms. The only drawback to Elk Rapids really having hundreds of tourists coming is the want of sufficient hotel accommodations. The management of the L. V. is perfection, and we only regret that a one hundred and fifty room hotel is not built.

08 05 81 A dancing party was given in Lake View Hall Tuesday evening in honor of the Niposink Club, of Rockford Ill. Sixteen of the members of which have been camping at this place. The Lake View Hall is a mighty pleasant one, and was made too look prettier by beautiful house plants scattered about the room.

08 12 81 The Hughes House has enjoyed a splendid business so far this summer- the house being filled with tourists nearly all the time since the season opened.

08 12 81 The Hughes House will provide accommodations to teachers who wish to attend the Institute for $1 per day.

09 02 81 The lamp which lights up the porch at the Lake View House burst Sunday night, and set fire to the house. It was discovered by F.R. Williams Esq., who came from his residence and subdued it. A moment more and the guests at the house would have been coming out "on a fly."

10 07 81 Mr. Joseph Drake gave a dance at his boarding house last evening.
The billiard tables and barber shop at the Lake View House have been removed from the basement to the office for the winter.

10 14 81 Charles Galligan of the barge *Leland,* and Lewis Bailey created a little disturbance last Sunday night at the Hughes House, by tearing up a map and generally throwing things in the office of that hotel. Mrs. Hughes, the proprietress, got out a warrant but no arrests were made. Both were under the influence of liquor which accounts for it.

10 21 81 Mr. Geo. A. Dyer has leased the Lake View House, and will manage it on his own account next season. It is not yet decided whether it will be open to the public during the winter or not...

03 17 82 The work of preparing the Cooper building for the post-office has been in progress some few days. A room 35x35 has been partitioned off, and will be completed at once for the P.O., stationery and news depot, and for C.D. Towne, Jeweler. The other work on the building, as proposed will give about 20 new rooms for the Lake View House; a large dancing hall and dining room. Now if the building could only be raised one story, and the post-office removed to the old Lake View House we could have a hotel that would accommodate 80 or 100 guests.

04 21 82 Mrs. David Spaulsbury intends building a large boarding house on Traverse avenue this spring we learn.

05 12 82 Frank Lewis, of the Lewis House, Torch Lake has a very pretty note head. It is a view of Torch Lake, with the steamer *Queen of the Lakes* lying at the dock. The envelope has a very correct litho. of the Lewis House.

05 19 82 A new aquarium has been built for the office of the Lake View House. It is 2x32 feet, and 18 inches in depth. As soon as it is placed in the office, several speckled trout will be put in, and they can be kept alive indefinitely, as a continuous stream of water will flow into it.

05 26 82 Several handsome rooms have been added to the Lake View House.

05 26 82 The basement at the Lake View House has been kalsomined and painted and the billiard table removed to that room.

05 26 82 Lewis House, Torch Lake - Wanted at the above hotel, one elderly woman for store keeper, four dinning room girls, two chamber girls, two laundry girls, and two for kitchen and to wash dishes. Wages $12.00 and $15.00 a month. I will sign contract to pay $1.50 a week to all help engaged from June 1 until July 1 that I do not want to use till July 1, and they may remain at home till needed. I have never failed to pay my help every dollar agreed. I want good, trusty help, and will pay liberally for such for the season of 1882. Please apply at once, in person if possible.

05 26 82 The aquarium in the Lake View House office, although small, is mighty slick. There is only one speckled trout in it now but it will soon contain several. Dyer knows how to make things pleasant for the Kentuckians if his hotel is small. Next season it will be double the capacity.

05 26 82 The rates of the Hughes House have been raised from $1.00 to $1.40 a day.

05 26 82 The spring work on the Hughes House such as painting, graining and kalsomining has all been accomplished and now this hotel is ready for the season's business.

06 02 82 The Hughes House has had the best business the past two weeks, of any time since it was first opened.

06 02 82 Geo. A. Dyer, of the Lake View House, did us the honor of using our fish catch on his letter heads, cards, envelopes, circulars, etc.

06 16 82 A special car brought the following prominent Nashville, Tenn., citizens to Traverse City, last Saturday night, who are now at the Lake View House; D.N. Brooks, Ticket Agent L.& N.R.R.; W.M. Duncan, Banker; Chas. E. Hillman, Iron Merchant; F. Furman, Dry Goods Merchant; E.D. Hicks, Sec. Commercial Insurance Co.; S.L. Demoville, Druggist; Wm. Porter, Wholesale Dry Goods; Edgar Jones, Cashier 3rd National Bank; Robert Thompson, Oil Manufacturing; L.F. Benson, Wholesale Carpets; E.S. Wheat, United States Marshall; J.M. Bass, Attorney at Law; Wm. W. Berry, Wholesale Druggist; J.P. Foard, Superintendent Hecla Coal Mines; also B.F. Wheat, Pres. 1st National Bank, Quincy, Mich.

06 23 82 The Lake View House dinner bill last Sunday was a new deal. Following the regular courses was the fish catch of the week from the *Progress.* This will be a regular feature every Sunday hereafter. It pleased the guests of the House, and Dyer never stops half way when the happiness and comfort of his guests can be increased. We forgot to mention that the dinner on Sunday, as usual, reflected credit on the management.

07 14 82 Geo. A. Dyer has added six handsome rooms to the Lake View House, and has had them all nicely furnished.

08 04 82 A pipe for conducting water to the new addition to the Lake View House was laid this week.

09 29 82 58 persons took dinner at the Hughes House Tuesday.

10 20 82 Geo. A. Dyer is building a kitchen onto the Cooper building.

Chapter 22
Kalkaska County

01 30 80 A new brick block is to be put up in Kalkaska the coming season.

05 14 80 Goldman and Yalomstein sold to J. B. Richard, of Wilson township, 40 acres of Kalkaska County land Monday for $100.

07 16 80 The Orange men celebrated at Kalkaska the 12th. Threats were made that if they did parade the village would be fired, but nothing occurred to interrupt the parade.

04 29 81 We learn that Bond's saw mill at Fife Lake burned Sunday last, and also a quantity of lumber. The fire is supposed to have caught from the slab pit. The loss is estimated at $40,000.

05 13 81 Ben. F. Davis, editor of the *Traverse Bay Progress*, was in town two or three days this week, and made us a pleasant visit. He is bound to have a railroad from Kalkaska to Elk Rapids, and we hope and believe his expectation will be realized. — *Kalkaskian*, Kalkaska.

Of course we are bound to have a railroad. Kalkaska is a thriving, busy town, and is rapidly growing. The route between Kalkaska and Elk Rapids is level, the roadbed would require little work done on it, and it would run through some of the very best farming land North. It is only a question of a few years before we'll have the road. We went over to Kalkaska on purpose to see Sweet about it.

Eight years ago the writer was in the village of Kalkaska, that was to be, when the town boasted of seven saloons, and one saw-mill and no dwelling houses. The Kalkaska village of to-day is wholly different. The town has a population of 697, is rapidly increasing in population and new houses are being rapidly built. One of the finest buildings is the "brick block," owned by,A.A. Bleazby, C.P. Sweet, A.E. Palmer and McVean & Beebe. It is the finest building in Grand Traverse Region and reflects great credit on the town. Two papers are published here- *Kalkaskian* and the *Leader* and both are doing a fine business. One improvement to the town would be a good hotel, and it would pay some energetic man to put one up there. Eight years ago there was not a dwelling house there but a great change has been made for the better. Kalkaska is now a fine thriving town, with good farming lands near and we predict for it a prosperous future.

10 07 81 William Copeland, of Barkers Creek, sends to the *Kalkaskian* the following "I noticed in your paper that Fred Ford cradled 1,134 bundles of oats in one day. W.H. Bockes cradled 1,632 bundles of wheat for me inside of ten hours, and Martin Moran raked and bound them. Beat that and we will set them up.

10 14 81 Considerable excitement was occasioned in Kalkaska this week on account of the sudden disappearance of O.S. Curtis, a prominent business man of this village. In company with his wife he attended the fair at Grand Rapids, and while there left for parts unknown.

From Chicago he sent a deed of all his property to his wife. His most intimate friends claim that the cause of his departure was domestic and financial difficulties; but it seems to us that financially he could have got along well enough had he attended to his business. His stock of hardware will more than pay all the claims against it, but the grocery establishment of Curtis &Cronin did not pan out so well.

When Curtis left he took and charged to himself between six and seven hundred dollars—which had been laid away to pay some of their bills. Freeman, Hawkins & Co., of Grand Rapids, had the largest claim against the stock, which they vied [sic] on and sold to McVean & Beebe. Mr. Cronin informs us that after everything belonging to the firm is turned over to the creditors it will leave him no less than $1,000 in debt.

Mr. Curtis has been a very popular man in Kalkaska, and from the organization of the county until last fall was County Clerk and Register of Deeds. We understand that the hardware store will soon be re-opened and operated by Mrs. Curtis.

12 02 81 The schools of Kalkaska have been closed on account of diphtheria. The board of health of that village has ordered notices to be posted on all buildings rendered dangerous by the presence of diphtheria.

05 12 82 *Kalkaskian:* We have counted seventeen new buildings about town, either in progress or about to be commenced.

The board of Supervisors, at its recent session, took the preliminary steps toward building a new court house.

06 16 82 Oliver Isbell, of Garfield, Kalkaska county, met with rather a sad accident Tuesday, while shooting hawks with a revolver. He had shot several times and thought all the cartridges had been discharged, and to make sure placed his eye in range with the chambers in the cylinder, which brought his mouth in close proximity with the muzzle of the weapon, when it went off the ball passing through his upper lip and lodging in the left side of his face, just under the cheek bone. Considerable difficulty will doubtless be encountered by the physicians ere the ball can be extracted. — *Fife Lake Eye.*

12 08 82 At a recent term of the circuit court at Kalkaska, Newell, who was charged with raping his own child, was acquitted.

Chapter 23
Village of Kewadin

04 21 82 G.D. Wyckoff intends removing soon to Indian Town and keeping a store in the place now occupied by E.H. Hale.

10 27 82   **MURDER !**

Last Saturday night word was brought to this village that a murder had been committed beyond Indian town. The Prosecuting Attorney, who was then at Traverse City, was informed of the fact arrived about 1 o'clock; Sunday morning. In the meantime Joseph P. Mullery, Christopher Hughes and Perry Stocking started for the scene and arrested Joseph Nah-sho-ga-she, better known as Joseph Wah-be-ska, and George Ge-wa-je-wan, son of Gabriel O-ge-ta-na-quet; more commonly called Pe-ton-ne-quet, as the ones supposed to have murdered Peter Pe-dwa-we-dam, commonly called Peter Ke-wa-din and nearly murdered Peter Mark Nah-we-ge-shig, usually called P.M. From one who saw them that night we glean the following facts: It seems that the four mentioned left this place late in the afternoon of said day, considerably under the influence of liquor, and when they arrived at Banninger's they filled with three pitchers of wine. Just before leaving the house, one of the accused called some one a vile name and Ke-wa-din remonstrated with him, and this is where the quarrel of the night commenced, although we learn that there had been previous ill feeling. When they arrived just this side of Hi Robinson's place some harsh words were interchanged when the two accused took heavy clubs from the fence and knocked the two others down and commenced beating them about the heads with their clubs.
Conrad Bachi, who lives near where the crime was committed, said that the Indians would pound them and then run around and whoop. Hi Robinson informs us that on Saturday night about 8 o'clock, Mary Ke-wa-din came to his house and told him that the Indians were killing her husband. Hurrying to the spot he met Wah-be-ska and Geo. Pe-ton-ne-quet, each carrying clubs, and upon going down the road some distance, found Peter Ke-wa-din and P.M. lying on the ground. Throwing the light of his lantern upon them he says he never saw such a sight. Ke-wa-din was lying in a pool of blood, and his face all covered with blood. Mr. Robinson says he went immediately for water and bathed Pe-ton-ne-quet's face, and found a fearful wound just above his right eye, the skull completely crushed in. After bathing his face he says that he lived about twenty minutes. The next morning on going to the spot he found a piece of the skull, which is now in Dr. Bailey's possession. P.M.'s wounds were of such a serious nature that he was thought to be dying several times. His skull was crushed in above his right eye, in almost the same place that Pe-ton-ne-quet's was, and it is said he cannot live. The prisoners waved examination Monday, and on Tuesday they were taken to Bellaire, where their trial will come off before the Circuit Court next December.

Chapter 24
Leelanau County

04 02 80 **MURDER AND SUICIDE.**
The Suspected Murderer Cuts His Throat.
— His Victims Body Found In A Well.

Special Telegram to the *Progress.*
Leland, Mich., Mar. 27, 1880.
Adam Deygenkolb, who some four months ago was suspected of foul dealings with his wife, who disappeared, and he reported that she was crazy, and had run away, killed himself last night by cutting his throat from ear to ear. A party of citizens from Northport and Leland went to his house to-day and surrounded it. He went up stairs to get his clothes, and soon a heavy fall was heard by those below, who rushed up to find him as above stated. Search of the premises was made and it was found that his well had been filled up. On removing the dirt the body of his wife was found with her throat cut and her face bruised considerably.

04 29 81 The *Leelanau Tribune* changes hands again and the paper has suspended publication for a few weeks.

05 06 81 The *Leelanau Tribune* will not hereafter be published at Suttons Bay. It will be published at Traverse City.

12 23 81 The Leelanau county seat removal question is beginning to agitate the minds of the residents of that county. A vote will be taken in the spring upon the question of its removal from Northport to Leland.

01 27 82 Large numbers of settlers are now coming into Leelanau county looking for farms upon which to establish permanent homes.
D.H. Day, manager for the Northern Michigan Co., at Glen Haven, informs us that he will get out about 1,000,000 feet of hardwood logs and about 4,000 cords of wood.
We are informed that the Leland Iron Co.'s furnace will, not go into blast until about the middle of February. They have been putting in new gas-pipes, and making other repairs which were needed.
The Leland Iron Co. has put up several new buildings at their camps this winter, one of which is the spacious and commodious building occupied by Mr. Charles Gillmore, foreman of camp No. 1

01 27 82 NORTHPORT, JAN. 26, 1882. — The town hall was burned this morning. The town library was burned, but the records, and town books were saved.

02 03 82 On Wednesday morning of last week, the court house at Northport, burned. The Probate records and the law library of Geo. A. Cutler, Esq., were burned. The county records and the Circuit Court records were in safes and were uninjured. The fire is thought to be the work of an incendiary.

03 24 82 *Suttons Bay Telephone:* One day last week the little son of Wm. Brown, of Leland, met with a narrow escape. He was in the furnace where they were breaking up iron when a small piece struck him on the cheek passing through his mouth and out through the other cheek, taking with it, two teeth.

03 24 82 *Suttons Bay Telephone:* The Leland Iron Co's furnace is now turning out from 36 to 39 tons of iron per day. The Company is preparing to rebuild their saw-mill, to fit up both tugs and two lighters, building new kilns, and a general boom in business is the outlook for Leland the coming season.

03 31 82 *Leelanau Enterprise:* The Leland Iron Co. are making between 35 and 40 tons of iron per day now which makes business lively at Leland.

12 08 82 The new court house for Leelanau county, furnished by the town of Leland is a neat and commodious building.

Chapter 25
Elk Rapids Township Library

05 28 80 The town library has been removed to the building east of theP.O.

10 28 81 There are now 28 members to the Elk Rapids Literary Society.

Chapter 26
Logging

03 29 78 *Benzie County Journal* says that J.J. Hubbell had a hemlock tree cut down recently at Benzonia, which was 462 years old.

10 18 78 H.E. Jackson of Custer had an elm tree cut recently which measured 7 feet at right angles across the stump and measured 14 feet in circumference 50 feet above the stump. There was also a basswood 65 feet to the first limb, 2 feet 6inches diameter 50 feet below the first limb.

01 02 80 Those getting out wood on the Elk Lake road now draw it on the road recently made, which is built through the woods on Mr.Steele's place and on other farms in this vicinity.

01 09 80 Traverse City has shipped to Chicago during the past season 21,504,000 feet of lumber. Frankfort shipped 11,152,000.

11 26 80 The Tittabawasee boom company ran out 575,000,000 feet of logs this season against 455,000,000 last season. In 1878 they ran out 328,000,000.

01 14 81 The largest maple log that has been scaled for Wadsworth & Thurston was put in by C.C. Coulter. It was 12 ft. long and contained 631 feet.

01 14 81 We have now had over 60 days good sleighing and expect to have 60 or 100 days more of the same sort. Some complain of too much snow in the woods for convenience in getting around with teams.

02 04 81 A car load of black walnut logs, the first ever brought into Traverse City, arrived from the southern part of the State, Thursday. They were purchased by G.F. Murray & Co., proprietors of the veneer mill, who will manufacture them into veneer.

02 11 81 Daniel Staley recently cut a basswood tree on his farm at South Arm Charlevoix county, which measured fifty-three inches in diameter at the butt, cut five twelve-foot logs and scaled 3,147 feet.

06 10 81 There is said to be 350,000,000 feet of logs in the Muskegon and its tributaries above Big Rapids, and the boom company intend to provide electric lights for night work in running out the logs.

01 20 82 The past ten days has been well improved by the lumber company of C.T. Scofield & Son Williamsburg, in getting logs into the yard as well as in moving lumber to the Follett landing on Elk Lake. Hereafter the lumber manufactured at this mill will be shipped by the way of the lake to Elk Rapids and pass through the hands of Dexter & Noble.

02 03 82 Some men who were chopping wood in the eastern part of Antrim county, cut into a hollow tree and were startled to find that it contained the skeleton of a man. —*Sentinel*, Charlevoix.

02 03 82 Wm. McDougal and Perry Stocking in twenty-two days cut 85 cords of wood and 12,000 feet of logs for Messrs. Hollenbeck & Frink of Milton. After the job was done Mr. Frink presented each of them with $2.00 apiece extra.

02 10 82 George Lackey, brought with one of Isaac Love's teams Monday, a load of green wood from Q. Thacker's farm at Yuba, which measured six cords of 18 inch wood. It was drawn a distance of five miles.

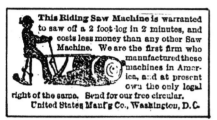

02 17 82 One day last week Mr. Geo. Steimel jr., of Suttons Bay cut a large oak tree. It was seven feet one inch across the stump and occupied three hours and a-half to cut it down. The next day two men were sent to cut it into saw logs and they sawed two hours without seeing each other, the timber was so tough and curly.

02 24 82 R.W. Coy, of Spencer Creek, put in a stick of board timber, on the bank of Torch Lake, (hauling the same 22 miles) which contained 275 cubic feet, equal to 2,750 feet of lumber. Who can beat it?

02 24 82 If there is a cord wood chopper in Antrim Co. that has not cut off a toe, or heel, or split a three cornered chip from his feet or ankles, this winter, let him come forward as a curiosity.

03 24 82 *Traverse City Herald* In D. McRaes' camp, near the head of Carp Lake, Leelanau county, there was recently cut a stick of fine timber squaring 29 inches and measuring 46 feet in length. Scale, 4,000 feet.

04 14 82 BELLAIRE—Our lumberman, James M. Wadsworth, has purchased and sold the following amount of logs and timber during the past winter: 1,200,000 feet of hardwood to the Elk Rapids Iron Co.; 600,000 feet of pine, and sold the same to the Iron Co.: and 80,000 cubic feet of board pine, and sold the same to Burton Bros., Barry, Ontario Canada. The whole number of feet, including hardwood and pine, is about 2,760,000 feet, costing him about $20,000. We learn that he intends to increase his business the coming year. He left to-day for Bellaire to commence breaking rollways along the river.

05 12 82 Pascal Kimball cut this winter on his farm in Grand Traverse county a sugar maple tree and from it took seven cords of block wood and one cord of four-foot wood, and there is one more cord of block wood to be yet taken from the tree. Our informant of the above, James R. Dean Sr., says that last winter he cut down a bass-wood tree which was six and one-half feet across the stump and that he cut it down in four hours and a half.

05 26 82 The timber passing down the river to the bay parted the water pipes leading to the residence of E.S. Noble and to the Chemical Laboratory of Norman M. Pierce, thereby causing great inconvenience to Mr. Noble and entirely stopping the chemical processes of Mr. Pierce.

05 26 82 The square timber now being loaded on the British barges and gotten out by James M. Wadsworth is of superior quality. It seems a pity that such valuable timber cannot be utilized at home.

06 09 82 Monday of this week 156 feet of basswood lumber was cut in Marsh's mill, Elgin, in 42 minutes, with 8 horse power.

06 23 82 A scow load of lumber went up the lake Tuesday morning- material for a cord-wood camp. Ten carpenters went on the tug to put up the camp, which is to be used by 50 Canadians, who are expected here to work for the Iron Co. this summer.

06 23 82 About $14,500 worth of square timber was shipped from here this spring.

08 25 82 A few days ago Merril L. Lake of Elmwood township, Leelanau county, cut 37 four feet rings of bark from one hemlock tree. The tree itself was only of medium diameter, but a straight and beautiful specimen of this wood, as indeed it must have been to have cut 148 running feet of bark.

10 20 82 At the present rate of consumption it is estimated that the supply of white pine timber in the United States will be exhausted in twelve years.

10 20 82 *The Northwestern Lumberman* advises the settlers of northern Michigan to "go slow" in the clearing of their land. It says that it seems like a great waste of natural wealth to cut and burn up the "majestic maples" for the only purpose of getting them out of the way, so that the land on which they grow can be cultivated, and that if the new settlers on Michigan forest lands would cut off the timber no faster than they can clear the land well, they would make money by raising better crops and saving their timber. Our advice is, clear just as fast as you can, clear the land well and cultivate it thoroughly- no faster. Turn to the best account the timber on the land you clear- it may be best to burn it up- and protect carefully your remaining woodland. The "majestic maples" are growing annually more valuable.

11 10 82 *Traverse City Eagle* –Broadfort & Carrier shipped nine sets of logging wheels away Wednesday morning. They are building these wheels at the rate of a complete set every day and we understand have a contract now in hand for forty sets.

08 11 82   GOOD BABIES.

`Tis a jolly day from East to West,
For children thrive, and mothers rest,
The darling girls all named Victoria,
And with the boys, they have Castoria.
It is a fact, there is no "may be,"
A mother's milk can't save the baby,
While sweet Castoria digests their food,
Gives them health and makes them good.

Chapter 27
Village of Mancelona

01 30 80 Perry Andress, of Mancelona, has purchased the Occidental House at Petoskey and has gone there to take charge of it. Jacob Passage has taken charge of the Mancelona House.

07 23 80 The Democrats at Mancelona formed a Hancock and English club on Saturday last with the following officers;

President	C.B. Person.
Secretary	Dr. E.E.C. Kellogg.
Treasurer	Peter Jackson.

08 20 80 The first number of Vol. 2 of *The Mancelona Herald* is at hand. We were glad to welcome its first number and we hope that its proprietors will make heaps 'o money. It has done good work in opening up and advertising the eastern portion of the county, and should be liberally supported. We have only one objection to it—its politics are bad.

10 01 80 L.C. Handy, of Mancelona, is shipping rye south, 500 bushels being the amount of his first shipment.

Work is progressing on the new Congregational church at Mancelona. It will be an ornament to the town when finished.

02 11 81 The Methodists of Mancelona have decided to build a house of worship the coming season. The society numbers about fifty persons. They contemplate building a church 32x55 which will cost not to exceed $1,200.

03 18 81 Perry Andress, of Petoskey, formerly proprietor of a hotel in Mancelona died last Thursday night.

03 25 81 The Citizen's Judicial Convention was assembled at Mancelona on Friday, the 18th inst...

08 05 81 The Mancelona House boasts of a boy who will "shine eyer boots for a nickel" in the most approved fashion.

08 25 81 The Mancelona Handle Co. is a fact and commenced operations. Tally one for Mancelona.

10 21 81 Something new: A first class furniture store in Mancelona.

10 28 81 Mr. N. McKechnie harvested 230 bushels of potatoes from one acre of ground, the timber from which was cut last April. The cost of the land was $7 an acre, and the crop sold for $140. The cost of labor on the crop up to the time of digging was $6.

11 04 81 During the past seven months thirteen new buildings have been erected in Mancelona.

182

12 02 81 MANCELONA—There are eighty pupils enrolled in our schools.

The building committee of the Congregational church report the total amount received from all sources, since June 24, 1881, $830.40. Total expenditures $837.36, making the amount paid out $7.06 more than received. The pledges unpaid amount $114.62, and the bills payable to $97.09, leaving a net balance in favor of the church when pledges are all paid, of $17.53. As some of these pledges will not be paid, it will be necessary to raise some money to meet this deficiency.

12 09 81 Mrs. Perry Andress has erected a beautiful monument on the Andress lot in the cemetery. Besides the Inscription it bears a Masonic emblem composed of the square and compass.

12 23 81 Parties in Mancelona are buying large quantities of maple and basswood logs, for the New England furniture company, of Grand Rapids.

On Friday evening last week, our citizens were called out to respond to a fire alarm. The new town hall proved to be on fire beneath the floor of the first story. By the prompt action of the citizens the fire was soon extinguished. The fire originated from a defective heater that had been set up to dry the plastering.

01 27 82 Mr. David Ward, of Detroit, has paid his taxes in Mancelona, to Treasurer Savage. The tax was $1,366.81

03 24 82 The *Mancelona Herald*: While assisting in placing a new collar on the "pet" bear at the Mancelona House on Tuesday last, Dr. Miller received a severe and painful wound on his left hand from the teeth of the brute, tearing the ligaments of the hand between the first and second fingers and badly crushing the index finger.

03 31 82 The *Mancelona Herald*: The "pet" bear that has so long reigned monarch of the back yard of the Mancelona House is no more.

Charlevoix Sentinel: Iron men said to be those of the Pine Lake Iron Co., have been during the past week looking up a site for a furnace along the northern portion of the G.R.& I.R.R. and have finally selected a location at Mancelona, at which place 40 acres of land has been pledged to them. Our informant was a Petoskey gentleman, who saw the dispatches announcing this result. Mancelona was selected because of the probability of a branch railroad from this place via the head of South Arm and Ironton to Charlevoix. The Petoskey gentleman referred to stated to the editor of this paper that he expected to see a locomotive in Charlevoix within 18 months. It certainly looks more that way than ever before.

04 07 82 *Mancelona Herald*: Judge Edwards has made an order appointing Mrs. Maggie M. Kellogg, of Mancelona a School Examiner in place of Mr.S.F. Hill who resigned. Mrs. Kellogg is a lady of refinement, eminently qualified for the position. She is a teacher of experience, being at the present time principal of the Mancelona schools. We can heartily recommend her to the older members of the board and to the teachers of Antrim county.

04 14 82 S.F. Hill, of Mancelona, was in town Wednesday and informed us that the furnace at that place was an assured thing, and that work on it had commenced. Mr. Hill also informed us that the furnace to be built would be the same size as the one here.

Let us predict a little. If that furnace goes up at Mancelona, in two years that town will be the largest town in the county. Eight years ago when the publisher of this paper was there, one log hotel and one store constituted the town. Now it has 13 stores with the prospect of the 14th, with a first-class hotel, and the town is on the road to a successful future.

04 14 82 C.S. Edward has sold his interest in The *Mancelona Herald* to L.E. Slussar the Junior partner of the firm. The *Herald* has gained a fine reputation under the old management, and we will have no doubt sustain its reputation under the new.

04 21 82 *Mancelona Herald*: Mancelona shows her enterprise in securing the location of the blast furnace at this place. Efforts were made by Boyne Falls and other points to secure it but without avail. The advantages offered by the excellent water supply, the splendid timber in the vicinity, and the interest manifested by our citizens in the enterprise, induced the gentlemen owning the furnace to favor its location here. The company have purchased forty acres of land situated on the bank of Passage's lake, and the citizens twenty more lying on the west side of the railroad and adjacent to that purchased by the company.

05 19 82 The Mancelona furnace company having imported a gang of negroes to work in their furnace business, the citizens of the village, or a portion of them at least, are indignant.

05 26 82 The *Mancelona Herald* says this about the twelve colored gentlemen who have located there: The squeamish ones are few and far between. However, if we have no worse people locate among us than the twelve colored gentlemen from Richmond, we may consider ourselves extremely lucky.

06 02 82 *Evening News*: Mancelona is now in the throes of a "religious war," which, as is usual in such disturbances, hasn't any too much religion in it. It appears that the Congregationalists imported a revivalist from Boston to stir up the dry bones, and he has done it with unexpected results. The Methodist pastor took occasion to make some remarks about the Bostonian or his work, and came down too heavy to suit some of the church folks, who got wrathy and sided with the revivalists. Then on Wednesday the later sailed into the Methodist pastor and let fly a broadside that made the whole village quake. The affair has since got so hot that the presiding Elder has arrived to see if he cannot cool down the fever a little and thus avoid what the world's people think is a most ungodly strife.

06 30 82 *Traverse City Herald*: Hon. C.S. Edwards, formerly of the *Mancelona Herald*, will, about the middle of July, establish a paper at Elmira, Otsego county, to be called the *Elmira Gazette*. It will be a six-column quarto. Judge Edwards is a good newspaper man and will give the people of that county an excellent paper.

08 11 82 Thirty Germans direct from Castle Garden arrived in Mancelona on Tuesday. Most of them are at work at the furnace.

08 25 82 W.R. Rice, a Justice of the peace, at Mancelona, has been charged with misconduct in office, and Gov.Serome has appointed a commission to investigate said charges.

09 15 82 A new meat market is being erected on State street.
A certain insurance agent, of this place has traded a good watch off for a good dog. Good trade.

     The fact that 85 good, substantial buildings have been erected in Mancelona during the past year is proof sufficient that the town is growing.

09 21 82 L.M. Handy, of Mancelona, is preparing to build a tasty and commodious house.

     The lime kilns at the Mancelona furnace are being built and will soon be ready for operations.

09 22 82 Wetzell Bros.' new mill arrived last week and will at once be put up. The firm intend to be in running order again in the course of 60 days.

10 05 82 We have a German Sunday school.

     C.W. Jones, the new M.E. Pastor, means business in his endeavor to raise the mortgage on the new church. He ought to succeed.

10 20 82 School will soon commence in the new school house.
Street lamps now shed their welcome "glimmer'" over the streets of this village.

10 27 82 Work on the Mancelona furnace is progressing slowly on account of an incompetent foreman.

     The Methodists of Mancelona have paid off their church debt and raised enough money to by a bell.

11 03 82 The furnace company intend getting their furnace in shape to go into blast some time in December.

     W.W. Sweet will clear his addition to this village during the winter. This is an improvement much needed.

11 10 82 Mancelona's "ball alley" will soon be in operation.

     The first load of iron ore for the Mancelona blast furnace arrived last Sunday.

11 17 82 W.S. Mesick, Esq., of Mancelona, received one vote for Prosecuting Attorney, at Mancelona. Mr. Mesick has a great many admirers.

     Rodenburg Bros. are fairly settled in their new store, down under the town hall.

     The brass band had a benefit last Friday evening. It was a dance at the town hall, and netted about $19.00. What would benefit some of the members more than a dance would be 18 years practice under an efficient instructor. However they are improving and can now play "Hold the Fort" in such a style that no regiment of veterans under heaven could be induced to undertake its capture when the band was inside playing.

11 24 82 Ed King goes to Alba to start a billiard hall.

One of our prominent builders took leave quickly for parts unknown last week. The interest comes in the fact that he took along a considerable amount of money belonging to building firm with which he was connected.

Quite a little excitement was occasioned last week by the discovery by Geo. Ricker, of a loss of a considerable quantity of goods from a chamber where they had been stored for safe keeping. They were finally found under the bed of one of our citizens. Some one took the goods, just for fun, and hid them there when he slept. In consideration of the fact that it was all a joke, we withhold names.

Evening News: Iron ore for the new furnace at Mancelona on the G.R.& I. railroad is now arriving at Mackinaw City from a mine on the Marquette, Houghton & Ontonagon railroad, thus going to the furnace without change of cars or breaking bulk.

Mancelona Herald: J.J. Otis, one of the proprietors of the Iron Furnace came nearly being the victim of a fatal accident last Monday morning. As it was, he received a severe scalp wound, produced by a triangular block of wood, falling from the elevator a distance of some fifty feet and striking him on the head.

12 15 82 School under the tuition of Prof. Simmons, from Albion, has commenced in the new school building.

Mancelona Herald: A serious accident happened at the furnace on Monday last, which may yet have a fatal termination. Call Williams, one of the carpenters employed on the building, was fastening some bolts in the bridge, which runs from the kilns to the top of the stack, when he lost his balance and fell a distance of 40 feet, alighting on a pile of scantling and striking on the right side of his head, producing a fracture of both tables of the skull, just back of the ear, and resulting in concussion of the brain. He has been in a semi-conscious condition since the accident and the attending physician has slight hopes of his recovery. As we go to press we learn the injured man is slowly improving.

12 22 82 J.H. Passage has sold his village plat of Mancelona, to D. St. John, of Fostoria, Ohio. Consideration $7,500. Mr. St. John is largely interested in lands, in that vicinity; is public spirited and has large means.

Chapter 28
Marine Activities

01 02 80 During the season the number of vessels at this port exclusive of the bay boats and those on the inland lakes, is 68. Those leaving this port 68. The tonnage received at this port for the same time, 20,000 gross tons. The number of tons shipped, 14,499. No. of small craft which came here 10, with a combined tonnage of 114 tons: making a total tonnage of 20,114 tons received and the total number of arrivals 78, exclusive of the inland lakes and bay boats.

01 02 80 The barge *Leland* came into port Tuesday night from Chicago with a load of hay together with general merchandise. We believe this is the last trip for the season and she will lay up here.

01 09 80 Messrs. Wadsworth & Thurston will place a steam yacht 34 feet long on Central and Intermediate lakes.

01 30 80 The barge *Leland* is being over hauled and repaired. Workmen have been employed the past week in enlarging the hatches and fixing the coal bins and making other necessary improvements.

02 06 80 Last Saturday night the barge *Leland* broke away from the dock by the parting of the head-lines. After some little work she was brought up all right.

03 05 80 The tug *Torch Lake* tried to force a passage through the ice on Elk Lake Wednesday, but the effort proved ineffectual.

03 05 80 The propeller, *A.C. VanRaalte*, which has run on Grand Traverse Bay for several seasons past, will, we see by the *Detroit Free Press*, tow barges the coming season.

03 05 80 The barge *Leland* is having quite extensive repairs made on her.
  The tug *Torch Lake* has been repaired and fitted up, and is now ready to commence her summer's work on the inland lakes.

03 12 80 The steamer *Jennie Sutton* has received a new coat of paint the past week and otherwise repaired for summer business.

03 12 80 The tug *Elk Lake* has been pumping out the wood scows preparatory to the coming season.

03 12 80 Owing to the scarcity of wood at the furnace the tug *Elk Lake* took men with axes up the river last Tuesday morning to break the ice so that she could take the scows to a banking ground for wood.

03 12 80 The steamer *Clara Belle* was at the dock yesterday afternoon with merchandise for Dexter & Noble.

03 19 80 The tug *Elk Lake* broke her rudder posts and chains Wednesday.

03 19 80 A canal three miles long was cut through the ice on Elk Lake this week, through ice ten inches thick, to allow the passage of the tug *Elk Lake* with her scows for wood, the Furnace being nearly out of it. Every morning the ice in the canal has been frozen to about a quarter of an inch, and it was this ice that broke the rudder chains and post of the tug. The tug has made trips every day and has brought back full loads of wood.

03 26 80 The *Clara Belle* is now making regular trips here.

03 26 80 During the violent storm last Tuesday the barge *Leland* parted her lines and came very near going ashore. By calling men from the furnace and elsewhere, she was brought back to the dock without damage to her. She had parted all her lines and was held by only the anchor which was dragging.

03 26 80 The late severe storm everlastingly ripped the deck off of the schooner *Two Fannies*. Her after deck has all been swept away to the main mast, and the port side of her forward deck is gone. We saw sometime ago in one of our exchanges something to the effect that some one was going to make some money out of that wreck. If we have many more such storms as Tuesday gave us, the divers will have hard work to find it.

03 26 80 Capt. Galligan arrived in town Monday to be here when the barge *Leland* starts.

03 26 80 The barge *Leland* will commence running between this place and Escanaba the 1st of April.

04 02 80 Messrs. Wadsworth & Thurston purchased some time ago a steam yacht to run on Clam and Grass Lakes. Mr. Wadsworth brought her from Traverse City to this place. She is 25 feet long and is a perfect beauty, with the name of *Snipe*. Wednesday she was taken to Torch Lake village.

04 02 80 Last Sunday the tug *Elk Lake* made a trip up Elk Lake for wood. After loading two scows the ice was seen moving, and before the tug could be turned around the ice came against them, sinking the two scows. The tug received only slight injury to her wheel.

04 09 80 A schooner supposed to be the *Holly* went down the bay Wednesday afternoon.

04 09 80 The barge *Leland* has been loaded with pig iron, and yesterday she started on her first trip to Chicago.

04 09 80 We stated last week that Messrs. Wadsworth & Thurston's yacht was to run on Grass and Clam lakes. We correct it by saying that she will run on the Intermediate chain of lakes, of which Central Lake is the foot. The name of the yacht has been changed to *Wah-wa-tay-see*, the meaning of which is "Firefly."

04 09 80 County Convention Round Trip. The steam yacht *Wahwataysee* will leave Bellaire (Green's Landing) for Central Lake, stopping at Cutler's, Bedell's and Snowflake, on Saturday, April 24th, 1880 at ten (10) o'clock a.m. Fare for round trip to and from the County Convention, fifty cents. –Wadsworth & Thurston.

04 16 80 The steamer *City of Traverse* arrived at Traverse City last Tuesday morning, took on a cargo of lumber, and left for Chicago Wednesday evening. She has been newly furnished, her accommodations nearly doubled, and is now as she always has been one of the best passenger boats on the great lakes.

04 23 80 The barge *V. Swain* with her consort came in Sunday night for a cargo of iron. The wind was blowing pretty fresh when she came in and it being dark she came near running foul of the *Two Fannies*.

Mr. R. Myers, of Chicago, the owner of the schooner *Two Fannies*, has been in town the past week. He will try to raise her.

04 23 80 During the fearful storm that passed over this region last Sunday the tug *Elk Lake* was coming down Elk Lake with two scows loaded with wood. The waves were running so high that the tug was obliged to let go her hold to keep from swamping. Thirty cords of wood were swept from the scows, which were driven ashore.

04 23 80 The barge *V. Swain* left this port Wednesday night for Milwaukee for a load of grain. She will call here for her consort, which is being loaded with iron and then go to Cleveland.

The barge *Leland* returned from Chicago Sunday with a part of a load of merchandise for Messrs. Dexter & Noble. She will load with iron and go to Cleveland.

04 23 80 The steamer *City of Traverse* has under gone some extensive repairs the past winter. Visiting Traverse City one day this week we took that opportunity to have a look at her. Her boilers have been removed from the main deck to her hold, and the deck hand's room from the promenade to the forward part of the main deck. The cabin which is elegantly fitted up, runs the entire length of her with staterooms on either side. She has now accommodations for 150 passengers, and is now one of the best passenger boats on the lakes.

The steamer *Queen of the Lakes* is being painted and otherwise refitted.

04 30 80 The schooner *Mary Ann*, Capt. Gallagher from Beaver Islands arrived here Tuesday.

The schooner *Reed Case* touched here Wednesday partly loaded with oats. She took on a deck load of iron and sailed Wednesday for Cleveland.

The steamer *City of Grand Rapids* made her appearance at this port Monday for the first time this season. As all of our readers know how elegantly she is fitted out, we will no more than mention that she has run on her old route the past week. On going aboard her Monday we were informed that her time would be changed from that of last year making the round trip between Traverse City and Petoskey in one day.

05 07 80 The barge *Leland* came in Wednesday with a cargo of coal.
The schooner *Melvina* made this port Wednesday with a cargo of lime stone.

The steamer *Queen of the Lakes* is receiving a new coat of paint and is being thoroughly fitted out for the season. Her run on the "Six Lakes" is a delightful one. She will commence making regular trips the latter part of the month.

The steamer *Jennie Sutton* will run this season the same as last between Elk Rapids and East Bay: Connecting with the *Queen of the Lakes* at this place for Torch Lake. The *Sutton* is nearly ready for the summer's business and will commence running the latter part of this month.

The schooner *C.R. Crawford* came here Saturday afternoon and took all the rigging from the *Two Fannies.* She also took the rigging which had been removed by orders of Mr. Henry Noble and left for the Beaver Islands Monday for 8,000 railroad ties to be delivered in Chicago. Captain Myers, the owner of the Two Fannies has contracted with R.W. Coy, of Spencer Creek, for 150 telegraph poles which will be put in the hold of the *Two Fannies* to raise her. After she is afloat the captain will have a steam pump from Chicago to pump the water from her. She will then be taken to Chicago where she will be placed in a dry-dock and repaired. The captain thinks her hull is good below the plancher.[sis]

05 14 80 The tug *Elk Lake* is being painted.

The schooner *Two Fannies* is at anchor off this place.

The tug *Torch Lake* has been fitted up and is now running with Joe Hawley as captain.

A raft of square timber is at the head of the river waiting for a schooner to take it to Quebec.

The schooner *Cora* of Benton Harbor, called at this port Wednesday, and took on a load of potatoes.

The schooner *Melvina* left this port with a load of iron for Buffalo. She was towed from the dock by the steamer *Clare Belle.*

05 21 80 The tug *Leviathan* and consort, cleared this port Wednesday.

The tug *Elk Lake* has been refitted and now looks like a new boat.

The steamer *Jennie Sutton* will be ready to run as soon as she gets an engineer.

The schooner, *E.M. Carrington,* came in Wednesday morning for a load of iron for Chicago.

The crew are all aboard of the *Queen of the Lakes,* and she is nearly ready to go into commission.

The tug *Leviathan* came to this place last Friday bringing with her a steam pump to be used in raising the *Two Fannies.*

05 21 80 The tug *Leviathan* left this port Wednesday in response to a telegram to assist the schooner *C.J. King* which had gone ashore at Gull Island.

James McClusky, wheelsman on the barge *Leland* fell through the hold from the main deck. He was quite badly injured but will be all right in a few days.

05 21 80 The Steamer *Jennie Silkman* brought down the last raft of square timber to this place, Thursday from up the lakes. It will be loaded here on the schooners and shipped to Quebec.

05 21 80 Capt. Myers returned to this place from Chicago this week to superintend raising the schooner *Two Fannies.*

06 04 80 The tug *Leviathan,* considering all things is making good progress with the wreck *Two Fannies.*

The steam yacht *Little Western* is making trips between this place and Bellaire.

The steamer *Jennie Sutton* commenced making regular trips to East Bay last Wednesday.

The steamer *Queen of the Lakes* made a short run into Elk Lake last Sunday to try her machinery.

The *Queen of the Lakes* has commenced making regular trips between Elk Rapids and Torch Lake, touching at intermediate points. She will make the round trip in two days for the present.

The wrecking tug *Levithan* and consort arrived here Monday afternoon. Last Thursday she arrived at Detroit with the schooner *C.G. King,* which she released from Gull Island on the 24th, in tow. The *King* was loaded with iron ore when she went on, and before being released 100 tons were thrown overboard and 70 tons lightered.

The two favorite passenger boats *Queen of the Lakes* and the *Jennie Sutton* never were in finer condition for the summers business than they are this season. Messrs., Dexter & Noble have spared no pains or expense to make them all that the traveling community can desire. The two popular captains, Johnson, of the *Queen,* and Bennett, of the *Jennie Sutton,* will be in command of the steamers respectively this season.

06 11 80 The steam pumps from the tug *Leviathan* commenced pumping the water from the schooner *Two Fannies* Wednesday. One pump was kept running all that night, and yesterday morning she was out of water so far that she could be towed to the dock. To us she looked like an undesirable piece of property with two stumps of masts, with no decks and with her stern knocked out, but in speaking to Capt. Myers, her owner, we were informed that he would not take $9,000. for her the way she was. It will take two or three days to fix the schooner up and she will be taken to Milwaukee and put in a dry dock.

06 18 80 While coming across the bay from Old Mission Wednesday, the mate on the *Sutton,* Thad Bailey, while emptying the ash bucket burned his hand quite badly. He dropped the bucket.

The tug *Little Western* took a scow of lumber up the lake.
Captain Hawley of the tug *Torch Lake* has been towing the square timber back to the head of the river this week.

The tug *Leviathan* with her lighter and the hull of the schooner *Two Fannies* left this port Sunday for Milwaukee. We are rather sorry to have the schooner leave us, as she has furnished us, when hard up, a local nearly every week since she went ashore. If it wasn't for the wickedness of it we would wish another schooner to go ashore.

06 26 80 The other day the steamer *Jennie Sutton* made the run between this place and Old Mission in 26 minutes- an average of over 16 miles per hour.

06 26 80 We take the following from the *Traverse City Eagle* of the date of June 23, under the heading of "New Departure":

Commencing on Monday morning there will be a daily line of boats each way between Traverse City and Little Traverse and intermediate points. Up to this time the *City of Grand Rapids* has been making the run down one day and back the next, and the *Clara Belle* has been making daily trips about the Bay. By the new arrangement the former boat will leave here Mondays, Wednesdays and Fridays, for Old Mission, Elk Rapids, Torch Lake, Northport, Norwood, Charlevoix, Petoskey and Little Traverse. She will return over the same route Tuesdays, Thursdays and Saturdays. The *Clara Belle* will leave Traverse City Tuesdays, Thursdays and Saturdays for Suttons Bay, Elk Rapids, Old Mission, Torch Lake, Norwood, Charlevoix, Petoskey and Little Traverse, returning over the same route upon the alternate days. By this arrangement the traveling public will be much better accommodated than if the round trip were made daily by one boat, as the time of departure and arrival would be necessarily much earlier in the morning and later at night than now. By this arrangement the boats will not leave here until eight o'clock A.M. and will arrive long before dark.

The steamer *Clara Belle* has been receiving a new coat of paint during the past two days, preparatory to starting in on her new route to Petoskey and Little Traverse. It has improved her looks wonderfully. The machinery of the boat is in better shape than ever before, and as the natural result she is making better time than ever before. On a recent run to Escanaba she made, with no unusual effort, a run of 58 miles in five hours.

06 26 80 Messrs. Wadsworth & Thurston will run their steam yacht *Wah-wah-tay-see* between Central Lake and Bellaire on the 5th of July. She will leave Central Lake at 7 o'clock A.M.; returning at 1 P.M. Leaving Central Lake at 4 P.M., returning at 9 P.M.

07 02 80 This week Mr. A.K. Dougherty has been engaged hauling the tug *Albatross* from the bay across to Elk River. Captain Mike Gay will command her. It will be two or three days before she will be launched.

07 02 80 We learn from Captain Bennett of the steamer *Jennie Sutton* that some fishermen drew up their nets on the beach at East Bay leaving a lot of fish there to decompose, making such a stench that it is almost impossible to land. We also learn that parties fishing back of the saw mill leave minnows and small fish on the *Sutton's* dock which makes it unpleasant to land there. The causes of these annoyances should be removed and stopped or sickness will be the result.

07 02 80 The barge *Leland* came into port last Saturday with a cargo of brick.

The barge *Leland* burst her cylinder head while in Saginaw Bay. Fortunately the tug *Albatross* was with her to tow her.

The Iron Co.'s new tug the *Albatross* arrived Saturday from Buffalo. She makes pretty good time- about 16 miles an hour.

07 02 80 The schooner *Prussia* of Kingston, Canada came in this morning. She will load with square timber.

07 09 80 The schooner *Melvina* came in Thursday with ore.

The schooner *Siberia* is here loading with square timber.

The schooner *Prussia* cleared this port Wednesday with square timber for Quebec.

The schooner *W.A. Smith* of Charlevoix, touched this port Tuesday and put off a quantity of shingles.

Commodore Ballard is putting his fleet in commission as fast as possible.

07 16 80 The tug *Albatross* was successfully launched into Elk River Monday afternoon.

Two schooners have been loaded with square timber here this spring. There are twelve more loads boomed in the river.

The steamer *Little Western* makes tri-weekly trips between this place and Bellaire. That is to say, she goes up one week and tries to come back the next.

07 23 80 Three tow barges arrived last night from Quebec for square timber.

The schooner *W.A. Smith* of Charlevoix unloaded a quantity of lath here this morning.

Commodore Ballard of the "Musquito Fleet" is repairing and painting some of his ships-o-the-line".

The yacht *Flora* of Traverse City was in the mill race Tuesday. She made the run from Traverse City here, stopping at Northport on the way, in two hours.

07 23 80 The tug *Albatross* had an extension put on her smoke stack Monday.

07 30 80   NEW ROUTE FOR TOURISTS.

The upper lakes of the Intermediate chain are now for the first time reached by steam.

The traveler, taking the steamer *Queen of the Lakes* from the Lewis House at 7 A.M., or from Elk Rapids at 2 P.M., for Russell's Landing on Torch Lake, finds there a conveyance for Central Lake, where are comfortable accommodations at the Central Lake House.

Starting after breakfast from this point by steam yacht "*Wahwataysee*," the tourist passes through Cedar, Hanley's, Sisson's, White's, Bower's, St. Clair's, and the Six Mile Lake to the head of steam navigation, returning in time for supper at Central Lake.

If desired, the Lewis House may be reached the same evening, or the trip up the lake and return may be made from the Lewis House the same day.

The traveler may leave Central Lake in the morning, connecting at Russell's with steamer *Queen of the Lakes* for Elk Rapids, or by boat and guide down the rapids, through Grass and Clam Lakes, taking the *Queen* at the mouth of Clam River for the Lewis House.

These lakes and rivers abound in fish. Parties not exceeding twelve in number can make the trip from Central Lake to the head of Six Mile Lake, passing through the most beautiful scenery in Northern Michigan, and returning to Central Lake, having steamed about sixty miles for twelve dollars. For further information address,

WADSWOJRTH & THURSTON,
Central Lake, Antrim Co., Mich., July, 1880.

07 30 80 Three barges left Wednesday with square timber for Quebec.

The barge *Leland* came in Sunday from Escanaba with ore.

The tug used by the Charlevoix Iron Co., was here Sunday.

Four steamers and five vessels were at the dock last Friday all at one time. Quite a fleet.

The tug *Metamora,* of Montreal, with her tow barges *H. Benson, Frank Russell,* and *G. Manler* were loaded with square timber at the dock this week.

The U.S. Steamer *Michigan* left Erie, Pa., last week on her annual trip up the great lakes. She will visit all ports between Erie and Chicago to enlist boys for the navy. The boys must be between 15 and 17 years of age, and have to serve until they are 21.

07 30 80 The yacht *Oriole* has had her machinery put in order and is now ready to run.

08 06 80 The wind last Sunday night raised such a sea on Torch Lake that the occupants of the boarding scow went ashore to escape being drowned.

08 06 80 The schooners *Siberia, Prussia* and *Norway* are at the dock loading with square timber.

08 06 80 The old saw says that a man who can sing a hymn while putting up a stovepipe should go to Heaven, but one of our steamboat engineers is of the opinion that the one that can burn fine coal without knocking chunks out of the commandment is sure of getting to that happy land.

08 13 80 Three ship loads of square timber left here this week.

The tug *Little Western* brought in a load of lumber Tuesday.

The tug *Torch Lake* was up the lake for a raft of logs this week.

The schooner *Barbarian* of Chicago came to the dock with a load of iron ore Tuesday morning.

08 20 80 If any boat ought to be well patronized it is that elegant steamer *City of Grand Rapids.* A band of five pieces accompany her every day and it plays finely. The steamer calls here every day, and every body rushes to the dock "When the band begins to play."

08 20 80 The tug *Torch Lake* sunk in Elk River one day this week by having too much iron placed on her forward while trying to repair some injury. They took a scow and lightened her and then were able to raise her.

08 27 80 The schooner *Experiment* came into port Wednesday with a load of ore.

The schooner *Metropolis* left Sunday morning for Racine with a cargo of iron.

Schooner *Flying Mist* came in Friday last with 2,000 bushels of corn, loaded with iron and left Monday morning for Buffalo.

09 03 80 A horse used on the schooner *Prussia* to draw the square timber into the hold fell through the hatch yesterday morning and broke its back. After firing 14 shots at the horse to put him out of his misery, he was dumped into the bay, which ought not to have been allowed.

09 03 80 The schooner *Prussia* came in Wednesday after a load of square timber.

09 17 80 Schooner *Barbarian* left this port Tuesday morning with a load of iron. She goes to Racine.

The schooner *Prussia* left here Saturday last for Kingston. She was loaded with square timber.

The schooner *Metropolis* arrived yesterday morning light. She will take a load of pig iron to Milwaukee.

While the barge *Leland* was coming from Escanaba last trip a small hose over the boiler became loose and as there was quite a sea at the time it struck against the steam pipe to which the small whistle is attached, thus let the steam from the boiler escape. The barge "swashed" around for about four hours before the injury was repaired, and then steamed for this dock.

09 24 80 Number of passengers carried on steamer *Jennie Sutton* from June 1st to Sept. 1st 1880, 1,556.

The steamer *City of Grand Rapids,* Capt. A.H. Bennett, did not make her regular trip to this place Tuesday on account of the storm, she having assisted the schooner *Dan Hayes.*

The schooner *Dan Hayes* dragged anchor in Northport Bay last night and went ashore. No lives lost.

The schooner *Dan Hayes* that went ashore here was gotten off on Wednesday. Amount of damage not known.

The propeller *Gordon Campbell* was obliged to run into this port this morning, being disabled. She was loaded with 34,500 bushels of corn and towing the schooner *Tom Scott,* loaded with 45,000 bushels of wheat. The *Campbell* was obliged to cut loose from her tow this morning, near the Manitous, the sea being too heavy to hold her. The *Campbell* shifted cargo and the water rushed in on her boiler, carrying the deck of her engine house away.

10 01 80 A scow loaded with railroad ties sunk in Round Lake Monday. The scow was being towed to this place by one of the Iron Co.'s. tugs.

10 08 80 Schooner *Fair Play* was at the dock Monday.

The schooner *Metropolis* arrived here Monday from Milwaukee.

The *Metropolis* is loading with railroad ties and pig iron.

The schooner *Six Brothers,* of Beaver Island, arrived here Monday with wheat.

The barge *Leland* came in Friday last from Chicago. She left Monday for Escanaba.

10 15 80 The schooner *Melvina* came into port Sunday morning with a load of iron ore. She loaded with pig iron and left Tuesday for Buffalo.

The schooner *Metropolis* left this port for Chicago last Saturday with a load of iron.

10 22 80 The steamer *Clara Belle* and barge *Leland* layed at anchor at Old Mission during the storm Sunday, Monday and Tuesday.

The schooners *David Vance, E. M. Carrington, F.L. Stroner,* and *Sloane,* and the scow *Brigham* are ashore at the South Manitous.

While coming by Manitowoc, Wis., CaptainCorbett, of the schooner *Metropolis*, sighted four vessels, two of them beached, one of them sunk and one dismasted.

The schooner *Metropolis* left this port last Saturday a week for Chicago with a load of iron, arriving there at 2 o'clock on Thursday. She left Chicago at 7:00 o'clock Sunday morning and arrived here Monday just as the furnace whistle was "ringing" for noon. Pretty good time.

The schooner *Hartzell* went ashore off Frankfort the 16th inst., loaded with ore for the Frankfort iron furnace. A line was shot off shore with mortar and six men were drawn on shore. A woman cook aboard could not be reached and she perished in the rigging. The schooner is a total wreck.

The schooner *Melvina*, of Kenosha, in tow of the tug *George N. Brady*, ran against the lower end of the government work in the St.Clair cut and sank in Canadian waters. The tug went on with the other vessel of her tow. The water then rose and the tug *Champion* being near could have taken her away had it not been for the blasted Canadian wrecking law. The *Melvina* was helpless and to prevent pounding the crew had to scuttle her. The *Melvina* was owned by E. G. Hazelton, of Kenosha, and her captain, A.. P. Read; rated A 22, and was insured for $6,000, her insurable value being $10,000. Her cargo consisted of 470 tons of pig-iron from Elk Rapids to Cleveland. —*Evening News.*

10 29 80   THE OLD FRIGATE *CONSTELLATION.*

An inspection of the ship-of-war *Constellation* has been ordered by the Secretary of the Navy. The vessel is not in very forward condition, having neither spar, sail, nor a single gun, and furniture is conspicuous by its absence.

The *Constellation* has a remarkable record. It was the second finished when the Navy of the United States was organized, and was launched at Baltimore Dec. 7, 1797. In the Mediterranean struggle of 1808, the vessel was in the Decatur Squadron; and in 1812 was rebuilt and twelve feet added to the length at the Washington Navy Yard. Returning from a long cruise in 1834 the *Constellation* was considered one of the finest war ships in the world, having ridden through a storm in the Mediterranean near where a French ship went down in sight of and under its admiral's flag.

The vessel was rebuilt again and transferred as a school-ship to Annapolis, taking out cadets on summer cruises. It was detailed in its eighty-first year by the Government to convey exhibits to the Paris exposition, arriving from Annapolis on March 19. Her tanks and bulkheads were taken out, the cargo was stored, and March 27 she sailed for Havre.

The *Constellation* returned to New York July 7, and shortly went back to Annapolis under orders. On Sept. 8, 1879 the vessel arrived to carry the relief officers and crew to the Mediterranean squadron and sailed with them Nov. 1, meeting the flag ship at Gibraltar. The *Constellation* was dismantled when it returned on Jan. 19 with the relieved officers and crew.

11 05 80 The Scow *James T. Petrie* is at the dock. The boys call it devil. It must be because it looks like the devil.

11 12 80 It was noised about town Saturday that the scow *James T. Petrie* came into this port Saturday after all the Democrats to take them up "Salt River." If the Democrats are as sick as the scow looks, they better go on it.

11 12 80 The *Collins,* a large and an elegant three-master leaves Torch Lake today with 250,000 feet of lumber and 150 cords of bark.

11 19 80 The steamer *Wahwataysee* sank at her moorings in the gale of Saturday last. The officers and crew were all ashore, and no lives were lost. As there were no injuries to the vessel the underwriters will not suffer, and she will soon again be ready for business.

11 26 80 Owing to the storm Wednesday evening the barge *Sheldon* made a run over to Old Mission. She came back Thursday morning and finished loading.

11 26 80 A large scow in tow of the *Jennie Silkman* loaded with goods for Wadsworth & Thruston of Central Lake, caught fire while on its way from Elk Rapids. The flames were as supposed extinguished, but about 7 P.M. while tied at the dock here the fire broke out again and was not overcome until about $25 or $35 worth of goods had been destroyed.

11 26 80 The barge *Leland* made her last trip to Escanaba Friday a week.
    The barge *S.E. Sheldon* came into port Thursday morning. She will load with 1000 tons of pig iron for Cleveland.
    The schooner *Thomas W. Ferry,* loaded with iron ore went ashore on the Beavers Saturday night. She is a total wreck. Crew all saved by aid of help from shore.
    The steamer *City of Traverse* is to have a new compound engine placed in her this winter. It is expected to put her in even better shape than ever before for passenger business. – *Eagle.*
    The steam barge *Fletcher* which left Chicago last Friday night for Buffalo with a cargo of 34,000 bushels of corn, owned by Niayew Francis Co., of Buffalo, went ashore on the south Fox Island Sunday night, during a blinding snow storm, at 5:30. She grounded in 15 feet of water. Several attempts were made on Sunday to get ashore with the crew, but all efforts proved futile on account of the heavy seas. On Monday morning, however, a successful attempt was made and the Captain succeed by the services of W.S. Warren, the light-house keeper, through whose untiring efforts the entire crew were saved. The smoke-stack and rigging were carried away when she struck. Her cargo is a total loss. She lies where she struck a mass of ice.

12 17 80 The barge *Leland* had a rough trip the last one to Milwaukee. She went through 75 miles of ice and had to throw overboard 30 tons of pig iron. She arrived in Chicago safely but a little demoralized, the sea taking the railing away in front of the pilot house.

12 17 80 We learn from the *Detroit Free Press* that Hannah Lay & Co. have purchased another steamer for the Bay route next season. Price paid $11,500.

01 06 81 Nelson & Farrand are building a steamer to run between Bellaire and Elk Rapids. It will have a 40 ft. keel and 12 ft. beam. It will be built on the Ohio River plan with paddle wheel behind.

03 11 81 Hannah Lay & Co., of Traverse City are spending $20,000 on the propeller *City of Traverse,* this winter. --*Sentinel*

Hannah Lay & Co. never do anything by halves. The *City of Traverse* was "magnificent last season."

03 11 81 New wheels are being made for the steamer *Queen of the Lakes.*

New wheels are being put on the Steamer *Jennie Sutton* and tugs *Torch Lake, Elk Lake* and *Albatross.* The wheels are of home manufacture and the hub is cast separate from the flukes, and the flukes are keyed in, so that in case of a breakage of a fluke another can be slipped in. The Buffalo wheels when broken are useless, which difficulty is overcome by the new wheel which is manufactured at the furnace.

03 18 81 Chas. W. Ferrand has just returned from Detroit, where he has purchased the boiler and other necessary apparatus for the new steamer now being built at Bellaire to run between that place and Elk Rapids.

04 22 81 Wadsworth & Thurston's steamer *Wahwahtaysee* is being painted at the furnace.

04 22 81 The tugs *Elk Lake* and *Torch Lake* are being painted.

05 06 81 Wadsworth & Thurston's yacht *Wahwahtaysee* has been thoroughly fitted out for the season's business, and was taken to Central Lake Monday.

05 06 81 Chas. Frame, formerly of this place, but lately of Chicago, arrived in town Thursday, a week, and will take charge of the tug *Elk Lake.*

05 06 81 The tug *Albatross* made her first trip in the wood business on Elk Lake last Monday. The *Torch Lake, Elk Lake,* and *Frank H. Petrie* will soon follow suit.

05 06 81 The E.R.I Co. have transferred the steamer scow *Frank H. Petrie* from the bay to Elk Lake and will carry about 60 cords of wood besides towing two or three loaded scows.

05 06 81 There will soon be an opportunity to test the device of T.H. Noble to facilitate the transfer of wood from the banking ground to scows. There can hardly be any question of its utility in this respect.

05 06 81 The scow *Frank H. Petrie,* which the Elk Rapids Iron Co. bought last fall, is being hauled over into Elk Lake.

05 13 81 The barge *Leland* made her first trip to this place, last Saturday morning, with merchandise for Dexter & Noble, machinery for the Iron Co., and some machinery for the chemical works.

05 13 81 The tug *Bob Stevenson* belonging to the Charlevoix Iron Company is laying up here a short time for repairs.

05 13 81 Steamer *Faxton,* of Traverse City, Messrs. Hannah Lay & Co.'s. elegant boat, came here Tuesday, bringing the Wildman & Peck's Opera Company.

05 20 81 The steam yacht *Oriole* is being painted.

The steamer *Jennie Sutton* is being painted.

The tug *Torch Lake* is having her boiler repaired.

Schooner *Metropolis,* of Chicago came into port Sunday

The steamer *Queen of the Lakes* is getting under way for the summer's business.

The schooner *Phenix,* of Kenosha, made this port last night, light, after a cargo of iron.

The steamer *Jennie Silkman* is making regular trips to this place, on Monday, Wednesday and Friday.

Schooner *Birdie Calkins* went ashore three miles South of Charlevoix Friday, a week, and was taken off the following Sunday.

Schooner *Metropolis,* Capt. Corbett, left Escanaba last Saturday morning at 7:30 o'clock and made this dock at 12 n. Sunday.

The steamers of the Northern Transportation Company's line running between Chicago and Mackinaw, will touch at Torch Lake, both ways this season.

The two Northern Transportation boats which will stop at Torch Lake this season are the *Lawrence* and the *Champlain.*

05 20 81 Joseph Parks is fitting out the steam raft *Frank Petrie* for sea.

05 27 81 The tug *Albatross* broke a bucket from one of her wheels Monday night and did not make her trip Tuesday morning. The bucket was removed Tuesday and she made her regular trip up the Lakes the afternoon of that day.

05 27 81 The captain of the tug *Albatross* picked up a calf in Elk Lake, about 40 rods from Schuler's point one day last week, and brought it to the furnace. The calf belonged to Jacob Gribi who was so delighted that he gave Captain Hawley $1.

05 27 81 The barge *Leland* left here Wednesday afternoon for Buffalo with a cargo of 550 tons of pig iron.

The Schooner *Gifford,* of Erie, Pa. made this port Tuesday, and will load with 800 tons of pig iron ford Buffalo.

The tug *Torch Lake* is having a coat of green paint put on her, The tug *Albatross* is painted white and the Elk Lake red.

The tug *Minnie Warren,* of Charlevoix, was at the dock Sunday. She came to have machinery repaired for Nicholls saw mill.

The schooner *Phenix* took on 62 tons of pig iron last Friday and left for Torch Lake where she loaded with hard wood lumber for Racine.

We learned that the steamer *Faxton* made her last trip here Monday, but she managed to come here Tuesday with a large load of freight.

The steam barge *Leland* arrived here last Friday from Escanaba with iron ore, unloaded her cargo and left Wednesday with a cargo of iron for Buffalo.

The tug *Bob Stevenson*, which has been here some days having its boiler and engine repaired, left this port for Charlevoix, Wednesday evening, where it is owned.

The steamer *Jennie Sutton* has been put in good trim and will run on the same route she did last season. The work, painting etc. was done by the noble captain, himself.

The steamer *Faxton* was three hours unloading freight for the Iron Co., Dexter & Noble, and the Michigan Chemical Co., at this place Monday. The *Clara Belle* was also loaded.

Some misunderstanding having occurred the steam tug *Leviathan* which was getting the schooner *W.R. Taylor* off shore at Northport left that place and went to the help of the schooner *Two Friends* which went ashore at North Bay. The tug *Winslow* will tow the *Taylor* to St. Catherine's.

06 03 81 Captain Fred Johnson, of the steamer *Queen of the Lakes*, is in town, and we learn that the above named boat will commence making regular trips between this point and Torch Lake about the 15th inst.

06 03 81 The schooner *Gifford* left this port last Friday with 800 tons of iron for Buffalo.

The tug *Minnie Warren* was here Sunday for machinery for Nicholls' saw mill at Charlevoix.

The steam scow *Petrie*, has its engine all set up and is ready for sea and will go to work either to-day or to-morrow. It was necessary to put her on the dry dock one day this week to repair her rudder.

06 03 81 The steamer *Brook Trout*, of Bellaire created a sensation by coming to this place yesterday.

06 10 81 Capt. Fred Johnson informs us that the *Queen of the Lakes* may make her first trip Monday next.

06 10 81 The *Little Western* is being taken across from Elk River to the bay.

The barge *Leland* returned from Buffalo, Tuesday with a miscellaneous cargo.

The tug *Albatross* had two new wheels put on her Tuesday and did not make her regular trips.

The steamer *Jennie Sutton* made her trial trip last Sunday and started on her regular trips Monday.

The tug *Metamora*, with two barges, the Russell and Benson came here Sunday after square timber for Quebec.

The schooner *C.A. King*, of Chicago, came to this port Monday, and will take 570 tons of iron to Buffalo.

We spoke of the steamer *Brook Trout*, of Bellaire coming to this place last week. The proper name of the steamer is the *Mah-shah-ma-go-sas.* If it does look like a cross between a wind mill and a dry goods box, it will probably do a nice business.

06 17 81 The Schooner *Duvall,* cleared Torch Lake Sunday morning with a cargo of lumber for Milwaukee.

The Prop. *Champlain* made her third appearance at Torch Lake Tuesday evening, bringing freight for Traverse City, Elk Rapids, Clam Lake. Eastport and Torch Lake parties. Her Capt. expects to touch here each trip on his way up to Mackinaw.

06 17 81 The elegant Yacht *Idler,* of Chicago is lying here and has been for some days.

06 24 81 The barge *Leland* is making regular trips to Escanaba.

The steamer *Faxton* still makes regular trips to this place, as does the *Clara Belle.*

The schooner *Fleet Wing,* of Charlevoix, made this port Monday, from Manistee, bringing lath and shingles for Dexter & Noble.

The steamer *Queen of the Lakes* is now making regular trips. She leaves this place in the morning at 7 o'clock for Torch Lake and returns at 7 P.M.

The schooner *Metropolis,* Capt. Corbett, came here Friday night with 451 tons of soft ore for the furnace.

The tug *Albatross* was disabled Wednesday by breaking her wheel, and the tug *Torch Lake* was sent to take her in tow.

The steam Yacht *Frank H. Petrie* will carry wood on Elk and Round lakes, making one trip a day. She will carry about 50 cords of dry wood.

07 01 81 The schooner *C.A. King,* left here Wednesday morning with pig iron for Chicago.

The schooner *Emma,* of Manistee, came in Tuesday morning loaded with shingles for the Chemical Co.

07 08 81 All day Sunday the steamers and vessels at our docks displayed their flags at half mast, and had black flyers above, on account of the attempted assassination of President Garfield.

07 08 81 Oscar and Sam Smith have bought the *Eastman* boat which has been laying below the saw mill, and intend fitting it up to take parties out sailing.

07 08 81 The Schooner *John Miner* came into port Sunday morning for iron.

The steam yacht *Oriole* has been put in Elk River and is now ready for sailing.

Wm. Briggs recently purchased of W. Parmalee, of Old Mission, a yacht which he is preparing and getting ready for sea.

The Steamer *Jennie Sutton* has been laid up for repairs. Her shaft becoming loose, her owners have had her drawn out and are having it repaired.

The steamer *Queen of the Lakes* made her regular trip the Fourth, and quite a number of people from this place attended the celebration at Spencer Creek.

07 22 81 The yacht *Viking* of Chicago called here Monday, on her way to Mackinaw.

The schooner *C.A. King* left here this morning with pig iron for Chicago.

07 29 81 The barge *Leland* is making regular trips to Escanaba.

The steam, tug *Metamora* with a tow barge arrived here Monday for square timber.

The schooner *Metropolis* came to this port last Friday with ore.

The steamer *Jennie Sutton* did not make her regular trip Tuesday morning on account of the heavy sea which was running, preventing her from leaving her slip.

The tug *Sarah E. Bryant* was here this week for a lighter, to assist in removing the machinery from the steam barge *Fletcher* which went ashore at South Fox Island last fall loaded with corn.

08 05 81 Those who attended to camp meeting at Bay View last Sunday had hard luck. Returning, the *City of Grand Rapids* did not make Northport until 11 o'clock Sunday morning, owing to the dense smoke from forest fires, and the steamer *Jennie Sutton* did not leave Northport until 4 o'clock Monday morning, reaching this place at 7 o'clock.

08 05 81 The schooner *Metropolis* left last Saturday morning for Chicago with a cargo of iron.

The tug *Sarah E. Bryant* was here Tuesday, bringing the lighter that was taken to the Foxes last week.

The steam yacht *Oriole* made a trip to Torch Lake on Monday to take a party of ladies and gentlemen to that place. It was the first trip of the season for her.

08 12 81 The tug *Minnie Warren,* of Charlevoix, is at this port for repairs.

The barge *Leland* made a trip to Traverse City last Sunday for castings for the furnace.

The schooner *W.H. Rounds,* of Buffalo, came into port Wednesday with a load of brick for the Iron Co. The *Rounds* will take out iron.

The steamer *City of Traverse* did not make her regular time Sunday. When forty miles out from Chicago the sea was so heavy she was obliged to turn back.

The barge *Leland* came in Wednesday. While coming from Escanaba the brasses of the connecting rod broke on the after engine, and is being repaired at the furnace machine ship.

The steamer *Queen of the Lakes* and tug *Torch Lake* had a very exciting race through Torch River Tuesday. The *Torch Lake* would run up to the *Queen* and then "slow down" and let the *Queen* get ahead. It was intensely exciting but the Capt. of the tug wishes the *Queen* to get out of the way next time.

08 16 81 William Briggs made a trip from Old Mission to this place last Saturday during a hard storm. Compliments from a great number of people on the excellent management of his sail boat.

08 16 81 A telegram, was received here late last night from Muskegon, that the little scow *Nellie,* fruit laden, and bound for Charlevoix capsized in a squall off that port and all hands were lost.

08 16 81 The steamer *Jennie A. Sutton* belonging to Messrs. Dexter & Noble was burned at her dock at this place last Sunday morning. The fire was discovered, but too late to save her. She was burned way down to the rail and the ribs and lining were burned out. It is thought that her engine or hull are not badly damaged. All day Sunday parties from the village visited her, as she was a great favorite with all our townspeople. She was a fast sailor and one of the prettiest models ever built. She was valued at $3,000, with no insurance. Origin of the fire unknown.

08 16 81 Vessels passing Saginaw bay last Friday and Saturday report large numbers dead birds afloat on the water, probably victims of the forest fires.

08 19 81 The schooner *Elizabeth Jones* arrived here the 12th light, and left the 16th for Cleveland with 945 tons of iron.

08 25 81 The schooner *C.A. King* left here Monday for Chicago with a load of iron.

The schooner *W.H. Rounds* left this place Saturday last for Buffalo with iron.

The tug *Bob Stevenson*, of Charlevoix, called here yesterday, put off a small pump and left for above place.

The schooner *Collins* came here Tuesday with a load of corn and oats for Messrs. Dexter & Noble, discharged her cargo and left last evening for Torch Lake, where she will take on a load of lumber for Milwaukee.

09 02 81 A big lamp should be placed on the dock.

The schooner *Two Fannies*, of Kenosha, arrived here Tuesday morning with a load of ore.

The schooner *Lookout*, of Kenosha, was anchored across the bay Sunday, taking on a load of cobble stone for pavements.

We find the following in the *Charlevoix Sentinel*:
The propeller *City of New York* en route from Escanaba to Ironton, ore-laden on Friday night last ran aground on Fisherman's reef, six miles west of this port. The captain had gone to his room some time previously, having given the mate the course to steer. During his absence from deck, the mate and wheelsman got into a dispute as to the course which the captain gave, and the mate yielded to the wheelsman's understanding of it, which was not the course ordered. Land was sighted, and the captain was called. He had not reached the pilot house when she struck. The captain secured assistance from this port, and after jettisoning about forty tons of ore, she was liberated, but not until Saturday evening. She goes into dry dock at Milwaukee next trip for inspection.

09 09 81 The schooner *Two Fannies* left here yesterday for Chicago with iron.

09 09 81 The scow *Petrie* is bringing railroad ties from Central Lake to this place for shipment to Chicago. Yesterday it brought 2,000.

10 07 81 The schooner *Six Brothers*, of Beaver Island is laying at the dock.

The barge *Leland* returned from Chicago Monday, stopping by way of Escanaba and bringing 575 tons of ore.

The propeller *Roanoke*, of Buffalo, arrived here last Friday for a cargo of iron for Buffalo, took on a cargo of 1,000 tons and left Monday for above place.

Before the propeller *Roanoke* reached this place last Friday, report had it was a new boat that Messrs. Dexter & Noble bought to run on the bay. It was 255 feet long and registered 1,400 tons which would make it a large bay boat. -- *Grand Rapids Daily Times*.

Harbor Springs, Mich., Oct. 4. - The propeller *Raonoke*, bound from Elk Rapids to Buffalo, met with an accident to her boiler near Beaver Island yesterday, which disabled her. A head wind prevented her from making Beaver harbor, and she turned toward Little Traverse harbor, getting within six miles of the point before becoming unmanageable. She was towed into the harbor last night, and is now being repaired. She will be able to resume her journey in a few days.

Mr. James Wadsworth, of Central Lake, has purchased the yacht *Ida*, of Smith Bros., Cheboygan, and she reached this place yesterday. She experienced rough weather coming across, Mr. Wadsworth informs us, being out in the blow we had the early part of the week. Mr. Wadsworth intends to run her between Bellaire and Torch Lake, connecting with the steamer *Queen of the Lakes* at Clam River, giving a direct communication between this place and the county seat during navigation. Mr. Wadsworth left on the *Queen* yesterday for home, and expects to return to-day with men to assist in taking the yacht from Elk Lake over into Elk River.

10 14 81 The schooner *Sophia Bonner*, of St. James is at the short dock.

The schooner *Six Brothers* made a trip to Old Mission Sunday taking over a pleasure party of about 30 persons.

Smith Brothers have sold their steam yacht *Ida* to parties from Charlevoix. She left Monday for that place and we understand is to be used in towing lighters for carrying wood from the upper lake in that county where only light draft tugs can be used. The purchasers we are informed, own forty scows and have a contract for furnishing a large amount of wood to the furnace company at Charlevoix. — *Tribune*, Cheboygan.

You are way off Mr. *Tribune*. The yacht was sold to Mr. James Wadsworth, of Central Lake, a notice of which we published last week.

10 21 81 The schooner *George Sherman*, of Cleveland arrived here Monday with 630 tons of lime stone. As she came in she struck on the bar in front of the village and the *Clara Belle* helped her off and brought her to the dock.

10 28 81 The hull of the steamer *Jennie Sutton* has been raised and her engine and boiler taken out.

The schooner *Six Brothers* of Beaver Island came in Wednesday with wheat for gristing, making the second time this season.

11 04 81 The schooner *Reindeer* is at anchor in the bay. She has coal from Milwaukee.

11 04 81 T.D. Smith sold the schooner *Fleet Wing* to Daniel S. May and Phil Caffrey for $1200 Monday. Daniel takes her out next trip, for Milwaukee, Phil continuing as captain of the schooner *Fair Play*.

11 11 81 The schooner *Reindeer* came in Sunday with a load of coal.

The steamer *Queen of the Lakes* has laid up for the season.

The tug *Maple Leaf* of Suttons Bay was in at the short dock yesterday with a load of produce.

The schooner *Metropolis* came into port Monday from Chicago with 10,000 bushels of grain for Dexter & Noble.

The schooner *Dunalle*, loading with lumber at Central Lake was driven ashore last night by the heavy sea. She was gotten off without much damage.

The steamer *City of Traverse* brought a full load of merchandise for our dealers on Monday. She loaded with lumber and left on Wednesday evening for Chicago, where she will go into winter quarters.

NORTHPORT — The steam barge *Gordon Campbell* from Chicago to Buffalo with a cargo of corn and flax seed, shipped her cargo last night about 10 o'clock in a heavy sea and rolled down to starboard until the water shipped on her upper deck. She is now all right

The schooner *Metropolis* left Traverse City Monday, a week, for Chicago. Arriving there she discharged the lumber with which she was loaded, took on 10,000 bushels of grain and enough sundries to make out her load and left for this port arriving here Monday, making the trip from Traverse City to Chicago and return to this dock in just one week.

11 18 81 The schooner *Reindeer*, was in Tuesday with 600 tons of lime stone from near Petoskey. She anchored in the bay Monday night and was out in the storm that night.

11 18 81 Larry Higgins, mate of the barge *Leland*, fell through the hatchway Tuesday night receiving severe injuries. He had gone from the cabin to call those below too supper when he fell through striking his head on the iron in the hold below.

11 25 81 The schooner *Reindeer* left for Petoskey Sunday night for a cargo of limestone.

The yacht *Oriole* has been hauled out of water and placed in the Cooper building.

The steamer *Jennie Silkman* has made several trips here lately from Torch Lake, bringing wheat for gristing.

The schooner *Thomas Parker*, of Chicago, arrived in port Monday, light, and will take on 13,000 tons of iron for Chicago.

The barge *Leland* left for Chicago Friday night with a load of iron. While making her last trip from Escanaba she lost her forward spar.

12 02 81 The barge *Leland* came back with a new spar.

The schooner *Thomas Parker* sailed Friday afternoon for Chicago with 1,300 tons of iron.

We last week made a local that the schooner *Thomas Parker* was to take out 13,000 tons of pig iron. For the benefit of the world at large we correct it by saying that we had it thirteen times too much.

CHARLEVOIX — The schooner *Charlottie Rubb* arrived the 29th for wood and bark.

The schooner *Sea Gem* arrived at Charlevoix the 28th from Milwaukee — making the run in 27 hours.

NORTHPORT — The schooner *James Platt*, of Detroit, with salt for Chicago, went ashore on South Fox Island last Friday and is now a total wreck. The captain and woman cook were lost after being exposed 48 hours. The balance of the crew were saved by the Light Keeper, and brought here in small boats. They were on the wreck from Friday until Sunday, before they could be gotten off. The Captain and cook died from exposure.

12 09 81 The steamer *Ida*, of Bellaire, has been laid up at this place.

The Barge *Leland* with her tow, schooner *Metropolis* left this port Sunday for Chicago.

The schooner *Metropolis* was loaded with 418 gross tons of iron Sunday from 8 A.M. to 4 P.M.

The *Leland* and the *Metropolis* left this port for Chicago on Sunday night, both loaded with iron. On Wednesday they were still laying in Northport harbor, waiting for the wind to subside.

12 16 81 Hannah, Lay & Co., have sold the little bay steamer *Clara Belle* to Stockman & Bartholomew of Charlevoix, who will place her upon Pine lake. She is an excellent boat and well calculated for that route. Traverse City people will be sorry to see the *Clara Belle* leave as she has always been a favorite boat here, but it has been apparent for a year or two that the bay trade and travel required a larger boat. The former owners of the *Clara Belle* have not yet decided what they will do in the matter, but we have no doubt they will be prepared another season to fully meet the rapidly increasing demands of the bay business.

12 23 81 The barge *Leland* left for Chicago last night with a cargo of iron and acetate of lime.

01 27 82 We are informed that Thomas White and Jimmie Morrison are engaged in the construction of an engine for a pleasure boat to run in the lakes. Mr. White has drawn the plans of the engine and expects to finish it at odd times this winter and Jimmie is on the lookout for the right kind of a boat.

02 10 82 Capt. Sandy Bennett went to Charlevoix last Saturday, and as a consequence he will run the *Clara Belle* next season.

02 24 82 On Wednesday, of last week, the vessel *Four Brothers*, went ashore off New Mission point. A telegram was sent to Greilick, of Traverse City, too come to their assistance as it was leaking badly. Mr. Greilick, sent his tug the *Chas. C. Ryan*, to their assistance and by throwing overboard her deck load, which was cord wood, the tug pulled her off and towed her into Northport harbor.

03 10 82 We learn that Messrs. Hannah Lay & Co.'s boats, the *Faxton* and *Grand Rapids* will run on the bay the coming season. From what we learn, they will ply between Petoskey and Traverse City, leaving out Mackinac. The bay trade is gaining every year.

Capt. Phil Caffery is rigging out the small schooner *Fair Play* to carry alcohol from Elk Rapids to Traverse City. He will enter at once upon the contract. — *Sentinel.*

The *Jennie Sutton's* boiler has been set up at the furnace to furnish steam for the pumps and the machine shop. Her engine is being repaired, and will probably do service in another field the coming season.

03 10 82 The tugs are being fitted up for the summer's work, the tug *Albatross* being the first one commenced upon. Her cylinder is at the machine shop at the furnace being bored out.

03 17 82 The barge *Leland* will leave Chicago for this port with merchandise for our people some day this week.

The tug *Charles C. Ryan*, of Traverse City, was here Saturday with a load of merchandise for our dealers.

J.M. Wadsworth has had his boats repaired throughout, and is ready for the opening of navigation.

The *Charles A. Ryan*, of Traverse City, made another trip to this port Monday bringing the locomotive for the Traverse Bay and Elk Rapids short line railroad, and merchandise for our dealers.

Hannah, Lay & Co.'s steamer, *City of Grand Rapids*, was towed from Grielick's to Traverse City, Wednesday by the tug *Ryan*, where she will be overhauled, and refitted for the season's business. She will commence business, it is expected, April 1st.

03 17 82 Bay View will rebuild the dock at that landing. It will be remembered that this dock as well as the one at Petoskey was taken away by one of our heavy storms. The Petoskey dock is also being rebuilt.

03 17 82 The tug *Winslow* passed through the straits of Mackinaw March 9, the first boat of the season.

03 17 82 The U.S. Signal Service commenced work on the Lakes the 15th inst.

03 24 82 We are glad some one owning a steam boat will put it on the route between Traverse City and this place the coming season. There is no better run in the country than between these two places, the *Faxton* will do a good business.

03 24 82 A representative of the *Progress* meandered over to the Iron Co.'s ship yard one day this week, and found A.K. Dougherty, foreman, and his men busy preparing the Company's floating stock ready for sea. One wood barge was out of the water being calked, and the bulwarks of the tug *Torch Lake* was being rebuilt. Mr. Dougherty informed us that the Company had 23 barges and four tugs which were to be got ready for the season's work. The tug *Albatross* has only to be painted which is but a small item of what has to be done.

03 24 82 Ed. Cooper and Joseph Butler had their sail boat rebuilt at Old Mission this winter, and received it on this side Sunday, and it is now in the river.

03 24 82 The tug *Ryan*, of Traverse City, made a trip to this port Sunday, bringing a scow load of lumber, oil barrels, and some merchandise for our dealers.

The barge *Leland*, Capt. D. Galligan, mate Larry Higgins, arrived here Monday afternoon from Chicago, making the trip in 30 hours. The Captain informs us they had a pleasant trip, with no obstacles of importance.

Hannah, Lay & Co.'s steamers, the *City of Traverse* and *Faxton* will leave Chicago the 30th, weather permitting. The *Faxton* will commence running between Traverse and Little Traverse touching at intermediate points. The *City of Grand Rapids* will make Traverse City and Mackinaw every other day.

03 31 82 Eugene Hall is fitting up the steamer *Ida*.

The screw of the *Mah-sha-mah-goos* has arrived, and C.W. is putting it in place. Other improvements will be made in the boat.

The schooner *Sea Gem* left Charlevoix Saturday evening for Milwaukee, with a load of ties. She will bring back merchandise for dealers at that place.

John E. French and C.A. Watson left for Cheboygan yesterday for the steamer *Valley Queen*, a steamer that John E. French & Co., bought of Smith & Watson, Wednesday of this week. The *Valley Queen* will be run from here to different points on the "six lakes," to accommodate fishermen, and pleasure parties, with no regular trips until after the season is over. An advertisement will appear in *The Progress* upon her arrival.

03 31 82 Tugs *Maple Leaf* and *Chas. Ryan* of Traverse City were in town this week. — *Enterprise*, Northport.

03 31 82 Capt. Jacob Johnson, owner of the schooner *E.M. Portch*, yesterday received a dispatch from Capt. Moore, master of the *Portch*, dated Sheboygan, Wis., saying that the *Portch* had a collision with the steam barge *Leland* and had been run into Sheboygan harbor, where she sank below decks. A dispatch from *The Tribune's* correspondent at Sheboygan last evening states that the collision took place off Centerville about 8 o'clock Sunday evening during a dense fog. The *Leland* struck the *Portch* on her port bow cutting her down to the water's edge. Immediately after the collision the *Leland* took the *Portch* in tow and towed her to Sheboygan. Three tugs were secured and attempted to tow the disabled schooner inside the harbor, but she filled and sank just alongside the south pier. A second dispatch from Capt. Moore to Capt. Johnson said that the *Portch* was in a bad place and asked that a diver, tug, and steam pump be immediately sent to her relief. Captain Peter Falcon, the marine diver, left by cars last evening, and the tug *Parker* will leave with a steam pump this morning. The *Portch* is valued at $10,000, has three masts, and rates A 22. She was built at Depere in 1867, and had extensive repairs made in 1880. There is no insurance on her. The *Portch* left this port Saturday evening light for Rawley's bay, and was on her third trip this season. The *Leland* was bound to this port with a cargo of wheat from Elk Rapids. She was due at this port yesterday, but up to a late hour last evening had not arrived, although after towing the *Portch* to Sheboygan she continued on her way. No anxiety, however, is felt for her safety, as nothing was said in the dispatches of her having been injured by the collision.   — From Tuesdays *Chicago Tribune*.

04 07 82 The steamer *Ida* is being painted and calked.

The steamer *Faxton* made her first trip here Monday, on her way from Chicago to Traverse City. The *Faxton* is a fast sailor and a fine boat for the Northern trade.

Tug *Torch Lake*, Captain Dumphrey, is receiving a coat of paint. Her hull is white with a green rail. The engine is painted green with gold trimming, same as the Albatross.

By a telegram from Bay City, John E. French informs us that he did not purchase the steamer *Valley Queen*, as per our announcement last week. Why the purchase was not made we have no idea as yet.

04 07 82 Tug *Albatross*, Captain Frame, has been thoroughly overhauled, and has been painted outside and in. The hull is white with the rail green, the engine and boiler house brown. The engine has been touched up in green and gold. The work was done by Martin Hanson.

A fine run for a steam boat is between Elk Rapids and Traverse City. A boat that could make twelve miles an hour, or one that could take the *Jennie Sutton's* old route could do a good business this summer, as the number of passengers between Traverse City and this place will be in excess of last year.

The schooner *Watertown*, of Chicago, bound for this port for a cargo of iron went ashore last night at about 10:30. She made a tack down the bay, and then ran on the bank just west of the dock. We learn that she tried to make no particular point, but was steered for the trees about town, and that they had no idea they were so near shore. The tug *Ryan*, of Traverse City, was telegraphed for, and at 9:45 this morning she started and at 10 o'clock she was way off. She was laying on shore in about 4 feet of water, with only her bow aground, and it is thought she is uninjured.

04 14 82 The schooner *Watertown* left this port for Chicago Saturday with a cargo of pig iron.

The tug *Albatross* is bringing wood from the lakes, and the tug *Torch Lake* is towing logs.

The steamer *Jennie Silkman* of Torch Lake, made her first trip to this port Monday. She will be pulled out and calked.

James M. Wadsworth commenced to-day to fit up the *Wahwataysee* for the season. Henry W. Smith will be the engineer.

Charles Hults of Torch Lake purchased the steamer *Valley Queen*, of Smith & Watson of Cheboygan. The steamer will run between Eastport and Elk Rapids this season, we learn.

Schooner *Lake Forest* dragged anchor at South Manitou Island and went ashore last Saturday night. Have sent to Milwaukee and Traverse City for tugs. She is high and dry but not damaged much yet.

04 21 82 The tug *Elk Lake* is being painted. The hull is black, with green rail.

The schooner *Cobb*, of Racine, Wis. arrived at this port this morning at about 8:30, after lumber.

Capt. Alexander Bennett, of the steamer *Jennie Sutton* left Tuesday for Charlevoix, where he takes the *Clare Belle*.

The *Faxton* had a big load of freight for this place, Tuesday. The captain informed us that she would make regular trips here this summer.

The tug *Elk Lake* will come out about the handsomest of any belonging to the Iron Co. She will be commanded this season by Capt. Kinney, formerly of the *Clara Belle*.

The tug *Albatross* caught on fire last Saturday afternoon under her pilot house. It is supposed that a spark from the fire box was blown under the wood work. The crew were just going to supper when the alarm was given, and while they were putting out the fire a dog belonging to Tom Noble ate up the meat. The damage done to the boat by fire was slight, but the meat was irrecoverably lost.

04 28 82 The steamer *Mah-sha-mah-goos* will hereafter be known as the *Bellaire*.

The schooner *City of Green Bay* left this port last night for Cleveland with a load of iron.

The steamer *Queen of the Lakes* is being painted for the summer travel on our inland lakes.

The schooner *A.P. Nichols*, of Racine, Wis., passed up East Bay Monday morning, on her way to Acme for lumber. She had lain at this dock since Friday.

The barge *Leland* made this port Wednesday, with a load of iron ore for the furnace. The barge laid six days at Escanaba before she could be loaded with ore.

The schooner *Floretta*, of Chicago, made this port Wednesday afternoon, for a cargo of iron for Cleveland. This schooner has had a hard time making this port, once after starting out from Chicago, small pox broke out among the crew and she was obliged to put back, and once she had to turn back on account of heavy weather.

From the *Chicago Inter-Ocean* we take the following, and shall publish something on the other side when we know more about it:

The loss of the schooner *E.M. Portch* was due to a collision with the steam barge *Leland*. Mr. Jacob Johnson, the owner of *Portch*, made a discovery yesterday that he deems a very important one. H.W. Magee is his lawyer, and Rea & Smith are for the Elk Rapids Iron Company, the owners of the *Leland*. Mr. Johnson says the company's lawyers have all along since the collision talked of a settlement, but that he discovered yesterday that they have been proceeding secretly. His loss is about $22,000, and the *Leland* would have to satisfy that. He says they got an order from Judge Blodgett's court to appraise the *Leland*: that J.B. Hall and E.M. Doolittle acted as such appraisers, and put the value of the *Leland* at only $7,665, which would be all the company would have to pay into court to satisfy his claim. All these proceedings Mr. Johnson says have been suppressed, and had it not been for his discovery yesterday of what was going on he would receive the amount stated in payment of his loss of $22,000. He says he can prove by any fair appraisers that the *Leland* is worth at least $25,000, and points at the Lloyd's Register, where the valuation of insurance is placed at $20,000. The *Leland* measures 325 tons, came out in 1873, and classed A2. "There's music in the air" for somebody.

05 05 82 Owing to the thorough overhauling of the steamer *Clare Belle* she will not be out yet for about two weeks. – *Charlevoix Sentinel*.

05 05 82 The schooner *Floretta*, of Chicago, left this port last Saturday for Cleveland with a cargo of iron.

The amount of pig iron and iron ore handled on Dexter & Noble's dock in six days ending May 1, was as follows: Barge *Leland*, 1,100 tons of ore; schooner *City of Green Bay*, 620 tons of ore and 640 tons of pig iron; schooner *Floretta*, 500 tons of pig iron; schooner *Metropolis*, 412 tons of pig iron; aggregating 3,311 tons of pig iron and iron ore.

05 12 82 TORCH LAKE — Capt. Chas. Hultz landed at the dock on Friday last, with his side wheel steam yacht, the *Valley Queen*. He will give her a new overskirt of paint and gilt trimmings when she will commence a daily trip from this port *via* Bellaire to Elk Rapids and return touching all intermediate landings.

05 12 82 The mate of the barge *Leland* says that the ore at the mines is so badly frozen that the barge has to lie for several days at Escanaba. The ore has to be blasted before it can be loaded.

05 12 82 The barge *Leland* came in Monday morning from Escanaba with ore.

The steamer *Valley Queen* was launched Tuesday morning, and after being painted will make a regular trip to-morrow.

The schooner *Watertown,* which tried to have a collision with E.S. Noble's chicken coop some two or three weeks ago, arrived in port Friday afternoon with ore. And left this morning with 500 tons of pig iron; 60 tons of acetate of lime and 41 barrels of wood alcohol. She goes to Chicago.

The little side wheel steamer *Valley Queen,* which Chas. Hultz recently purchased of Cheboygan parties, arrived on Friday last, and Saturday Mesas, Dexter & Noble's men and teams succeeded in getting her half way over from the bay to Elk River. We learn that this steamer will run between Eastport and Elk Rapids, leaving the above place at the same time that the steamer *Queen of the Lakes* leaves Elk Rapids, thus forming a line of two boats a day between these two places. The more boats on the "Nineteen Lakes" the better.

Larry Higgins, mate on the barge *Leland,* has entirely recovered from the severe injuries received last season by falling through the hatch of the *Leland.*

05 19 82 The engines of the tug *Elk Lake* are being fitted.

The barge *Leland* has a new top mast.

The schooner *Floretta,* of Chicago, arrived last Friday morning with ore.

Philander Bailey, of this place, is porter on the steamer, *T.S. Faxton.*

The steamer *Bellaire* was on the dry dock Wednesday, having a new wheel put on.

The fine little steamer, *Gazelle,* Capt. Dodge, of Detroit, was laying at the dock Sunday and Monday. It is chartered by the Interior Circus.

It has been hinted to us that the steamer, *Gazelle,* Capt. Dodge, might run on the bay this season, after taking the circus to Pt. St. Ignace. As she is somewhat larger than the *Grand Rapids* she would make an elegant bay boat.

The little steam yacht *J.J. Morley,* of Detroit, was at the dock Monday. She was built for Waterman, the real estate agent of the above city, at a cost of $15,000, and was recently purchased of him by Capt. Long who was on the Faxton last season.

Evening News: A steamer plying on the lakes in Antrim county was named the "Mah-sha-mah-goos," but it wouldn't work. They couldn't get all the name on her side without making her longer, and if they made her longer she couldn't turn around in Antrim county. A compromise was effected by giving her a shorter name.

05 19 82 The steamer *Bellaire* will have her cabin lowered two feet.

Henry Peters is fitting out the engines of the *Queen of the Lakes.*

05 19 82 From the *Charlevoix Sentinel,* we learn that Capt. Pillip Caffrey, of the schooner *Fair Play,* was foully murdered and his body was found in Nawbinway bay. No clue to the murderer has been discovered.

05 19 82 We learn that the elegant little steamer, *J.J. Morley* will take the *Jennie Sutton's* old route for this season and will commence making regular trips next Monday. This boat is finely fitted up for passengers, and can also stow away considerable freight.

05 19 82 Elk Rapids people will liberally patronize the little steamer *J.J. Morley*.

05 26 82 The schooner *C. Collingwood* of Chicago, arrived on Friday last for lumber, and left Tuesday night for Chicago.

The tug *Metamora*, of Montreal, with barges *F. Russell, G. Manley* and *H. Benson*, of Quebec arrived in last Saturday morning for square timber.

05 26 82 The little steamer, *J.J. Morley* will not run on East Bay this season, but between Boyne City and Petoskey.

05 26 82 Last week we made a local to the effect that the *J.J. Morley* would take the *Jennie Sutton's* old route on East bay. We were induced to do so by the owner and captain telling us that was his intention. We have made several mistakes lately by publishing unreliable news, and this time we are going to let it drop where it belongs.

06 02 82 *Petoskey Record:* According to posters, the inland line of steamers are now on their daily route between Petoskey, Cheboygan, Mackinac and St. Ignace. One of the side-wheel steamers *City of Cheboygan* or *Northern Belle,* leaves Crooked Lake on arrival of the train from Petoskey, for the above named places. The train leaves Petoskey at 9 A.M.

06 02 82 The steamer *City of Traverse* left Chicago one day late last trip. High winds and heavy sea.

The tug *Metamora* with the barges *F. Russell, G. Manley* and *H. Benson* left this port Saturday for Quebec with square timber.

The schooner *Green Bay* is ashore at South Fox island, loaded with lumber. She has been scuttled and is lying very easy. A tug from Charlevoix has gone to her assistance.

The officers of Hannah, Lay & Co.'s steamer, *City of Traverse,* appeared last Friday in their new uniform, and they presented a fine appearance. They are a jolly crowd of fellows, and should wear soft cloths.

Wednesday morning when the *T.S. Faxton* was about a mile off from Northport, she became unmanageable owing to the braking of her engine. Her anchor became foul and she commenced to drift. The steamer *Grand Rapids* was telegraphed to, which was at Charlevoix, and she towed the *Faxton* back to Traverse City.

06 09 82 The old *Albatross* engine is being repaired for the brick yard.

06 09 82 The *Valley Queen* has hauled off to be thoroughly repaired and fitted up.

06 09 82 The route through the lakes that outflow at this place, is becoming one of the most popular of any in the Northwest. Five passenger steamers are now plying on the inland lakes, and the scenery to be met at all points is truly beautiful. Come and ride over our fifteen lakes.

06 09 82 Wm. Debbingham fell overboard from the steamer, *Queen of the Lakes,* Monday. If it had been in the middle of Lake Michigan he might have drowned.

Captain Johnson, of the *Queen of the Lakes,* informs us that the first trip of the season was thoroughly enjoyable.

A new piston head for the steamer *T.S. Faxton* is being cast at the Iron Co.'s foundry.

The *Metropolis* took out 449 tons of iron and 35 barrels of alcohol.

The steamer *Bellaire* has been painted and is much improved in appearance.

Since navigation opened 24 vessels have loaded and unloaded at Dexter & Noble's dock.

The tug *Maple Leaf,* of Suttons Bay, called at the dock yesterday. Left for Traverse City, last night.

The schooner *Reindeer* arrived on Tuesday with groceries and provision for Dexter & Noble. She will take out lumber.

Detroit Free Press. The schooner *J.P. DeCoudres* went ashore at Milwaukee Saturday morning and became a total loss. The crew were brought in a life-car by the life-saving crew. The *DeCoudres* measured 146 tons and was built in 1873 on the bottom of the old schooner *Appleton.* She was rebuilt last winter and was valued at $5,000. Carpenter, Bartholomew, Bleyer & Mason of Charlevoix, were her owners. She was uninsured.

The elegant side wheel steamer, *Queen of the Lake,* Captain Fred Johnson, made her trial trip Monday and commenced regular trips on Tuesday. This steamer was built for Dexter & Noble and arrived here 10 years ago the 13th of July, and looks to-day as fine as when she first left the builder's hands. She is first class in every respect, and will make regular trips between Elk Rapids and Torch Lake, stopping at intermediate points; leaving Elk Rapids at 8 A.M. and returning at 6 P.M.

06 16 82 A.K. Dougherty covered the hull of the *Sutton* Wednesday, to keep off the rain and sun.

The deepest place in East Bay is between Elk Rapids and Old Mission, about half way between these two places. The water is 103 fathoms at this point.

Capt. Kinney, of the tug *Elk Lake,* has accepted the position of first mate on the steamer *City of Grand Rapids.* He made many friends while here, and we are sorry to see him go. Joseph Hawley will command the *Elk Lake.*

06 16 82 The tug *Maple Leaf,* of Suttons Bay, came here Sunday, bringing a scow load of freight, among which was the machinery for the new saw mill to be built at Eastport.

The schooner *Reindeer* was towed out Sunday by the tug *Maple Leaf.*
The *Reindeer* was loaded with hardwood lumber and left for Racine.

06 23 82 The tug *Metamora* and barge *Manley* left Tuesday afternoon for Kingston, with square timber.

The steamer *Valley Queen* has been painted, and has had her engine repaired. She left Tuesday afternoon for Torch Lake.

The elegant yacht *Idler*, of Chicago, came in Friday and anchored at the end of the pier. She ran over to Old Mission Sunday and returned here Monday.

Wheels for the *Albatross* are being manufactured at the Iron Co.'s shops. The hubs are of cast steel and are cast separate from the paddles or flukes, which renders it convenient when one of the flukes break to replace it easily. The flukes are keyed in the hub so they do not work loose. We believe that for shallow draft tugs like those belonging to the Iron Co., these wheels are much preferred.

06 30 82 The schooner Reindeer came into port Tuesday after a load of iron and lumber.

06 30 82 The schooner *Metropolis* came in Friday with limestone.

06 30 82 The schooner *Metropolis* left last night with part of a load of iron, 60 barrels of alcohol and 375,000 pounds of acetate of lime. She goes to Chicago.

06 30 82 The tug *Albatross* was hauled out Saturday. Her wheels will be set back further so as to give her more speed.

06 30 82 Weather permitting, the steamer *Clara Belle* will give an excursion from Charlevoix to this place next Sunday, we learn.

07 07 82 The schooner *Reindeer* left Wednesday night for Chicago with a load of lumber and iron.

The yacht *Douglas*, of Chicago, was at the dock Wednesday.

07 14 82 The schooner Metropolis, Capt. Corbett, arrived from Chicago, via Escanaba, Tuesday night with ore and grain.

07 14 82 The steamer Ida has laid up for repairs — having new flues put in her boilers.

07 14 82 C.W. Farrand has sold the steamer *Bellaire* to J.M. Wadsworth and Mr. Wadsworth has sold the *Snipe* to Mr. Farrand. The *Bellaire* is to be run on Intermediate Lake, and the *Snipe* will ply on the lower lakes. —*Breeze*.

07 21 82 The propeller Fountain City made its entrance into Charlevoix harbor last Friday, which was quite an event in the history of Charlevoix.

07 21 82 The schooner *Christiana Nilsen* was towed out by the steamer *Faxton*, last Friday. She took a load of iron to Buffalo.

07 28 82 There are three Buffalo boats a week stopping at Northport, and there should be a small boat running from Old Mission and Elk Rapids to connect with them.

07 28 82 Kessler Smith, of Cincinnati, and Ben and Max Yalomstein bought Wm. Briggs' sail boat, Tuesday, for $50 which was a bargain.

07 28 82 Through trips can now be made to Bellaire by steamers *Queen of the Lakes* and *Ida*. At Bellaire close connection can be made with the *Belle* which will convey you to Central Lake.

07 28 82 The yacht *Vicking*, of Chicago was at anchor near the dock, Wednesday.

08 04 82 If the steamboat men on Torch, Clam, and Intermediate lakes would spend a few dollars on printing ink, their boats might pay more. People in the eastern part of the county and at Traverse City, say that they know nothing about the time cards of the boats, and it is not to be wondered at.

08 04 82 H.E. Lyon has the contract to complete the Clam river bridge, which heretofore has been more show than profit.

08 04 82 One hundred and seventy-five persons went to Petoskey on the propeller *Leland*, Sunday, and report a fine time.

08 04 82 Monday another scow load of lumber from Scofield & Son, Williamsburg, arrived at the River dock. The lumber is being shipped to Racine.

08 11 82 The schooner *City of Chicago*, came in Monday night for iron.
    The schooner *Christiana Nilson* came in Saturday night last.

08 11 82 The tugs *Elk, Torch* and *Albatross* have each new quarter-boards, with newly painted names.

08 18 82 The following vessels were at the dock this week: Schooner *Granger*, for Buffalo with 620 tons of iron, acetate and alcohol; schooner *Lottie Mason*, from Petoskey with a cargo of lime stone; schooner *Fleetwing* for Racine with 350,000 feet of maple lumber; schooner *Reindeer* for Racine with a cargo of maple lumber; schooner *Metropolis* 455 tons of iron to Cleveland; barge *Leland* a cargo of ore; schooner *City of Chicago* for Buffalo with iron, acetate and alcohol.

08 18 82 The schooners *Reindeer* and *Fleetwing*, arrived in port last Saturday, for lumber.

08 18 82 The steamer *Granger*, of Milwaukee, made this port Saturday last.
    The *Lottie Mason*, of Charlevoix, came in Saturday last, with a load of lime stone from Petoskey.

08 18 82 The steamer *Mermaid* will give an excursion from Elk Rapids to the Indian camp ground at Northport on Sunday August 20, leaving Elk Rapids at 8 A.M. Fare for round trip 75 cents.

08 25 82 The steamer *City of Traverse* has now a handsome Hallett & Greenston piano.

08 25 82 A number of the Charlevoix tugs and steamers have laid up- some of them temporarily, and one of them for the season.

08 25 82 Some one stole John E. French's sail boat Monday night, and it was seen going towards Northport. French left for the above place Tuesday.

09 01 82 The *Valley Queen* has been laid up during the last week for repairs and for want of an engineer.

09 01 82 Commodore, Chas. Howard, of Traverse City, visited our place in his new yacht, *Kittie Cline*, on Friday evening enroute from his farm on the west bank of East Bay, to Traverse...

09 08 82 *Charlevoix Sentinel:* The Crosses, fishermen, returning from their nets, Saturday, ran afoul of the hurricane deck of a propeller; with pails lashed to it, and the roof of a vessel's cabin, a door, and several blankets. Nothing was found to disclose the names of the crafts, but the debris had every appearance of being the result of a collision, between a steamer and vessel, in the fog which prevailed two days previous. The debris was found about twelve miles this side of Beaver Island.

09 08 82 The *Metropolis* had 700 barrels of oil for Traverse City, Wednesday. She will be here in a day or two.

09 15 82 During the month of August 235 schooners, propellers, etc., cleared Manistee, and the total number of entries for the same time, 238.

10 05 82 The *Maria* of Charlevoix, made this port yesterday morning.

10 13 82 The schooner *Ellen Spry*, of Chicago, came in Sunday morning for iron.

10 20 82 The barge *Leland* left for Pt. St. Ignace this morning, for ore.

10 20 82 The propeller *Fountain City* went into Old Mission yesterday for a load of potatoes.
   The schooner Reindeer left yesterday for Racine with lumber, iron and wood tar.

10 20 82 Talk about the *Jennie Sutton* being rebuilt this winter, and being put on the East Bay route next season. It would be a good thing for Elk Rapids and a profitable investment for her owners. We should have a bay boat and one owned by Elk Rapids men.

10 27 82 The Propeller *Florence* of the Northern Michigan line ran aground on Harbor Point in Little Traverse Bay Wednesday morning. The damage was slight.

11 03 82 *Charlevoix Sentinel:* The steamer M.W. Wright has been hauled off her Petoskey and South Arm route and has been employed by Chas. and Eugene Cross in the fishing business at $35 per week. The Crosses are running 100 nets.
   The steam barge *Truesdell*, owned by the Pine Lake Iron Company, went ashore at Charlevoix Wednesday night of last week, and was badly damaged. She had on 450 tons of iron for Chicago.

11 10 82 The schooner *Sophia Bonnel* came in last week with 1,400 bushels of wheat for gristing at Dexter & Noble's mill.

11 17 82 On the 13th the barge *Sylvanus G. Macey*, of Detroit, came into port for iron.

The *City of Grand Rapids* has gone into winter quarters at Traverse City. The *Faxton* will run about a week longer.

11 24 82 The barge *Macey*, of Detroit, left for Cleveland, Friday with iron.

The tug *Mermaid*, of Northport, came into this port on Wednesday with passengers. She is probably closing up the business left undone by the regular lines, which have gone into winter quarters.

12 01 82 The barge *Leland* left Tuesday for Chicago with lumber and iron. She will bring back merchandise for Dexter & Noble, Rushmore & Holbrook and other dealers about town.

The schooner *Montauk*, loaded with coal, ran ashore last Thursday night, on the north point of North Manitou Island. She has broken up and gone to pieces. All the crew safe and left here to-day on the propeller *Champlain*. Propeller *Champlain* and *Lawrence* passed down to-day.

12 08 82 Captain Galligan telegraphed that the barge *Leland* would leave Wednesday morning, from Chicago, and she probably ran into some lake port during the storm.

12 08 82 The schooner *Metropolis*, loaded with a miscellaneous cargo, left this port for Chicago early Wednesday morning. If the present weather continues her prospects for reaching her destination soon are not very encouraging. A telegram was received here yesterday, from Northport, stating that a schooner, closely resembling the *Metropolis*, had gone ashore at Light House Point. The telegram also stated that lumber, with which the schooner was loaded was being thrown overboard. The *Metropolis* left here with a fair wind, and it hardly seems possible that she got no farther than Northport. We wonder when the time will come when men will not risk life and property in such hazardous undertakings as sailing a vessel on the great lakes at this season of the year.

12 15 82 The schooner *Metropolis* went ashore at Weiderman's south of light house point.

12 29 82 The barge *Leland* on her last trip when about two miles out of Chicago got entangled in a field of ice and was obliged to call a tug to extricate her. The ice stove a hole in her bows and otherwise damaged her which will make it necessary for her to go into dry dock for repairs.

12 29 82 The steamer *Mermaid* sunk at her dock, at Northport, on Sunday morning, week. Her cabin and upper works have gone to pieces, but her hull and machinery remain.

Chapter 29
Milton Township

04 30 80 Last Tuesday a young boy of Joseph Paradise' started for the head of Torch Lake to see about some shingles belonging to his father. When near Mr. Amisiker's, between this place and Torch Lake village he passed by a lot of colts in the road when one of them turned and kicked him in the side. He was carried into Mr. Amisiker's house where he commenced spitting blood. It is thought perhaps he may not live.

04 30 80 The people of Milton voted that colts could run at large. After the accident to Joseph Paradise it probably changed some of their minds.

07 16 80 The population of Milton is 654.

07 30 80 Farmers are busy gathering their crops in the day time, such as wheat and oats. Thieves are busy too at night. I would advise that family to try that game on me again. I don't live by stealing. I get my living by hard labor, and if any of my neighbors are out of lumber to build their houses they upset privies and take all the lumber off and build their own house with it. Free country.- S. G. Ne-qua-goh-mog.

12 03 80 Alexander O. Campbell is teaching school in district No. 1 in Milton, and has 40 scholars.
    F.L. Church of Banks, is teaching the Peaslee school in the Township of Milton and we learn that he has a good attendance.
    Hollenback & Frink, of Milton, propose getting out a good many cords of cord-wood this winter, having 10 men chopping and two teams hauling wood to banking ground at Indian Town.

12 17 80 Our population has increased some what in the last few weeks. Four families from Canada have moved here for the purpose of settlement, and others from the same locality are looking for suitable homes to bring their families to. They can find but few places in Northern Michigan better adapted for stock and fruit raising than can be found in Antrim county.

01 06 81 A singing school has been organized under the leadership of C.E. Smith, District No. 1, with about 25 scholars.
Preparations have been made to build a Methodist church on the State Road two miles north of Indian Town. Some money has been raised, and the probability is that it will be built in the Spring.
Christmas in this township was generally observed. They had a Christmas tree at Mr. Barnes' and the children of the neighborhood were invited. This was on Christmas eve. Christmas night an oyster supper was had at the same place for the old folks. There was also a Christmas tree at Indian town and a good time was had.

02 11 81 There will be a donation at the Milton School House, Dist. No. 1, on the evening of the 16th inst. Doors open at 7 P.M. supper at 7:30, after which will be a short program, consisting of singing and speaking. - By order of Comm.

The Methodists North of this place along the State Road are contemplating building a church in the spring. Pledges to the amount of several hundred dollars have been secured. A ladies aid society has been formed and they are busy at work holding socials quite often. Last Saturday evening they held one at the house of Mr. Cameron and the proceeds of the evening were $12.85. Wednesday evening the 16th inst. there will be an oyster supper at the house of Frink and Hollenbeck, the proceeds to go to the building fund. A general invitation is given and all that want to have a good time and help forward a good cause can do so by attending this supper.

02 18 81 At the donation given Rev. Blanchard last Wednesday evening, at Milton, the amount of $26 was raised.

03 25 81 H. Robinson has commenced work on his dwelling house again. He commenced the foundation last fall but had to stop operations during the winter on account of the severe weather.

The Methodists have commenced to move material for their new church onto the ground. It is to be erected early in the coming summer on ground donated by Mr. Barnes. It will be within a few rods of the State Road and about two miles north of Indian Town.

04 01 81 John Winters and his father, 61 years old and brother 14, cut from the 5th of Dec. to 23rd of March, 330 cords of wood on Hollenbeck & Frink's farm. - Beat this if you can.

05 06 81 Hollenbek & Frink got out 1,100 cords of wood last winter. Next! Hollenbeck & Frink, intend to clear 50 acres of land this summer.

07 29 81 Mr. S.H. Marsh formerly of Kalamazoo, intends putting up a saw mill in Milton township for custom work. It will be a circular mill, and will be in operation after harvest. Mr. Marsh has brought the first steam thresher that has ever been in this country.

12 16 81 The new Methodist church in Milton north of Indian town will be so far completed as to be opened for religious service on Christmas day. A Christmas tree and sugar social will also be held in the same place on Christmas eve.

02 17 82 Messrs. Hollenbeck & Frink, of Milton have let the contract for the building of their new barn to Mr. John Sage. The building will be 50x36.

04 07 82 Alex. Campbell was elected Supervisor of Milton, and Eldridge Barnes, Treasurer.

04 14 82 At a logging bee last week Frink & Hollenbeck had six or seven acres cleared.

Chester Hollenbeck has just moved into his new house on his farm ¾ of a mile from Indian Town.

Mr. Rockfellow, of Elk Rapids, has purchased what is known as the Johnson farm in South Milton. Compensation, $1,200.

Mr. Marsh has started up his steam saw mill on Torch Lake, and is now able to do better work and more of it than heretofore, having just received and got in running order a new saw. Lumber sawed on halves. Bring on your logs.

04 21 82 The new church in Milton is being completed but will not be ready to occupy for some weeks yet.

Mr. Hirts has donated one acre of land to the town for a burying ground, and it will be immediately fenced and made ready for occupancy.

06 02 82 An exhibition was given in the new Milton M.E. Church, Wednesday evening, to defray expenses incurred in the building. Receipts $16.00. The church had a new pulpit presented on that eve.

06 16 82 Fred Kaiser is doing a good job on the road in front of HiRobinson's farm. The grading is 18 feet between the ditches.

06 16 82 The school has been in session about a month, under the charge of Miss Johnson, of Old Mission.

07 14 82 W.L. Frink of Milton, has a fine new barn completed.
Hollenbeck & Frink, who have been in partnership for three years divided up and dissolved partnership last Monday night, in about a half an hour, without any disagreement. Together they owned 360 acres of land and that was cut in two. C.D. Hollenbeck taking one half and W.L. Frink taking the other. In the three years they have been in the county, they have cleared 125 acres of land and now both own splendid farms.

08 04 82 Monday the 24th inst., while the hands employed at Marsh's mill were at dinner, fire broke out in a pile of slabs near the mill and when discovered was under such headway that it took the united efforts of all hands to save the mill. But for the timely aid of neighbors the mill would have undoubtedly been destroyed, but as it is the loss is small, a few hundred feet of lumber perhaps. The fire is supposed to have originated from sparks from the engine.

11 10 82 School at the new school house has commenced with Miss Emma Gates as teacher. At the Russell school house Miss C. Johnson as teacher. North Milton feels assured of good schools the coming winter.

11 17 82 P.M. the Indian so badly pounded by two other Indians a week or so ago, is now recovering and may possibly recover.

11 24 82 About forty of the neighbors met at Thomas Russell's last week, and husked about 100 bushels of corn, and had a good time generally.

02 26 81
It was a bold, rash census man
  Approached a lady true;
"How many kids?" said he, and she
  Said, "What is that to you?"
"Its my business," and she screamed;
  "Come here a minute, Dan?"
And a burly person came and put
  A head on the census man.

Chapter 30
Miscellaneous

01 23 80 The arrivals of all classes of Ocean craft for the year 1879 is officially given as 21,421. Probably this is the largest on record.

03 05 80 Idaho has a go-as-you-please town. It is a place called Beaver, situated at the mouth of Beaver Canon,[sic] is a sort of kangaroo city, which has jumped along as far as the railroad advanced, thirty or forty miles at a time. A year ago it was called Oneida, and was one hundred and twenty miles from Ogden, since which time it has changed its base and name several times, and is now one hundred and forty miles from its former base. When the town takes a spring, the hotel, saloons, dwelling houses, and shops are packed up and moved along and are set down again just as they started. In each new locality the streets and signs appear the same, so that a visitor at one place is at home, without asking, in the new. The inhabitants seem to take kindly to this municipal nomadic life, and Barney O'Niel, the hotel keeper, says, "Ivery time she jumps she jumps aisier."[sic]

04 09 80 If Friday never deserved to be called hangman's day before, it certainly did last Friday, as eight men were hung in this country on that day.

04 16 80 To prevent being annoyed by fleas at night, put two under sheets on the bed, and lay fresh tansy [sic] leaves between. This will not stain, and is not as unpleasant as the companionship of the tormentors.

05 07 80 Captain Edward Doherty, who commanded the detachment which made John Wilkes Booth a prisoner, is a street contractor at New Orleans. He got a reward of $75,000 for the capture.

06 04 80 In Scribner's "Bric-a-Brac" for June, attention is called to the fact that the phonograph is not a new invention, but- if we are to believeCyrano Bergerac, a French traveler — was in constant use in the moon two centuries ago. That wicked Edison!

10 29 80 A prominent Republican said to us Monday that ifHancock was elected President he would, some day we might select, stand on his head in front of the post-office. We expect to advertise by posters that a dignified Republican, Mr._____ will stand on his head in front of the post-office in honor of Hancock's election. The name of the gentleman and the day of the performance will be given on small bills.

10 29 80   VOTE RIGHT.
Vote For Honest Hancock.
If you want another four years like Grant's last term, vote for Garfield.
Vote for Hancock next Tuesday and you will kill sectionalism, and secure a more perfect union of the States.
Vote for General Hancock, the Soldier and Statesman, next Tuesday, and

you will have peace, union and prosperity.

The Republican party elected their President by fraud. Are you honest men to say amen to it by voting for De Golyer Garfield?

If you wish to say amen to the stealing of the Presidency in 1876 vote for Garfield. No honest man knowing the history of that crime, can do it.

11 05 80 Lots of sick office-seers. This is not a good year for Democrats.

11 05 80 A Saginaw supervisor drew his pay, went on a voyage of discovery about town, and at the close of the cruise accused a woman of the town of having robbed him. That's the kind of shaky timber they make supervisors of, sometimes.

11 05 80 It will be remembered that we mentioned lately that a prominent Republican in town said to us that if Hancock was elected he would stand on his head in front of the post office in honor, and we were to advertise the same. Things look as though there would be no use for these hand-bills. We don't care any thing about Hancock's election, (sour grapes) but we would like "thundering well" to see the gentleman stand on his head under those circumstances.

11 12 80   "The melancholy days have come,
           The saddest of the year."
Yea! The saddest we have seen in four years. We have searched the Democratic papers for many days and find no ray of hope to us poor disconsolates. We sought our Bible for words of comfort and read "Oh! Lord thou knowest our down-sittings and our uprisings. Yes he saw us uprise in the early part of the campaign, saw the bright promises that lured us on, and then saw the Reps. sit down on us unmercifully. But this did not revive our drooping spirits we tried again. "There is hope of a tree if it is cut down that it will sprout again." We verily believe David was a Democrat when he chanted his consoling sentiments to a disconsolate host. Being exultant we read a line or two more. "But man giveth up the ghost and where is he?" A still small voice walked forth on the balmy air, from away up that saline rivulet and gently echoed, Where?"

03 18 81 The growing popularity of the postal-card as a means of correspondence is something wonderful. The entire number manufactured and used during the first year of their introduction was 100,000,500, and during the year which has just closed the aggregate number sent out was 246,063,060. This latter number is an increase over the number issued in 1878 of 36,879,060.

05 13 81 The Fuel of the Future – The *Nautical Gazette* makes the following announcement in regard to the use of petroleum as fuel: We shall soon be able to announce a wonderful stride in the mechanical appliances for using liquid fuel for generating steam in both marine and land boilers. The matter is in the hands of practical men who will soon demonstrate that they can make 18 to 30 gallons of crude petroleum costing from 85 to 90 cents, do the work of a ton of coal, costing from $4 to $4.25, and without dirt or smoke, and when, as in the case of a large steamer carrying from forty to forty-five men in the fire-room, one man in each will be abundantly able to keep up a uniform pressure of steam at all times.

Liquid fuel is the intervening step between coal and electricity which will in due season furnish motion for the world. But until we arrive at a thorough knowledge of this subject and of motive power liquid fuel will have had its day and generation, wiping out the last remnant of barbarism coal. The fireman of the future can wear broadcloth in the fire-room, while the coal-passer will have laid down his "shovel and hoe" to become memories of the past. This condition of things is near at hand.

05 13 81 Wexford county is trying to move its county seat from Sherman to Manton, and has got the prisoners as far along as the Cadillac lock-up, which the supervisors have declared the official jail of the county. The people voted at the last election to change the county seat to Manton, and at the next election they will vote on the question of moving it to Cadillac.

05 20 81 A lump of native copper nearly pure, and weighing five and three quarter pounds, was found the other day in Vernon township, Shiawassee county.

06 10 81 Grand Rapids proposes to try the experiment of lighting the city with towers and, electric lights. The first tower will rise 96 feet above the eaves of the building and will have five lights.

06 17 81 The city of Ludington was destroyed by fire Monday. The telegraph office, churches and business places were burned. About 75 families were left houseless, and the loss to the city is put at $200,000. The entire business portion was destroyed.

06 17 81 The coming Sunday will be one of unusual interest to those who believe in signs and seasons. At 8:45 of that morning, six of the planets are at or very near the nearest point of their orbits to the sun. The earth is on the opposite side of the sun and near its farthest distance from it. This brings several planets on almost a direct line with six of them exerting their combined attraction on the sun. Astrologers and superstitious people regard this as a harbinger of war, pestilence, earthquakes, and upheavals in society and governments. Some are even afraid that the combined attractions of the planets will so disturb the solar system as to bring a grand crash and put an end to things in general. Scientists are interested because it is a phenomenon which appears only at very long intervals. Only three of these planets are visible to the naked eye. These may be seen any morning between three and four o'clock as three bright morning stars. The large one is Venus. The pale yellow is Saturn and the bright red one is Jupiter.

07 08 81 As the President (Garfield) was entering the depot at the Baltimore and Potomac Railroad at Washington, last Saturday, to take the train for Long Branch, he was shot twice by a scoundrel named Charles Jules Guiteau...

08 05 81 The Muskegon salt well is a success, and two more will be sunk at once.
A 15 ton mass of pure copper is being taken out of the Mass mine, in Ontonagon county.

226

Cadillac has a boat house and opera house combined-boat house down stairs, on a level with the lake; and opera house up stairs.

08 12 81 The building in which most of the Grand Rapids lawyers have their offices is known as the "Robber's Roost."

08 16 81 It is estimated that it will require 50,000 bushels of seed wheat to replace that was destroyed by the fire storm in Eastern Michigan.

09 02 81 The fish hatchery buildings at Crystal Springs, which cost this state a snug sum of money, were sold for $1.30. The knot holes were worth more than that.

09 23 81 PRESIDENT GARFIELD IS DEAD...While his death has been expected for some weeks, still the shock was very great...

09 30 81 MEMORIAL ADDRESS--(for President Garfield) Delivered in the Presbyterian Church, Monday Sept. 20, by Rev. L.M. Belden.

We are met to-day, in obedience to the proclamation of the Governor of the State, to pay the last tribute of respect to the memory of our late President, James A. Garfield...

LIFE and DEATH of JAMES A. GARFIELD
A correct History of his Life and full Particulars of the **Assassination** of our martyred President. A most remarkable and critical **AGENTS WANTED** The **BEST SELLING BOOK** record of a noble man. **AGENTS WANTED** of the AGE. Circulars Free.
50 per cent. discount to Agents on orders for 20 copies or more. Sample Book by mail, $1.00. CINCINNATI PUB. CO., 174 W. 4th St., Cincinnati, O.

10 07 81 A relic reported to be a ring belonging to Father Marquette was found at Old Mackinaw... —*Cheboygan Tribune.*

10 21 81 Dr. M.L. Leach, of Charlevoix, leaves to-day for South Arm, at which point he will cross over to the head of Intermediate Lake and go down the chain to Elk Rapids. The object of the expedition is to write up the route for *The Chicago American Field.* His articles will embrace the geological and botanical features of the region, as well as that of the game and scenery. He will be absent three weeks.

11 04 81 On Oct.13, a funeral service was held in Berlin in the memory of our late President.

11 11 81 Halloween, the evening preceding all Saints' day, comes but once a year in this country, and we presume that a good many folks are glad of it. The celebration of this important (?) occasion was duly attended to in this city last Monday evening, according to the testimony of some of our citizens on the following morning. Gates, signs, barber poles, etc., wandered from their homes and became located in neighboring yards and other strange places; lawyers became doctors and doctors became lawyers; millinery establishments made use of barber poles to advertise their business, and the cute Big Rapids youth winked in his sleeve when he thought how too cute for anything he had been. —*Current,* Big Rapids.

The Elk Rapids citizens can bear witness that Holloween was celebrated at this place.

03 31 82 Henry W. Longfellow, the renowned poet died at Boston, March 24 ...

04 07 82 It is now reported that Jesse James has really been killed. The murder was committed April 4, at St. Joseph, Mo., by Robert and Charles Ford, members of the police force, and who have been with James' gang since November.

04 28 82 Don't get in the way of A busy man or A buzz saw.

04 28 82 A million pounds of buffalo meat were shipped from the plains last year and the railways have carried 10,000.000 pounds of buffalo bones and 6,000,000 pounds of hides to eastern markets.

05 05 82 Sullivan, the champion pugilist, was sentenced by the Boston police court to three months in the house of correction for his assault on Robbins in a saloon row. Sullivan appealed and was put under bonds for trial at the superior court in May.

05 05 82 A dastardly attempt was made at New York, April 29, by some miscreants on the lives of W. H. Vanderbilt and Cyrus W. Field by sending them explosives through the mails. Fortunately the dangerous character of the packages were discovered enroute to the post-office station, and so a probable loss of life prevented.

05 05 82 A Milwaukee girl wants $5,000 damages because she wasn't quite ready to be kissed when a man kissed her. He ought to have blown a horn or rung a bell and given her thirty seconds warning.

05 05 82 Jefferson Daves' daughter Varina is a great belle in the South. She is pale, slender and reserved. At a recent ball she appeared as the Margravine of Beiruth in a rose pink velvet and satin costume.

06 30 82 GUITEAU – We delay our paper for a short time to-day to furnish our readers with a few telegraphic dispatches concerning the wretched death of the assassin. There is precious little satisfaction in taking the cur's life, although he did not hesitate to take the life of the Chief Magistrate of this nation (President Garfield).

Washington, D.C., June 30, 1882.
    The drop fell at 12:30 and death ensued instantly. He partook of a hearty breakfast, bathed, shaved, and had his boots blacked, and dressed previous to ascending scaffold, which was accomplished with a firm step. After prayer by

Rev. Hicks, he delivered the dying prayer, and read a few verses, breaking down twice, recovered well and shouted, "Glory". With the black cap drawn over his head he gave the signal himself. The drop fell and he was dead in three minutes, with broken neck. The crowd rushed forward and viewed the remains in the casket, which will be buried in the jail yard after autopsy. Every thing as regards the hanging successful in every particular. Guiteau's brother viewed the hanging, and his sister will view the remains to-morrow.

07 07 82 The Manistee *Times* calls the hanging of Guiteau, the "necktie social." Guiteau was buried in the Northeast corridor of the District of Columbia jail. The corridor is opposite the one in which he was hung.

07 07 82 A man in public office may be — no matter how great a success; the man who follows him will be a successor.

07 21 82 Mrs. Lincoln, widow of the late President Lincoln, is dead.

07 21 82 John L. Sullivan, the Boston pugilist and Tug Wilson, the English Champion, fought a hard glove contest in the Madison Square Garden, New York, Monday night. Sullivan failed to knock Wilson out of time in four rounds and thereby lost $1,000.

08 11 82 Effects of Latin on the Hair — Mr. Alden has discovered that the teaching of Latin has a tendency to make the hair curl, as illustrated by the schoolmarm's of Massachusetts and other Eastern States. He omits to note, however, that this curl becomes so tight in the case of the masculine pedagogues that the hair becomes self-extractive, which accounts for their baldness. This also explains the lack of hair on Caesar, who learned Latin in his early youth, and spoke it habitually in his more advanced years.

08 18 82 A new party has been formed in Detroit, in the interest of free trade, and made their bow through the *News* last Saturday. A strong list of names have already been pledged, and the party will gain in power. The platform as set forth is...

08 18 82 The Science of Kissing -- Science in the last few years has gained a terrible foothold in this world. It has rattled the dry bones of oldfogyism, made pi out of worn-out theories, upset ideas which have been established for centuries. The latest and most astonishing fact that has been developed is that there is a scientific mode of kissing.

The day when a young man could grab a girl round the neck and gobble a kiss in a rough, but comfortable manner, is past. The time when he could encircle her waist with one arm, get his shirt bosom full of hairoil, and pirouette his lips over every square inch of her countenance, is no more.

Science has proclaimed against it, and man shudders, but remains silent. The old style of kissing, which sounds like some one tearing a clapboard off a smoke house, is now considered bad taste, and, consequently, is rapidly going out of fashion, although the majority of girls admit that science has cruelly destroyed all the comfort of a long lingering, heart-thrilling kiss, and causes them to express no little regret at the change.

The improved scientific method of kissing is to throw the right arm languidly around the fair one's shoulder, tilt her chin up with the left hand until her nose is pointed at an angle of forty-five degrees; or, rather, until it has an aspect resembling the bowsprit of a clipper-built sloop, then stoop slowly, and, grazing about her lips in a quiet, subdued sort of way, tickle her nose with your mustache until she cries "ouch!" This is scientific kissing, but there is no consolation in it. It is flat, lukewarm; it lacks substance, and if not stale it is at least unprofitable.

12 08 82 It is proposed to carve a new township out of the northern part of Manistique county. The present townships up in that region are about as large as the state of Rhode Island.

04 01 81
He softly kissed his sleeping wife,
  And then with a lingering look
Of fond affection straightway went
  And kissed her pretty cook,
Alas for him, the gentle wife
  He thought asleep, was not,
And for her cook and hubby, too,
  She made it mighty hot.
He softly kissed his sleeping wife,
  Then with a lingering look

Chapter 31
People

01 02 80 A number of young people of this place attended the ball at Traverse City Wednesday evening.

01 02 80 Mr. Jas. J. McLaughlin is clearing a large piece of land opposite Mr. Geo. E. Steele's place. A fine view can now be had of Elk Lake from the highway.

01 02 80 A new carriage team for Mr.H.H. Noble came on the *Leland* Wednesday morning.

01 09 80 Last Saturday Mr. James Davidson traded horses with some one, we don't know who, and going out to feed his new horse next morning found it so far gone that he was obliged to kill it. Some sharper had evidently played him a trick.

01 09 80 While working on the spile driver near the furnace Thursday morning Emile Gribi had his foot badly crushed. The injury will probably lay him up for some weeks.

01 16 80 Over 100 people enjoyed the skating on Bass Lake last night. With a beautiful evening, splendid ice, big bon-fire on the shore, good company a good time was had. Some of the young men can waltz very nicely on skates. Several quadrilles were danced and every body had a tip top time.

01 16 80 We notice in the *Detroit Free Press* that Mayor Lewis, of London, Ont., brother of Mr. James Lewis of this place, has donated his entire salary of $1,200 to the poor.

01 16 80 Mrs. Lodema Wyckoff recently purchased the Belden farm on the Elk Lake road of Christian Diefenbach.

01 16 80 There is a girl not many miles from here who fixed Christmas day to be married, but postponed it because her mother could not get any eggs to make the wedding cake.

01 23 80 Last Friday evening John Spencer had a leg broken while scuffling in Newton's Saloon. It is not serious, however, but will probably lay him up for a month or so.

01 23 80 Mr. John Denahy was quite seriously injured by an explosion Wednesday last. A doctor was called who pronounced the injuries slight. It was one of these patent curtain rollers that went off and John was more frightened than hurt. No damage was done.

01 23 80 David Spaulsbury has about two hundred cords of wood cut and has had the past week six teams drawing wood from his place to the Furnace.

01 23 80 Get out your snow shovel and set the small boy to work.

01 30 80 A number of people were awakened Monday night by the cry of Fire! Murder! etc., by some persons on the street. We think a night in the lock up would be good for them. It would evidently keep them sober while there.

01 30 80 The social at the residence of Mrs. John Cooper last Tuesday evening was not behind those already given, socially. With mind-reading, charades and story telling, those present regretted much when the hour for departure came.

01 30 80 The happy couple that were "saranayded" [sic] last Wednesday evening, if they have any ear for music, will long remember the night. It was their wedding eve and the boys everlastingly made the music until the happy groom came out to "set, em up," which he did in a right royal manner. After he had "set' em up" the boys gave them a parting salute and returned to their homes.

01 30 80 Gus Myers last Sunday went into Charles Grammel's Saloon on River Street to clear'er up when he was followed by two persons and because he would not give them beer they broke the windows. This is second hand.

01 30 80 A few people on the street last Sunday evening noticed flames issuing from what they supposed was the residence of Mr.H.H. Noble. On going there it was found to be the ash-house.

01 30 80 Hi Robinson has recently moved the empty building near the brewery up along side of Chas. Grammel's house, which will be rebuilt by Grammel for a dwelling house.

02 06 80 Last Saturday some young fellows from Elgin, after getting pretty high, came a good joke on O.B. Sackett of this place. One of them engaged in conversation with him while the others stole a ham from his meat wagon. Mr. Sackett said nothing, but Monday Sheriff Cameron went up to see them and they paid damages, costs, and for the ham. Rather an expensive joke.

02 06 80 Last Wednesday evening a party was given at the Hughes House to celebrate the birthday of Miss Mary Hughes. It was one of the pleasantest parties given in Elk Rapids for many a day. The music was good, the room for dancing a pleasant one, and the company present thoroughly enjoyed themselves. Miss Mary is at present at Lynville, Ill. but her friends remembered her.

02 13 80 Last Tuesday a young fellow by the name of Frank Olney hired a rig from Power's Livery Stable to go to Traverse City, and was to return the same day. The horse and buggy was let him, but he did not return until Wednesday about 11 o'clock. On returning instead of taking the rig to the barn he stopped at the Hughes House, ordered his horse put out and said that the horse was warm and did not need feed. After getting his dinner he "lit out" without paying Mr. Powers for the use of the livery. Mr. Powers was notified that the horse was at the Hotel, and now he feels as though he could make it hot for Mr.Olney.

02 13 80 Charles Deverny was found nearly dead on Wednesday morning near the Furnace. He was in the Casting room the evening before. Leaving there he went but a short distance before he fell. We have not yet learned the cause.

02 13 80 Some of the young people at the Furnace went up to Mr. John Goddard's last Tuesday evening, had a pleasant little dance and returned home late.

02 13 80 Most of the people at Elgin are busily engaged in getting out wood for the Elk Rapids Iron Co.

02 20 80 Mr. Cameron our County Sheriff conducted a trade for Mr. F.J. Lewis, of Torch Lake, with Mr. Bill Dingman (a man who never trades horses except for the accommodation of other people) paying $5 and taking his choice. After the bargain was closed our Sheriff was kindly informed that it was the same horse he owned two years ago, having kicked himself clear through Torch Lake and the northwest corner of Antrim Co., destroying several shade trees and miles of rail fence between Traverse City and Charlevoix. Being dark Mr. Cameron did not recognize his old friend until next morning when after trying to harness up, with the help of a pitchfork finally succeeded in hitching to the wagon. The result was part of Mrs. Hughes hay-loft gone, wagon smashed and $5 to trade back. Mr. Lewis left for home in the afternoon, $10 having made himself and Mr. Cameron sadder but wiser men.

02 20 80 Geo. H. Bailey was arrested last Saturday afternoon on a charge of whipping his wife. The case was adjourned until the 24th of this month and will be tried before Justice McLaughlin.

02 20 80 Last Saturday night about 9 o'clock Goodley Laubscher with his father and uncle were crossing Elk Lake. Goodley skating and pushing his uncle and father on a sled. It being a little dark he did not notice the crack in the ice near Stony Point and pushed them both in. A good wetting to both of them was the result.

02 27 80 On Wednesday of this week after 1 P.M. Joe Schuler, a 14 year old son of Fred Schuler, was crossing Elk Lake to pick up some block wood that had been left on the ice and take home some cedar posts he had cut. When he came to the place where Mr. Smith lost his horse, he broke through the ice. Jas. Miller saw him when he broke through, but the ice was so weak that he could not go to him. He came to town and Mr. Skinner sent some men up from the Furnace. They procured a boat but before they could reach him, the little fellow went down. He had broken about three rods of ice in trying to get out. After some little time the body was recovered in about 10 feet of water.

02 27 80 The trial of Doc. Bailey for whipping his wife took place as per adjournment on last Tuesday which resulted in a disagreement of the Jury. A second trial for the same offense was had on Thursday at which trial the Doc. was acquitted. The Doc. characterizes the whole affair as persecution, naming ourselves among others as one of the persecutors. Mrs. Bailey told us her husband had whipped her which we would have sworn to if we had not been choked off by the Court. But if we have done the Doc. injury by believing the statement of his wife that he whipped her, we beg pardon and will make all the reparation in our power, which is;

> He has our free and full consent
> To whale her to his hearts content.

02 27 80 A gentleman hailing from Indiana while crossing Elk Lake yesterday broke through the ice and with difficulty succeeded in getting out.

Ben McCreadey's team broke through the ice on Elk Lake last Monday. With the assistance of Amos Wood and others the team was gotten out.

Charles Smith, of Milton, lost one of his horses last Tuesday. While driving across Elk Lake, they broke through. One of them was lifted out but the harness, wagon and the other went down. It was a narrow escape for Mr. Smith too we learn, as he was pitched head foremost into the water. He was driving near where they have been getting out ice and the ice is quite thin at that place.

03 05 80 A. Lieberthal arrived here Tuesday from, Bay City, and is salesman in the clothing house of Mr. S. Goldman.

03 05 80 About 17 years ago a Prussian named Lawrence Garrett came to this country and after saving to the amount of $600 he returned home to the island of Foehr, which belongs to Prussia. With the money he purchased property there, but having some debts he returned here last October and commenced working for the Iron Co. About two weeks ago he was taken with typhoid and pneumonia, which resulted in his death last Monday. He leaves a wife and two children who are now in the Old Country.

03 05 80 As many of the young gentlemen in our town love to waltz, we take the following little note from an exchange which may probably interest them: "One man waltzes with his head in the air and much the expression worn by a dog when he is howling at the sound of music. Another has a bend in the middle, which looks as uncomfortable as it is ungraceful. One genuflects [sic] at every turn and slides out one of his feet as if to trip up rival dancers. An even more dangerous performer works his left hand up and down as if it were a pump-handle. A tall man, with a top-heavy kind of a stoop, leans over his partner like a great hen taking a chicken under his wings. One man holds his partner as if he were afraid she would slip from his grasp, while another looks as if he wished he were rid of his bargain.

03 12 80 The case of the people *vs.* Charles Wendell did not come to trial last Monday on account of the non-appearance of G.H. Bailey, the complainant. Wendell was formerly in the employ of Bailey, and after the trial of Bailey for wife beating was commenced, Wendell, who was the principle witness against Bailey was arrested for larceny. On Monday last Wendell gave himself up to the sheriff and was discharged by Justice McLaughlin.

03 12 80 A party of three men, probably from the lumber woods, passed through this place last Wednesday on a vehicle resembling a cross between a circus wagon and a milk cart.

03 12 80 While using the lathe at the Furnace Monday Mr. John Thompson was struck on the head by the stick he was turning, which cut quite a large gash in his forehead. Dr. Evans was called and dressed the wound.

03 12 80 We had nearly forgotten the town of Bellaire until we heard that James Rankin had located there.

03 19 80 A free fight was had in front of Newton's Saloon last Saturday, in which one or two persons were pretty badly bruised. It would be a good thing if men when they get drunk would settle their difficulties some where else than in the front streets, and when they do make a rumpus of that kind on the front street they should be promptly arrested and put in the Cooler.

03 26 80 Thursday Louie Roberts and an Indian after partaking of a little of the "Oh! be joyful" started to cross Elk Lake, when Roberts fell and received a "tunk" on his head. A physician was called who pronounced the injuries slight, but recommended that he be allowed to sober off. The Indian was quite communicative and said that Roberts drank eleven glasses of beer and one glass of whisky, and that he, the Indian, drank just as much as Roberts did. It is known where the Indian got the beer and whisky, too.

03 26 80 In coming from Kalkaska on Monday last O.J. Powers was obliged to come on foot from the head of Round Lake. He thought he would take the shortest route here which was to cross Round and Elk Lakes, which he did, but not however without making a hole through the ice a little larger than it would seem necessary for him to crawl out of, which he did very promptly, and coolly and cautiously, and went his lonely way rejoicing.

03 26 80 Tuesday night about half past eleven a shock something similar to an earthquake was felt in the vicinity of the furnace. It caused considerable alarm, but on investigation it was found to be nothing but a poor Englishman indulging in a quiet snore.

03 26 80 James Cameron, our worthy sheriff has measured the distance between here and Indian town, and found the same to be four miles. He also found the distance between this place and his father's farm to be 82 miles. There was some little dispute as to the distance between Elk Rapids and Mr. Cameron's place, so the sheriff tied a rag on the wheel of his buggy and counted the revolutions.

04 02 80 For several days past there has been (with out food, clothing, or shelter from the cold either day or night) two pigs. One died in the road near Mr. Carns from starvation, the other one, George Gee Jr., took home, feed and clothed and took care of it. Owner can have it by paying charges.—Henry Gee.

04 02 80 William Deering fell off the end of the dock into the bay one day this week, and Adam Lobscher in his efforts to save him wished to throw him a pig of iron for a float.

04 30 80 If the person or persons who broke into our office some weeks ago will repair the window we shall appreciate his or their kindness. A person that would break into a printing office is considered a fit candidate for a lunatic asylum, as there is nothing that would benefit anyone. But Chas. Wendell rented some weeks ago a window in it and his bench was not passed by, for they took two watch works, one of them belonging to Rev. Mr. Bradey, and the other one belonging to some one else. The works have been returned, but a lathe belonging to Wendell has not. The "business" will be ferreted out. It has got to be quite a common thing in this county to murder, commit rape, burglary, and to do anything that is damnable and disagreeable. Wendell made proper restitution to Mr. Bradey and other persons loosing by the theft. The burglary was committed in the night of April 6th, and it is thought that the guilty parties will be brought to justice, but we hope they will fix that window.

04 30 80 An amusing occurrence happened at the flouring mill of Dexter & Noble one day this week. Uncle James Davidson, our accommodating drayman, called at the mill for some feed with a couple of bags, one in the other. After stating what he wanted he thrust his hand into the bag containing the other and as quickly withdrew it and began jumping and striking one side and the other to the dismay of the miller, who knowing that the old gentleman had been out of health for some time past, thought he had been seized with a fit of some kind; but when he gasped "mouse", the miller knew one had run up his coat sleeve, and they had a hearty laugh at his expense. The mouse must have been half starved as he began to eat the old man as soon as he got to a good stopping place.

04 30 80 One of the most disgraceful affairs that has been our lot to witness was enacted on our streets yesterday.

Charles Wendell was walking along quietly minding his own business, when Harry Alplern come along and without the slightest provocation struck him twice, once with his fist and once with the handle of an umbrella. Wendell retaliated by hitting Alpern on the side of the head with a stone.

What Wendell had previously done to Alpern we do not know; but we do know that he had no provocation at the time.

05 07 80 Samuel Mitchell, of Winnebago City, Minn., who visits this place every spring and who was formerly a resident of this place, opened the fishing season Tuesday by spearing an immense pickerel which weighed 16 pounds and was 3 feet and 2 inches in length.

05 07 80 BORN – A daughter to Mr. and Mrs. H.E. Gemberling, Friday, April 30th, 1880. Mother and child doing well. – *Albion Recorder.*

Considering the high price of paper, "roller composition" and the time required, we are glad to hear that Mr. Gemberling has at last a "gal-ly."

05 07 80 It is said that Adam was the first man. This town is blessed with an Adam who is said to be a lineal descendant of the first Adam, but unlike him, our Adam is a painter. Adam the first had a rib extracted from his side and a partner made for him. Our Adam on the contrary, judging from his frequent visits to Traverse City, is contemplating adding a couple of ribs to his anatomy. We write by request of Adam, and we suppose if it isn't all right he will raise Cain as soon as he is Able, but then we don't care A-dam.

05 14 80 Mr. Chas. Hickox received on the barge *Leland*, a fine looking cream colored mare which he had sent home for.

05 14 80 We took a short ride in the country last Tuesday, and could not help noticing the beautiful farms along the road. Among the many was the Mr. Sours' farm, situated about two miles from this place on the east side of the road, Mr. Sours has a good many acres under cultivation, and the wheat is looking finely on his farm. He as a large orchard of young trees which all bear fruit. His house is a neat two-story frame building. Everything about the place is in the best of order. Mr. Carnes has a fine farm on this road and also has some fine fields of wheat. He has a large brick farm house which a person would not expect to see "up north in the pine woods". Mr. Shermans' farm extends from the Elk Lake road. His house is built near the lake and every thing about shows evidence of a master hand.

05 21 80 Charles Wendell who has been in this place for some time repairing watches and jewelry left Wednesday for Charlevoix where he will establish himself in the jewelry business. Wendell did some good work in his line.

05 21 80 Mr. John Hughes who has been absent from Elk Rapids for the past two years returned home last Saturday.

06 04 80 About forty Swedes left this place Tuesday on the Clara Belle, bound for Escanaba.

06 04 80 A little son of Rudolph Guyer fell in the river at the chute on Monday last and in falling received a contusion of the head. He was rescued and permitted to start for home alone, and in crossing the bridge above the saw mill, somewhat dazed by his hurt, fell in the river again, and would have been drowned but for the timely aid of Mr. H.H. Cooper who discovered him, and with some difficulty succeeded in saving him.

06 04 80 Young man, don't swear. There is no occasion for swearing outside of a newspaper office, where it is useful in proof reading, and indispensably necessary in getting forms to press. It has been known also materially to assist an editor in looking over the paper after it is printed. But otherwise it is a very foolish habit. – Ed.

06 11 80 Oliver Powers went out in the country this morning to arrest Jim Coleman who was seen to pick the pockets yesterday of an Indian named Jim Fisher.

06 18 80 Obituary of Archibald Cameron, of Creswell...
    Jim Colman who was arrested last week for picking an Indian's pocket was examined before Justice LaForge last Friday and was placed under $500 bail to appear at the circuit court.

06 26 80 The past few days of warm weather has warmed the water so the boys go along the street holding two fingers up—an invitation to go in swimming.

07 02 80 W.S. Mesick of Mancelona, was in town Wednesday. He had "come down" that morning from Bellaire, and his description of the place was any thing but good. We sincerely hope that the people have selected a good point for a county seat; but we fear not.

07 02 80 One of the employees at C.A. Newton's Livery Stable made a bet with another employee Tuesday night that after the *Jennie Sutton's* last whistle was blown he could harness the horses, hitch them to the bus and drive them to the dock before the *Sutton* was tied up. He harnessed the horses, hitched them to the bus and turned the corner by the post office in three minutes and a half; but failed to get to the dock before the *Sutton* was tied up, and so lost a "V".

07 9 80 Kearney came near being chawed up lately on the sand lots by some angry Democratic workingmen. The police rescued him.

07 09 80 A man got shot at R.W. Bagot's store the other day.

07 09 80 Mr. J.W. Davis met with an accident last Friday after noon which might have been fatal. He had gone upstairs in Messrs. Dexter & Noble's flouring mill to look at the machinery when his coat caught on the line shaft. It was impossible for him to extricate himself as the wheel was going pretty fast. After being taken around as it seemed to him an indefinite number of times, it seemed to him that the motion of the wheel was slower and by and extra effort he succeeded in getting his shoulder against a post that was near and being a very powerful man he succeeded in stopping the wheel. He then called to Willie Moore, a young lad who was working in the mill at the time, who shut the water off. Mr. Davis had his clothes torn badly and received two or three bruises, but was not seriously injured. He does not care for another such experience, and he and his friends are very thankful for his escape from what might have been his death if it had not been for the young boy mentioned above, as his strength was nearly gone when the boy happened to come upstairs.

07 09 80 To-day Misses Mary Noble, Maria Norris, Celia Davis, Clara Ballard and Messrs., T.H. Noble, Henry Durkee will start on a camping expedition to Rapid River. They will be absent a week.

07 16 80 When we wrote that article about our Adam a few weeks ago we did not think our predictions would be verified so soon; but it seems that they are, or are about to be. He was seen the other day coming up the street laboring under the burden of a full grown cradle. Poor Adam- but it is the way of all the world.

07 16 80 Messrs. N. Sid Platt and George Deering of Louisville, Ky., accompanied with their wives, fished at Follett's mill Monday and caught a beautiful lot of trout. We learn that it was the best string that had been brought to the Lake View House this season.

07 16 80 W. Riley of the Lake View House barber shop has not been able to shave his customers this week because his wife presented him with a little shaver Monday morning.

07 16 80 Manda M. Smith was born in the state of New York June 1, 1881; died July 13, 1880, [sic]...

07 23 80 Mr. H.H. Noble is having a neat picket fence built in front of his lawn.

07 23 80 The matrimonial market has been very unsteady for the past month, but there are now indications of its assuming the standard basis. Stock has been to a very high figure lately, a recent transaction being quoted above fifty; but it is now coming down, and a certain case soon to be disposed of will probably go about 23-19, while in a case in which negotiations are now pending it will probably drop to 20-16.

07 23 80 The "camping out" party, Misses Mary Noble, Maria Norris, Delia T. Davis, and Messrs. Durkee, T.H. and E.S.Noble, returned home Saturday last from their trip on Intermediate Lake. They had a "glowyous [sic] time."

07 30 80 Charlie Noble, a 4-year old son of Mr. H.H. Noble, nearly met with death last Friday afternoon. He stepped on to a board that was loose just above the saw mill and fell into the water near the wheels. He caught hold of a timber by one hand and was just slipping from his hold when he was pulled out. A moment more and he would have been crushed by the wheels as the mill was running at the time.

07 30 80 George Wocott, a German employed by the Elk Rapids Iron Co., was sun-struck Sunday while working in the wood yard at the furnace at 4:30 P.M. A physician was called but he died about 7 o'clock that evening. He had a wife and two children, who are in Germany.

07 30 80 We have said a good deal about our Adam lately, because his welfare lies nearest our 'art. He intends going to Kalamazoo before long — not to the insane asylum but to see a little 'sylkum of his own. For
　　　The bells were ringing for Sarah, Sarah, Sarah.
　　　　The bells were ringing for Sarah,
　　　From morning until night.

07 30 80 Guests in town do not wish it published that they fell into the River or not as the case may be, so we will not publish that Miss Grace Clark did.
　　　We shall not say anything about whether Miss Mary Lee Alexander fell into the River the other evening or not. We shall not say that we heard that she fell in, or that any of the guests at the Lake View were joking her about it. We are going to be perfectly mum on the subject, we are.

07 30 80 Last night while walking thoughtfully along we espied our Adam standing alone by the side of a little cradle, gazing sadly at the vacant place where nestled no sweet little face among the pillows. Tenderly, and with solicitude we asked, "Adam, why sorrowest thou. Has the little cherub, the imprint of whose tiny form is still distinct upon that little bed; is he—" "Oh," said

Adam, "he's too big." And as we passed along we meditated upon it, and came to the conclusion that he had,

> Put away the little cradle,
> Where the darling used to sleep
> He'll not want it any longer,
> 'Caust the little cuss can creep.

08 06 80 Mr. E.A. Kemp received yesterday by mail a beautiful bird of the Gwengowia species. These birds are particularly valuable from the fact that they sing nothing but bass solos.

08 06 80 Last Sunday morning a large gray eagle came down in Mr. E.S. Noble's lawn. Hr. Noble fired two or three shots at him, but none of these took effect so that it could be captured. It was a very large bird and it being a very warm day it is supposed that it had come so far that it had to light from sheer exhaustion.

08 06 80 Prof. Jonas called this morning to inform us that he intends going down the chute this afternoon, wind and weather permitting. It will be a grand and imposing sight, and will probably be witnessed by thousands (of fish).

08 13 80 Ever since Henry Ballard went down the chute everybody has been talking about his great feat. We always knew that Henry had rather large feet, but then we don't think it is quite right for people to talk about them.

08 13 80 McAllen, the "Sweet Singer of Michigan", is in town and his melodious voice can be heard far and near.

08 27 80 All the boys in town are polishing stones. On the beach can be found stones of a coral formation which when ground and polished make very pretty ornaments. We believe that there are persons at Petoskey who follow a regular business of gathering, cutting and polishing the stones and offering them for sale, and as we said before every boy in town is running around with a lot of stones in his pocket or in his hand, which he has polished and wants ten cents for.

09 17 80 The marriage of Capt. Duncan Corbett, of the schooner *Metropolis*, and Miss Mary Hughes which took place at the Hughes House, Sept. 17, was a very pleasant event. A number of invited friends were present to enjoy the occasion. Eight o'clock was the appointed time, and punctual to that hour the ceremony was performed. After the congratulations the guests adjourned to the dining hall to enjoy the bounteous repast placed before them. A number of elegant presents were given. The happy couple sailed at 12 P.M. on the schooner *Metropolis*. And all their friends wish that their voyage through life may be as beautiful as was the night they left our shores.

10 01 80 It is getting to be fashionable in town for young ladies to wear gloves in the house as well as out of doors.

10 08 80 Mrs. Duncan Corbett returned to her old home Monday, to make a visit here before going abroad. As soon as navigation closes on the lakes Captain

Corbett and wife will visit the old world where they both have relatives.

10 08 80 Mr. Jacob Winkler has been engaged the past few days fencing the lot on River street opposite Mr. E.S. Noble's residence.

10 08 80 Last Sunday while Mr. and Mrs. James Davidson were returning from a drive in the country, and were coming down Yuba hill, the buggy broke down, throwing them both out, dislocating Mrs. Davidson's shoulder and otherwise injuring her. Mr. Davidson also received some bruises.

10 08 80 Mr. and Mrs. R.W. Bagot left town Wednesday for Stafford, N.Y. Mr. Bagot will buy his fall stock of goods while away.

10 15 80 Baptist Resignolle, the young lad that was accidentally shot by Herbert Frame last week, is getting along nicely and well-grounded hopes are entertained of his ultimate recovery.

10 22 80 M. Payment, the machinist at the furnace has been away the past week.

10 29 80 We are grieved to learn that Mr. Charles Durkee lost a valuable horse lately. We learn that the horse was a beauty. Mr. Durkee takes the loss very quietly, and receives the condolence of his friends with equanimity.

11 05 80 If the party who took a rubber cloth umbrella with a silver name plate on handle, from the hallway of the Lake View House will be kind enough to return the same at once the owner will be- Oh! So glad!

11 12 80 Adam Schuler, Esq., is having a stone foundation built under his house.

11 12 80 Charles Victor Lawson a 11 year old boy left town Tuesday morning for a prolonged visit at Lansing where he will become a guest at the State Reform School. He was born in Sweden, and his father and mother are both dead. Not having any one to look after him he had fallen into ways of helping himself to eatables that happened to be near, and has for some time slept around the furnace. His friends thinking that the Reform School was a good place for him, a complaint was made and the necessary papers made out Monday which will keep him in Lansing until he is 21 years old.

11 19 80 Charles Victor Lawson the young gent that was sent to Lansing to become an inmate of the Reform School, last Tuesday, returned to this place Wednesday. The commitment papers were made out wrong and thus his return.

11 19 80 A "recherhe Chocolate"[sic] was given by Mr. James Lewis at his rooms last Sunday. Only the elite of the city were invited who pronounced the entertainment magnificent. Mr. Lewis has the happy faculty of making his guests have a charming time.

11 26 80 Joseph Shaw had a collision with a mule's hind legs one day this week. The mule kicked him once in the side and tried to repeat the caress but his hoofs were not close enough together and he only managed to knock off Joseph's hat. The first kick would probably have been fatal had the mule been shod. Not any more for Joseph.

12 03 80 Some of our young folks took dinner at Traverse City Sunday. The sleighing being fine a number rode up in the morning and came back that evening.

12 03 80 Yesterday the south stage left a cook stove and some house keeping utensils in front of the *Progress* office and several persons interested in our well-fare, stopped and read on the card attached, and others came in and congratulated us. We can inform them that we have no such intentions and that the house-hold property belonged to other parties as those who read the card found out.

    "Oh! The lonely old bach,
     The unmarried man,
    Who fain would be happy,
     But, Alas! never can,
    Life's burdens are lighter,
     For two than for one,
    And its pleasures less sweet,
     When partaken alone."

12 03 80 Some sharp aleck piled our storm house full of wood last night. Instead of annoying us we wish they would fill it every night as it saves us bringing in wood. That much work at home would probably make them awful tired. Come again boys, you can't plague us.

12 03 80 A young son of Dr. Pennock was run over by a sleigh the other day, which happened to be not loaded. For a minute he had a pain under his apron but was soon catching on to bobs again.

12 03 80 Hon. George E. Steele recently sold his farm on the Elk Lake road to a Mr. Kaiser, who recently came over from Switzerland. The newcomer returned to Switzerland after his family and Mr. Steele has removed to Traverse City. Mr. Steele will be greatly missed in this place as he has numerous friends. We congratulate Traverse City on the acquisition of such a good citizen.

12 03 80 Elk Rapids, Dec. 2nd, 1880.
   The undersigned has no desire to make an answer privately. Any thing contrary to the following: one forty acre to my stepmother, one forty acre to George Gee, Jun. and one forty acre to myself, is not the will of my father, George Gee. Sen.
Where was Haman after feeling so joyous on the supposed morning of the execution of Mordecai.
           Your well wiser,
           Henry Gee.

12 03 80 Our young folks indulged in a sleigh-ride to Torch Lake last evening, and after reaching that delightful hotel, the Frank Lewis House, they indulged in a bit of a dance, and returned home early this morning.

12 03 80 Joseph Cox traded one of his horses Tuesday. A trader stumped him and Mr. Cox said he would for $5 boot, and that his horse had four sound legs and a sound body. The trade was made without seeing the horses and then it was found that the horse that Mr. Cox traded was a four legged saw-horse. Mr. Cox made a way out of the operation but the man, whose name was Ewalt, kept his horse, and was a saw-horse ahead.

01 21 81 Lewis Bailey lost a pocket book containing forty-three dollars one day last week. Moral: Run a country newspaper and you won't be troubled with the stuff.

01 21 81 Henry Ballard, (Commodore of the mosquito fleet, in the Summer) returned to Trenton, Mich. Wednesday, where he will remain permanently. We are sorry that he is to leave us, but we suppose his reasons for so doing is that he will be nearer to "Edith." We hope, however, that we may have a visit from him occasionally.

01 21 81 Obituary of Joseph Cox...

01 21 81 Last Tuesday night yells were heard in the rear of Messrs. Dexter & Nobles store, and several persons going as an investigating committee, found Charles Mickleson in the river. It being quite dark, he had backed his cutter into the river, but the horse was not inclined to go. Mickleson's business is that of a fisherman and his cutter contained fish, and man and fish were floating about when help came. By prompt aid he was brought to land and most of his crop of fish saved. If it had not been for the prompt action on the part of Mr. Milton Lang he would have been drowned, as he was wound up in a quilt, and his overcoat, weighted 50 pounds, water-soaked, enough to pull pretty hard.

01 28 81 We don't like to appear proud or conceited or as though we were the worst abused man in town, but when we got right down to "bucking cord-wood" this morning it took all the good nature and conceit out of us. What poor, erring, frail creatures we are- but we have a job for some good man.

02 26 81 People *vs.* H.A. Taylor- before James J. McLaughlin, Justice of the Peace.
   This is an action for assault and battery in which the accused is charged with taking indecent liberties with the person of a little girl. Defendant has not been found.

02 26 81 Monday night some persons went to the house of H.A. Taylor for the purpose of giving him a coat of tar and feathers for the alleged crime of trying to rape a little girl eight or ten years old. Either they had no "sand" or he had too much gunpowder, for they did not do the job, or get away before he had put a charge of shot into one Mr. Arm, who was going home from work, and was passing the house when the shot was fired. The whole charge struck him between the knee and the thigh. Sixty-two No. 2 shot went through his pants and forty went nearly through his leg. Taylor left Tuesday for parts unknown.

03 18 81 The first gathering of "Old Settlers" at Elk Rapids, March 15, 1881 was a success, ninety-two persons present...

03 18 81 Obituary of Rev. Albert C. Lewis...

04 08 81 We are not troubled by the sweet song of mosquito; or by the hopping of the festive flea; or the warbling of the tuneful frog; or the midnight serenade of the big Thomas cat. We are not troubled with any of these we say—but give us all the above in preference to our neighbor's accordion.

W.J. Mills has commenced building his house on Traverse Avenue.

04 15 81 A span of horses belonging to H.K. Brinkman broke through the ice on the bay yesterday morning about 7 o'clock. They were in the water about three quarters of an hour. They broke through near the shore in about four feet of water. The team was gotten out all right.

04 15 81 Joseph F. Underwood, of Chicago, who has been working on the dock, and boarding at the Hughes House, skipped the town and his board bill last Friday. The matter was put into Sheriff Acker's hands who went to Traverse City and made Underwood shell out the ducats. He made tracks rather lively after he had paid the bill with the boys after him.

04 22 81 We published an item some time ago to the effect that Perry Beckwith, who formerly resided here was lost in a fishing boat, while out from Grand Haven. Our information was not correct as he was seen at Traverse City last week, by Wm. Briggs of this place.

04 22 81 Prof. Henry Gordon, of Flat Rock, Mich. is in town, and it is his intention to organize a class in singing, and to give private instruction on voice culture to all who desire it. Mr. Gordon has had classes in Charlevoix and Traverse City with evident success. We hope our music loving people will assist him in his undertaking.

04 22 81 It is sometimes said that to be initiated into, masonry one has to ride a billy goat, but to become a member of the Young Folks Literary Society one has to slide down the banisters at the Court house successfully.

04 22 81 At the meeting held at the Court House last evening, for the purpose of organizing a class in singing, twenty persons joined. A committee was appointed of three persons, Mrs. C.D. Towne, Miss Phoebe Ahnefeldt, and Ben. F. Davis, to receive names of new members. Prof. Gordon, the conductor promises to give good satisfaction, and we have no doubt but that he will, as we know that his reputation as a teacher of vocal music is first class. The tuition for 15 lessons is $2, and the time for holding meetings will be Thursday, Friday and Saturday nights. In connection we will say that Prof. Gordon will give private lessons to those who wish them.

04 22 81 According to the *New York Herald*, politicians and filth mean about the same thing in New York City. The only difference we can discover is one taint the moral Atmosphere the other the natural and both are unhealthy in the region of their respective influence.

04 22 81 Michael Welch, who was lodged in jail some time in the winter for incest made his escape Wednesday. He had been allowed too much breathing room, and he probably concluded that he was not wanted long and so he left. And was brought back Thursday.

04 22 81 Henry Guyer, a 6-year old son of Rudolph Guyer fell into Elk River yesterday, and would probably have been drowned, had it not been for Mr. R.J. Archbold who helped him out.

04 22 81 The jail birds in the Washington, (D.C.) jail among other things have petitioned the Senate to change places with them for a week, promising to break the dead lock, and confirm all the appointments of President Garfield in that time. The said J. B's thought a week's time spent in their domicile would cure the Senators of their penchant for dead locks for a while.

04 29 81 Tuesday afternoon, John Vann got into a difficulty with Thomas Kelly, and hit him in the mouth with a shovel cutting him in a fearful manner, after doing which he came to town and had Tom arrested. About dusk Tom retaliated by giving Vann a whack over the head with his shillaly.

05 06 81 Wednesday evening, Norman Hawley speared a brook trout, that measured sixteen and one-half inches in length, and weighed one pound and nine ounces.

05 06 81 The singing class of Prof. Gordon is making rapid advancement under the able instruction of the Prof. He is evidently the right man in the right place. There are some excellent voices among our young people here, that only need cultivation to give those possessing them prominence as singers.

05 20 81 Christopher Hughes has purchased the dwelling house opposite the Court House and has removed there with his family.

05 20 81 Geo. A. Dyer is moving into the vacant house on River street, next to the Elk Lake road.

05 20 81 Mr. Ranger talks of having this sign put on his residence: The preacher doesn't live here. It is a matter of self defense.

05 20 81 20 births and 5 deaths in the township of Elk Rapids during the year 1880.

05 20 81 Ansel Atwood, of Acme, was arrested some time ago and lodged in jail at Traverse City for counterfeiting. Last Wednesday, a week, he broke jail and it is pretty generally known who helped him out. Last Saturday Atwood was arrested at Saginaw in company with Charles Wright, of Acme, and both were lodged in jail. Charles Wright formerly lived here.
05 20 81 Obituary of Mrs. Linda Spaulding...

05 20 81 W.N. Bartlett seems to have all the painting jobs in town, he having two or three contracts for painting buildings.

05 27 81 We heard it mentioned that Elk Rapids was blessed (?) by having several "soiled doves" in town.

05 27 81 C.A. Newton has a $25 dog.

05 27 81 We have heretofore spoken of the great beauty of some of the stones picked up on the shore of the bay, but we had no idea of the exquisite beauty of them until last Tuesday, when Mr.L.W. Skinner showed us over two hundred which he had ground and polished. In this collection there were finger rings, crescents, coffins, crosses, charms for chains, plumb bobs, and paper weights. Mr. Skinner has traveled extensively, having been in every country in the world, and takes great delight in fashioning these ornaments as he did years ago in making them from shells from the ocean and in ivory, and he says in all his travels in every division of the globe he has never found anything that would compare with these stones for ornaments and jewelry. They are certainly beautiful and we hope Mr. Skinner will place them on exhibition some where.

06 03 81 The singing class under the instruction of Prof. Henry Gordon, has made rapid progress, and we hope after Mr. Gordon leaves the class will meet occasionally. Every one in our village should be interested in the musical welfare of it.

06 03 81 Samuel Mitchell, of Winnebago City, Minn., is in town. Mr. Mitchell is an old resident of this place, and makes the village an annual visit.

06 17 81 Mr. Edward Hart, of Cincinnati, lost a charm from his watch chain Wednesday below the chute and offered a reward of $5.00 for its recovery. John Morrison dove and brought it up and received his 'V'.

06 17 81 Oliver Powers has bought the corner lot opposite the chapel, and will build this summer. He has the shingles already on the ground.

06 24 81 Janet Gardener, a young daughter of George Gardener, was badly bitten by a dog belonging to Charles Grammel Tuesday morning.

07 01 81 Willard J. Spaulding met with quite an accident last Saturday at his slaughter house. While drawing a beef up, the crank on the windlass flew off, striking him in the face, cutting through his upper lip, and bruising his face in a shocking manner.

07 01 81 Last Sunday Fred Pennock constructed a raft, which he was propelling at the mouth of the river, when it got in the current and took Master Fred out in the bay. A young lad hearing his cries informed his father, Dr.Pennock, who sent two boys in a row boat to bring him in. When very near the raft they asked Fred where he was going, he politely told them he was going to- Sunday School or some such place. He was taken from the raft and brought on shore.

07 01 81 Mr. Amos Wood is preparing to build a new house on his farm about three miles east of the village on the shore of Elk Lake. Mr. Jno. Horton, of Pine Lake will do the carpenter work.

07 08 81 Charles Frame and James Dougherty rowed a race with small boats Tuesday morning from the end of the dock to the mouth of Elk River, the distance of nearly a mile, for $5.00 a side. Frame won by several yards. The judges were Captain Bennett, of the steamer *Jennie Sutton*, and Larry Higgins, mate of the barge *Leland*.

07 15 81 There has been considerable sickness in and around the village during the last two weeks, but nearly all are now in a fair way to recovery.

07 29 81 Mrs. Mary McVicker, mother of Mrs. Jas. P. Brand, died last night at 8 o'clock at the residence of her son-in-law, Mr. James P. Brand. The funeral will be held to-day at the family residence.

08 05 81 Geo. M. Jackson, the photographer, has pulled up stakes and gone to Kalkaska.

08 05 81 An ugly tramp giving his name as Andrew Anderson, alias Charlie Peterson came along River Street yesterday, throwing stones at passers by, threatening the lives of different persons. He was taken into custody, and necessary papers made out for threatening to kill Samuel Crummie. In the evening he had his examination before Justice LaForge and was taken to Bellaire.

08 12 81 Last Friday Truman Carns had a very narrow escape from which might have been a fearful death. He was oiling the power of his threshing machine when the horses started and his clothing caught on the coupling rod and tore every stitch of clothing from his body, excepting his boots. Mr. Carns was only bruised a little but does not wish to be undressed in such a manner again.

08 12 81 The fearful fires which have passed over a portion of this state have left thousands of people homeless, and a cry has been sent up help us or we perish. If it ever so little, you can give. Any contributions left at Messrs. Dexter & Noble's or Messrs. Rushmore & Holbrook's stores will be forwarded to the relief of the sufferers

08 12 81 What Shall We Do With Our Daughters?
Teach them self-reliance.
Teach them to make bread.
Teach them to make shirts.
Teach them to foot up store bills.
Teach them not to wear false hair.
Teach them how to cook a good meal.
Teach them to wear thick, warm shoes.
Bring them up in the way they should go.
Teach them how to wash and iron clothes.
Teach them how to make their own dresses.

248

Teach them that a dollar is only 100 cents.
Teach them how to darn stockings and to sew on buttons.
Teach them every day, dry, hard practical common sense.
Teach them to say No, and mean it; or Yes, and stick to it.
Teach them to wear calico dresses, and do it like queens.
Give them a good, substantial, common-school education.
Teach them that a good rosy romp is worth fifty consumptives.
Teach them to regard the morals and not the money of their
    suitors.
Teach them all the mysteries of the kitchen, the dining-room and
    the parlor.
Teach them that the more one lives within his income the more he
    will save.
Teach them to have nothing to do with intemperate young men.
Teach them that the farther one lives beyond his income the nearer
    he gets to the poorhouse.
Rely upon it that upon your teaching depends, in a measure, the
    weal or woe of their after life.
Teach them that a good steady mechanic without a cent is worth a
    dozen loafers in broadcloth.
Teach them the accomplishments of music, painting, drawing, if
    you have time and money to do it with.
Teach them that God made them in His own image, and no amount
    of tight lacing will improve the model.

08 19 81 Mr. Tom Noble thinks that the clearing house at the works would make a beautiful baby farm. His plan would be to cushion the huge tank on the inside and put four or five children in each, and he thinks there would be no danger of their getting hurt. Brilliant idea! But how many babies will Mr. Noble furnish?

08 91 81 The reception given by Mr. E.S. Noble on Wednesday evening last, in honor of Mr. and Mrs. Charles N. Hurlbut, was one of the events that even an overcrowded memory will retain as one of the most complete and enjoyable occasions that ever occurred, at all events in Elk Rapids...

09 02 81 Mr. John Hughes, who has been at St. Ignace for some time, returned home Saturday.

09 02 81 Charles Deverney hacked his shin with an adz Wednesday.

09 02 81 John Johnson who left this village for Iceland early this spring returned yesterday with 26 Icelanders.

09 09 81 Hon. Henry Ford, of Lawton, was in our village yesterday looking over the furnace. We learn he was formerly superintendent of the Bangor furnace.

09 09 81 Rev. Luther Pardee, of Chicago, entertained quite a crowd of ladies and gentlemen Wednesday by going down the chute in his canoe.

10 07 81 Leave your contributions at Messrs. Dexter & Noble or Rushmore & Holbrook's stores for the sufferers of the forest fires. Give clothing, farming tools, money, seed wheat, and it will be forwarded to their relief. The railroads carry all contributions free.

Elzor Fortin, Esq., dubbed "Joe Minnie," by the tourists left Thursday for a visit to Montreal and other places in Canada, and will remain some time.

10 14 81 On Wednesday night as Joshua Ulrick, who is in the employ of Mr. Charles Grammel, was going to the brewery a man sprang out from the bushes and struck at him with either a knife or an ax cutting him across the fingers of the left hand. As the person struck, Ulrick started back and ran for the village and the scoundrel ran into the bushes. Ulrick could not recognize him and no clue can be found as to whom it was.

10 14 81 Monday night Bertrand Villieneuvo, a German, was stabbed in the back, and horribly pounded over the head and face. In telling his story of the affair, he says that Gotlieb Peterson, otherwise known as "Big Goodley" told him that a friend of his at the brickyard wished to see him and together they started for that place, which is about half a mile from the village. When about a quarter of the distance, Villeneuvo says they sat down on a lumber pile and that Peterson took a bottle of whiskey from his pocket and invited him to drink, which he refused. Peterson then took a drink and then asked him again. Villenevo then touched the bottle to his lips and handed it back. Peterson then asked if he had any money and Villeneuvo replied that he had a little but he wished to go to Traverse City. Immediately after this Peterson struck him over the head with a club which knocked him insenible. When he come to his senses he made his way to the brick yard and found that he had been robbed of all his money and had a stab in his back. Dr. Bailey in dressing the wound said if it had gone an inch below it would have caused his death. Peterson skipped out the next day and has not been seen since.

10 14 81 Obituary of Peter L. Winnie...

10 21 81 Last Saturday Mr. Oliver Powers went after Gotlieb Peterson who made the assault and robbed the German named Bertrand Villeneuvo. He found him loading scows up the lakes and arrested him. Peterson managed to escape and left for Charlevoix where Mr. Powers found him Tuesday, and brought him to this place Wednesday.

10 28 81 Adam Laubscher has left the Lake View House and is in the employ of the Chemical Company.

Paul Gates, a seven year old son of Mr. M.F. Gates, picked up 30 bushels of potatoes last Friday.

11 04 81 Chewing "taffy tulu" is one of the enjoyments of us poor mortals up North.

All the boys are walking on stilts now-a-days.

Hi. Robinson has some tasty looking chimneys erected on his new house across Elk Lake.

11 04 81 O. Stafford, while under the influence of liquor Tuesday night knocked his wife down three times on River street. Thomas Kiniard who was near then knocked Stafford down.

11 04 81 Last Saturday while working at the Chemical works, Nelson Bartlett had his left hand crushed by a buck-stay weighing about 300 pounds falling on it.

11 11 81 Some person cut the telephone wire between the Lake View House and Messrs. Rushmore & Holbrook's store Sunday night which was a despicable trick.

11 25 81 We are pleased to learn that Larry Higgins mate of the *Leland* is improving. For a time it was thought that he received serious internal injuries, but we are glad to note that he is improving rapidly.

11 25 81 Last Sunday night when the tug *Albatross* was nearly through Torch River, the captain heard the cries of a person, and rang the bell for the engineer to "Slow up." The person from whom the cries came was C.D. Petes, who lives near Spencer Creek, and he was found in a half frozen condition, nearly dead from hunger and cold. It seems that Mr. Peters started out in the morning on a deer hunt and not over-taking the deer towards night, started to return, as he thought towards home, but instead he wandered in a different direction into the swamp near the above river. He was minus a coat not taking any with him in the morning, and if the tug had not come down that night, sad would have been his lot, for it was a fearfully chilly night and he would have died of exposure before morning.

11 25 81 Very good skating was found on the pond below Elk Rapids. We heard of several boys being there who, we learn, were not at Sunday School.

12 02 81 The small-pox is creating considerable excitement among the Indians and they are scattering in all directions. No white person has had the disease yet, and precautions are being wisely taken.

Whoever reported that there was small-pox in this village to the State Board of Health did it maliciously or else he did not know much about the geography of his own town. All the cases that are known of in the county have been in Milton township.

12 09 81 At bass Lake Sunday Ben and Max Yalomstien, Phy Bailey, Henry Campbell, Andrew Dougherty, Alson Landon, Herbert Frame, and George Johnson, were standing on the ice when it gave away, and the boys received a good ducking. Henry Campbell went down twice before being rescued. We promised the boys that we would say nothing about there being skating on the Lake so we mention none of the particulars.

12 23 81 Mr. Peter Morrison and family arrived from Scotland Monday, and has leased the farm of Mrs. John Hughes, east of the village. Mrs. Morrison is sister of Capt. Duncan Corbett, of the schooner *Metropolis*.

12 23 81 A wood sawing match between Alfred Varley and John Boyington takes place today. Boyington betting that he can saw with a buck-saw 5 cords of wood in ten hours and Valley betting that he cannot. From present prospects Boyington will win. $10 is the amount of the stakes.

12 23 81 Charles Rex who is in the employ of Manwarring & Kramer knows more about shoeing oxen than he would choose to divulge.

12 23 81 Mrs. Peter Johnson Who lives near the Brand school house is very ill.

12 30 81 We spoke of the wood-sawing match last week between John Boynton and Alfred Valley, in which Boynton bet $10.00 that he could saw five cords of four-foot wood once in two in ten hours. Boynton sawed five and one half cords in nine hours and six minutes, and during the period ate three times, and got "high" in the afternoon. We shall here speak of the contemptible meanness of some whelp who threw sand on the wood, besides driving tacks in a good many sticks. The person who did it is as mean as Guiteau.

01 06 82 We here tell a story of a pickerel which Geo. M. Ewing, of the *Fife Lake Eye* will vouch for. Ewing went down in Cass county a fishing and caught Miss Dora Belle Pickerel, of Calvin Mich., and they were married Dec. 24, 1881.

01 06 82 Ed. Cornwall is recovering from his last week's skate. He sat down on the ice, and drove his back-bone through the top of his head, several inches, more or less.

01 13 82 Misses Josephine and Mary Ahnefeldt left for home last Saturday after a visit to their sister, Mrs. C.N. Hurlbut.

01 13 82 Obituary Mrs. Peter (Flora Jane) Johnson...

01 13 82 Ned Noble received by stage last Saturday morning, a Shetland pony.

01 20 82 Some of the young boys about town are getting to be experienced shop lifters. If they keep on the way they are going, "behind the bars" will be their abode a few years hence.

01 27 82 Obituary of Gotlieb Laubscher...

01 27 82 Amos Wood crossed Elk Lake with a team Monday, the first of the season. The ice is not, however, considered perfectly safe.

01 27 82 Six years ago Tom Palmer in attempting to cross to Old Mission fell so many times on the ice that his nervous system received a severe shock. His unsteady walk causes many to think him intoxicated. He is an industrious, steady man as all know who have employed him. Should one overtake him on the road, a pleasant "how are you," jump in, and ride, would be appreciated, and a "God bless you" would be booked by the recording Angel. But when a man charges him 3 shillings for a few miles ride and refuses to give back the change, when given a half dollar, we feel like calling him a highway robber, and on the road to a hotter place than Torch Lake.

01 27 82 Mr. Wilson Rushmore has left the employ of Messrs. Dexter & Noble after a service of 14 years, and will pay closer attention to the business of Rushmore & Holbrook than formerly.

01 27 82 We are glad to learn that Horatio Lewis, son of the late Rev. A.C. Lewis, of Elk Rapids, has been promoted. He is now one of the assistant book-keepers in the dry goods house of Marshall, Fields & Co., Chicago. He is capable, and though young to start on his way in the world, we predict he will make a success of what he undertakes. –*Eagle,* Traverse City.

02 03 82 Considerable talk has been occasioned by the disappearance of a young man by the name of Charley Warren, who has lived here for some time. It has been said that he was foully dealt with and an investigation of the matter should be made.

02 10 82 Last week we mentioned the sudden disappearance of Charley Warren, and that it was the common talk that he had been foully dealt with. We have inquired of his relatives who say they know nothing of him, he having ceased to come to see them for some time. The story of his death as we hear it is that he was murdered on the sand hills back of the furnace, and after cutting his throat they buried him in the sand. We do not know how much truth there is in the story, but the young man is evidently missing, and has been for some months.

02 17 82 The stories in regard to Charley Warren, we learn are quite untrue. We have it that he is living at Cross Village.
Oliver Powers is getting ready to commence the building of his house — the stone for the foundation is being drawn this week.

02 24 82 Obituary of Mr. Henry Beekman Graham. He was connected with the firm of N.K. Fairbank & Co...

03 03 82 Obituary of David Spaulsbury...
Obituary of John Horton, age 19...

03 03 82 The boys in town have purchased four pairs of boxing gloves, and the scalped noses and black eyes that can be seen reach a good number.

03 10 82   OLD BOOKS.
We have been permitted through the politeness of Mr. Charles Marriott to examine some old books in his possession. Though some what mutilated they are in good condition considering their age. One, a complete history of the Bible by Lawrence Clark. This work is in as fair state of preservation and profusely illustrated. Each illustration being dedicated to some illustrious personage of that time. This book is about 143 years old being printed in the year 1739.
Another work comprising several volumes entitled the "World Displayed," by different authors, must have been a work of great interest at the time of its

publication between the years of 1740 and 1750. These books like the history of the Bible regarding their age, are in a good state of preservation, some of them are preserved entire. These are also illustrated. We could not help being struck by the great improvements in the art of illustration between that period and the present time. In reading up the search for a North West passage by the Arctic Navigator, Davis, we found after discovering the Straits bearing his name, he returned to England, reporting the ultimate discovery of the North West passage as a dead, sure thing, in which it is hardly necessary for us to say he was egregiously [sic] mistaken.

Mr. Marriott also has a collection of coins, something over eighty in number. One is an Irish penny of the date of 1820, and one Colonial penny with no date; one Wellington half-penny with no date; one Hamburg shilling of 1726. The one that struck us as being quite a keepsake was a Confederate coin of brass, dated 1860. On one side in bass relief was a palmetto, kegs of powder and a cannon, and the words, "No submission to the Union." On the other side were the words, "The Wealth of the South," and "Rice, Tobacco, Sugar, Cotton."

We have a few more old things in town, that have a history, and shall give them from time to time as circumstances will admit.

03 10 82 A well known resident of Elk Rapids, a young married man, (we withhold his name for fear somebody might kill him), when showing off the good points of his nine months old boy to a friend the other evening, was asked the name of the bright little fellow. "Samuel", was the answer. Samuel queried the friend. "You don't expect him to be a prophet?" With a slight dropping of the under jaw, the heartless father replied, "More loss than profit, I guess."

03 10 82 My wife having left my bed and board, without just cause or provocation. I hereby caution people trusting her on my account, as I will pay no debts contracted by her after this date.
Isaac Love, March 1, 1882.

03 17 82 The boys have purchased two more pairs of boxing gloves.

03 17 82 The Biting End –"You did wrong to shoot that man's dog. You might have pushed him off with the butt of your gun," said the *Galveston Recorder* to a man who was charged with shooting a neighbor's dog. "I would have done that," replied the prisoner, "if the dog had come at me tail first, but he came at me with his biting end."

03 31 82 M.F. Gates sent us a large butterfly Wednesday. It must have been a very handsome one when caught, but whipped its wings off in the basket in which it was confined.

03 31 82 Joseph Drake will build a house on lot 152, First street. The work will be commenced April 1st.

04 07 82 Charles Mariott showed us 13 arrow heads, one evening this week, eight of which he picked up about town. One of them was of white flint.

04 07 82 Mrs. John Hughes, in company with her father, Mr. Edward Deering, returned from their visits in Illinois Monday. Christopher Hughes who has been in Louisville, Ky. the present winter returned also.

04 07 82 Monday afternoon smoke was seen issuing from Benj. Dunning's house. The cry of fire soon brought a large crowd of people to the spot, and willing hands soon brought water enough from the river to subdue the flames. The fire caught in the cellar in some unknown way, and the house being old and dry, the flames quickly spread so that at one time it was doubtful if the house could be saved, and all of the household goods were taken to a place of safety. The damage done is quite serious, not only by the fire, but by axes used to find out where the fire was located. There was no insurance.

04 07 82 Mr. and Mrs. Benj. Dunning desire to express through the *Progress* their sincere thanks to those who saved their house from destruction by fire Monday; also for the valuable assistance afterwards.

04 14 82 A very romantic marriage occurred on the steamer *Jennie Silkman,* while she was making her first trip to this place.

04 14 82 P.S. Brinkerhoff lost his pocket book one day last week which contained $55.00. Monday he came to this office and had bills struck offering $10.00 for the return of the same and contents. In the afternoon it was returned to this office by Robert Forster, who found it Saturday on River Streets. The publisher of the *Progress* went with Mr. Forster to find the owner of the pocket book, when Mr. Forster was made $5.00 richer- he refusing to take more than that amount.

04 14 82 N.R. Morman is getting material together on the ground to build a house on the lot just West of the M.E. Church block. W.M. King has the contract.

04 21 82 Oliver Powers has commenced building his dwelling house on the lot in front of St. Paul's Church. The size of the main part is 26x26; wing 16x16. The foundation of stone with the two upper stories of brick if they can be obtained.

04 21 82 Mrs. John Norris, of Norrisville, has given birth to another pair of twins. We say another because this is the fourth time, and the whole crowd are alive and kicking.

04 21 82 A. Pollock is building a house on Church street beyond the school house. The wing is all he will finish at present, which is 16x24 in size.
04 21 82 "Deacon Jake" Carns left on the *Faxton,* Tuesday for Charlevoix. He proposes to travel around the Region to take photos.

04 28 82 Thos. Holt has sold his house and lot on Traverse Avenue to Mrs. Cox, for $600 and he will remove to Traverse City at once and build again.

04 28 82 N.R. Morman commenced work Monday morning, on his new house just west of the M.E. Church. The upright will be 16x28 feet with a wing on the east side, 8 feet front, with verandah, and runs south 34 feet connecting a wing on the south end of upright of 11 feet, making a total size on the ground of 24x39.

05 05 82 Fred Nackerman is building a dwelling house about a half mile south of the furnace.

05 05 82 Charles Rex intends building a house on Traverse Avenue. The material for the same being on the ground.

05 05 82 Wm. H. Smith is building a neat fence around his house and lot on Traverse Avenue. The example of Mr. Smith might be followed by others in town.

05 05 82 Mrs. J. Cox is having a fence built around the house and lot she recently bought of Thomas Holt.

05 12 82 John Denahy is at his old work on D.& N's dock. John has been in the employ of Dexter & Noble for over twenty years, and there is probably no man better known in this country than John Denahy.

05 12 82 Joseph Parks went fishing in a peculiar manner one day this week. He was walking along the track, by the furnace when he stubbed his toe and fell headlong into Elk River, and either was after fish or went down to inspect the hull of the *Petrie*. Got out and not injured.

05 19 82 James Miller lost $40 in cash at the circus Monday, besides about $150 in notes. He has no idea how his pocket book got out of the side pocket in his coat.

05 19 82 Securely lock your houses, because burglars are on the war-path.
     S. Goldman recently sold his house and lot on River street to Mrs. Duncan Corbett for $1,500.

05 19 82 The furnace boys read the *Progress* earnestly week before last, to see if *Progress* Ben mentioned the ducking he received at their hands one day last week.

05 19 82 Casper Schuler left Monday for his old home in Switzerland and will remain away about six months.
05 19 82 Mrs. Hughes lost a valuable cow last Saturday. She died.

05 19 82 John Hughes returned Sunday. We were glad to see him back.

06 02 82 John Hughes is employed at the Elk Rapids Iron Co.'s blacksmith shop.

06 02 82 Gotlieb Peterson, who was arrested for robbery and tried at the last term of the circuit court was discharged.

06 02 82 To Ed. *Progress*: How is this for an item? Last Saturday E. Martindale hauled with one of my teams at one load, 160 bushels of coal, from here to the E.R. furnace—about 6 miles. Yesterday he took about 170 bushels and thinks it the largest load ever taken in to the furnace. He is waiting for some one to equal this and then he will take 200 bushels at a load.

Yours,
Quincy Thacker

06 02 82 S. Goldman has purchased of John Denahy his fine little property on River street for $1,800. The property consists of a pretty little house and lot.

06 09 82 James S. Lewis has shown us some very pretty sketches he has made of residences, and other buildings about town, which have decided merit.

06 09 82 While coming from Bellaire, Tuesday morning, Capt. Hall, of the steamer *Ida*, picked up three children of E. Wood, in a skiff. When he took them to the shore the oldest politely thanked him for their ride. The children had been playing marbles in the boat and seemed as unconcerned as if they had been on shore.

06 09 82 H.A. Taylor, of North Ridgeville, O., is the new leader of the band and we learn that he is much liked by its members. Mr. Taylor is a new comer and is employed by the Chemical Co.

06 16 82 Andrew Anderson, of Creswell, recently bought a 105 acre farm on the west shore of Torch Lake, of Henry Rosswell. It is beautifully located on sec. 30, town 30, range 8, and is for sale.

06 23 82 While breaking the ground preparatory to building his house, Charles Mariott found several pieces of ancient pottery.

06 23 82 John Lickly fell over board the *Queen of the Lakes* Sunday morning. If he had held his head long enough under water, he might have been drowned.

06 30 82 Mrs. H.H. Noble now drives in a pretty new phaeton.

07 07 82 Capt. Fulton and Mrs. Fulton, of the *Reindeer*, attended the Methodist Church Sunday evening, of which they are members.

07 14 82 Mrs. H.H. Noble now drives a very handsome gray in front of her pretty new phaeton.

07 28 82 Fred and Joe Nackerman, and William Briggs, left for Bangor, Tuesday, where they will do some mason work for the Chemical Co., at that place.

07 28 82 Charles Durkee is getting lumber on the ground preparatory to building his house.

07 28 82 Julius Hannah, of Traverse City, drove his fancy gray team here last Sabbath. The attraction was not so much the fine fruit and quiet surroundings as it was the young ladies' society, probably.

08 04 82 Miss Puss and Lolu Germaine, of Traverse City, were in town Saturday. Two cases of typhoid fever in town- children of Geo. A.Stimers.

08 04 82 Capt. Corbett, of the schooner *Metropolis,* is having considerable work done on his house, on River street.

08 04 82 Thomas Turk, of Pontiac, called on us this morning. Mr. Turk was with the original surveyors, and was here forty-three years ago.

08 11 82 During the severe storm of Tuesday and Wednesday, the bay shore in front of R.W. Bagot and Dr. Pierce's residences was badly washed away, and several more of those handsome trees were destroyed. Unless a breakwater is at once constructed we fear for the houses of these gentlemen.

08 11 82 Newton *vs.* Anderson – Assumpsit. Tried before Justice McLaughlin last Friday. Judgment, no cause of action, and costs for defendant. After the decision, the defendant excused some of his statements upon the witness stand on the ground that he was not yet fully recovered from the effects of a severe attack of sunstroke, and was not therefore responsible.

08 11 82 By years of patient toil and privation we at last gathered together five dollars, which we lost the same day we received it, on Monday last, between F.R. Williams' law office and Dexter & Noble's store. With this amount we intended taking a trip to Europe. If any one found a stray V that day they will not cheat us out of our proposed pleasure, but will promptly bring it back, with no questions asked, but will receive the prayers of a poor printer.

08 11 82 In the walking matches on Wednesday and Saturday evenings last, between May Marshall and Harry Stockng, the former was beaten each time.

08 18 82 "Conquer or die," is the motto of Jake Carns. He attempted to ride a bicycle, and although he did not succeed at first, he kept on trying over and over again, until at last he became its conqueror.
    — *Charlevoix Sentinel.*

08 25 82 Charlie Russell has really went and got married. The happy bride is Miss Mary Peatre, of Echo. It seems that Charlie does not appreciate music much, for he was so afraid of the rattle of the tin pans and the blow of the dinner horn that he gave a dance on Friday evening, at the residence of H. Russell, where a goodly number repaired and 'tripped the light fantastic toe' until the weesma' hours of the morning, to the music of the Johnson band.

08 25 82 Mark M. King came in last Friday and offered us the cigars upon the advent of a 8-pound son on the morning of said day. We always did like to smoke with Kings.

08 25 82 Miss Lillie Semple, of Louisville, an accomplished lawn-tennis player, is initiating the guests of the Lake View House into the mysteries of that fascinating game.

09 01 82 Mr. and Mrs. Lee Smith, of Cincinnati, returned home last Friday. Their departure was noticed by the firing of the village cannon and other demonstrations.

09 01 82 J.A. Scott, received a peculiar injury Wednesday morning at Dexter & Noble's grist mill. He was in the wheel house, where a workman, Mr.Fitzgerald was using a mallet, which slipped from his hand striking Mr. Scott on the arm, driving a part of his sleeve supporter into his arm making an ugly wound.

09 01 82 Wm. M. King handed us the cigars yesterday morning. By looking at the marriage notice in another column, a reason will be given. Again we smoked with a King.

09 01 82 Oliver Powers has his house up about one story, and he will have the nobbiest little place in town. The brick used of Elk Rapids manufacture are of fine quality.

09 01 82 "Let there be Light." Mr. and Mrs. W.J. Light, Wednesday, Aug. 29, 1882, an 8-pound son. "And immediately a Light appeared."

09 08 82 Ben. Davis, of the *Elk Rapids Progress,* advertises for a wife in the last number of that paper. —*Traverse City Eagle.*
    All of which is untrue.

09 15 82 Casper Schuler returned from Ruti, Switzerland, Monday, where he has been the past summer visiting friends and relatives.

09 22 82 John Corbett, a brother of Capt. Corbett, of the *Metropolis,* fell through the hatchway of that vessel last Thursday afternoon and received several severe bruises, but only one bone in his right leg was broken. Several pigs of iron with which the schooner was being loaded dropped on him before his presence in the hold was known.

09 22 82 One day last week three women (we with-hold their names) were blackberrying near town, when one of them wandered away a short distance, and was met by some rascal and insulted and abused in a shameful manner. She begged him to desist, because she was an old woman, and he told her "he did not care a damn if she was." She finally made her escape, not however until he had robbed her of a pail of berries.

09 22 82 On the evening of the 12th the friends of Conrad Banninger met at his place and enjoyed the evening in tripping the light fantastic toe, all in honor of Conrad's safe return from his visit to Switzerland.

09 22 82 Ben. Davis, of the *Progress,* now denies that he advertised for a wife in his paper. If this denial of responsibility for the very first item at the head of the column on the local page, published without signature, is not the most cheeky thing on the part of an editor we have ever come across in all our newspaper experience! If this is the kind of a young man he is we don't wonder all the girls "fight shy" of him, and we advise them that should he hereafter become so desperate as to even fill his whole paper with frantic appeals to the fair daughters of Eve to have pity on him, that they pay no attention whatever to his raving. He is evidently of too unstable a disposition for any girl to tie to.   – *Eagle*.

We published the item spoken of just as we did another in the same position, some months ago entitled 'Our Baby', and it is now a wonder to us that the *Eagle* did not make mention that Ben Davis of the *Progress* had given birth to a baby. If the girls fight shy of us we are sorry because we love them all. We are glad though that we have done something cheeky, because we are naturally of a modest and retiring nature.

09 22 82 North Milton – We think the *Progress* is getting quite poetical. We hope some one else will come forward and propose for a wife so as to furnish the *Progress* with lots of poetry; but we hope he will have more courage than to back out, as the editor did.

09 29 82 Twenty-five Germans arrived here Tuesday, coming over with J.J. Winkler. They will settle near Elk Rapids. Sixteen came whenCaspar Schuler arrived, all of whom live near here.

10 05 82 J.J. McLaughlin is building a house on Traverse Ave.

10 13 82 An Indian banged Goodly Peterson with a piece of cinder night before last. Goodly now carries his head in a rag.

10 20 82   A Living Faith.
The following is a truthful history of the life of Henry Gee — Abridged.
The affairs, or co-partnership between Henry Gee, of the Township of Whitwater, Grand Traverse Co., State of Michigan, and his father George Gee Sr., of the same Township, County and State.
My father had not a day in school in his life, my mother had her instruction in a Sunday school only, my wife had 9 years in a Sunday school, and myself (Henry Gee) had only 9 months- good opportunity to learn. Always my mind has been centered upon farming so that by the aforementioned it will be observable that I am posted pretty well, on proportion to my education, on the use of the hoe, rake, fork &c. In all other matters I am ignorant and do not expect that lawyers are obliged to supply people with brains. But they are going beyond their bounds when they approve of a plan, or scheme, whereby boys are defrauded of their compensation, of labor. I am about 5,000 miles away from the place of my nativity. Vice was not the cause of change. As my father, mother, brothers and sisters are all in their graves, I have no desire to say anything more than, dust they was, and unto dust they are returned.
The leading cause of this abridgment are as follows, showing great attachment between me and my father, Geo. Gee Sr...Lastly there was a floating account between my father and myself when I came to America, and that was the first cause of our attention to the letters we received in England, and on the 8[h] day of June, 1880 my father promised me the top 40, instead of the one originally intended for George...

The Unabridged History of the above can be found in these few words, saying :
My object was progression,
And peace was my delight,
To labor in the day time,
And have quietude at night.
Henry Gee.

10 27 82 Wm. M. King returned from Chicago, Monday. Just as the *City of Traverse* was leaving the dock at Chicago, he fell in the calm and beautiful Chicago river.

11 03 82   NOT 'A LIVING FAITH' BUT THE TRUTH.
In the *Progress* of October 20, 1882 is an article entitled "A Living Faith," in which the relations of George Gee and his son Henry, are discussed by the latter... Some years ago my grandfather George Gee, gave to Henry Gee, his son, the forty acres agreed upon between them. Afterwards George Gee made a will giving to Henry only twenty dollars; to Henry's son George nothing, and to others of his kin the residue of his real and personal property...

11 10 82 The two persons arrested on suspicion for burglarizing Dexter & Noble's safe were released last week. A. McManus, of Traverse City, was bailed, and Wm. Wiley was discharged.

11 24 82 Ned and Charlie Noble, sons of Mr. and Mrs. H.H. Noble, have been furnished with a beautiful dog cart suitable to be drawn by their Lilliputian Shetland pony. They appear on the streets every day rain or snow, to the admiration of all the small boys in town.

11 24 82 R.W. Bagot has succeeded in putting in a drive well on his lot, with a good supply of excellent water. More wells should be put down and less river water drank.

11 24 82 William Brush has finished his new house west of the M.E. Church and is occupying the same.

12 01 82 Obituary of June Spaulding, only daughter of Mr. Willard Spaulding...

12 01 82 Last Friday John Hugli a German boy living in East Elk Rapids, just for fun made himself rather free with the rear end of one of M.F. Gate's mules, running at large. The mule not liking the familiarity lifted a hoof and planted it under John's jaw. The boy was not killed but the performance came to a sudden stop. Moral: Don't fool with a mule.

Chapter 32
The Island House

07 23 80 Mr. E.S. Noble set out last year some grape vines on a side hill on the east side of his lawn, and they are this year about two feet high and have several large clusters of grapes on them. He is having a trellis built for them to grow on. They will probably bear a full crop next year.

08 20 80 Mr. E.S. Noble has just "gone in" for fine gates. The one in front of his bridge on River Street is "a thing of beauty."

05 12 82 E.S. Noble has planted willows on the little island in Elk River in front of his residence.

06 16 82 E.S. Noble has planted numerous small trees on his already beautiful grounds.

07 28 82 E.S. Noble has removed the old picket fence from the top of the hill, and is having a wire fence built down on the banks of the river. The old fence is doing duty around the barn.

Chapter 33
Poems

SOLD AT AUCTION

Auction is up for this place to-day.
So put out the things in tempting array;
Put out these chairs in which poor, mamma sat,
Sell them all off for the most you can get.
Now bring out the lounge and set it down here,
To offer such things it seems rather queer;
But never mind that, they all must be sold,
And turned quickly into glittering gold.

Now here some blankets that kept us so snug;
And here some vases, and here a nice rug;
Set out this rocker, she'll want it no more
To rock lullabys as in the days of yore.

These carpets, these pictures, and here this bed,
These cooking utensils — this trough for bread,
Pile them up well, and get all in good trim,
All must be sold by the auctioneer's vim.

Put them all up, sir, and talk them off plain,
No matter how keenly we feel the pain;
They all must be sold, she'll want them no more,
For she has left us and gone on before.

Sad are our hearts, as we sadly look on ,
And hear the tones of "Going, going- gone!"
Our hearts fill with sadness, our eyes with tears,
To see them sold, her collection of years.

Our dear mamma's treasures are now all sold-
Carpets, rugs, lounges — all turned into gold;
So close up the house, she'll want it no more,
For she sleeps now on that echoless shore.

PEOPLE WILL TALK

You may get through the world, but it will be slow
If you listen to all that is said as you go;
You'll be worried and fretted and kept in a stew,
For meddlesome tongues must have some thing to do.

And most people will talk

If quiet and modest; you'll have it presumed
That your humble position is only assumed,
You're a wolf in sheep's clothing, or else you're a fool.
 But don't get excited keep perfectly cool,

And most people will talk

And then if you show the least boldness of heart
Or a slight inclination to take your own part,
They will callyou an upstart, conceited and vain.
But keep straight ahead – don't stop to explain,

And most people will talk

If threadbare your dress or old fashioned your hat,
Some one will surely take notice of that,
And hint rather strong that you can't pay your way.
But don't get excited, whatever they say,

And most people will talk

If you dress in the fashion, don't think to escape.
For they criticize them in a different shape;
You're ahead of your means, or your tailor's unpaid,
But mind your own business – there's nought to be made.

And most people will talk

Now, the best way to do, is to do as you please,
For your mind, if you have one, will then be at ease.
Of course you will meet with all sorts of abuse.
But don't think to stop them – it ain't any use,

And most people will talk

03 25 81   THE STREAMLET'S MESSAGE.

By S. ST. C.

She held a fair rose in her hand
  And softly on the stream
Dropped crimson petals, one by one.
  As frail as poet's dream.
"Oh, water, laughing water,
  I pray you tell him low,
As soft you bear this freight so fair,
  I answer "Yes" not "No!"

She laid a lily on her breast,
  Then smiled, and to the wave.
With parted lip and fluttering breath,
  The fragile blossom gave,
  "Oh, water, dancing water,
Bear him this lovely flower;
  And as the trees bend to the breeze
I yield to love's sweet power !"

She pressed a viole to her lip,
  With blushes like the dawn;
Then, on the streamlet's sparkling breast
  The modest flower was gone.
"Oh, water, lisping water,
  I kiss your silvery rim,
While soft and low my fond words go;
  I give my self to him!"

THE HIGHWAY COW

The hue of her hide was a dusky brown
  Her body was lean and her neck was slim,
One horn turned up and the other down.
  She was keen of vision and long of limb;
With a Roman nose and a short stump tail.
And ribs like the hoops of a home-made pail.

Many a mark did her old body wear;
  She had been a target for all things known;
On many a scar the dusky hair
  Would grow no more where once it had grown
Many a passionate, parting shot
Had left upon her a lasting spot.

Many and many a well-aimed stone,
  Many a brickbat of goodly size.
And many a cudgel, swiftly thrown,
  Had brought the tears to her bovine eyes;
Or had bounded off from her bony back,
With a noise like the sound of a rifle crack.

Many a day had she passed in the pound,
  for helping herself to her neighbor's corn.
Many a cowardly cur and hound
  Had been transfixed on her crumpled horn;
Many a tea-pot and old tin pail
  Had the farmer boys tied to her time-worn tail.
Old Deacon Gray was a pious man.
  Though sometimes tempted to be profane.
When many a weary mile he ran
  To drive her out of his growing grain.
Sharp pranks she used to play
  To get her fill and to get away.

She knew when the deacon went to town.
  She wisely watched him when he went by;
He never passed her without a frown
  And an evil gleam in each angry eye.
He would crack his whip in a surly way
And drive along in his "one-horse shay."

Then at his homestead she loved to call.
  Lifting his bars with her crumpled horn,
Nimbly scaling his garden wall.
  Helping herself to his standing corn.
Eating his cabbages one by one,
Hurrying home when her work was done.

Often the deacon homeward came,
  Humming a hymn from the house of prayer,
His hopeful heart in a tranquil frame,
  His soul as calm as the evening air.
Redder and redder his face would grow,
  And after the creature he would go.

Over the garden round and round,
  Breaking his pear and apple trees;
Tramping his melons into the ground.
  Overturning his hives of bees;
Leaving him angry and badly stung.
Wishing the old cow's neck was wrung.

The mosses grew on the garden wall,
  The years went by with their work and play.
The boys of the village grew strong and tall,
  And the gray haired farmers passed away
One by one as the red leaves fall.
But the highway cow outlived them all.

All earthly creatures must have their day,
  And some must have their months and years;
Some in dying will long delay,
  There is a climax to all careers,
And the highway cow at last was slain,
In running a race with a railway train.

All into pieces at last she went,
  Just like the savings banks when they fail;
Out of the world she was swiftly sent,
  Little was left but her old stumpy tail.
The farmer's cornfields and gardens now
  Are haunted no more by the highway cow.

—Eugene T. Hayes

TWO WOMEN.

A grandma sits on her great arm chair:
Balmy sweet is the soft spring air

Through the latticed lilac shadowed pane
She looks to the orchard beyond the lane.

And she catches the gleam of a woman's dress,
As it flutters about in the wind's caress.

"That child is glad as the day is long-
Her lover is coming, her life's a song."

Up from the orchard's flowery bloom
Floats fragrance faint to the dark'ning room

Where grandma dreams, till a tender grace
And a softer light steal into her face.

For once again she is young and fair,
And twining roses in her hair.

Once again, blithe as the lark above,
She is only a girl, and a girl in love!

The years drop from their weary pain:
She is clasped in her lover's arms again:

The last faint glimmers of daylight die:
Stars tremble out of the purple sky

Ere' Dora flits up the garden path,
Sadly afraid of the grandma's wrath.

With roes-red cheeks and flying hair
She nestles down by the old arm chair.

"Grandma, Dick says, may we-may-I-"
The faltering voice grows strangely shy,

But grandma presses the little hand;
"Yes, my dearie, I understand!

"He may have you darling!" Not all in vain
Did Grandma dream she was a girl again!

She gently twisted a shining curl:
Ah, me! the philosophy of a girl!

"Take the world's treasures- its noblest, best-
And love will outweigh all the rest!"

And through the casement the moonlight cold
Streams on two heads- one of gray, one gold.

10 20 82   AGNES.

Agnes as a little flower,
  Came and went as a morning shower;
She did not here long with us stay,
  Till God called her from Earth away.

In pain severe she suffered here;
  Canker prostrated our little dear,
At last its spirit took its flight,
  To dwell with angels in delight.

Now, Agnes is freed from all Earthly cares.
  No pain of body or limb she feels,
Now let her rest beneath the sod,
  While her spirit dwells with its Maker, God.

As friends we look forward to that future day,
  Where Agnes we'll meet in splendor arrayed;
Oh, now as her friends have bid her adieu,
  We hope to share with her the glory she views.

(In memory of 4 yr. old Agnes Arno.)

05 19 82   ODE ON SPRING.

The following pretty little song was written a few days ago by Rev. J.E. Davis, of Davis, Mich., who is in his 95th year. As the composer is the grandfather of the publisher of this paper, we take pleasure in placing it before our readers, with the hope that we can give them something from his pen when he reaches his 100th year. The ode was composed and written in 20 minutes.

Now behold the spring returning,
  Nature paints a pleasing scene,
See the rosy-spangled morning
  Breathing odors o'er the plain.
View the glad creation smiling,
  See the meadows all arrayed,
Now the frugal bees are toiling;
  O'er the blooming flowery glade.

Lo! the prospect now increases,
  See the orchards all in bloom,
Softly play the fragrant breezes,
  Wafting round a rich perfume.
Now the lambs in sportive gambols,
  O'er the verdant pastures play,
Ever harmless in their rambles,
  Always innocent and gay.

Hear the sound of bubbling fountains
  Purling through the flowery vale,
See the green embellished mountains
  Wavering to a balmy gale.
Now the grateful hymns of nature
  Seem profusely poured abroad,
Pleasure smiles in every creature,
  Every thing displays a God.
        J. E. D. Davis,
      Macomb Co., Mich., May 7, 1882.

07 07 82

THE HEARTS CHOICE.
By Fenry A. Lavely.

A painter quickly seized his brush
And on the canvas wrought
The sweetest image of his soul
His heart's most secret thought.

A minstrel gently struck his lyre,
And wondrous notes I heard
Which burned and thrilled and soothed by turns
And all my being stirred.

A singer sang a simple song
The echo of his soul:
It vibrates still through all my life
And lifts me to its goal.

A poet took his pen and wrote
A line of hope and love,
It was a heaven-born thought and breathed
Of purest joys above.

A man of God what time my heart
Was weighed with sorrow down.
Spoke golden words of faith and trust
And they became my crown.

I see the painters picture still,
I hear the minstrel's lyre,
The singer's song, the poet's thought
Still glow with sacred fire.

But in my heart's most hallowed realm
The good man's words do live,
And through my life a perfume breathe
That nought of earth can give

SHADOWS ON THE CURTAIN.

by Eugene J. Hall.

I am a bachelor, merry and gay.
With nothing to trouble me here.
I have seen at a window, just over the way,
The changes of many a year.
When the curtain is down, at the close of the day,
There are shadows that often appear,
Shall I tell you the story? Ah well! you will find.
It is only a tale of the commonest kind.
I was romantic and young- you may smile!
A very "Beau Brummel" in manner and style.
My features were ruddy, my teeth were like pearls,
I was handsome and fond of the beautiful girls.
Till an incident happened, I faintly recall,
I loved and I lost- but I lived through it all.

What comfort it was in those dull days of gloom,
As I silently sat in my desolate room,
When my labor was done at the end of the day,
And gazed at that window, just over the way.
Where a pair of young lovers, devoted and true.
Had built them a "nest" and were hidden from view;
For the curtain was down and nobody could see,
But their "tattle-tale" shadows presented to me,
Such pictures of rapture, of joy and delight,
I forgot my own griefs at beholding the sight.

Many months passed away, many changes and care,
I could see, o'er the way, in my neighbor's affairs;
Their kisses grew scanty, their curtain unclean.
And seldom together the lovers were seen.
Then came o'er that curtain new forms of delight,
Like imps in a bottle, that appeared in my sight.
Some chidings, low spoken, were brought to my ear
That I was reluctant and sorry to hear,
While loud cries of children, in rage and affright.
Were wafted away on the winds of the night,
There were shadows of cares that were novel to me,
That made me rejoice that my spirit was free,

That my life was untrammeled by fetters and bars
That my peace was unbroken by family jars.

The window is down, but my neighbors are there;
The lover is living without any hair,
For his round chunky head, both behind and before,

Is as smooth and as bare as the knob of a door!
His ringlets have vanished and gone to decay,
For fingers, once tender have torn them away;
The daughters are married, the sons all are grown,
The lovers are left in their dwelling alone;
Loud cries of contention are brought to my ear.
Discordant, unpleasant, and frightful to hear;
The wife seems triumphant; I hear her command,
The husband submits as she clenches her hand,
And the sounds that I hear and the sight that I see
Bring comfort, delight, and contentment to me;
For the woman I loved is still living to-day,
The wife of my neighbor just over the way.

08 04 82   IN EVERY SOUND.
                              By May Probyn

In every sound I think I hear her feet-
  And still I wend my altered way alone,
And still I say, "To-morrow we shall meet."

I watch the shadows on the crowded street-
  Each passing face I follow one by one-
In every sound I think I hear her feet.

And months go by- bleak March and May-day heat-
  Harvest is over- winter well-nigh done-
And still I say, "To-morrow we shall meet."

Among the city squares, when flowers are sweet,
  With every breath a sigh of hers seems blown-
In every sound I think I hear her feet.

Belfry and clock the unending hours repeat,
  From twelve to twelve- and still she comes in none-
And still I say, "To-morrow we shall meet."

O, long-delayed to-morrow! hearts that beat
  Measure the length of every minute gone-
In every sound I think I hear her feet.

Ever the suns rise, tardily or fleet,
  And light the letters on a churchyard stone,
And still I say, "To-morrow we shall meet."

And still from out her unknown, far retreat
  She haunts me with her tender undertone-
In every sound I think I hear her feet-
And still I say. "To-morrow we shall meet."

08 25 82   THE THREE SCARS.

by Walter Thornbury

This I got on the day that Goring
Fought through York, like a wild beast roaring-
The roofs were black and the streets were full,
The doors built up with packs of wool;
But our pikes made way through a storm of shot.
Barrel to barrel till locks grew hot;
Frere fell dead, and Lucas was gone,
But the drum still beat and the flag went on.

This I caught from a swinging sabre,
All I had from a long night's labor;
When Chester flamed, and the streets were red,
In splashing shower fell the molten lead;
The fire sprang up, and the old roof split,
The fire-ball burst in the middle of it';
With a clash and clang the troopers they ran,
For the siege was over ere well began.

This I got from a pistol butt,
(Lucky my head's not a hazel-nut);
The horse they raced, and scudded, and swore;
There were Leicestershire gentlemen, seventy score;
Up came the "Lobsters," covered with steel-
Down we went with a stagger and reel;
Smash at the flag, I tore it to rag,
And carried it off in my foraging bag.

AEI.

by May Probyn

"Look not long on the face of the dead;
Leave the Past in the Past," they said.
"Dig some grave for the old despair;
Bury it far out of sight and sound:
 The years bring nothing but sorrow and care-
Bury the last ere the next comes round,
 Or the burden will grow too great to bear."

I said not yea, and I said not nay,
But I wept when they carried the corpse away.
 I flung to the wind the flowers that were dead:
I covered their places with new-turned mold;
 I watched and watered the empty bed
Through the dark, and the dearth, and the biting cold,
 But, lo! no others came up instead.

I locked the door on the unused stair;
I broke in pieces the vacant chair;
 I looked not back as the days went by;
I let the grass grow over the Past.
 I could not smile, and I would not sigh-
I thought that I should forget at last;
 I would not believe that I wished to die.

Till, behold! one day I awoke to find
That the whole of my life was left behind,
 That I walked alone in a world of air,
A world of all sound and speech bereft.
 The Past may hold but a song of despair,
But take it away, and there's nothing left,
 Only the silence everywhere.

I wandered back to the desolate place;
I looked again on the dear dead face.
 I counted the sorrows the years had sown;
I kissed them, and gathered them into my heart;
 And I felt they were mine, my all, my own,
That I and my Past could never part,
 Flesh of my flesh, and bone of my bone.

OPENING WEEK AT A SUMMER RESORT.

by A Flirt

Yes, I've been here a week. I've had just one
Flirtation, and already it is done.
The gentleman was Mr. Harry May,
We happened to arrive the self-same day.
We got acquainted, had a quiet talk,
And, in the evening, took a pleasant walk.
He came as an advance guard, so to speak,
Said Mrs. May was coming down next week.
When he said that, I vowed my lady fine
Should find him kneeling at another shrine.
To flirt with single fellows is a bore,
Unless they've other sweetheart to make roar;
But, when you chance to catch a married one
To flirt is naughty. Then it's lots of fun
Especially if you can make his wife
So jealous that she's very tired of life,
Well, during this past week I played each card
To capture him. I never tried so hard
To make a mash. And great was my success;
He won't get over it for years, I guess-
And I was at the height of ecstasy
To think how angry Mrs. May would be.
To-night she came, and I was all prepared
To show her she was hated. Somewhat scared
At what might happen, though, I was, I own.
I let him meet her, at the stage, alone.
And it was after tea, an hour or two.
Before he took me to an interview,
I never was so mad in all my life.
The lady was his mother, not his wife?

My Betrothed.

by Eugene A. Basset.

All the day my fair lady goes singing the praise
Of the costumes and manners of old-fashioned ways
Of the people who lived in the colonial days.

She has shut off the gas and burns only candles,
She declares with a sigh that people are Vandals.
Who chose that their teacups be furnished with handles.

For she drinks from a cup of old blue willow-ware,
And she sits in a flag-bottomed, fiddle-backed chair,
And she wears a shell comb in her pretty brown hair.

Her silken flowered gown has big "mutton-leg" sleeves,
And her laces are sweet with dried damask-rose leaves;
Modern perfumes and powders she calls "make-believes."

She will dance but one dance, the "Virginia Reel,"
And she is learning to spin on a shady old wheel,
And she fastens her letters with wax and seal.

She disdainfully tilted her little straight nose
When I brought her a beautiful Marechal Neil rose,
With queer orchids and ferns and rich, deep jacqueminots.

She confessed that she hated a florist's "bouquets,"
And displayed what she called a bewitching "nose gay;"
'Twas six straggling sweet peas with a southern wood spray.

So sometimes I tremble lest she grow disgusted
Because I'm not mouldy, or faded or rusted,
And think me too modern, too young to be trusted.

Still, if I must share her dear heart with another,
'Tis most reassuring to know that that other,
Is only the shade of her great-great grand-mother.

Chapter 33
Elk Rapids Newspapers

01 09 80 The Old Year is out and the New Year steps in. Let "Progress" be the password for 1880. — *Kalkaska Leader.*

That is just the thing. Let the Progress be the password for 1880. If you subscribe for it you will be always happy and that will make us happy too.

03 19 80 Mr. Will Lewis, who has been in the *Progress* office for the past year, has accepted the position of Cashier in Messrs. Dexter & Noble's store, and will enter on his new duties Monday next.

03 26 80 Our Special Artist has made another trip to Bellaire. His adventures will appear next week.

04 16 80 From the *Mancelona Herald* the *Traverse Bay Progress* came to us last week dressed in mourning, on account of Elk Rapids loosing county seat.

The 13 15 14 puzzle makes no impression on the mental faculties of the editor of the *Progress,* but the "Keno" business has produced a melancholy effect.

We feel in regard to the above a good deal as an old member of the Ohio Legislature did when a young squirt belabored him in a two hours speech. The old gentleman heard the young member patiently and when he had concluded slowly arose and said he supposed he ought to make some reply, but it always wrenched him terribly to kick at nothing.

04 23 80 To quiet all feeling in the matter we will remark that the wood-cuts that have recently appeared in this paper were made at this office. We shall at times have other cuts which will be unfolded to the admiring gaze of the Kenoites.

06 04 80 Mr. Benjamin Franklin Davis, of this paper left last Monday evening on the steamer *City of Traverse* to attend the Republican National Convention at Chicago.

06 11 80 Owing to our absence from town several errors appeared in *The Progress* last week such as changing our name to Franklin and making fire-crackers read fine crockery.

06 18 80 The *Detroit Post & Tribune* has the following:

This is the best story that the *Traverse Bay Progress* could tell about the recent storm at Elk Rapids, and we all know that the *Traverse Bay Progress* never tells anything but the truth: During the storm last Saturday night the wind blew the nuts off from a cast iron stove which was riding at anchor on the walk between S. Yalomstein's store and the Lake View House.

This is not so for we can tell a better one: During the storm on that Saturday night an outhouse back of Casper Schuler's store was blown over. Some persons wishing to have some fun at Casper's expense telegraphed to him at Charlevoix, where he lives, that his house had been blown over. Casper took the first boat to this place, and the air was blue with sulfurous words when he found which house it was. This is getting to be a cruel world as the *Progress* hasn't got as much right to lie as the *Detroit & Tribune*, but the above are truths.

07 02 80 C.E. Dolph of this office, has been sick the past week with the measles, and has not been able to assist us, which accounts for the short-comings of the *Progress*. We have had enough work for a half a dozen and only one to do it. We hope to present the paper in better shape hereafter.

    A North Carolina editor declares that "the man who will read a newspaper three or four years without paying for it will pasture a goat on the grave of his grandfather."

07 23 80 The *Elk Rapids Progress* is coming out for Hancock & English. It hasn't got far to jump, for it has been lingering around the enemy's camp since its birth, lending aid and comfort. It might better put at the head of its columns.Hancock and Noble, or Dexter and English.

–Sentinel, Charlevoix, Mich.

    The *Traverse Bay Progress* faintly 'peeps' for Tilden, Hancock, English & Co. this week. The Republican party is perfectly willing that the Democrats should have the influence of wildcat papers of that stamp.

– Kalkaskian, Kalkaska, Mich.

07 23 80 Our exchanges generally have spoken respectfully of us in regard to our late departure from an independent to a conservative Democratic paper but the *Kalkaskian* and the *Sentinel* are the first to bray. All we have to say in reply is, that they that have ears long enough to entitle them to the practice of the habit, have our unlimited consent to bray as long and as loud as they like.

07 30 80 Our contemporary the *Traverse Bay Progress* has taken a new departure and has come out Democratic, flying the names of Hancock and English at its mast-head. We believe it is commendable in the *Progress*, to show its political faith squarely, and, although it hangs out the Democratic ensign, we wish it prosperity and success in all things, (politics excepted).   —*Herald*, Mancelona Mich.

08 06 80 The *Charlevoix Sentinel* rightfully says that the *Traverse Bay Progress"* might better put at the head of its columns the names of Noble andHancock or Dexter and English." The *Progress* man is evidently so closely wedded to the firm of Dexter & Noble that its real preference would be as the Sentinel says. For instance, in its last issue the *Progress* mentions the name and interests of the firm eight times, and speals of individual members of some four times. — *Kalkaskian,* Kalkaska.

After the long eared specimen of the *Kalkaskian* had found the name of Dexter & Noble eight times and the names of individual members four times in the locals he should have begun in the advertisements. If that don't suit he should come down here and peruse the nine years files of the *Progress,* and then he should see how many times he could say it, and he might get down to steady work by seeing how long he could sing it.

08 13 80 If you wish to be happy in this world and stand a good show of being happy in the next you want to take The *Progress.*

08 20 80 The *Enterprise* of Northport, takes us up because we happened to make a typographical error and spelled Hancock—Haacock. We should not have noticed it, if the *Detroit Evening News* had not once said that the *Enterprise* looked as though it used shoe-pegs for type and was printed on a threshing machine.

08 27 80 There is one thing that we try to be very particular about in conducting the *Progress,* and that is to have our locals, what we can manufacture in this small town, as near the truth as possible. We never publish rumors.

08 27 80 It makes us glad to have some of our subscribers pay up their subscriptions so soon after harvest. One of them came to see the printer first, and said although he had over a hundred dollars with him, (we wish it had been ten times one hundred dollars) that very little of it would be left in an hour's time; but he thought he would sleep sweeter now that the printer and the others were paid. What horrible dreams some of our subscribers must have. We shudder to think of them.

08 27 80 The *Holton Banner* came to us this week as the Bolton Hanner. We hope that Hanner won't bolt any more, because it might hurt the poor girl if she wasn't used to it. Nearpass should see that his Hanner should stop a Bolton.

10 08 80 The *Progress* is printed to give the local news of the town and county, and to make a little money for the publisher, and that is the platform we stand on.

10 15 80 2,591,375,496,111,513,129,672,476,532.13 bushels of wheat taken on subscription. We can get along without so much wheat, but then if it will accommodate any body, we're right on it.

10 15 80 1,000,500,375,100,575,212,123,375,3722 cords of wood wanted on subscription.

10 22 80   <u>P</u>UPLISHERS <u>A</u>NNOUNCEMENT.

> Business locals, five cents a line.
> Special Notices, three cents a line.
> Communications of a local character solicited.
> The *Progress* is devoted chiefly to local news.
> Entered at the Elk Rapids post office as second-class matter.

11 05 80 A good many subscribers will be without papers this week. The only excuse we can offer is that we do not propose to send them another year without pay, their subscription having run out two years or more ago.

11 05 80 We are going to have a correspondent in every town, and we invite every one interested in their towns to send us news from their respective places.

11 05 80 The advertising patronage of the *Progress* continues to grow larger although it is not the "official" paper of the county. People begin to realize that the *Progress* is not simply an Elk Rapids paper, but is interested in the towns of Milton, Torch Lake, Eastport. Central Lake, Norwood, Spencer Creek, Mancelona, and every other town in the county.

C. D. had a new adv. for this issue, but "Progress" had TOO MUCH WORK on hand to change it. Will appear next week.
C. D. Towne.

11 26 80 We shall earnestly strive too make the *Progress* a good local paper whether we are punctual in publishing it or not. This failing will be obviated in time, and don't you forget it.

12 03 80 The *Eagle* of last week wanted us to take back a few inches that snow was 3 feet on the level in Charlevoix county. That is just the way with all of them. Just as soon as the *Progress* gets hold of a good local, some one or other has to "set down on us." The snow is over three feet deep in Charlevoix county! If this don't suit the editor of the *Eagle* we will keep on raising.

12 10 80 The building in which the *Progress* is published caught fire from a defective chimney last Wednesday night, but timely efforts subdued the flames. Betwixt the heat and cold the *Progress* is very late this week. We hope for more comfortable quarters in the future. Had the fire not been put out as it was it would have swept the town as a gale was blowing at the time in a Westerly direction.

12 10 80 A representative of the *Progress* ate broiled fresh cod fish at the Lake View House Monday and it was a big cod—for a newspaper man up north to have a good square meal.

12 17 80 "Uncle Harry" they now call Harry Briggs of this office, and he is now two uncles—Mrs. William Briggs presented her husband with a fine boy baby Wednesday morning.

01 28 81 A youth, just launching out in trade,
  Unto a wealthy merchant said:
      "Pray tell me, sir, what you profess
      To call the secret of success?"
    The nabob's eyes with pleasure shone,
      As he replied in earnest tone:
    "The secret simple is, I think,
      You'll find it, sir, in printer's ink."

02 11 81 There is one man in this town that never comes into this office without stealing something. There is never much to steal, but he takes advantage of what there is.

02 26 81 According to the *Progress,* the sportsman at Elk Rapids are enjoying themselves duck shooting at the mouth of Elk River. How about the game laws, friend Davis? –*Eagle.*
    They are all right or at least they were the last time we looked. But the "D" of it is there ain't any more ducks around the mouth of the River. We would inform our readers that the *Eagle* man wants them to study the game laws before they go duck shooting.

04 15 81 The *Progress* is published at Elk Rapids on Fridays reaches us eight days later.– *Herald.*
    May be the *Progress* is as long getting around to its subscribers as the editor of the *Herald* was in selling the Antrim county poor farm, and may be not.

04 15 81 The building which is now called the M.E. Chapel, will in a short time be known as the *Progress* office, as we shall as soon as convenient remove into better quarters. We begin to feel more subdued as the time draws nigh for us to

284

"pull up stakes" and we hope that the atmosphere in the Chapel will have a warmer if not a "softening" influence, not only on us but on our inks, than we have experienced this winter.

04 29 81 Grass Lake is beginning to open near the mouth. –*Herald*.

It takes its cue from the *Herald* men probably.

The *T.C. Herald* men talk glibly of idiotic people. If they want any farther information on the subject we would advise them to consult their mothers, they having had considerable experience in raising that specimen of the*genus homo,* we should judge.

The *Herald* – Republican (?) paper. Ought to call it poor farm paper.
– *Progress*

We suggest that the board of supervisors purchase a poor farm and turn the *Progress* calf out to pasture.–*Herald*.

The calf of the *Progress* rises on its hind legs to remark that if it takes the Board of Supervisors as long to buy the farm as it did for Antrim county to get the money from the sale of the old poor farm, it will seek new pastures.

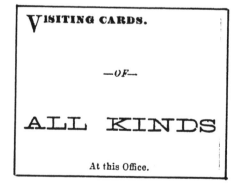

05 20 81 We expect to remain in our present place of abode for some time, as we have sold the M.E. Chapel to the Episcopal Church, and they will hold services there shortly.

06 24 81 We offer the following prayer for the benefit of our subscribers who won't pay up. Some of you have 'planked down' all right, but the one who can and won't, may imagine us on our knees praying thusly:

May he never be permitted to kiss a handsome woman.

May 2:40 nightmares trot quarter races over his stomach every night.

May his coffee be sweetened with flies, and his sauce seasoned with caterpillars.

May his boots leak, his gun hang fire and his fish line break.

May his best friend run off with his wife, and his children take the whooping cough.

May the famine-stricken ghost of an editor's baby, haunt his slumbers and hiss murder in his sleeping ear.

May his cattle have wolves in 'em, his mules the blind staggers and the pigs destroy his garden.

May a troop of printer's devils, lean, lank and hungry dog his heels each day, and a regiment of infernal cats caterwaul under his window each night.

May his cow give dry milk and his churn rancid butter; and in conclusion good Lord, may his daughter marry a one-eyed, hunch-backed editor, his business go to ruin, and he go to____,
Amen.

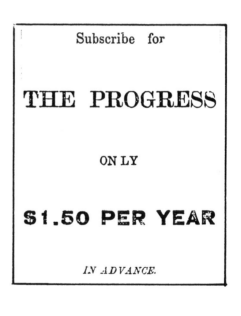

08 16 81 We have received the second number of the *Fife Lake Eye*. It is a seven column folio, patent outsides and a neat newsy paper, edited by Geo. M. Ewing. We hardly see the necessity of a paper at that place, with two splendid county papers in that county, but perhaps it will make a live.

09 02 81 We do not belong to our patrons;

Our paper is wholly our own;

Whoever may like it may take it,

Who don't may just let it alone.

09 09 81 The new paper to be published at Bellaire will, we learn, be a Republican paper. This will be an agreeable surprise to the Republicans of this county, as they have been deprived that luxury these many years. As the new paper will without doubt be a finely printed sheet, we bespeak for it a liberal support.

09 16 81 The name of this paper is to be changed next month to *Elk Rapids Progress.*

10 07 81 The *Progress* is enjoying a rapidly increasing circulation. Subscribe for it and send it to your friends. (The name of the *Progress* has been changed to *Elk Rapids Progress.* Ed.)

10 07 81 The oldest welcomes the youngest paper in the county. We to-day speak of the *Bellaire Breeze,* a neat all printed at home, five column folio, edited and published by A.S. Abbott. *The Breeze* blows that in politics it will be Republican— firmly advocating the principals it believes to be right.

10 14 81 It (the *Breeze*) is the smallest paper in Antrim county, but by no means the least. —*Herald,* Mancelona.
   We are glad the *Herald* acknowledges its littleness.

10 28 81 The *Bellaire Breeze* is the "official" paper of the county. The *Breeze* is a mighty good little paper, but we do not see what particular good can come out of being the "official" paper when it only gets 54 a folio for publishing the proceedings of the Board.

10 28 81 A good many printers find it inconvenient to set up a leach every time they want lye, and thus resort to concentrated lye which is very injurious to type, and we will give them as "receipt" for making lye which will clean type quickly and the articles will take up very little room. By a common wooden water pail; bore four or five holes in the bottom, put in some straw and then fill with ashes. Then take a common tin pail and set the wooden one in it and pour the water on. You can then every week make enough lye to wash forms without any trouble to you. This is free. We do not charge for it.

10 28 81 Don't know what will become of that *Progress* man at Elk Rapids. His last is a birch root one hundred and ten feet long pulled up by a drag in that vicinity. —*Leader,* Kalkaska.
   Come over and we will take you up to see that root. It is on the farm of Hollenbeck & Frink, of Milton.

10 28 81 We do not propose to enlarge the *Progress,* by having one side printed in Chicago. The *Progress* is all printed at home, and will continue to be. When we enlarge this paper we shall make a perceptible enlargement and it will be a all-at-home print and not patent "internally" or "externally."

11 04 81 *The Echo* ought to have a thousand subscribers in this county. It will form an admirable companion and supplement to the *Progress,* which of course has first claim on the reading public of Antrim county. It is only 75 cents a year and can be had three months on trial for 10 cents.

11 11 81 The remarks made by the *Mancelona Herald* on the *Progress* are about as truthful as the one made by a person in the eastern part of Antrim county that the *Bellaire Breeze* was printed on a wooden press.

11 11 81 Dennis, of the Kalkaska *Leader* preaches a bit of a sermon to his "flock" about the sin of jealousy and enviousness. Who is it, old cock, that thus aspires to editorial honors, and would take from you your exalted position of slinging the ink, wielding the shears and wearing big holes in their pantaloon? Let 'em envy, Dennis, let 'em envy. they know not what they do.

12 09 81 How far can the letter C?
> "*Boz.*" How far did the letter Go - *The Plain-dealer*
> As far as I can fly. - *Bradford Star.*
> How much did the letter O?
> Next, and be careful. - *Jamestown Leader.*
> There you had better letter B. - *Bellaire Breeze*
> For several reasons, which we are loath to enumerate it
> would bejust as well to letter P.

12 16 81 We announce to our readers that Christmas comes on the 25th this year. We have know this for sometime, but did not wish to mention it before, reserving it as one of the pleasant surprises to the *Progress* readers.

12 23 81 246,350,000 gallons of water run through the Elk Rapids chute in 24 hours. The *Progress* editor measured it the other day. - *Herald*, Traverse City.
> We did not measure it in a pint cup, like we should the *Herald* editor.

12 23 81 The *Grand Rapids Times* quotes the Traverse City *Herald* on some subject or other. We wonder how this great (?) paper could come down to speak of a "Weakly Weekly," or a country newspaper, It 'do beat all.

12 23 81 The editor of the *Mancelona Herald* calls the *Bellaire Breeze* man a liar or a fool, whever he likes best. We suppose now the *Breeze* man will put a chip on his shoulder for the other fellow to knock off, and the *Progress* will stand off and see the fun and hold the stakes. Whoop'er up Edward ! Whoop'er up Abbott !

12 23 81 Always look at your local papers when you want to deal with a business man in the village. If you don't find his advertisement, never hunt up the man.

12 30 81 The *Breeze* man says he would not believe the editor of the *Mancelona Herald* under oath. Such little pleasantries are so refreshing.
> The *Belaire Breeze* man calls Edwards, of the *Mancelona Herald*, both liar and fool, dubbed him Deacon. *The Progress* loves to hear the childish prattle of those little folks, and would tell them that 'whichever comes out ahead will win." Wade right in Edward ! Wade right in Abbott ! we'll see that you both have fair play.

01 06 82 Our dear brethren of the press are wading right into each other. The *Herald* calls the *Breeze* one and the *Breeze* says that the *Herald* is another. The *Progress* watches the war of words with becoming dignity, and hopes that no one will get hurt.

01 20 82 H.E. Gemberling, editor of the *Albion Recorder* places us under obligations for copies of the new daily he has commenced the publication of in that City...

02 24 82 Elk Rapids has a newspaper — the *Progress* – which many of our contemporaries in this section of the state might imitate with profit. It is a clean, newsy sheet, all printed at home, and bears the marks of a deserved prosperity. Our verdict is that the northern press, taken as a whole, far excels in its character and general conduct that of any other part of the state. —*Ovid Union.*

    The *Progress* does not often print complimentary notices, but the above is so unexpected and from so remote a quarter that we give it place in our columns, and at the same time thanking the handsome sheet that printed the graceful words.

03 03 82 Owing to the increase in our job work we have purchased a new job press. We can now do work in a quick and satisfactory manner.

03 10 82 Our new job press works tip-top, and now as we have three, bring on your job work.

04 07 82 The Elk Rapids correspondent of the *Mancelona Herald* says:

    In our article on Elk Rapids last week the writer neglected to mention that a newspaper is published here. Its called the *Elk Rapids Progress,* and is edited by a rising young man of rare ability and genius whose gems of thought and pithy editorials are making for this journal fame and fortune.

04 07 82 We are not posted as to the price of "taffy" yet, though this is a heavy 'chunk' we are willing to pay for it on presentation of bill.

05 05 82 There are some of our exchanges from which we should delight to copy had they any local news; but it is wholly impossible for us to do it unless they publish some.

05 05 82 The *Bellaire Breeze* has a first rate correspondent in Elk Rapids. We won't mention his name, as he might not wish to blush on being congratulated upon his editorial ability.

05 05 82 W.G. Thompson, M.C. sends us some Pub. Doc's, with the envelope directed — Rapid *Progress,* Elk. Antrim Co., Mich. We can tell the old fellow that we should have been more rapid in opening the envelope if it had contained $1.50 for a years' subscription, but as it is we think that we shall be slow reading that long winded speech.

05 12 82 When a country newspaper is hard pressed for news about this time of year it generally gets up one grand excitement by nominating some grand scallawag for office, and makes out perhaps a quarter of a column of "news."

05 19 82 We send two copies of the *Progress* to Zerich and one to Ruti, Switzerland, but shall not open a publication office there this season. All remittances for subscriptions, advertisements, etc., should be sent to the home office.

06 02 82 It seems to us that the more we give pleasant notices to some people — the meaner they are to us. We propose to shut up hereafter.

06 30 82 We received a note from one of our subscribers Wednesday to "Please discontinue the *Progress* when my prescription is out". This leaves us in a bad predicament as we do not know exactly how big a dose he got.

08 04 82 Every week from Elk Rapids, way up there in Antrim county, comes to us the *Elk Rapids Progress*, a neat six column folio sheet, all printed at the home office, and looking just as clean, fresh and winsome as a new schoolmarm. The *Progress* is the property of Benjamin F. Davis, who reads with reason, knows a good thing when he sees it, prints the paper for money, and as a consequence manufactures in the line of local and general news just what his readers want; all of which is not only in keeping with a successful pioneer publisher, but it indicates progress. — *Ovid Union.*

09 08 82 We will offer the *Progress* from now until after the election for only 10 cents, and if any one wishes to continue it after that date we shall be pleased to send it. Cash or stamps must accompany the order.

10 20 82 B.F. Davis purchased the house, office and lot on River street, known as the Sprague place, last Saturday for $1,300. Good judges say it was a bargain.

10 20 82 The *Progress* by a dexterous piece of political juggling converts the straight greenback ticket, nominated at Central Lake, into a "Union Ticket." Will the Greenbackers thus permit themselves to be swallowed by the Democracy? — *Herald.*

      Not such a dexterous piece of juggling after all, but which may appear so to the editor of the *Herald*. The *Progress* received the minutes of the convention directly from the unionists themselves. We are not desirous of seeing any of that ticket elected except Charles T. Hickox, for Prosecuting Attorney, and he is a straight out-and- out Republican.

11 17 82 The *Progress* office is now one door west of where it has been.

Chapter 35
Elk River

05 21 80 The old logs and boards which have been accumulating above the chute were sent down stream.

06 04 80 The sticks and stones have been cleared off from the lot near the mouth of the river preparatory to making a garden.

06 11 80 Last Saturday night the raft of square timber which was boomed on up Elk River broke away and came down and completely fills the river from the chute to the furnace.

06 18 80 This season the water in Elk Lake and River is very high, and Monday it was so high and the pressure so great that it pushed away some of the timbers of the flume near the grist mill. If it had not been for a pile driven between the chute and the flume the whole side of the flume would have been washed away.

06 26 80 A very neat railing has been put across the bridge at the chute.

02 18 81 Last evening about eight o'clock a span of horses belonging to Jule Ewalt, of Kalkaska, were drowned in Elk River. Ewalt left here about 7:30 o'clock for Spencer Creek and when near Mr. Grebee's he went on the ice on Elk Lake and instead of going toward Spencer Creek drove towards this place, by following the shore around Schuler's point and drove down into the river, about half way between the old ice house and the furnace. Several persons hearing cries went to the relief and Mr. John Denahy was unlucky enough to fall through the ice, and take a bath in the clear, cold and beautiful waters of Elk Lake. Ewalt fell in three times and was hauled out. The loss of the horses is a serious one to him as they were worth about $250.

02 26 81 Jule Ewalt came here Wednesday for the purpose of removing his horses from Elk River.

06 10 81 The *Traverse Bay Progress* says that last week William Dumphrey, of Elk Rapids, speared a two-pound trout. Mr. Dumphrey is probably not aware that there is a law prohibiting killing speckled trout in this manner.–*Kalkaskian*, Kalkaska.

That depends, my dear boy. That depends. The law says in inland waters, and the fish was not speared in inland waters. See?

10 14 81 The amount of water which passes through the chute every twenty-four hours from the "six lakes" is estimated at 180,000,000 gallons, which is twice the amount of the Croton aqueduct which supplies the whole of New York City with water. This does not allow for wastage or the amount used by the grist or saw mill. The pressure of this body of water is equal to about 300 horse power. Year after year this immense amount of water is running to waste where there should be nearly every kind of manufacturing.

10 14 81 The water in Elk River becoming so high having the saw mill race dammed that a large hole was cut in the grist mill flume, Monday, west of the chute for the passage of water.

10 28 81 THAT CHUTE AGAIN — Mr. Norman Pierce, Chemist of the Furnace and Chemical Companies, who furnished us the data concerning the amount of water passing through the chute (found in our issue of two weeks since), also gives us the following rule for computing the quantity of the flow and horse power of any stream of water:

1. To calculate the amount of water passing over a dam in a given time. Find depth of water at crest of dam in inches. Then by referring to tables found in almost any books on engineering, the amount of water in cu. feet for every inch in depth, will be found. This multiplied by the number of feet the crest is in width will give the amount of water discharged in cubic feet per minute. If gallons are desired, the cu. ft. are reduced to inches and divided by 231. (No. of cu. in. in one gallon). Example – Depth of crest of dam 20 ft. width is 4 ft. By turning to table we find that 1,800 cu. ft. of water pass over the crest for every foot width. Then 1800 x 20 =36,000 cu. ft. the total flow per minute. Or 36000 x 1728 divided by 231 =269,298 gals. per min.

2. To calculate the Horse Power of a given stream. First find the quantity of water (by Rule 1,) flowing over the crest in cu. ft. per minute. Then ascertain the head or fall in feet. Now we know that 1 cubic foot of water weighs 62.33 lb., consequently the quantity of water multiplied by the known factor 62.33 will give the No. of lb. raised 1 foot per minute or dynamos. This continued product divided by 33000 the No. of "foot pounds" in horse power will give the horse power of the stream. Example - Continuing our former illustration we have (calling the head 7½ feet,) 36000 x 62.33 x 7½ divided by 33000 = 510 H.P.

In our article two weeks ago we gave the amount of water which passes through the chute from the "six lakes," namely, Elk, Round, Torch, Clam, Grass and Intermediate lakes, as 18,000,000 gallons every twenty-four hours or twice the amount of water which passes through Croton aqueduct, which supplies the city of New York with water, in the same length of time. The amount of water passing through the chute every twenty-four hours at this writing is 387,789,120 gallons according to the above calculations. The reason of the increase is owing to the mill-race being dammed up so that work on the saw-mill can be pursued, and also to the recent fall rains. We repeat, it seems a pity that this immense power should be wasted, where there should be almost every kind of manufacturing.

12 09 81 The average flow of water through the chute, during the week ending 6 P.M. on Thursday, Dec.8, was — 246,350,000 gallons per day. Equivalent to about 450 horse power.

12 16 81 We venture to say that the water in the bay will be next season a foot higher than it is this year. Every seven years the water raises and then lowers in the bay. If it raises a foot next season the shore should be protected so that damage to it could not be done. The pond formed by the river breaking through the bank will probably be all bay next summer, for if the bay raises the small bank of sand dividing the bay and pond will be washed away.

12 30 81 Some thing should be done so that the bridge crossing Elk River will be more safe than at present. A new bridge with a railing would be the right thing.

12 30 81 The bridge over Elk River is in bad shape and should be rebuilt.

03 03 82 It is the intention of Mr. John French to build a boat house and office 70 feet long facing Elk River. The frame of the office has been built and the siding will be done as soon as it can be got.

03 24 82 The bridge over Elk River should be repaired and a railing should be placed on each side of the proposed new bridge. We will give our consent, also to a lamp being placed there on dark nights.

04 14 82 The Iron Co. has torn away all its plank dock on Elk River, and are replacing it by driving spiles along the water front and filling in with slag from the furnace. When the work is done it will be a great improvement.

05 05 82 John F. French & Co. have one of the nobbiest little boat houses in the country.
05 26 82 Dexter & Noble are making thorough repairs on the bridge crossing Elk River at the chute.

06 02 82 The chute is shut off now nearly every day so that the workmen can build the new bridge over the river. When completed it will be a daisy.

06 02 82 Dexter & Noble are building a new bridge over Elk River at the chute, and a neat one at that.

07 21 82 The Iron Co., have had spiles driven in Elk River and intend extending the revetment from the stock house to Dexter & Noble's hardware storehouse. If a revetment could be built along the west side of the river and one of the bay hills on the east side dumped into the low water there it would be a great blessing.

09 15 82 Spiles are being driven at the west side of the mouth of the river, to protect E.S. Noble's grounds from the heavy north seas.

10 20 82 Logs belonging to the Iron Co., are being taken from the river at the rate of about 100 a day. We learn that it will take about six weeks to finish the job.

Chapter 36
Railroads

03 05 80 Tuesday morning when the passenger train was near Traverse City the forward axle of the baggage car broke. The passengers rode to that place on the engine as the passenger car could not be taken.

01 14 81 Elk Rapids wants a railroad.– *Herald,* Mancelona.
　　　When Elk Rapids wants a railroad real bad, Elk Rapids will have one; "and don't you forget it."

01 28 81 The *Kalkaskian* has spoken for our railroad to come from Kalkaska and that place to be the junction. Can't do it Sweet! It's coming from a different direction. Smith of *The Sentinel* and ourselves are putting this road through – in our minds.

01 28 81 Say, Smith! (of the *Sentinel*) Lets have that road run from Petoskey to Charlevoix, and from Charlevoix to Elk Rapids and on to Traverse City. Whatd'y say? The amount of freight from both Charlevoix and Elk Rapids will be more than doubled in another year.

02 18 81 That proposed railroad which is to meander around from Petoskey through Charlevoix, down by Elk Rapids and Traverse City and join around Robin Hood's barn, will, if industriously worked up, pan out several newspaper items yet.– *Evening News.*
　　　We hope to give the *News* more reliable information in regard to that road to Elk Rapids. It may be "all talk" but from present indications we think that this place will be favored if Robin Hood's barnain't. Don't get in a "perspiration" sonny, there may be more in the "proposed" road than you think. If the road is not here to-day or to-morrow, we are of the opinion that it will come before that comet "knocks the stufin" out of the Sun. There is lots of consolation in this.

03 11 81 We are now in favor of a branch road from Kalkaska to this place, and we are perfectly willing to "go in" with Sweet to build the road. The "lay of the land" and everything is favorable.

03 11 81 The most favorable route for a railroad in the Region is a branch from Kalkaska to this place. Our freight every day will be an immense one. Messrs. Dexter & Noble have thousands of acres of pine on the Manistee which will be harvested some day, and our iron business, and the chemical works which are too come would insure an immense amount of freight each day. Let us estimate the amount of manufactured product each day. The furnace averages about 40 tons of iron a day. The Chemical Works will turn out several tons a day and it is expected that the saw mill will cut 10,000,000 ft. of lumber a year. The amount of grain shipped from here is not small. There is not a town in this whole region that ships annually abroad as much manufactured products as this.

03 11 81 We propose that sign boards be put on the depots of the G.R. & I.R.R. which will have on them the words "Closed for the Season", (*a la* Summer hotel) for no trains reached Traverse City for a week. (Because of the storm).

03 11 81 The last train into Traverse City arrived one week ago last Wednesday night the non-arrival of which is owing to the great fall of snow, which fell during the severe storm which passed over this section two weeks ago. There is now a force of seventy-five men shoveling snow from the track. One day last week the snow plow was ditched and on Wednesday of this week it ran off the track, nearly demolishing the engine. Traverse City receives mail matter every day, which is brought by stage from Kalkaska, and is distributed there for points north, Mail closes at Traverse City at 9 o'clock A.M., for Kalkaska.

05 06 81 Work is being pushed on the Lake View and Harbor Springs railroad around Little Traverse Bay, and it is expected that cars will be running to Harbor Springs by June 15.

05 20 81 We would like to bet a loaf of bread against a big brick house that a boom had struck this town. We are about to build that railroad from Kalkaska here.

05 27 81
      'All aboard', for train going to Kalkaska !

05 27 81 The *Kalkaskaian* and *Progress* are talking confidently of a railroad from, Kalkaska to Elk Rapids. The *Progress* says the route between Kalkaska and Elk Rapids is level, the road-bed would require little work on it and it would run through some of the very best farming land north. The Progress thinks it only is a question of time. – *Charlevoix Sentinel.*
      You can 'just bet your boots' that it is only a question of time. Railroad companies are slow to take 'new departures', but the amount of freight that any company would be guaranteed for ten years from this place would be immense. Dexter & Noble have a large tract of pine on the Manistee which would be harvested, the furnace makes her 40 tons of iron a day. The Chemical Works will yield as vast amount of freight, and other industries are talked of, of which we are not permitted to speak. Elk Rapids is 'on the move' now and we don't expect it to be 'paralyzed' again.

05 27 81 Kalkaska and Elk Rapids to be connected by rail. Elk Rapids people pretty sure, and Kalkasians hopeful.

05 27 81 The Kalkaska and Elk Rapids Railroad--how familiarly it sounds.

06 10 81 The agitation in regard to a railroad from Kalkaska to Elk Rapids is not the result of any mythical project, by any means. The absolute necessity of the road to the inhabitants of the country through which it would pass, and the reward certain to be reaped by the company that will build it, the level and easy grade, rendering the cost of the construction comparatively light, are guarantees that we have not long to wait for direct communication with Elk Rapids by rail.

Of course its speedy construction will depend somewhat upon the portion of the burden the people of the two towns will be able to bear, but in view of the great benefits and advantages to be realized from the enterprise, we confidently believe that they will not let the opportunity pass by unimproved. -*Kalkaskian.*

06 10 81 A sure thing—
> The K. & E.R.R.R.
> The business demands it,
> We are anxious to have it,
> And our expectations will be realized. -*Kalkaskian,* Kalkaska.
> So mote it be.

06 17 81 We cannot give our readers the exact date when work will be commenced on the Kalkaska & Elk Rapids Railroad, but we hope to some time in the dim future.

07 01 81 The *Progress* and *Kalkaskian* are busily engaged in building a railroad from Kalkaska to Elk Rapids. We wish them success, for Elk Rapids certainly needs a railroad, but talk alone will neither grade, iron, stock or operate one. — *Eagle,* Traverse City.

But, Bro. Sprague, there is considerably more to our railroad than you are aware. It isn't all wind, by any means. Elk Rapids people must have their mail more frequent than once a week in the winter time, and they are going to have it *via* Kalkaska. It would also be more convenient for the citizens of Traverse City if the Traverse City railroad connected with the G.R.& I. at Kalkaska. If it were so, the inconveniences of last winter would not be repeated. The building of the Kalkaska and Elk Rapids railroad in the near future is a certainty. Prominent railroad men have looked into the matter, are convinced of the feasibility of the project, and express themselves as being confident that it will soon be carried out.
— *Kalkaskian,* Kalkaska.

The *Kalkaskian* is quite right. Prominent railroad officials have said upon visiting this place. "We must have our rails in here." In fact, men in the employ of the railroad company have looked over the route between this place and Kalkaska and have remarked about the easy grade, and the cheapness of constructing a road this short distance. We have gone without our mail one whole week, and that is anything but agreeable.

08 25 81 Are we to have that railroad? Yes! the business men need it; all the people want it; and Kalkaska will have it. Don't you hear the whistle; the running of the wheels on the track; the hiss of the steam; the ringing of the bell? You don't? No? Neither do we.

10 07 81 That railroad from Kalkaska will, we think be a reality by this time next fall.

12 16 81 The *Traverse City Herald* in another column thinks that a road from Traverse City to Elk Rapids and Charlevoix would pay. There is no doubt of it. We did prefer one from Kalkaska, but are now perfectly willing to take one from any direction.

01 27 82 The *Kalkaska Leader* rises to remark that the *Progress* editor is coming to his senses on the railroad question," because we wish one from Kalkaska. In truth that would be a good point, and we do, and have wished for one for some time.

02 24 82 We have another route on our list of railroads which will no doubt be put through some day. It is an extension of the Chicago & W. Michigan from Pentwater, which would give us almost an air line to Chicago. The road to leave Pentwater and strike the counties of Mason, Manistee, Wexford, Grand Traverse and Antrim, touching at Elk Rapids and then on to Petoskey through Charlevoix county.

02 24 82 The *Elk Rapids Progress* wants an air line railroad to Chicago *via* Kalkaska and Bay City!   —*Breeze.*

It is so seldom that the *Progress* makes a "ball of it," that two or three of our exchanges copied that local entire without comments, so the *Breeze* is welcome to all the meat it can get out of it.

03 03 82 We had always supposed that an "air line", was a straight line, but since the *Progress* has commenced talking about an "air line" railroad from Elk Rapids to Chicago, by the way of Kalkaska and Bay City, we have come to the conclusion that the *Progress* man did not study the same dictionary that we did.-- *Eagle,* Traverse City.

This is pretty thin in the *Eagle,* considering the fact that it published our item without knowing the mistake until we pointed it out.

03 03 82 If Elk Rapids citizens wish to invest their filthy lucre [sic] in a railroad they should put in one from here to Roscommon to connect with the Michigan Central and make Kalkaska a junction.

03 03 82 Elk Rapids has a railroad- from the furnace to the dock. The locomotive has been purchased, and "off brakes" will next be heard. Take cars from dock to furnace, 10 minutes ride. The E.R.I. Co., have purchased a dummy engine to convey their ore from the dock to the furnace.

03 03 82 Traverse Bay newspapers are talking about a hope they feel that some day a railroad may be built from Elk Rapids to Kalkaska and through the counties of Roscommon, Gladwin and Bay, to connect with the Lake Shore & Michigan Southern at Bay City, giving us an air line to Chicago. By the time they find the Lake Shore & Michigan Southern at Bay City and make an air line of an ox-bow route. Traverse Bay will have evaporated. —*Evening News*, Detroit.

All we have to say in regard to this is, we need a railroad so bad that an "air line" to Detroit or Chicago *via* the north pole, would be a godsend.

03 03 82 Steps have been taken to survey the proposed route for a railroad from Ovid to Grand Traverse Bay, and another route is to be surveyed from Logansport, Indiana, to the Bay. The objective point of both these schemes seems to be the Bay, not Traverse City nor Elk Rapids particularly. The proper thing for one or both of these roads to do would be to build their roads to this point *via* Elk Rapids. Just pause a moment, gentlemen, and investigate the matter. —*Sentinel.*

03 17 82 Stand up like a man Ben., and face the music. We published your item and called attention to your "air line" from Elk Rapids to Chicago, by way of Kalkaska and Bay City, never intending to convey the idea that you didn't know an "air line" when you saw one. The trouble is you see so many that you get a little confused like, and forget which is which. Now this last one "to Detroit or Chicago *via* the north pole," which you say Elk Rapids would be so glad to get, will only serve to more entangle you. We wouldn't try for an "air line" if we were you, but take some other kind, a clothes line for instance. – *Eagle.*

Pretty thin in the *Eagle* trying to wiggle out on the end of a clothes line. It published our item in one week's issue, and did not see the mistake until we corrected it, and has wiggled on the end of that clothes line ever since. Wiggle on, oh gentle *Eagle!* Wiggle on!

03 17 82 The dummy engine lately purchased by the Elk Rapids Iron Co., has quite a history. A few years ago it was used in New York City on the 9th Avenue elevated railway, and later by H.O. Rose, of Petoskey, on his road between that town and Crooked Lake.

03 17 82 The *Charles A. Ryan,* of Traverse City, made another trip to this port Monday bringing the locomotive for the Traverse Bay and Elk Rapids short line railroad, and merchandise for our dealers.

03 17 82 The Riverside, the engine for use on the Traverse Bay & Elk Rapids short line was taken to the machine shop at the furnace to be overhauled. When the track for cars and engine is completed from the dock to the furnace, Chemical works, saw mill, grist mill, store, etc., the facilities for transporting freight from all these points will be perfect, employing a less number of hands, and doing the work in a much shorter time.

03 24 82 In our local last week in regard to the dummy engine, "of Petoskey," should have been inserted after the name of H.O. Rose. We hope friend Sprague will see the mistake before he copies it.

04 14 82 *Kalkaska Leader.* After mature reflection and without selfish motives, but looking only for the best good of the largest number, and the best returns o the investment, the citizens of Kalkaska have concluded to pass theOvid & Traverse Bay Railroad, so-called, through this place to Elk Rapids and Charlevoix. Of all the routes suggested this would be the best, and to we respectfully call the attention of the company, and assure that substantial aid awaits them at this end of the line.

05 12 82 The fact that the G.R.& I.R.R. Company has purchased the Traverse City branch makes us think more than ever that theOvid road will touch at this place, as the company who are building that would be very foolish to run a line parallel to the G.R.& I.R.R. when another better route could be found. Of course the first road into the place will get the biggest whack, in the shape of right of way and freights. Our companies do not believe in laying a track for some one else to own, but we have not a particle of doubt but that they would do the handsome thing by any road.

05 12 82 We learn that Ben. Davis of the *Progress,* wants a railroad at Elk Rapids. Well Ben. why don't you collect in your delinquent subscription and build one?- *Herald.*

"Cos" our delinq's seem to think they need the cash more than any one else.

05 19 82 2,503 miles of railroad have been constructed so far this year, not counting the road from Traverse City to this place, or the Ovid & Traverse Bay railroad.

07 14 82 A passenger train was badly wrecked near Petoskey last Saturday evening, and some of the passengers were slightly injured. The wreck was caused by a tree on the track. Engineer Hoff was quite badly scalded.

Chapter 37
Elk Rapids School District

01 02 80 The sixty new seats for the High School room came on the last trip of the *Leland* and are now being placed in the building. The school board have ordered a partition built through the center of the high school room, making a room for the principal and one for his assistant.

01 09 80 The Antrim County Teacher's Association held its Seventh Annual meeting at Central Lake...

01 09 80 The High School room looks much better with its rows of patent desks than it formerly did with only tables and chairs. A partition has been put across one side of the room thus making a recitation room.

01 09 80 The School Board are putting in ventilators in all the rooms of the School House, which will make the already pleasant and attractive rooms more so.

01 23 80 On account of sickness Joseph Butler was not able to attend to his duties as teacher in the Spaulsbury school. Edwin Cooper taught in his place.

02 06 80 Names of pupils who have been neither absent nor tardy for the month of January.
Intermediate Department.
    Lena Goldman, Harry Noble, Willie Rhodes.
Names of pupils who stood highest in their classes for the month of Jan.
        "A" Class—Ettie Briggs, Wm. Rhodes.
        "B" Class.—Fred Morton.

03 26 80 The Principal's report to the School Board but one visitor to the High School department this term. That one was not a native of these parts either. If there are poor schools in the village they need looking after better. If there is a good one a little encouragement would not injure the teachers.

03 26 80 The schools of the village close to-day for a week's vacation. The enrollment for term has been: High School, 36; IntermediateDep't, 27; Primary, 31. The branch schools have enrolled 31. While the diphtheria prevailed in the village the schools were quite small. They rallied again during the last month, and school closes with but few less than the enrollment.

04 09 80 Prof,. C.M. Ranger of this place, will have charge of the Secular Teacher's Institute which meets at Island Park, Ind., next July. The Institute is conducted on the Chatuaqua plan and is supported and encouraged by the ablest men in the country.

05 21 80 SCHOOL MONEY.   Elk Rapids, Mich., 1880.
Apportionment of primary school money for the county of Antrim.

	No. of children	Amount
Banks	237	$111.39
Central Lake	131	61.57
Chestonia	59	27.73
Custer	97	45.59
Echo	111	52.17
Elk Rapids	207	97.29
Forest Home	28	13.16
Helena	141	66.27
Jordan	117	54.99
Kearney	61	28.67
Mancelona	101	47.47
Milton	184	86.48
Torch Lake	39	18.33
	1513	711.11

The township Treasurers will be paid as above by calling on the county Treasurer, W.Bagot.

05 28 80 The South School closed to day. We learn that Joseph Butler has had good success as teacher.

06 18 80 We are pleased to announce that the School Board has engaged for next year the same teachers we had last. This year the school has reached the highest point of excellence, and a continuation of the same will no doubt be appreciated by our people. The names and departments are as follows: C.M. Ranger, Principal; Miss Phebe Ahnefeldt, Assistant; Miss Josephine Ahnefeldt, Intermediate; Miss Ellsa Walter, Primary.

07 30 80 School closed in District No. 1 in Milton July 23. Number of scholars enrolled during the term 54. Average daily attendance 31.58. I have had monthly examinations during the term, the last months' work being a general review. Average per cent, 92.45.   C.E. Smith.

09 03 80 The schools under the professorship of C.M. Ranger, assisted by the Misses Ahnefeldt and Miss Ella Walter, have reached the highest point of excellence, and we do not doubt but that in the future, as in the past they will be the same. In this column we give the general list of studies that will be pursued the next school year. We hope that parents will interest themselves in the school; visit it occasionally, and you will help the teachers in their work, and the scholars will pursue their studies with greater zeal if you show them that you are interested in what they are doing. School commences next Monday, and we hope that we can publish that more than one person visited the school during the school year of 1880-81.

The school year of 1880-81 opens Sept. 6th. The following classes will be formed in the High School department at the beginning of the term:

D Grade	Rudiments of Arithmetic.
	Geography,
	Language Lessons.

C Grade	Practical Arith. (beginning),
	Geography,
	Grammar and Analysis.

B Grade	Review of Arithmetic,
	Review Gram. and Analysis,
	History, U.S.,
	Algebra (beginning).

A Grade	Philosophy,
	Astronomy,
	Geometry,
	Algebra.

Reading and spelling in the D. C. and B grades.
Free hand drawing in the D and C grades.
Writing in all grades.
There will be two classes in Latin—a beginners class and one doing the 2 years'
work. The classes in Book keeping, Physiology, Orthography and English
Literature will be started at the beginning of the winter term.

C.M. J.R. Ranger, Principal.

11 12 80 Mr. John Cassy has resigned the position as janitor of the High School.
The teachers of the school miss him very much. Here is a chance for some good
man.

11 26 80 The school board are putting furnaces in the Union School house- a
furnace for every room. The school house has been closed at different times on
account of insufficient warmth in the building. The rooms will now be warm, and
there will be no reason for the scholars staying at home.

12 24 80 The Principal of the school has sent circulars to the patrons requesting
them to send all scholars who will enter the lowest grade of the Primary Dept.
before the close of the third week of the term. The Board approved of the request
and have adopted the following as a rule of the school: Scholars who cannot read
must enter school before the close of the 3rd week of a term.

04 22 81 The spring term of school opened with 141 scholars in the central
building. This enrollment is larger by twenty than any previous one during the
past two years.

05 20 81 The Young Folk's Literary Society had their last meeting Tuesday night,
they having adjourned until Sept. 10th . The Society have had some pretty good
debates this season and the members have thoroughly enjoyed them.

06 24 81 The School will give an excursion next Tuesday evening on the steamer *Queen of the Lakes.* Everybody invited. See advertisement in another column.

07 01 81 The High School Excursion on the steamer *Queen of the Lakes* last Tuesday evening was a remarkably pleasant one. There were 171 persons on the boat and all enjoyed themselves thoroughly. The Elk Rapids Band was in attendance and played very nicely. The refreshments were remarkably fine, and consisted principally of spruce gum.

08 25 81 The teachers of the schools for the next year will be:

Principal	Prof. C.M. Ranger.
Assistant	Mrs. C.N. Hurlbut.
Intermediate	Miss A.C. Updike.
Primary	Miss Ella Walter.
Brand's School	Miss Mary Craw.
Sours	Miss Julia Berg.

09 09 81 The school census has increased 35 per cent this year.

09 09 81   SCHOOL MATTERS.

Report of School Dist. No. One, Elk Rapids.

Sept. 6, 1880, money on hand	995.02
Received from one mill tax	479.38
Primary school fund	222.60
By district tax	3,000.00
From non resident pupils	4.00
Total receipts including money on hand	$4701.00
Paid teachers salaries	2333.00
Contingent expenses	1181.45
Total expenses	$3641.45
Sept. 5, 1881 by balance on hand	1186.54
	$4701.00

The sum of $2,000 for teachers salaries, $800 for contingent expenses and $200 for a bell ($3,000) was the amount appropriated by vote of the district for schools for the coming year.

The Brand school opened Monday last.

The enrollment at the Central school Monday was 124.

The Central building is to have a new bell—a large one.

F.R. Williams Esq., was re-elected Assessor at the annual meeting.

The school year at the Central building was shortened to nine and one half months.

The two branch schools have been repaired and painted and have been supplied with patent seats.

In the Central building all the rooms have beenalabastined and the seats and wood work varnished.

We challenge any village in the state to show so well preserved a school house as the Central building after 7 years wear.

The Brand school will have a year the same length as thatof the Central school and that of the South school will be increased to 8 months.

The number of scholars enrolled in the school this term in the different departments is; High School, 26; Intermediate, 36; Primary, 62.

Through a failure to make the proper records when the school house site was changed to that of the chapel, the district has had no title to the land on which the Central building stands. At the meeting Monday evening, the necessary steps were taken to empower the Board to make the transfer of the old site for the present one.

10 07 81 Mr. John Archibold applied for and received the position as teacher in the Spaulsbury school, and will commence his school work Monday next.

12 09 81 The new bell for the Central School building came on the *Clara Belle* Monday and has been placed in the cupola.

12 23 81 The Port Huron school board's committee on punishment has reported in favor of the use of a strap, an inch and three-quarters wide. The *News* will furnish a man who will give $5 for the privilege of using that strap two minutes on any of those committeemen.
    — *Evening News*, Detroit
    And we'll give one dollar to see the *News* man use the strap.

05 12 82 Chas. W. Pickell, of Bronson, Mich., sends us a short note informing us that he will take charge of the public schools in this place next year.

07 28 82 The teachers engaged for the public schools for next year are as follows: Chas. W. Pickell, Principal; Mrs. Chas. W. Pickell, Assistant; Miss Minnie Updike, Intermediate department; Miss Annie C. Timpson, Primary; Miss Mary L. Craw, East primary; Miss Mary Cassey, South primary.

10 05 82 Report of the public schools of Elk Rapids, for September.

ENTIRE NUMBER OF PUPILS ENROLLED.

High School	30
Intermediate Department	43
Primary Department	84
East Primary	46
South Primary	4
Total	207

10 13 82 The East Primary is rapidly filling up. Almost every pupil is a foreigner, Great credit is due Miss Craw for her excellent management of the school.

10 20 82 Nearly 90 scholars in the Primary department. Too many for one teacher.

10 27 82 True education consists of more than a mere smattering of reading, writing and arithmetic- something more than a mere superficial development.

Education consists in unfolding and expanding the whole nature of the child and fitting him for a useful and virtuous life. True teachers are those whose highest aim is to educate to this standard. Not that the six hours of time may be used, not that the pupil may go so far in geography or grammar, but that the child may be taught to think, speak and act aright. Actions should be taught as well as words or thoughts. Teachers need the highest, best preparation for their work. The time is fast approaching when a teacher will not be employed unless he has been professionally prepared for the work. When mothers and fathers will be so deeply interested that they will personally investigate the work of educating their children.

11 03 82 It will be remembered that some time ago the school board appropriated $100 for school library, $60 were spent for AmericanCyclopedia. The remaining $40 have just been spent for books of general information and interest.

11 03 82 The Primary Department has been so crowded this term that the board deemed it advisable to divide it. The Episcopal chapel has been secured for the accommodation of the pupils and Miss Julia Berg employed as teacher. In the reports hereafter the Supt. will designate this as the North Primary.

11 03 82 The school board have purchased the Episcopal chapel for $300. We hope that when the needs of the district calls for more school room the board will build either at the west or east end of the town instead of adding too the central building as has been talked. It would be more convenient for the smaller scholars not to have so much walking to do.

12 15 82 There are at present forty-two volumes in the school library.

Chapter 38
Service Organizations

08 13 80 A meeting will be held in Cooper's Hall Wednesday evening, August 18, for the purpose of organizing a Hancock and English club. All voters irrespective of former party ties are invited to attend. — John Denahy, Edwin S. Noble and J. Ward Davis.

01 21 81 The Masonic ball at Torch Lake last Friday night was a complete success. It took place at Frank Lewis' popular summer hotel, and every one knows that you can't go there to a ball or not without having the best kind of a time. We learn that an elegant supper was served and the party broke up about 9 o'clock Saturday morning.

03 03 82 March 1st opened bright and sunshiny just the kind of a day for the Old Settlers to come together. The roads leading to town were in bad condition else the attendance would have been greater. There were 43 persons at dinner at the Lake View House and all were perfectly satisfied with the treatment received. Their Chairman, not being present, Mr. John McDonald was temporarily elected. The business of nominating officers for the coming year, resulted in the following:

Alex. Campbell	Chairman.
Jered Arnold	Secretary.
Committee:	John McDonald, Chas. Russell, James P. Brand, Geo. Lardie, Sr., Enoch Wait, Mrs. Joseph Sours, Mrs. John M. Goddard, Mrs. W. Golden and Miss Lizzie Stone.

The Chairman and James P. Brand were appointed a committee to draft a constitution and bye laws to be presented at the next meeting for adoption or rejection.

04 07 82 A lodge of Good Templars was organized Sunday night with the following officers:

W.C.T	J.P.C. Church,
W.F.S	Miss Ella Walter,
W. Sec	W.C. Lewis.
W. Treas	G.M. Jackson,
W.F. Treas	Miss Julia Landon,
W.M.	Andrew LaForge,
Chaplain	Rev. Belden,
W.C.G.	Miss Martha Hughes,
W.O.G.W.	S. Spaulding,

Lodge Deputy Rev. Blanchard.
The next meeting of the Good Templars will be held next Monday evening in Masonic Hall.

04 21 82 K. of H. - Regular meetings first and third Tuesdays of each month.
F. & A.M. – Regular Communication Thursday evenings, on or before the full of the moon.

06 09 82 The lodge of good templars increased its membership by 12 new names Monday night.

The lodge of good templars has a membership of 60 in town.

08 18 82 The Installation of Officers in the Good Templars Lodge took place Monday evening. The following are the officers for the ensuing Quarter: W.C.T. — A. LaForge; W.V.T. — Martha Hughes; W.S. — J.E. Cooper; W.T. — W.M. King; W.M. — Jas. Dougherty; W.I.G. — Mrs. J. Cox; W.O.G. — Jas. Davidson; R.H.S. — Cordelia Davidson; L.H.S. — Hannah Drake; W.C. — S.G. Blanchard; W.A.S. — Juila B. Landon; W.F.S. — Mrs. J.P.C. Church; W.D.M. — Katie Wood; P.W.C.T. — J.P.C. Church.

09 01 82 The Elk Rapids Lodge of Good Templars numbers sixty members.

09 22 82 The Knights of Honor, Masons, and Good Templars will soon have for their use a hall over the Cox building on River street. The work of remodeling part of the building commenced Monday.

12 15 82 The Masons will hereafter hold their meetings in their new hall in the Cox building. This room has been expressly prepared for them, is roomy, and a pleasant place for their deliberations.

Chapter 39
Traverse City

02 27 80 A.M. Houghton, lumberman from Fife Lake, committed suicide by taking morphine, at the Front Street House, Traverse City, last Monday night...

03 19 80 New hotel in Traverse City...the Park Place...

06 26 80 The work of tearing out the old machinery and putting in the new at Messrs. Hannah Lay & Co.'s flouring mill is well under way. As we have before stated, the establishment is to be thoroughly overhauled from top to bottom and new and latest improved machinery put in. A large portion of the machinery that is being removed is good, but is taken out to be replaced with that of more modern style. The design of the owners is to make it the very best flouring mill in Northern Michigan and equal to any in the Union for the manufacture of flour.
> — *Eagle.*

08 19 81 From the *Herald* we learn that Traverse City will have water works for supplying the city with water, and that they will be on the bay shore, not far from the Bay House.

11 11 81 Traverse City has been chosen by the commissioners as a site for the location of the new insane asylum. The commission will purchase 399 acres of land for $21,991. The asylum will cost nearly $500,000 and Traverse City is just the place for it. The climate of Northern Michigan is healthful and the scenery fine.

11 11 81 We learn that Messrs. Hannnah, Lay & Co. of Traverse City, will build in the Spring their new store. We suppose when completed it will be a splendid monument to the enterprise, industry and public spirit always shown by this great firm.

12 02 81 The flats at the head of Boardman lake have for many years given Hannah, Lay & Co. much trouble in running their logs, as the river bed fills with sand every spring. They are now building a big scow 24x60 feet in size to be used in handling a dredge with which the river bed will be kept clear each spring hereafter.

01 20 82 We learned that Messrs. Hannah Lay & Co.'s new store, at Traverse City, will be 240 feet long and 90 feet wide, with three stories, heated by steam, and lighted by electric light. In fact, we learn that it will scoop any store building in the State.

01 27 82 Messrs. L.O. Sayler and J.T. Hannah started Thursday morning for Cuba. Will probably be gone two or three months.

02 10 82 *Eagle*: During the year 1880 over eighty new buildings were erected in Traverse City, in 1881 the number exceeded one hundred. From present indications the number that will be built in 1882 will be greater than any preceding year.

02 24 82 J.W. Hilton has been staking out the ground for Messrs. Hannah, Lay & Co.'s new store at Traverse City this week. The work on it will begin about April 1st. Mr. Hilton will have the supervision of the inside work.

03 03 82 The final arrangements for the construction of Hannah, Lay & Co.'s new brick block has been completed. The building is to be 208 feet in length, 112 feet deep, and three stories high. The first floor will be used for the retail trade, and will be divided as follows; First, on the southwest corner will be located the bank, 30x40 ft., which will be furnished with a fire and burglar proof vault built from the ground. In the rear of the bank will be a room for hardware with an entrance from Union street. Next to the banking room will be the main hardware salesroom, 30 ft. in width, and parallel to this will be the boot and shoe department, 30 ft. in width and next to this the dry goods room 50 ft. in width, then two grocery rooms, each 30 ft. wide, all extending back the entire depth of the building. All the rooms have double doors front and rear, and will be lighted front and rear with fine plate glass windows. The second story and basement are to accommodate the wholesale trade, while the third story will be devoted mostly to light storage. The first and second floors will be supported by iron columns, the third by wood. The whole building will be warmed by steam and furnished with steam elevators.

On all sides of the building will be a side-walk ten feet in width, and the basement extended under this gives an opportunity to light from the walk.

The outside walls will be put up of the best pressed brick, manufactured here, and already on the ground. They are a fine color, lighter than the celebrated Milwaukee brick. In the construction of this building there will be about 1,800,000 brick used, and about 200 cords of stone. A large amount of stone is already on the ground. The estimated cost of the building is $80,000.

The architects are Robinson & Barnaby, of Grand Rapids.

03 24 82 *Traverse City Herald*: About 10,000,000 brick will be required in the construction of the new asylum building.

03 31 82 Messrs. Hannah, Lay & Co., of Traverse City, are building a large shingle mill, says the *Eagle*. The building stands on a foundation of solid stone work, and the size of the main part is 36x50, two stories high, with engine and boiler room 24x42, one story. The mill will turn out 100,000 shingles a day, and will furnish employment for 18 hands.

04 07 82 Ground was broken on Tuesday morning, the 28th, for Hannah, Lay Co.'s new block. Seven thousand yards of earth will have to be removed for the basement excavation.—*Traverse City Herald.*

04 07 82 Thomas Holt, of this place, is doing the painting, graining, etc., on Park Place hotel, Traverse City. Having purchased a lot in the above town he will build a house on it and remove there from this place.

05 05 82 We were unable to print last week the following from the *Detroit Free Press* in regard to the asylum to be located at Traverse City:

The enter front line of the projected hospital is 920 feet in length, but is not a continuous line, and far from a straight one. First there is a section that stands prominently to the front; then a section that has retired from the foreground, then another section standing out boldly; another retiring section, an so on alternately for over a sixth of a mile...

05 26 82 Hannah, Lay & Co., Traverse City, are getting along splendidly with their new building. It will take about $100,000 to build it.

06 02 82 Traverse City people fought forest fires early Tuesday morning, near the fair grounds.

06 09 82 Hannah, Lay & Co., of Traverse City, were quite heavy losers by forest fires recently. Some pine on their Long Lake tract was burned.

06 30 82 E.L. Sprague has purchased James Spencer's interest in the *Traverse City Eagle,* and is now sole proprietor of that establishment.

07 07 82 Hannah, Lay & Co., of Traverse City, are building another dock. It will be 250 feet wide and 500 feet long.

07 21 82 An engine, boiler and machines have been shipped by the D.L. & N.R.R. to Traverse City for W.E. Avery, of Detroit, and J.S. Farr, of Grand Rapids, who have the contract for making and furnishing all the brick to be used in the Northern asylum for the insane, to be built at that place. *—Evening News.*

11 17 82 Last Friday night the Democrats of Traverse City had a jollification and during the festivities a cannon burst fracturing the arm of PeterGaverick. Several prominent citizens were standing near by but not injured.

11 17 82 The *Traverse City Herald,* takes the Republican defeat, hard. The *Eagle* gets up on its hind legs and howls.

Chapter 40
The Temperance Movement

10 22 80 The National Association of the W.C.T.U. having published a request that Saturday the 23rd inst. be observed as a day of prayer in connection with the temperance work, it is desired that those ladies who are interested in the temperance cause will meet at the M.E. Chapel at three o'clock on Saturday afternoon.

04 01 81 J.N. Cadeaux, of Muskegon, will lecture on the subject of Temperance, in the Methodist Chapel, Tuesday and Wednesday evenings, April 5th and 6th and accompany his lectures with interesting experiments. These lectures are highly commended by the press throughout the State. All are invited. Give the Doctor a full house.

05 27 81 The grand total of dealers in beer and whiskey in this state for the year 1880 was, according to a report sent to the House of Representatives by the Auditor General 3,700 and the tax paid by them amounted to $487,563.59.

07 08 81 At C.A. Newtons Saloon the front and back door was open all day the Fourth of July. Here is a chance for some one to try and find out if the Fourth is a legal holiday.

07 08 81 Several fights occurred on the Fourth, caused by too much "fire water."

08 05 81 Col. Geo. W. Lee, of Ypsilanti, Indian Agent, was in town this week, and says if he can find out who sells liquor to Indians he will make them sorry for it. It is punishable by imprisonment and a fine of $1,000 by the United States law.

08 12 81 Messrs. Hughes & Ward, of South Bend, Ind., commenced their series of Temperance lectures at the Methodist Church Tuesday evening to a fair audience.
C.A. Newton's saloon was closed last Saturday by the authorities on account of one of his bondsmen removing from the village.

08 19 81 The saloons are doing a poor business. Almost every man in town that frequents them having signed the pledge.

08 25 81 330 people have signed the pledge since Messrs. Hughes and Ward have been here.
Tuesday one of our liveliest saloons had at 4 o'clock P.M. taken in the enormous amount of 154.
A movement is on foot to organize a society to make complaint and arrest every drunken man on our streets.
Hughes and Ward, the temperance revivalists, are at Elk Rapids. The field is large in that corner of Antrim county-*Kalkaskian.*
Yes that is a fact. The saloonists have a big trade with Kalkaska, four large orders at one house Tuesday.

09 02 81 We hope that the authorities will see to it that the saloons of this village do stop selling liquor to Indians. Every time a saloonist or his agent sell a glass of liquor to a minor, or a habitual drunkard or an Indian he violates his bonds. A saloon can make enough profit by living right up to the requirements of the law, and we hope that an effort will be made to have them. Farther than that we have nothing to say.

11 04 81 More attention should be paid to having a more orderly town. When a drunken man appears on the street he should be promptly arrested and put into a lock up, which should be provided by the town.

01 20 82 There is probably more liquor drank in this village at the present time, than at any time since it was named.

02 10 82 The Mayor of Grand Rapids has been arrested for selling liquor by the drink in his drug store.

02 17 82 A drunken woman on the streets yesterday was an unusual and disgusting sight.

02 24 82 Some complaints have reached us about the saloons being open Sundays and after hours. This should be stopped as the bonds are violated when a saloon is open Sundays or after 10 P.M.

03 17 82 It is expected that Charles P. Russell will lecture on Temperance in the Methodist Church Sunday evening. Look out for small bills posted about town the last of this week. Mr. Russell is Grand Worthy Chief of Grand Lodge of Good Templars and an acknowledged temperance orator.

06 02 82 Elk Rapids now has two whisky and one beer saloons running.

06 09 82 Saloon men in town should see to it that no drunken rows occur in their saloons. There is nothing in the business that is note-worthy, much less when a fight or two a week is noticed.

07 07 82 The saloons of Elk Rapids were closed on the Fourth, thereby exhibiting respect for the law and the public.

07 21 82 Mrs. Boise, the popular temperance reformer, so well and widely known throughout this and other States, has been holding temperance meetings since last Tuesday night in the M.E. and Presbyterian Churches under the auspices of the Lodge of Good Templars of this place. The lady is a fluent and impressive speaker and is thoroughly acquainted with her subject in all its bearings, religious, political and moral. She imparts new life and interest to the subject of temperance, by her eloquent and earnest manner in presenting it.

07 28 82 People *vs* Charles A. Newton- Assault and battery. Charles Moody, complainant. This case was to have been held before Justice LaForge yesterday afternoon, a week, but the Justice dismissed the case on account of the complainant's feebleness, caused by over-indulgence of the wine cup.

08 11 82 We hope that some one will get shoved up for filling the Indians with liquor. For some time the saloons gave them none, but now we learn that they can get it at some places.

A saloon row occurred at John Acker's saloon Saturday night, but which subsided as soon as the proprietor hove in sight.

10 27 82 Something should be done to stop the drunkenness on our streets. It is absolutely unsafe for ladies to walk on the streets after nightfall.

11 24 82 The drunkenness in Elk Rapids is greatly to be deplored by every temperance man and woman in the country. And we think with Ed. of the *Progress,* something must be done and that immediately. Now that election is over, citizens, temperance people, all over the country, let us to work with a will, and do something to save our otherwise pleasant and prosperous village from the curse of liquor, which is demoralizing and ruining it. What has been the cause of nearly all the crimes committed in Antrim county? It is whiskey, which has been sold at Elk Rapids. It is not only citizens of Elk Rapids, but respectable farmers all over the country, are being ruined. Friends of temperance, let us commence at the cause of this evil. As long as there is liquor sold, there will be drunkenness. What are we going to do to save our fathers, husbands and sons from this evil?

Chapter 41
Tragedies

01 30 80 C.S. Abbot, of Portage, Mich., met with a sad accident last Saturday. He was chopping near Torch River in company with H.K.Ingersoll, both being on the same log, when Abbott turned suddenly just as Ingersoll was striking a heavy blow. The ax descended, striking Abbott on the wrist almost severing his left hand from his body. As soon as struck he took hold of his arm above the cut and pressed it to prevent the loss of blood and ran a mile and a half to procure a conveyance to bring them to this place a distance of eleven miles. Dr. Bailey dressed the wound.

03 05 80 A few days ago while two little children of H.Robinson were playing together one of them picked up a hatchet by some misfortune struck the other one on the hand, severing two fingers. One child was two and the other four years.

03 12 80 Last Wednesday a man by the name of John Parker started to cross Torch Lake from the village of that name. He has not been heard from since and the supposition is that he broke through the ice and was drowned. His dog came home without its master which further leads to this supposition.

03 19 80 A young man at the Furnace got his foot smashed last Sunday afternoon between the floor and the platform of the elevator. Dr.Evans was called and dressed it. At last accounts he was doing very well.

04 16 80 A 16 year old daughter of George Lardi, of Old Mission, was burned to death last Friday. She went to the bush with her sister, where they had been making sugar, for the purpose of making some maple wax. Her clothes caught fire, and telling her sister to go for help, she commenced rolling on the ground to extinguish the fire. In her efforts to put out the fire, she rolled into a brush heap which took fire and she literally burned to death.

07 30 80 Mr. H. Mellen's saw mill at Bagley Otsego Co., blew up Tuesday morning of this week killing two men and seriously injuring several others. The owner of the mill was among the injured. The explosion was caused by a defective boiler. It will be remembered that Mr. and Mrs.Mellen with their daughter, Miss Marion visited Mr. J. Ward Davis and family a few weeks ago. Miss Ella Mellen who visited Miss Delia Davis last summer was a victim of the disaster on the *Evening News* excursion.

08 06 80 Last Friday Harry Wells of Mancelona was killed by the falling of a tree.

10 08 80 Wednesday evening a report was about town that a six year old son of B. Resignolle, who is employed at the furnace, had been shot by Herbert Frame, a son of Charles Frame, who lives on the Craw farm, a boy about fourteen years old. As near as we could gather the boys had a revolver, and as is usual in such circumstances, did not know that it was loaded, and as a natural consequence some one had to catch it. The boy was facing Herbert when the shot was fired, and the bullet took him nearly in front of the neck and went through the windpipe and anchored, it is thought, in the back of his neck. Every thing was done for the sufferer that could be and last night he was yet alive.

12 10 80 Harry Robinson a son of Hi. Robinson, seriously cut his foot Monday morning. He was chopping wood at the time and the ax glanced and very nearly cut his foot off. He was about a mile and a half from his father's house and Joseph Paradise who was near carried him home.

12 24 80 Last Wednesday after noon Elmar Wealch came near being drowned. He attempted to cross Elk Lake on the ice from Amos Wood's place to his own. When out about eighty rods from shore he broke through, his cries arrested the attention of Charlie McLaughlin who was skating about eighty rods south of him. Charlie took a fence rail the first thing he could get and went to his relief but could not get near enough to help him out but pushed the rail near enough to Wealch so that the latter could catch hold of it and support himself until Charlie went back to where Amos Wood was standing and got a cane fishing rod, which he reached to Wealch, who grasped it with both hands and held on until he was pulled out, which was a very difficult job for the ice was soglarey that a person could scarcely stand at all and it was only by kicking a hole in the ice with his skates that Charlie could stand to pull him out. When he was rescued he was nearly perished having been in the water almost half an hour.

01 28 81 Last Saturday while John Shaw was drawing a load of wood to the furnace, he slipped and fell and the runner of thehindermost bob run over his leg. On the runners there is welded a sharp piece of iron about a quarter of an inch thick, to keep the sled from sliding from one side to the other, which with the weight of the wood made a very serious wound on Mr. Shaw's leg. The accident happened about a mile from town.

03 11 81 Perry Beckwith, who formerly lived here, is supposed to have been lost, among several others, who went out from Grand Haven in a fish boat last fall during a severe storm.

04 22 81 A house belonging to Orin Atwood, of East Bay, burned on the night of the 10th inst. Chas. B. Wright and family were living in the house at the time, and all their house hold goods, clothing, etc., were burned.

12 16 81 A Sad Occurrence– Several weeks ago a Mrs. McKinsey, who resided east of Central Lake was brought to this place in a bed, for medical treatment. She has been stopping with a lady attendant, in Mr. Cristopher Hughes' house, opposite the Methodist Church. For the last ten days she has failed rapidly. Her husband was sent for as soon as the danger was perceived, and he arrived with all dispatch on Sunday last, and at her urgent request, decided to start for home with her next morning, as she was very anxious to see her little family of three small children once more. Her strength rapidly failed as she moved homeward, and she died on her bed in the wagon when within two miles of her home. Her disease was dropsy besides two or three dangerous abscesses. The neighbor women have done all they could for her since learning the serious nature of her affliction, but the care of friends and medical skill were alike unavailing. She had for some time anticipated death.

01 27 82 Two brothers by the name of William and Charles Bence were killed by the cars Saturday evening last, at Fife Lake. They were crossing the track, and the team was also killed. Their father, who was with them escaped uninjured. The same family lost four children two years ago with diphtheria.

02 10 82 A sad accident occurred yesterday to Wallace Clow, of Central Lake. While cutting a small sapling the ax went over the pole and the bit went into his leg severing the ankle bone. Dr. Coolman was summoned, and performed the surgical operation. The patient is suffering considerable pain.

02 24 82 Johnathan B. Sherman, of Southfield, Charlevoix Co., met with a fatal accident last Saturday. While chopping in his woods he undertook to fell a dead tree which had lodged against another and remained in a leaning position. In felling the upright one the tree dislodged and fell, and striking Sherman on the back of the head and neck must have killed him instantly. His son, who had been to the house with a load of wood found his father under the debris of the fallen tree, his face and head jammed into an unrecognizable mass. The body was extricated with the assistance of neighbors.

03 03 82 Near tragedy–Joseph Shaw has a Winchester rifle, sixteen shot. A few days ago he took it down to clean it. He chose the kitchen as the proper locality for that purpose and proceeded to empty the cartridges with which it was loaded, on the floor, until he supposed the chambers were all empty. Letting the hammer fall presently after, the rifle was discharged, to the amazement and danger of several who were in the room. The ball passed through the sleeves of two coats that hung on the wall, then through the partition into the pantry, passing directly through a pan of milk from one side to the other, and thence through another partition into a bedroom, and from there its further progress could not be traced. No one was injured beyond the fright all necessarily sustained, so what might have been a matter of very serious character terminated in a little pleasantry, especially when the milk and cream were discovered deposited in all directions in the pantry from the perforated pan.
Too great caution cannot be exercised in the handling of firearms.

03 17 82 *Fife Lake Eye:* Mr. Bence, father of the two unfortunates whose mangled bodies told tales of deep distress at the hands of the express train, several weeks ago, received of the railroad company $150, enough to defray the expenses incurred by the sad event. Mr. Bence did not request their bestowal of even this much, and has no thought of taking action to procure more.

04 07 82 Robert Rust, of Chestonia, was instantly killed on his farm while chopping, on Tuesday last. It seem that he was falling timber not far from his house, and Mrs. Rust called him to dinner at noon, receiving an answer. She waited dinner about an hour and then called again. No answer was received and upon her going to the chopping she found him lying with a limb of a tree across his head, his skull crushed in and the brains oozing out. He leaves a wife and a babe about four months old. – Mancelona *Herald*.

06 02 82 William McAuley, a two year old son of Mr. and Mrs. Edward McAuley was instantly killed at the furnace Sunday afternoon. He and five other children were playing in the furnace yard, and while there, they espied a bird's nest in one of the large flasks used in the foundry. Clambering up on the flask it commenced to rock and all the children ran away but the little fellow, who could not escape before the heavy framework fell, crushing him to the earth. The cries of the children brought Samuel Crampton to the spot, when the cruel timbers were taken off the poor child, but nothing could avail as life had left the body. The funeral was held on the following Monday.

06 30 82 *Fife Lake Eye:* One of the most heart-rending accidents that has ever occurred in our village happened Friday, by which a little five-year-old daughter of C.F. Lancaster met with a horrible death. The child strayed away from home in the forenoon and was seen upon the principle street, and was requested by several of our business men to return home which she declined to do. Soon she was seen walking down in the direction of the railroad track, this was the last seen of her until the town was shocked by the news that she had been killed by the noon freight bound north. She was walking by the side of the track only a few rods ahead of the engine, and when within about a rod of the little one she stepped upon the track, only to be hurled into eternity by the ponderous wheels. Death was instantaneous.

07 07 82 An item of news lately received here in connection with the family of Rev, Peter Dougherty, well known in the Grand Traverse region for thirty years of its earliest history, will be of interest to old settlers. Two daughters of Mr. Dougherty, Bessie and Minnie, left their home in Wisconsin a few years ago, to finish their musical education in the city of Boston. While there they became acquainted with two lawyers, cousins, both widowers, and each left with one child. The gentlemen they subsequently married, the double wedding occurring at the same time and place. Recently the husbands were out riding together, when the horses ran away and both gentlemen received injuries which proved fatal. Mr. Dougherty's family in the west were busily making preparations for a visit from their children and their husbands, which latter they had never seen, instead of which the two young widows came back to their father's house crushed by the weight of their terrible double bereavement. –T.C. *Hearld*

07 28 82 Willie Garmire, a little four years old boy fell off the dock, at Torch Lake, into Torch lake and was drowned Saturday. C. Eagleton saw him in the water on his hands and knees and jumped in and pulled him out, but all attempts to resuscitate him were without avail.

09 01 82   **MURDER**
Martin Martinson stabs Charlie Rangstedt.
The Murderer Arrested and Held for Trial.
On Sunday morning last the town was shocked by hearing that a fearful crime had been committed here. Nothing particular was done until afternoon,

when Justice Davis impaneled a jury and proceeded to the furnace where the murder was committed. Upon reaching the furnace quite a crowd had collected, who were in groups talking over the affair. The house where the crime took place stands Northeast of the furnace, and does not differ from the rest of the houses near by. It is a rough board, one story, with shingled roof with a storm house in front of the outer door...On the night of August 26 a dance was given in the house above mentioned of which there were invited about 20 persons. Among those present was Charles Rangstedt, one of the owners of the house and Martin Martinson, the murderer. About 11 o'clock Martinson by constant drinking became noisy and was told by Rangstedt that he must be quiet or go out doors, and as he was not quiet Rangstedt put him out...Rangstedt placed his hands on Martinson's shoulders and pushed him from the room...Martinson made a sudden movement down with his left hand. About two minutes after they left the room Rangstedt appeared at the door and placing his hand on his left leg, said "Eastburn has cut me."...on Sunday afternoon after viewing the corpse the jury adjourned to the Iron Co.'s carpenter shop, where a medical examination was made by Drs. Conklin and Bailey. The wound was ten inches long, extending from four inches above the knee upward ten inches on the inner side of the thigh...He bled to death. (two column story.)

09 29 82 A man by the name of Charles Newell has recently been arrested in Wilson township, Kalkaska county, for raping his own child- a little 8 year old girl. The girl stated that about two weeks ago her father had ravished her in a most brutal manner, and threatened to cut her throat if she made any outcry. Newell has been arrested, and held for trial. If the charge brought against him is true there should be a neck-tie social at Kalkaska.

10 20 82 A terrible accident occurred at Kalkaska, Tuesday, in Baker's saw mill, resulting in the death of Jas. M. Harris an employee. Harris was standing on the log carriage stabbing a log with an ax, and the ax caught upon a rope, throwing the unfortunate man back upon the saw, cutting off his head, right arm and both legs. Harris leaves a wife and three children.

12 01 82 Last Sunday morning a little boy, son of Mr. and Mrs. William Moron, living on Traverse Avenue, got possession of a bottle containing chloroform and ether accidentally left within his reach and drank nearly all of the contents. The poison took immediate effect. The frightened parents with the assistance of the neighbors succeeded in keeping the little fellow partially awake until Dr. Conklin, who was promptly sent for arrived, and administered the proper remedies, in such cases, no doubt saving the lad's life. Parents with small children cannot be too careful with dangerous drugs.

Chapter 42
Weddings

Autherson, Joseph and Jennie Drake	07 25 1882
Broderick, Jacob & Rebecca March	04 06 1881
Brodrick, Jacob & Rebecca Marsh	03 11 1881
Brodrick, Jacob & Rebecca Marsh	03 11 1881
Cameron, Jas. & Retta Engleton	12 25 1880
Carson, Benjamin F. and Martha E. Love	03 25 1882
Child, J.R. and Mrs. M.M. Powers	11 18 1880
Corbett, Capt. Duncan & Mary Hughes	09 17 1880
Edwards, C.S. and Sarah Young	11 30 1882
Geary, Alfred & Florence Swift	04 06 1881
Harsha, Wm. & Belle Cameron	04 17 1880
Hawley, Joseph & Eliza A. Morrison	06 12 1880
Hicking, William and Louise Gribi	10 21 1882
Hosley, Frank & Anna Hailer	04 22 1880
Howe, Frank and Kate Heathcote	09 30 1882
Hurlbut, Charles H. and Phebe Ahnefeldt	08 02 1881
Keech, Jesse H. and Laura L. Allen	11 26 1882
Keeney, James T. and Hattie Hannah	11 23 1882
King, Wm. M. and Elizabeth Beird	08 30 1882
Larouche, Louis and Ellen Goodhew	07 10 1882
Madill, John, & Sarah Norton	06 05 1880
Marriott, Charles and Elizobeth Durochuer	12 02 1880
Pusey, Fred S. and Ardella Fife	08 12 1882
Ranger, C.M. & Lillie C. Robertson	08 25 1880
Reed, Cowper and Mary Cameron	10 26 1882
Russell, Charlie and Mary Peatre	08 18 1882
See, Fred and Clara Spaulsbury	10 ?? 1882
Silver, Allen and Ella Woodrow	06 28 1882
Smith, Wm. N. and Maggie J. Munroe	02 22 1882
Sours, Lowell D. and Emma J. Sherman	11 23 1880
Terry, I.C. and Hatty M. Bishop	09 19 1882
Way, Simon & Hattie Deam	02 25 1880
Willis, Alexander and Inis B. Baldwin	12 28 1881
Wood, George E. and Sarah Jane O'Brien	03 24 1882
Wood, Harry W. and Ada Minnie Chandler	09 06 1882

.

Chapter 43
Births

Angell, 9½ pounds without the wings to J.D.A.		09 ?? 1882
Briggs, baby boy,	Mrs. Wm. B.	12 15 1880
Briggs, a girl	Mrs. Wm. B.	12 11 1882
Burr, twin boys	Mrs. James B.	01 17 1880
Corbett, a girl,	Capt. and Mrs. C.	12 02 1882
Cross, a girl	Celon C.	10 ?? 1882
Dean, son	Pershall D.	03 ?? 1882
Drake, a boy	Joseph D.	06 28 1882
Gemberling, a girl	Mrs. H.E. G.	04 30 1880
Hurlbut, a boy	Mrs. C.N.H.	09 07 1882
Kimball, boy	Mrs. Pascall K.	02 07 1881
King, a boy	Mrs. Mark K.	08 18 1882
Kramer, son	Mrs. Frank K.	01 12 1880
Light, a boy	Mrs. W.J.L.	08 29 1882
Meriott, a boy	Mrs. Charles	05 25 1881
Pearl, a girl	Mrs. Jno. P.	05 0? 1881
Pierce, a boy	Mrs. H.M.P.	09 04 1882
Ranger, a son	Mrs. C.M. R.	07 11 1881
Riley, _____	Mrs. W. R.	07 11 1880
Russell, a girl	Mrs. John R.	12 ?? 1882
Smith, a son	Mrs. Wm. S.	10 18 1882

Chapter 44
Obituary's

Anderson, Joseph T.			11 11 1882
Arnold,	young son of Jas. A.		10 ?? 1882
Buck, Harvey	son of F.C.B.		10 27 1882
Cameron, Archibald		age 76	06 09 1880
Coleman, Joseph E.		age 22	10 30 1882
Cooper, Eliza			03 26 1880
Garrett, Lawrence			03 01 1880
Graham, Henry B.		age 44	02 18 1882
Johnson, Mrs. Flora Jane		age 23	01 05 1882
Jordan, Mrs. Sarah			07 24 1882
Levi,	a young boy		10 06 1882
Moffatt, Amelia H.			08 09 1882
Phillips, Orpha	infant of Daniel P.		02 02 1882
Schuler, Joe		age 14	02 25 1880
Silkman, Samual H.			07 01 1882
Smith,	young son of H. Smith		03 ?? 1882
Spaulding, June		age 5	11 24 1882
Spaulding, Mrs. Wm. S.			05 13 1881
Thompson, John		age 70	03 19 1880
Wadsworth, Alfred		age 2	01 02 1880
Wadsworth, Daisey		age 4	01 23 1880
Waldron,	a young man		09 18 1882